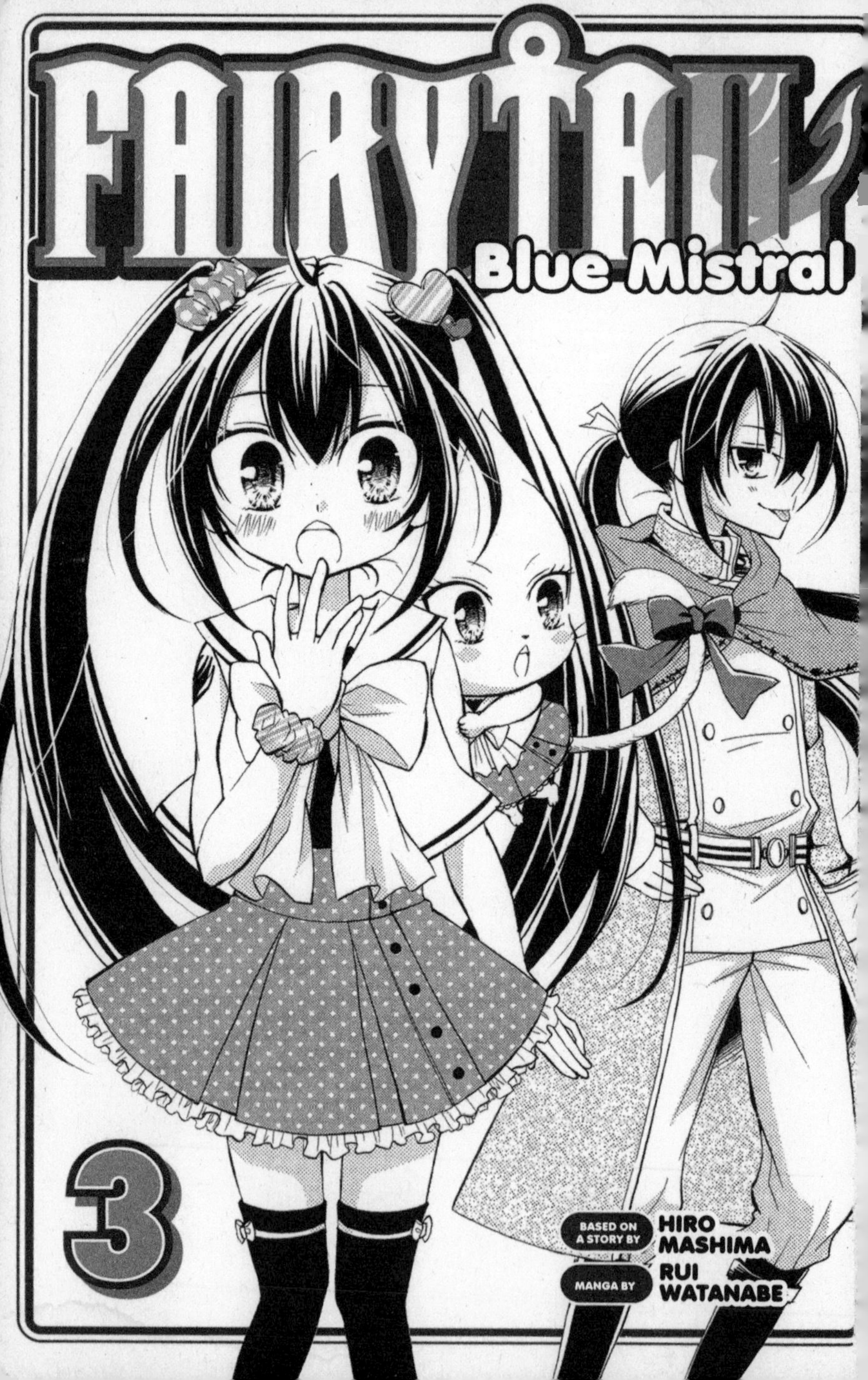
FAIRY TAIL
Blue Mistral
3
BASED ON A STORY BY HIRO MASHIMA
MANGA BY RUI WATANABE

FAIRY TAIL Blue Mistral

Dragon Slayer Magic...

It is accomplished by allowing your own body to take on aspects of a dragon.

It is an Ancient Spell...

There once appeared a young girl who could perform Dragon Slayer Magic!

And that power could shake the sky and cause the ground to tremble...

What is FAIRY TAIL?

It's the guild that Wendy and Carla are in. They call it the most powerful guild in the Kingdom of Fiore.

What is A GUILD?

It's a place where wizards gather. The guild is where the wizards get information on jobs they can take on.

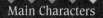

Main Characters

Wendy Marvell

A 12-year-old Dragon Slayer wizard who specializes in a magic that uses air, Sky Magic. When she was very little, she was raised by a dragon. She loves Carla. She hates pickled plums.

Carla

A creature that looks very much like a cat, which was born from an egg that Wendy once found. She loves English-style tea. She can sprout wings and fly through the sky.

The Story So Far

★This takes place about the time Wendy entered the Fairy Tail wizard's guild.

★For her very first solo job, she went to the village of Nanalu to discover the truth behind the "ghost of a dragon." On her way back, she encountered the mystery of a cursed mansion, and had to get to the bottom of both! With both incidents behind her, she returns reminded of how nice it is to be among friends.

★With her return to Fairy Tail, Wendy gets back into the fun daily routine she enjoyed before. But it seems there's a whiff of a new mystery out there...?! Just a tiny bit wiser, Wendy's brand-new adventure is about to begin!!

Contents

The Adventures of Wendell

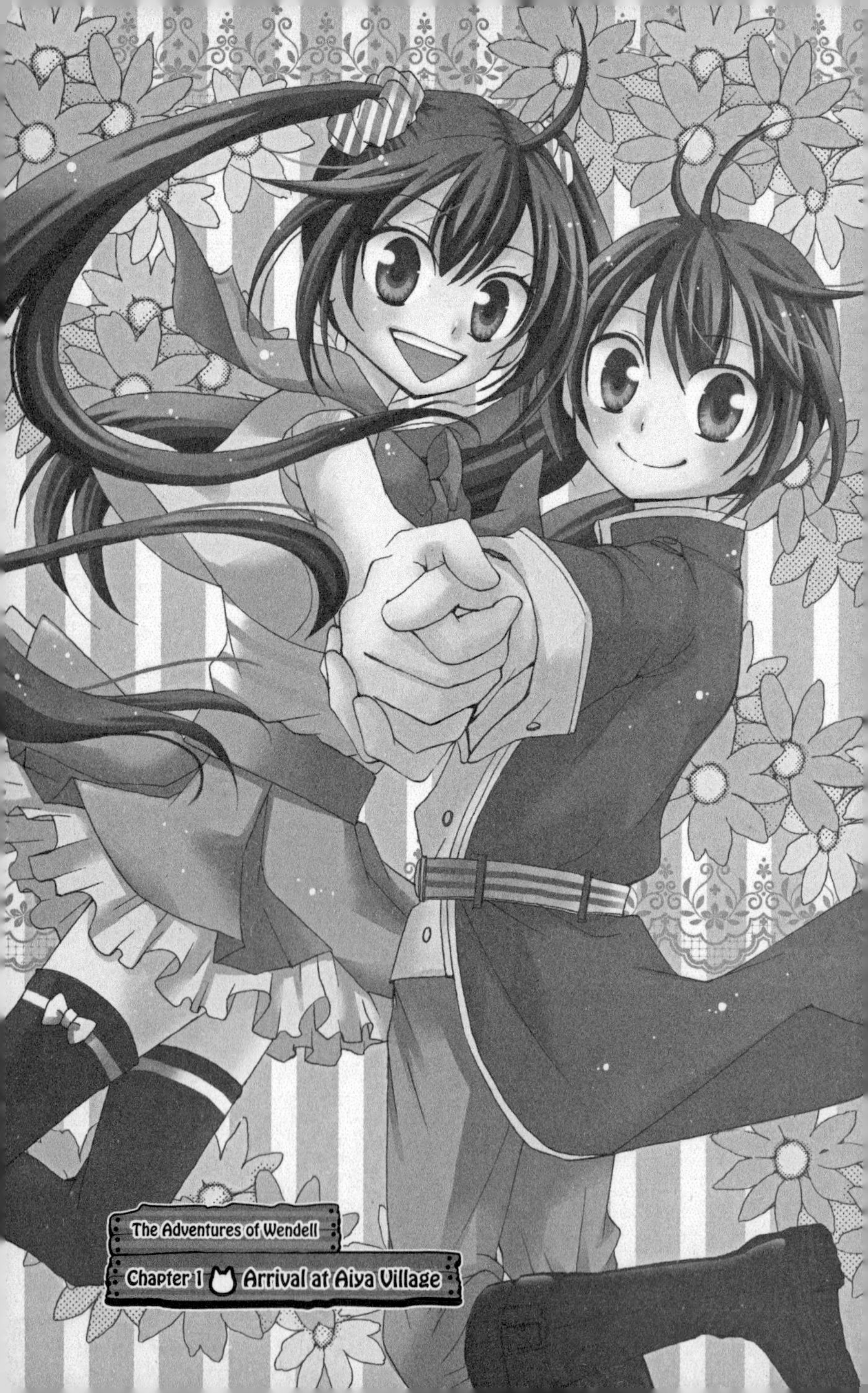
The Adventures of Wendell
Chapter 1 Arrival at Aiya Village

FAIRY TAIL

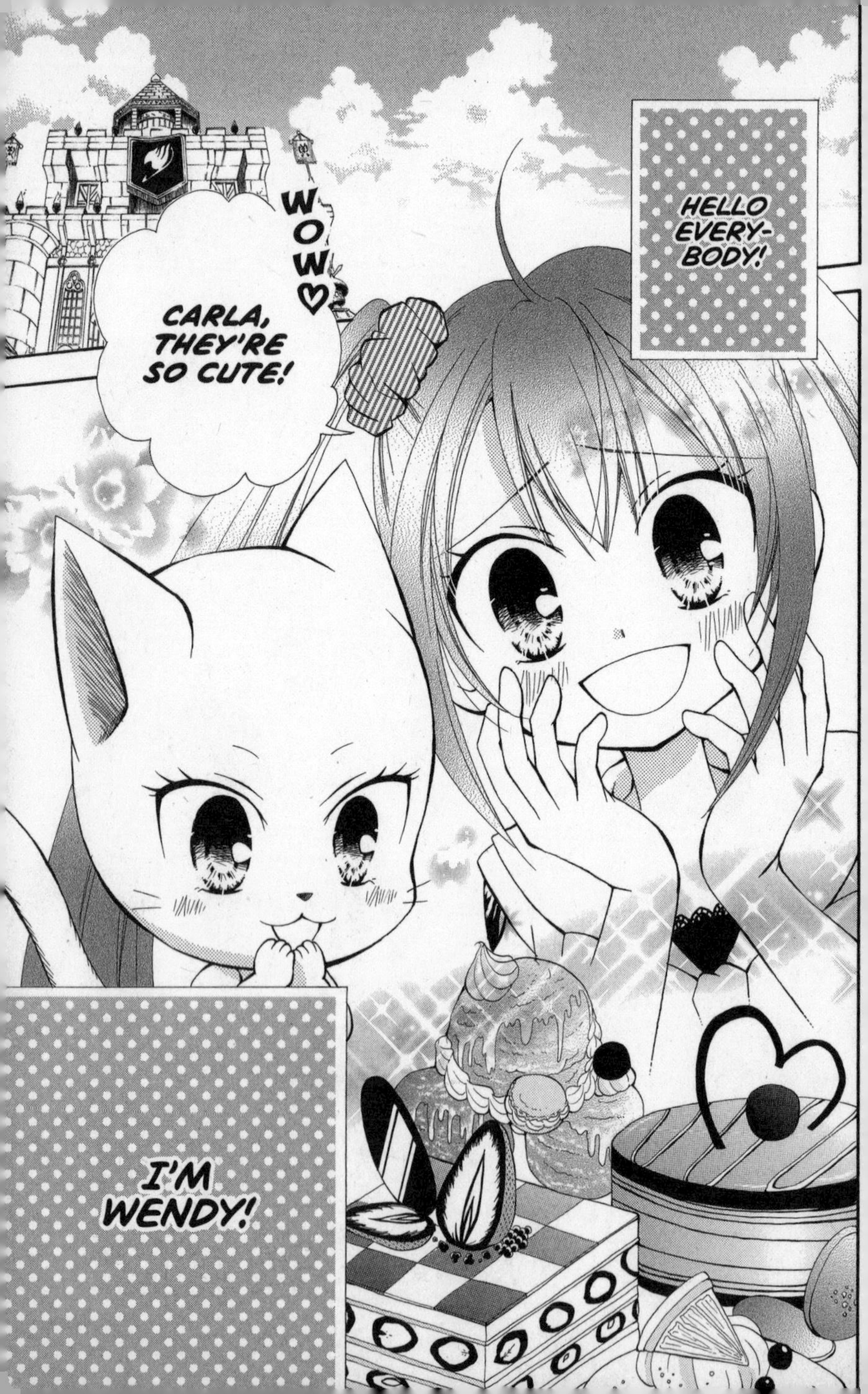
HELLO EVERY-BODY!
WOW♡
CARLA, THEY'RE SO CUTE!
I'M WENDY!

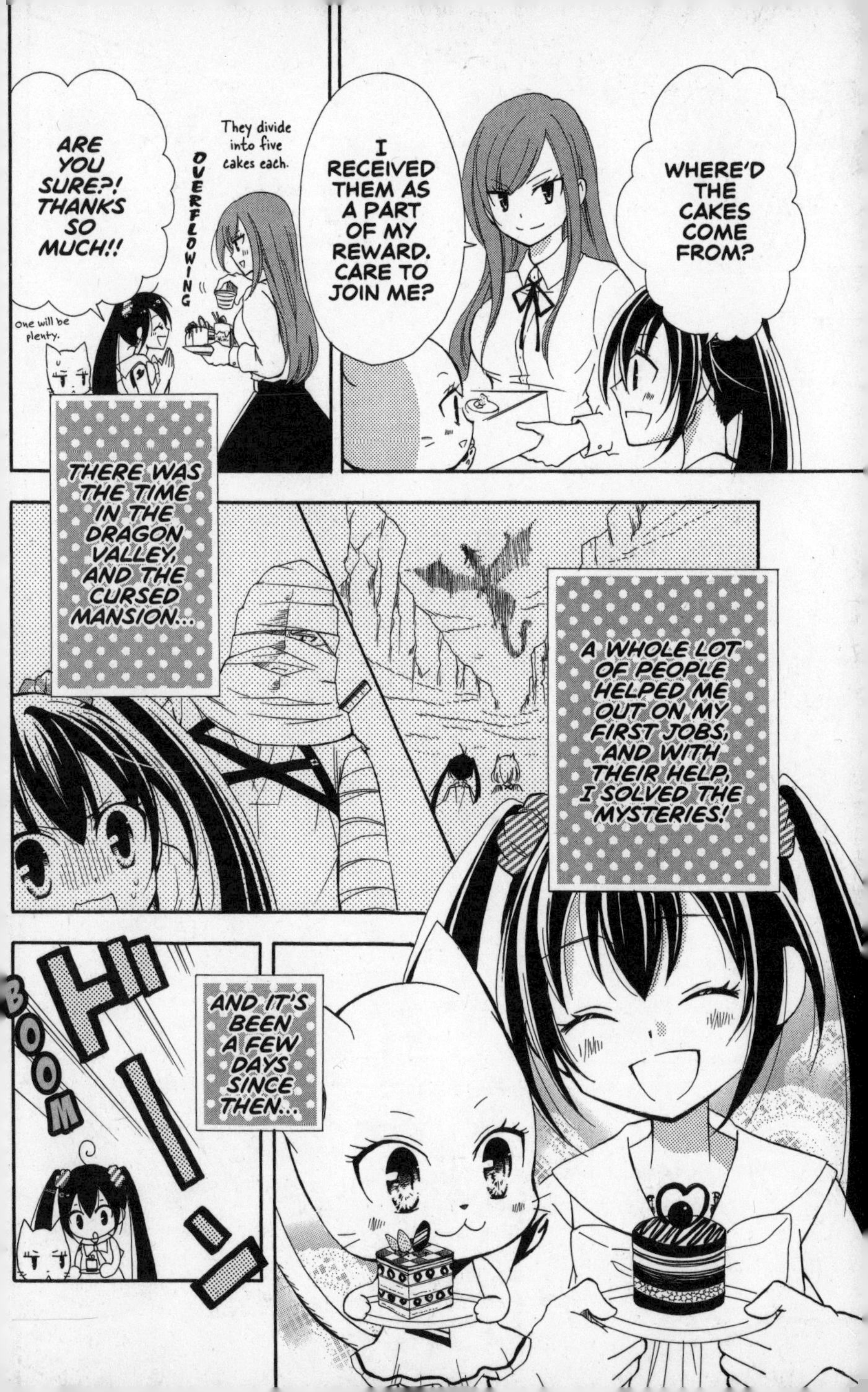
WHERE'D THE CAKES COME FROM?
I RECEIVED THEM AS A PART OF MY REWARD. CARE TO JOIN ME?
They divide into five cakes each.
OVERFLOWING
ARE YOU SURE?! THANKS SO MUCH!!
One will be plenty.
THERE WAS THE TIME IN THE DRAGON VALLEY, AND THE CURSED MANSION...
A WHOLE LOT OF PEOPLE HELPED ME OUT ON MY FIRST JOBS, AND WITH THEIR HELP, I SOLVED THE MYSTERIES!
AND IT'S BEEN A FEW DAYS SINCE THEN...
BOOM

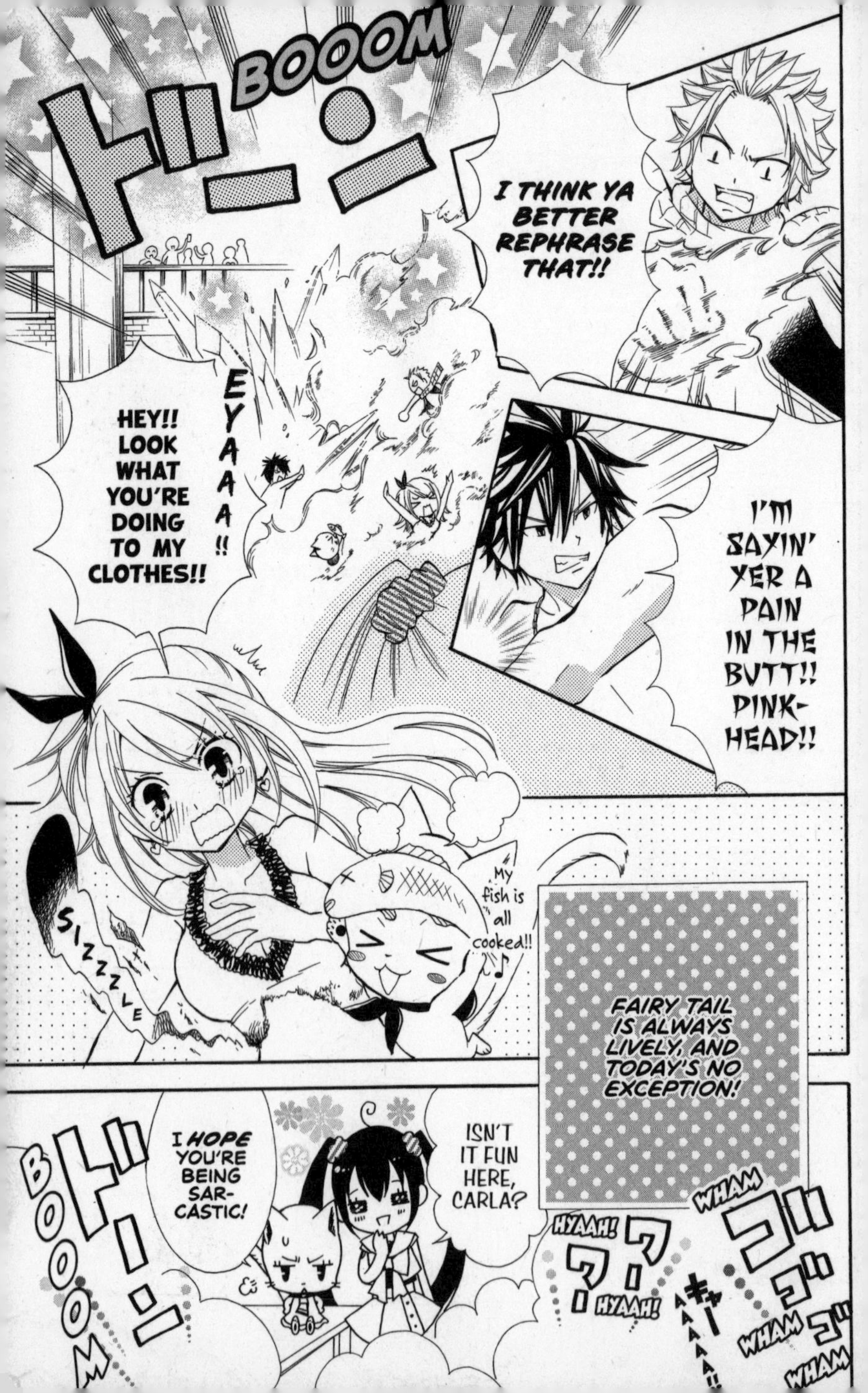

I THINK YA BETTER REPHRASE THAT!!
BOOOM
I'M SAYIN' YER A PAIN IN THE BUTT!! PINK-HEAD!!
EYAAAA!!
HEY!! LOOK WHAT YOU'RE DOING TO MY CLOTHES!!
My fish is all cooked!!
SIZZZZLE
FAIRY TAIL IS ALWAYS LIVELY, AND TODAY'S NO EXCEPTION!
WHAM WHAM WHAM WHAM
HYAAH! HYAAH!
ISN'T IT FUN HERE, CARLA?
I *HOPE* YOU'RE BEING SAR-CASTIC!
BOOOOM

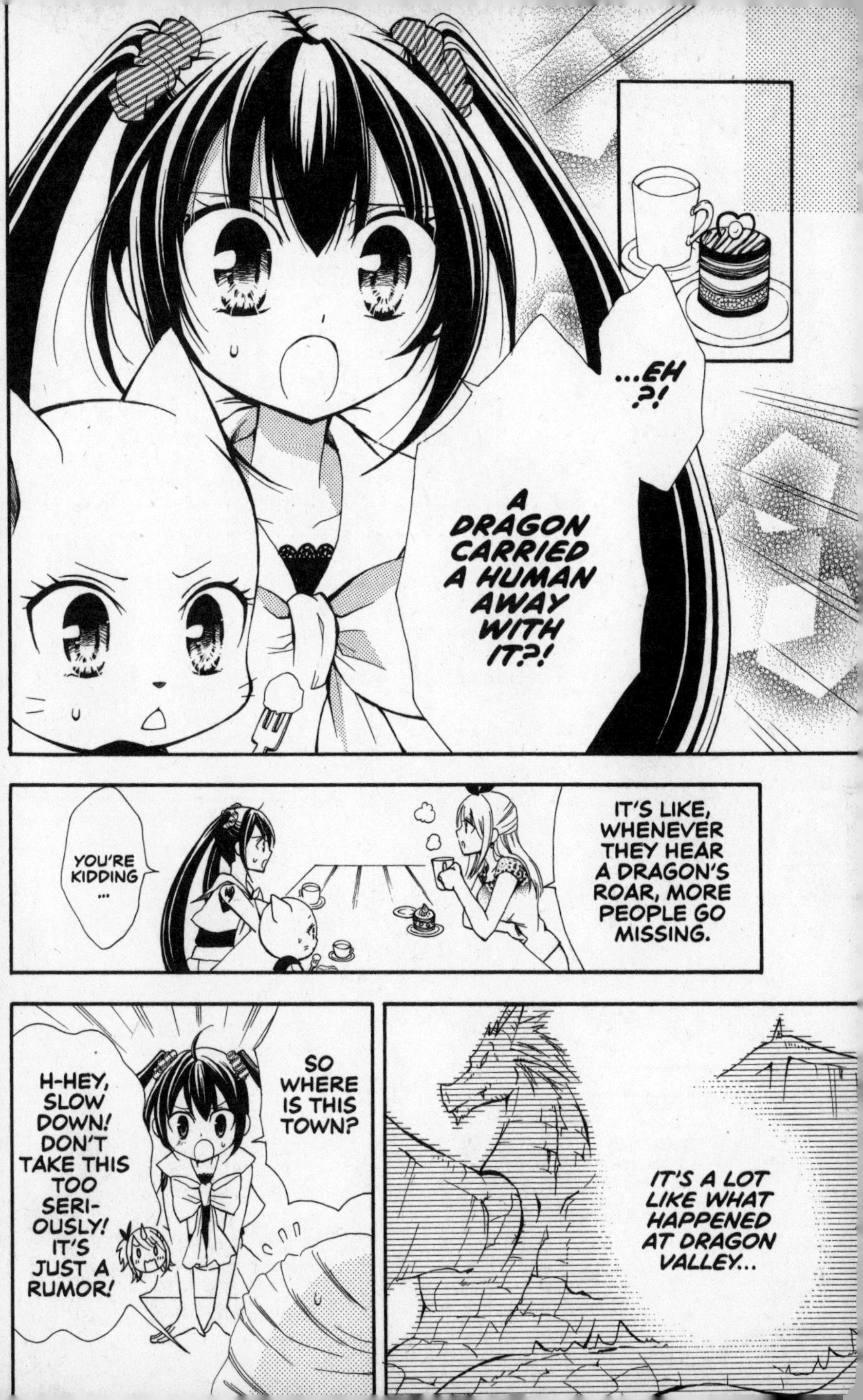
...EH ?!
A DRAGON CARRIED A HUMAN AWAY WITH IT?!
IT'S LIKE, WHENEVER THEY HEAR A DRAGON'S ROAR, MORE PEOPLE GO MISSING.
YOU'RE KIDDING ...
IT'S A LOT LIKE WHAT HAPPENED AT DRAGON VALLEY...
SO WHERE IS THIS TOWN?
H-HEY, SLOW DOWN! DON'T TAKE THIS TOO SERI-OUSLY! IT'S JUST A RUMOR!

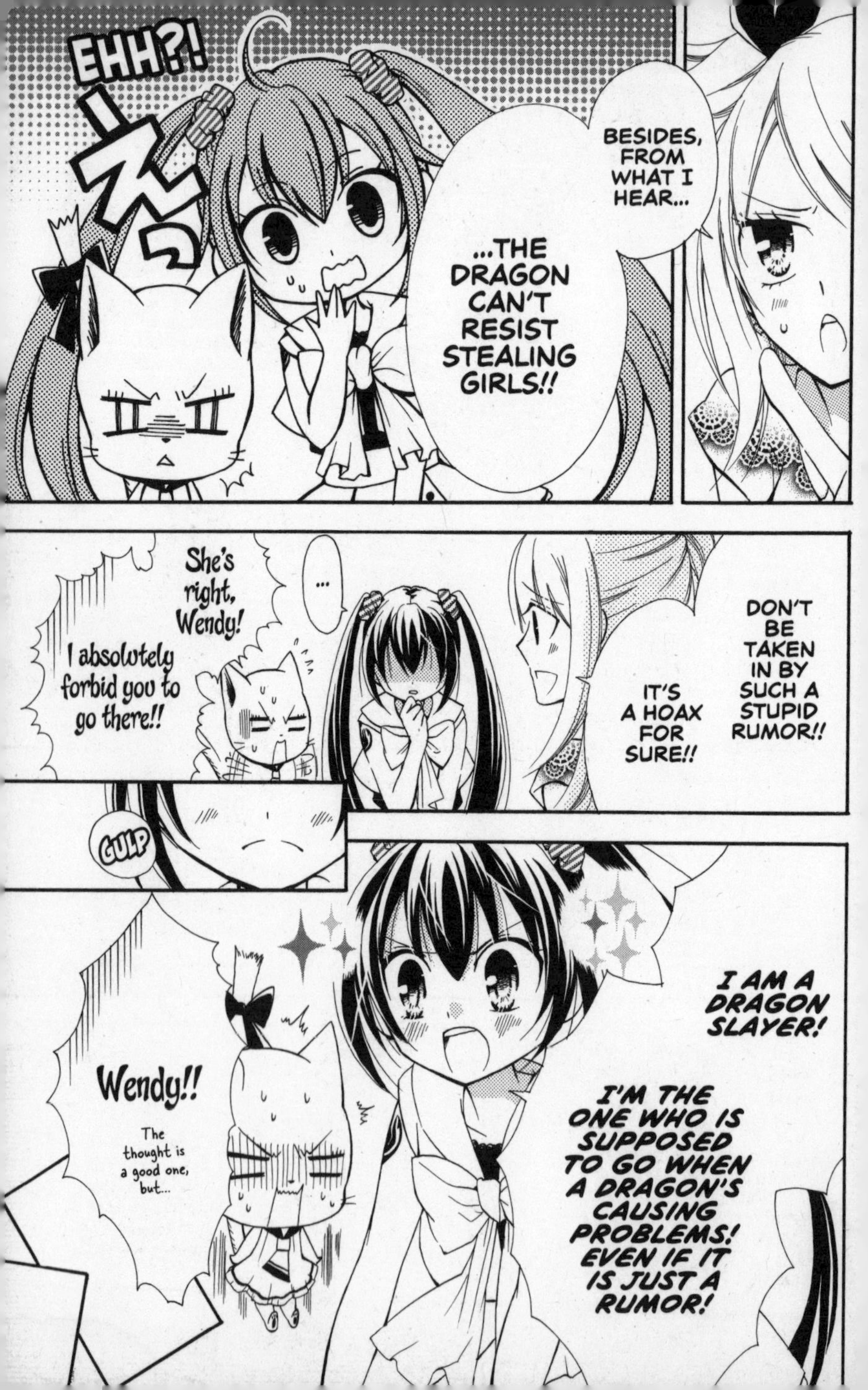
BESIDES, FROM WHAT I HEAR...
...THE DRAGON CAN'T RESIST STEALING GIRLS!!
EHH?!
DON'T BE TAKEN IN BY SUCH A STUPID RUMOR!!
IT'S A HOAX FOR SURE!!
...
She's right, Wendy!
I absolutely forbid you to go there!!
GULP
I AM A DRAGON SLAYER!
I'M THE ONE WHO IS SUPPOSED TO GO WHEN A DRAGON'S CAUSING PROBLEMS! EVEN IF IT IS JUST A RUMOR!
Wendy!!
The thought is a good one, but...

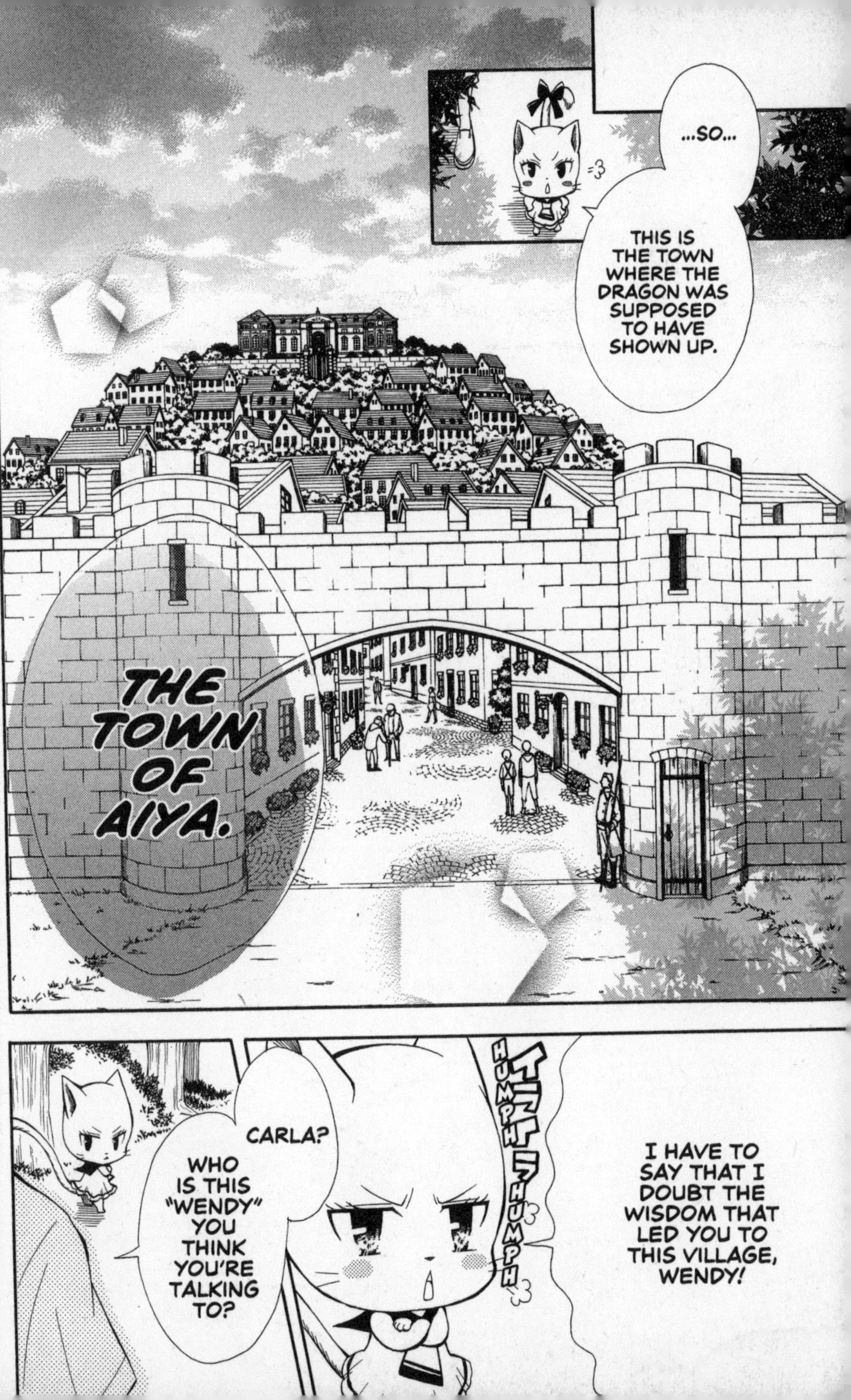
...SO...
THIS IS THE TOWN WHERE THE DRAGON WAS SUPPOSED TO HAVE SHOWN UP.
THE TOWN OF AIYA.
I HAVE TO SAY THAT I DOUBT THE WISDOM THAT LED YOU TO THIS VILLAGE, WENDY!
HUMPH HUMPH
CARLA?
WHO IS THIS "WENDY" YOU THINK YOU'RE TALKING TO?

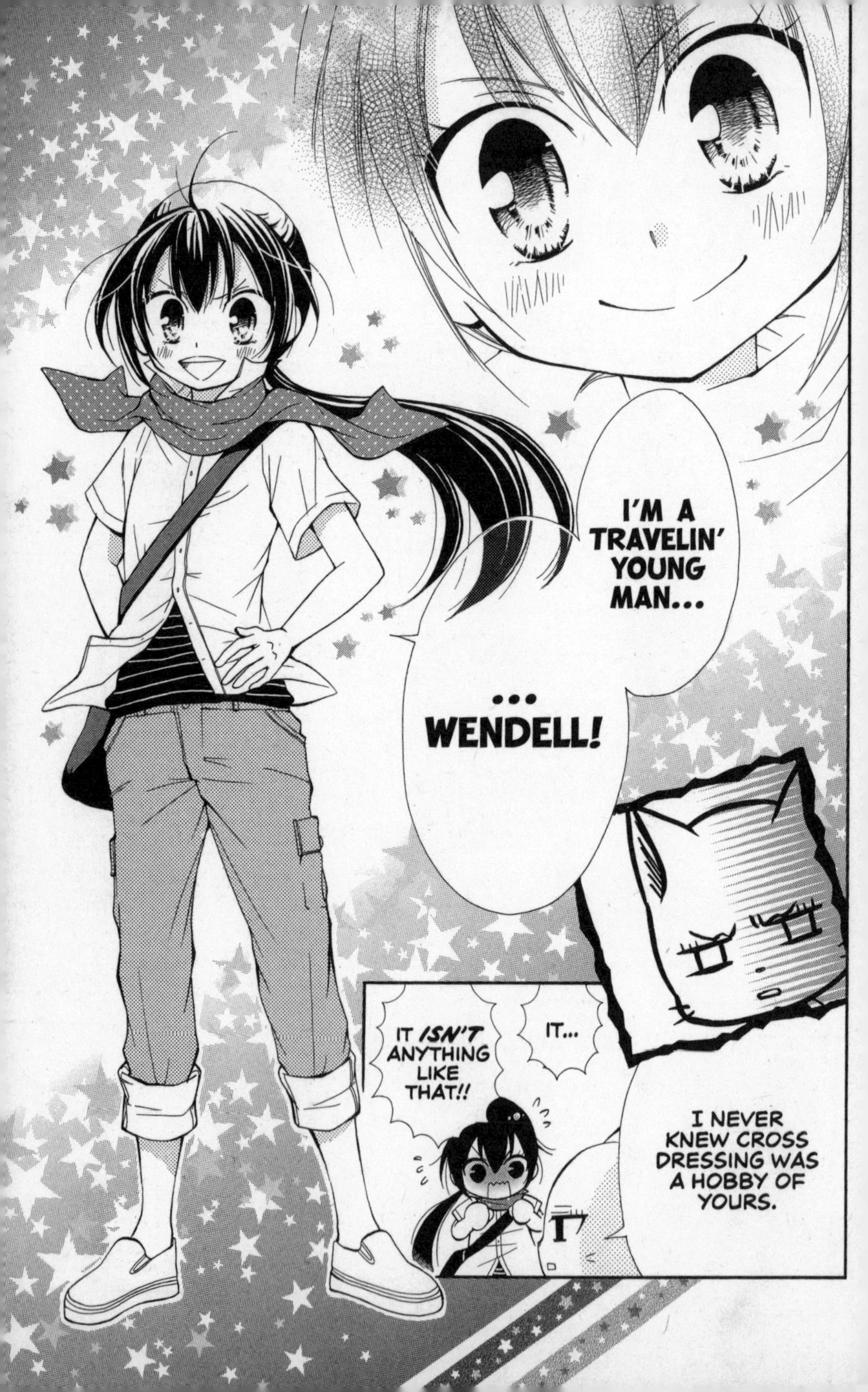
I'M A TRAVELIN' YOUNG MAN...
...WENDELL!
I NEVER KNEW CROSS DRESSING WAS A HOBBY OF YOURS.
IT...
IT *ISN'T* ANYTHING LIKE THAT!!

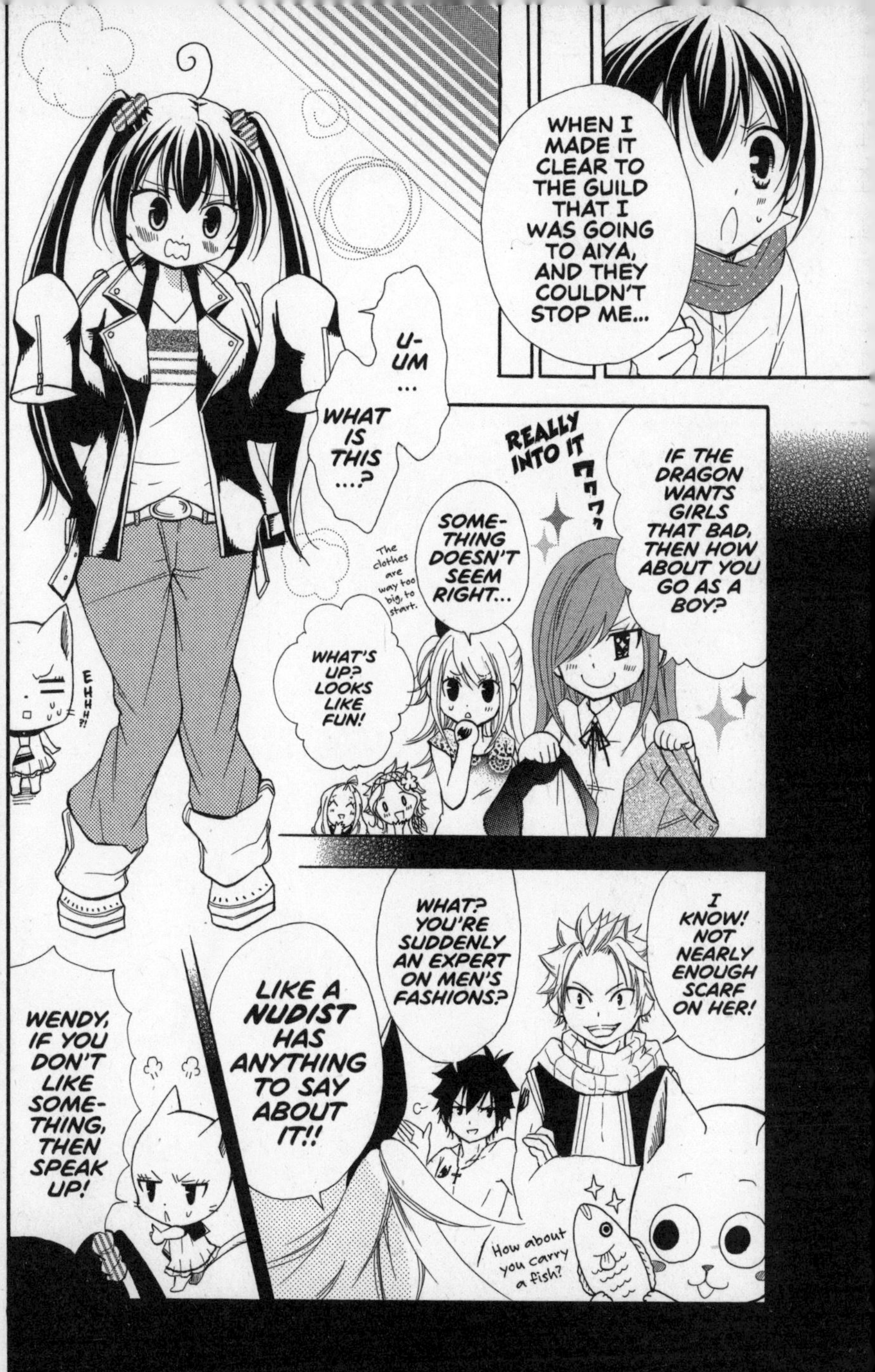
WHEN I MADE IT CLEAR TO THE GUILD THAT I WAS GOING TO AIYA, AND THEY COULDN'T STOP ME...
REALLY INTO IT
IF THE DRAGON WANTS GIRLS THAT BAD, THEN HOW ABOUT YOU GO AS A BOY?
SOME-THING DOESN'T SEEM RIGHT...
The clothes are way too big, to start.
WHAT'S UP? LOOKS LIKE FUN!
U-UM... WHAT IS THIS...?
EHHH?!
I KNOW! NOT NEARLY ENOUGH SCARF ON HER!
WHAT? YOU'RE SUDDENLY AN EXPERT ON MEN'S FASHIONS?
LIKE A NUDIST HAS ANYTHING TO SAY ABOUT IT!!
WENDY, IF YOU DON'T LIKE SOME-THING, THEN SPEAK UP!
How about you carry a fish?

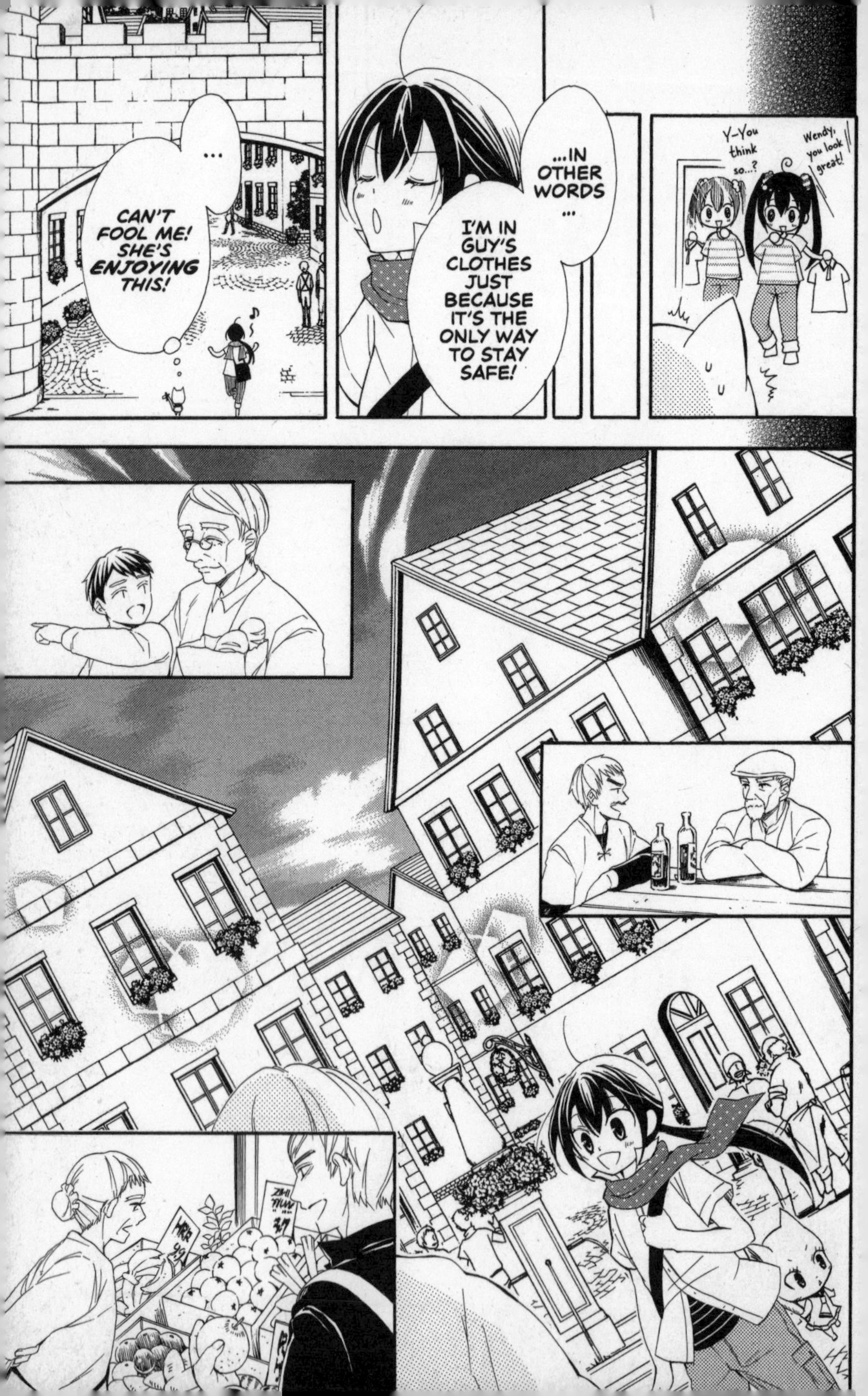
Wendy, you look great!
Y-You think so...?
...IN OTHER WORDS ...
I'M IN GUY'S CLOTHES JUST BECAUSE IT'S THE ONLY WAY TO STAY SAFE!
...
CAN'T FOOL ME! SHE'S ENJOYING THIS!

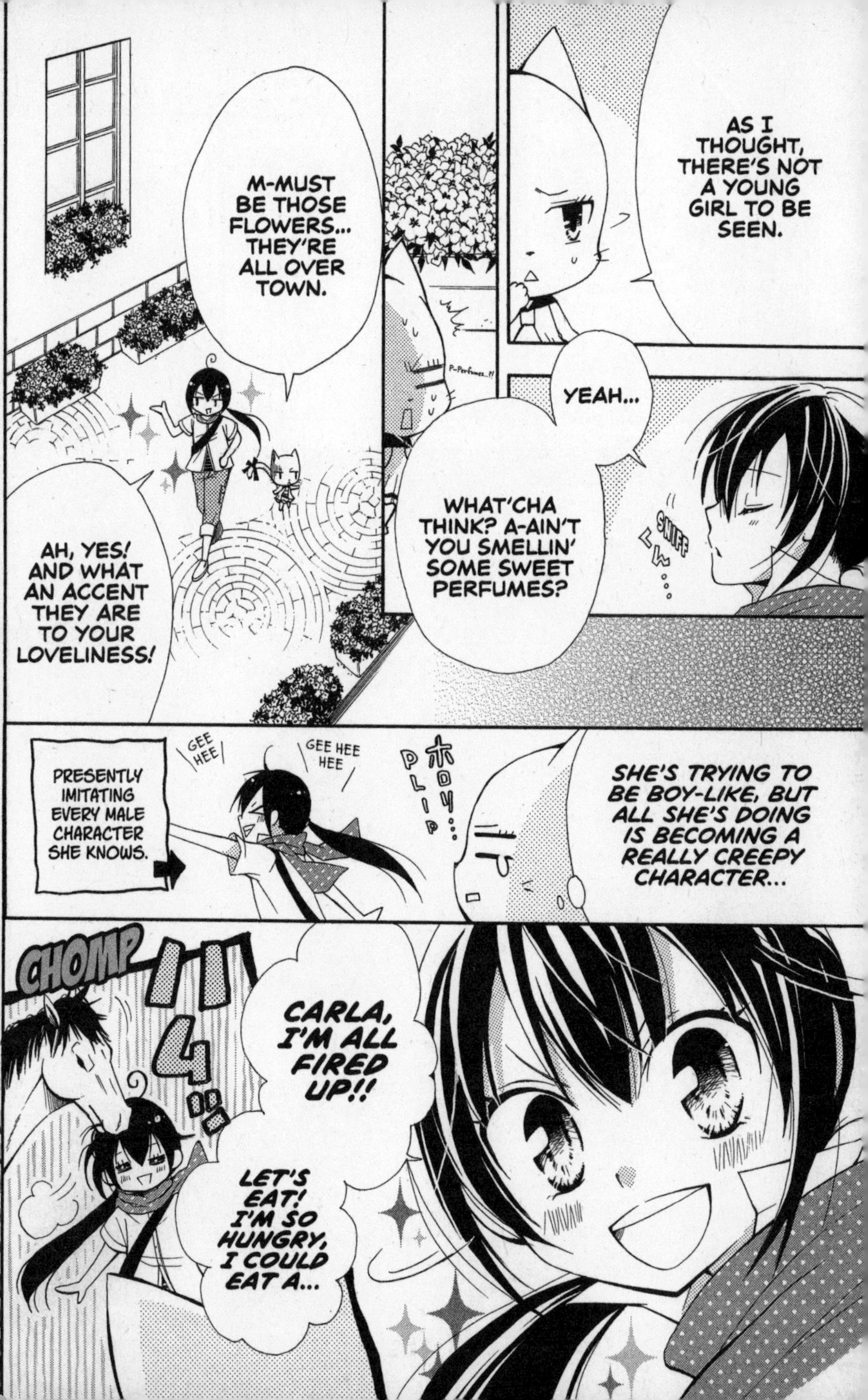
AS I THOUGHT, THERE'S NOT A YOUNG GIRL TO BE SEEN.
YEAH...
WHAT'CHA THINK? A-AIN'T YOU SMELLIN' SOME SWEET PERFUMES?
SNIFF
P-Perfumes..?!
M-MUST BE THOSE FLOWERS... THEY'RE ALL OVER TOWN.
AH, YES! AND WHAT AN ACCENT THEY ARE TO YOUR LOVELINESS!
SHE'S TRYING TO BE BOY-LIKE, BUT ALL SHE'S DOING IS BECOMING A REALLY CREEPY CHARACTER...
PLIP
GEE HEE HEE
GEE HEE
PRESENTLY IMITATING EVERY MALE CHARACTER SHE KNOWS.
CARLA, I'M ALL FIRED UP!!
LET'S EAT! I'M SO HUNGRY, I COULD EAT A...
CHOMP

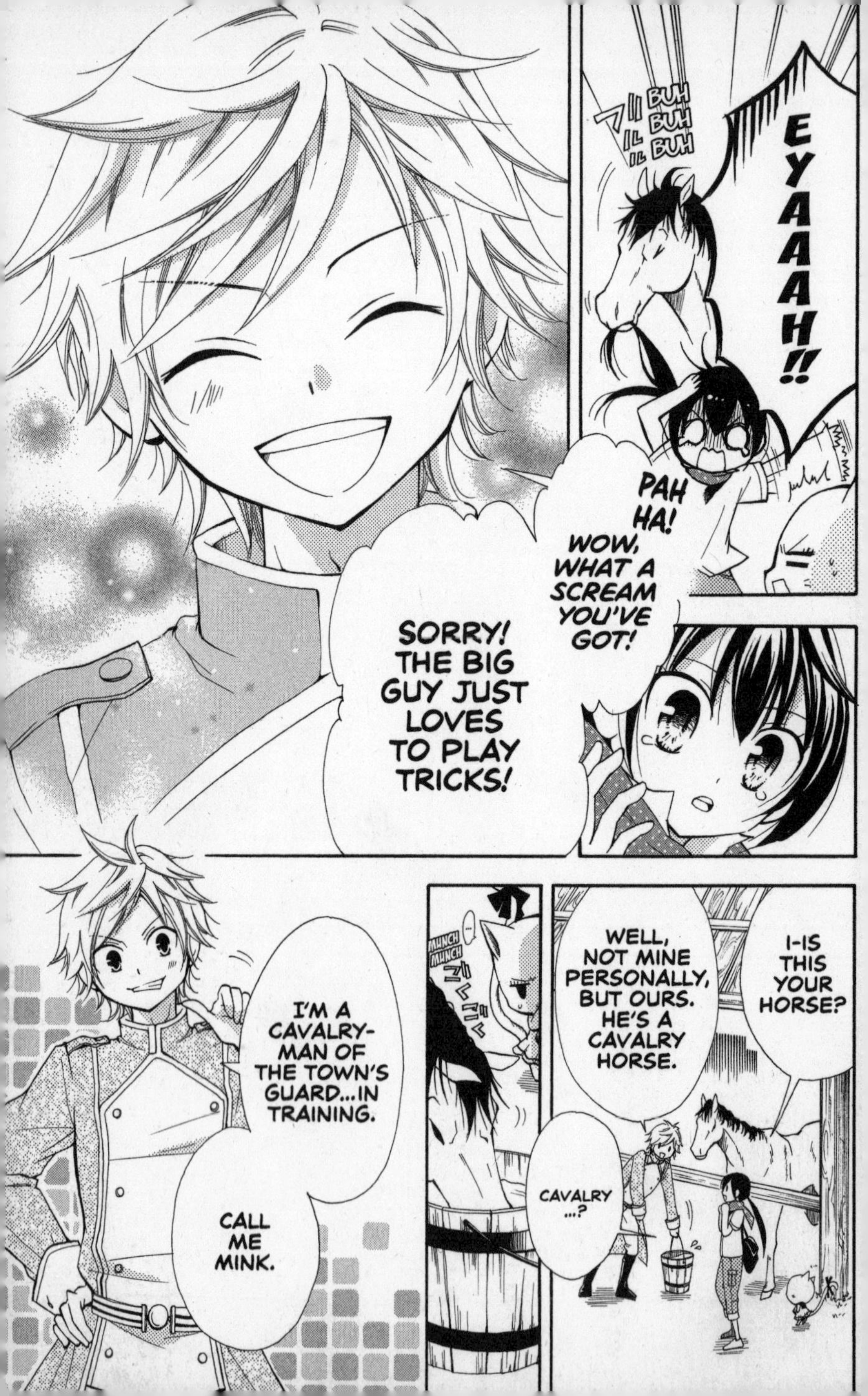
EYAAAAH!!
BUH BUH BUH
PAH HA! WOW, WHAT A SCREAM YOU'VE GOT!
SORRY! THE BIG GUY JUST LOVES TO PLAY TRICKS!
I-IS THIS YOUR HORSE?
WELL, NOT MINE PERSONALLY, BUT OURS. HE'S A CAVALRY HORSE.
CAVALRY ...?
MUNCH MUNCH
...
I'M A CAVALRY-MAN OF THE TOWN'S GUARD...IN TRAINING.
CALL ME MINK.

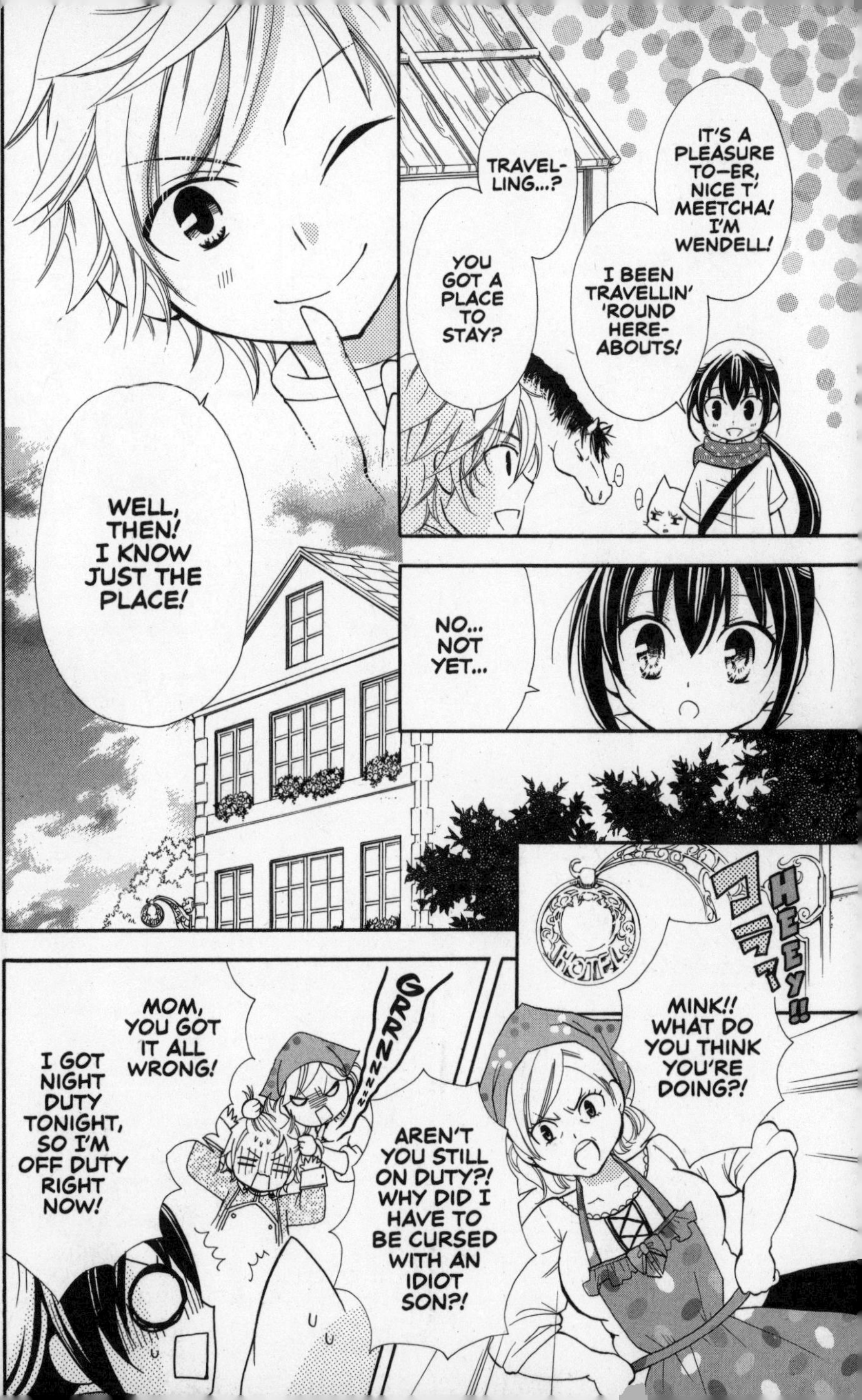
IT'S A PLEASURE TO—ER, NICE T' MEETCHA! I'M WENDELL!
I BEEN TRAVELLIN' 'ROUND HERE-ABOUTS!
TRAVEL-LING...?
YOU GOT A PLACE TO STAY?
NO... NOT YET...
WELL, THEN! I KNOW JUST THE PLACE!
HOTEL
HEEY!!
MINK!! WHAT DO YOU THINK YOU'RE DOING?!
AREN'T YOU STILL ON DUTY?! WHY DID I HAVE TO BE CURSED WITH AN IDIOT SON?!
GRRNNN
MOM, YOU GOT IT ALL WRONG!
I GOT NIGHT DUTY TONIGHT, SO I'M OFF DUTY RIGHT NOW!

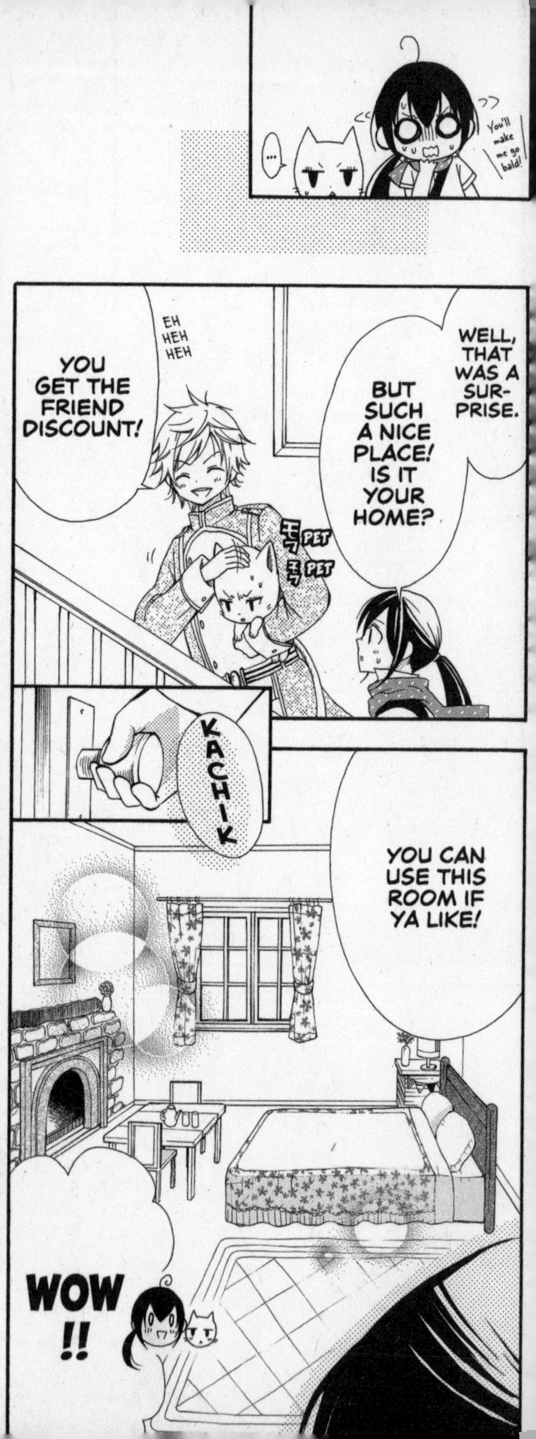
...
You'll make me go bald!
WELL, THAT WAS A SURPRISE.
BUT SUCH A NICE PLACE! IS IT YOUR HOME?
EH HEH HEH
YOU GET THE FRIEND DISCOUNT!
PET
PET
KACHIK
YOU CAN USE THIS ROOM IF YA LIKE!
WOW!!

BONUS MANGA 1

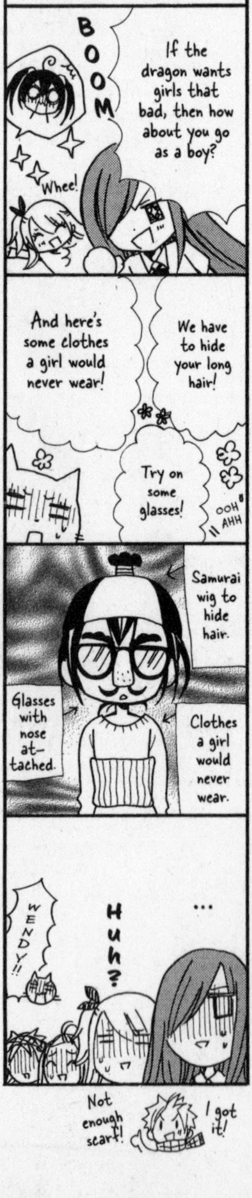
If the dragon wants girls that bad, then how about you go as a boy?
BOOM
Whee!
We have to hide your long hair!
And here's some clothes a girl would never wear!
Try on some glasses!
OOH AHH
Samurai wig to hide hair.
Clothes a girl would never wear.
Glasses with nose attached.
...
Huh?
WENDY!!
I got it!
Not enough scarf!

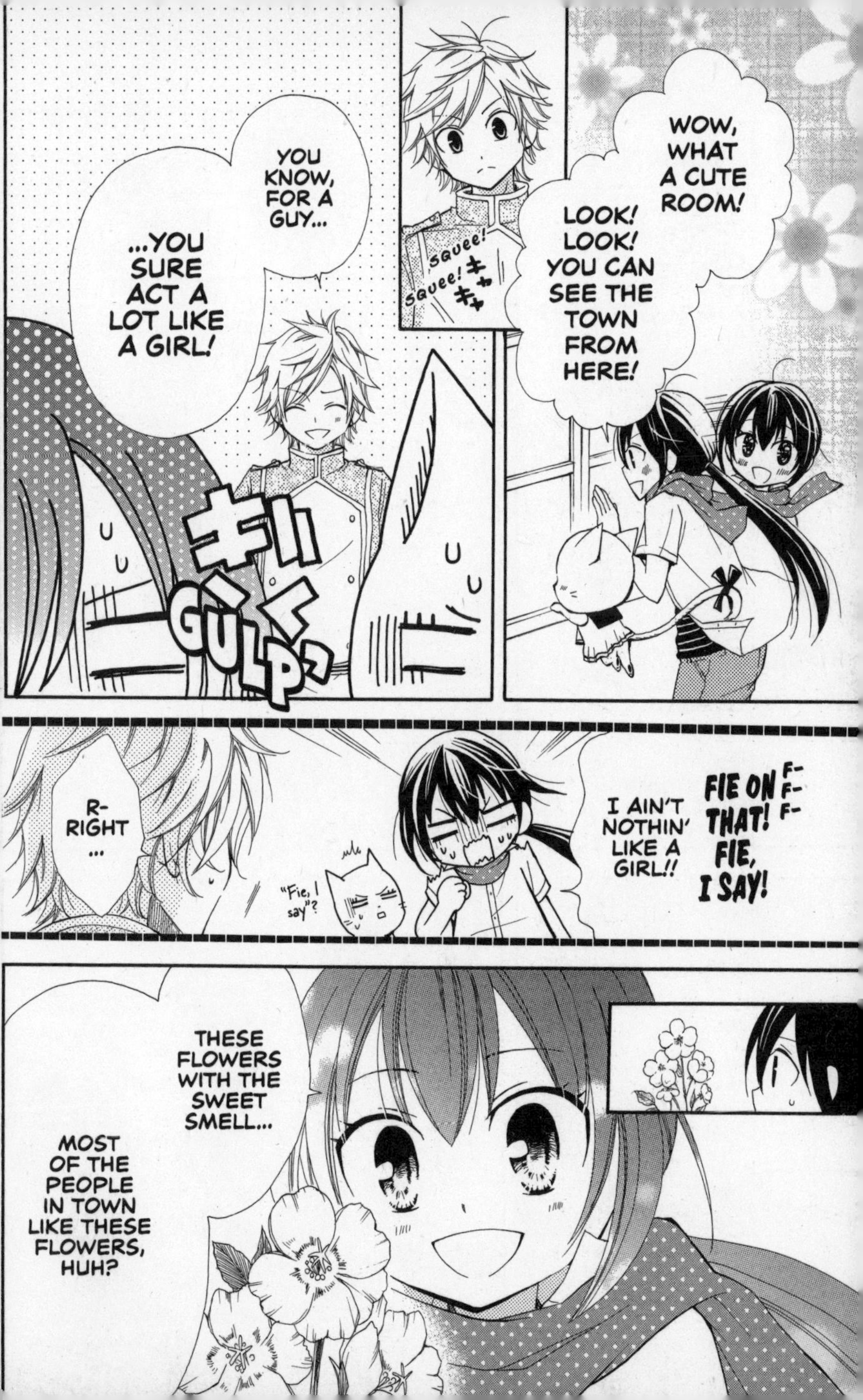
WOW, WHAT A CUTE ROOM!
LOOK! LOOK! YOU CAN SEE THE TOWN FROM HERE!
SQUEE! SQUEE!
YOU KNOW, FOR A GUY...
...YOU SURE ACT A LOT LIKE A GIRL!
GULP
FIE ON THAT! FIE, I SAY!
F- F- F-
I AIN'T NOTHIN' LIKE A GIRL!!
"Fie, I say"?
R-RIGHT...
THESE FLOWERS WITH THE SWEET SMELL...
MOST OF THE PEOPLE IN TOWN LIKE THESE FLOWERS, HUH?

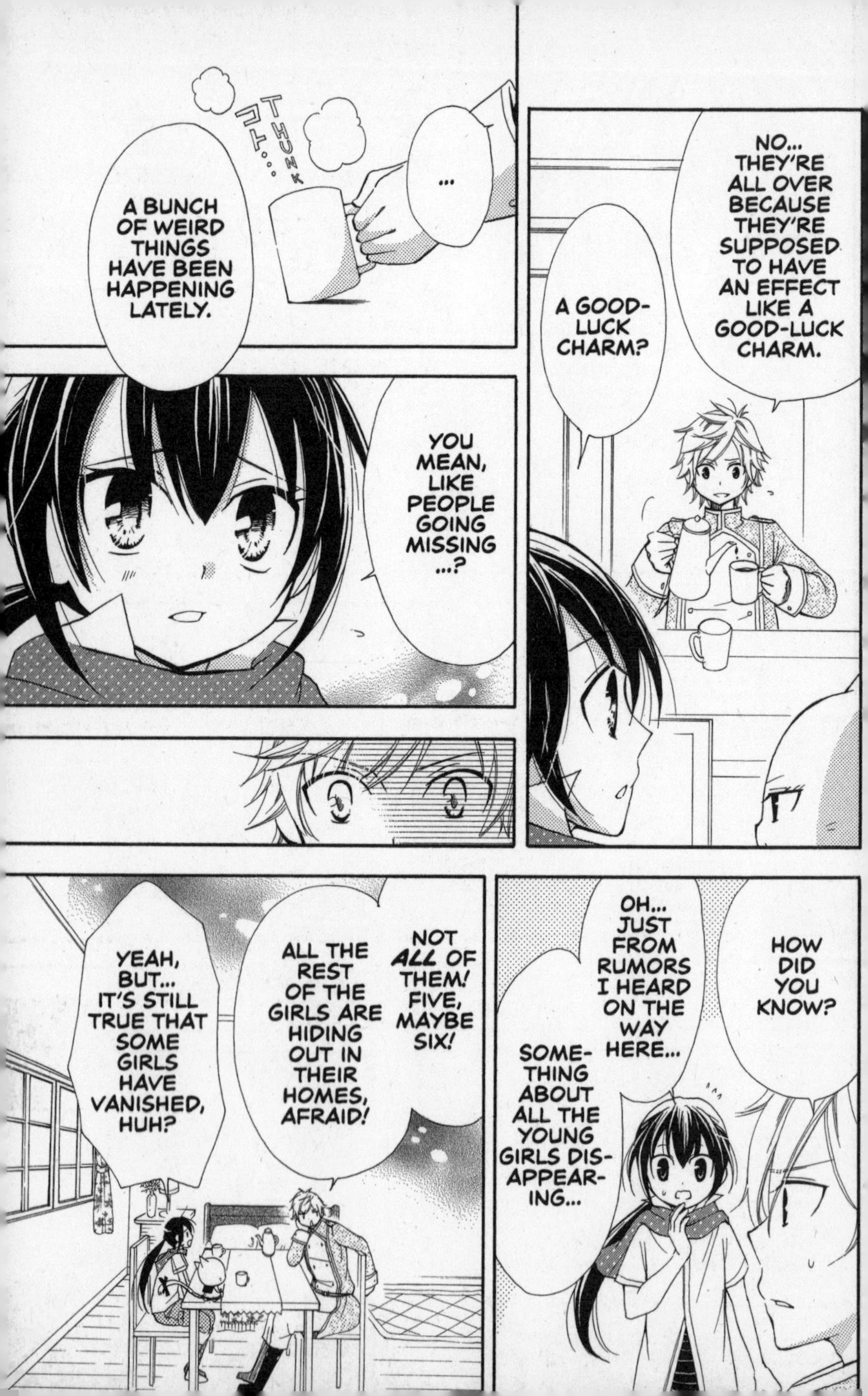
NO... THEY'RE ALL OVER BECAUSE THEY'RE SUPPOSED TO HAVE AN EFFECT LIKE A GOOD-LUCK CHARM.
A GOOD-LUCK CHARM?
THUNK
コト...
...
A BUNCH OF WEIRD THINGS HAVE BEEN HAPPENING LATELY.
YOU MEAN, LIKE PEOPLE GOING MISSING ...?
HOW DID YOU KNOW?
OH... JUST FROM RUMORS I HEARD ON THE WAY HERE...
SOME-THING ABOUT ALL THE YOUNG GIRLS DIS-APPEAR-ING...
NOT *ALL* OF THEM! FIVE, MAYBE SIX!
ALL THE REST OF THE GIRLS ARE HIDING OUT IN THEIR HOMES, AFRAID!
YEAH, BUT... IT'S STILL TRUE THAT SOME GIRLS HAVE VANISHED, HUH?

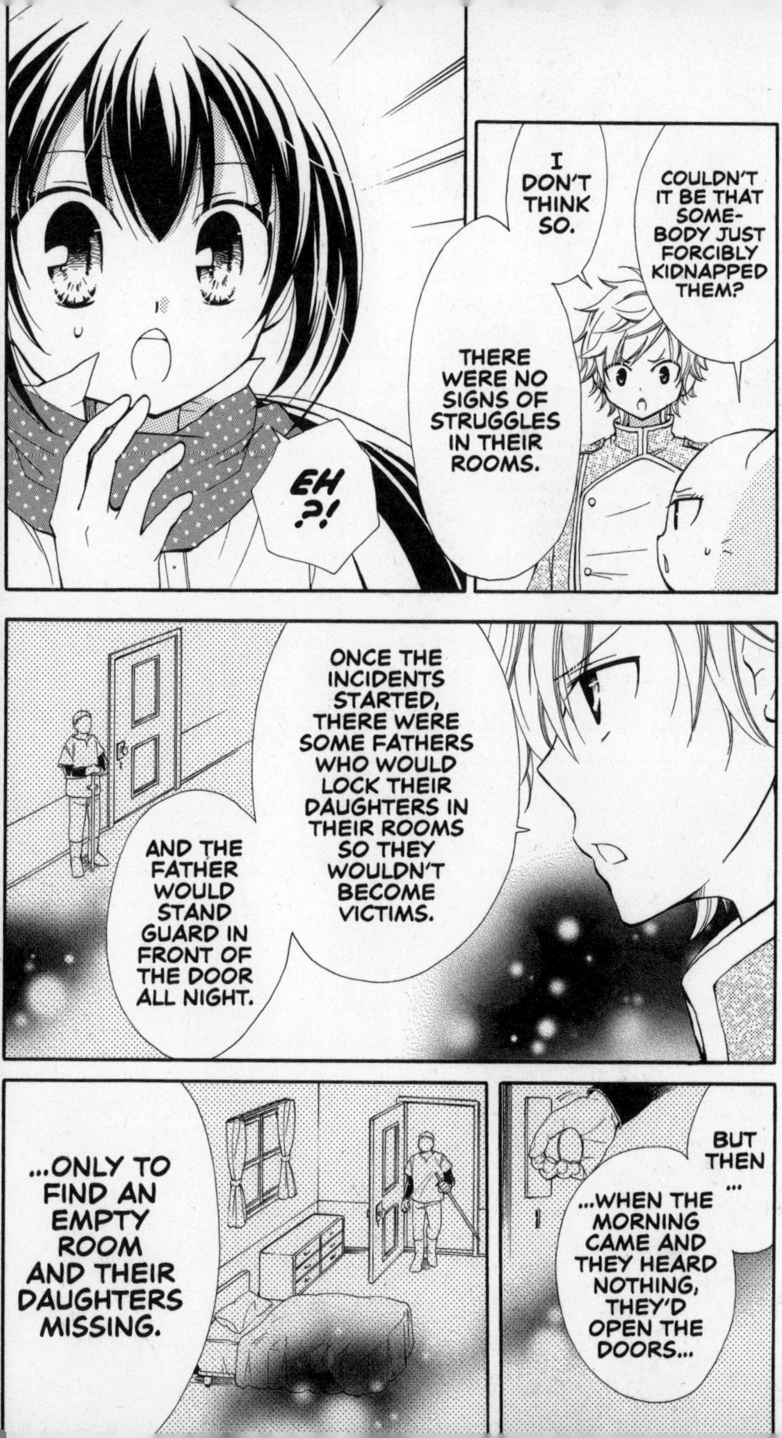
COULDN'T IT BE THAT SOMEBODY JUST FORCIBLY KIDNAPPED THEM?
I DON'T THINK SO.
THERE WERE NO SIGNS OF STRUGGLES IN THEIR ROOMS.
EH ?!
ONCE THE INCIDENTS STARTED, THERE WERE SOME FATHERS WHO WOULD LOCK THEIR DAUGHTERS IN THEIR ROOMS SO THEY WOULDN'T BECOME VICTIMS.
AND THE FATHER WOULD STAND GUARD IN FRONT OF THE DOOR ALL NIGHT.
BUT THEN...
...WHEN THE MORNING CAME AND THEY HEARD NOTHING, THEY'D OPEN THE DOORS...
...ONLY TO FIND AN EMPTY ROOM AND THEIR DAUGHTERS MISSING.

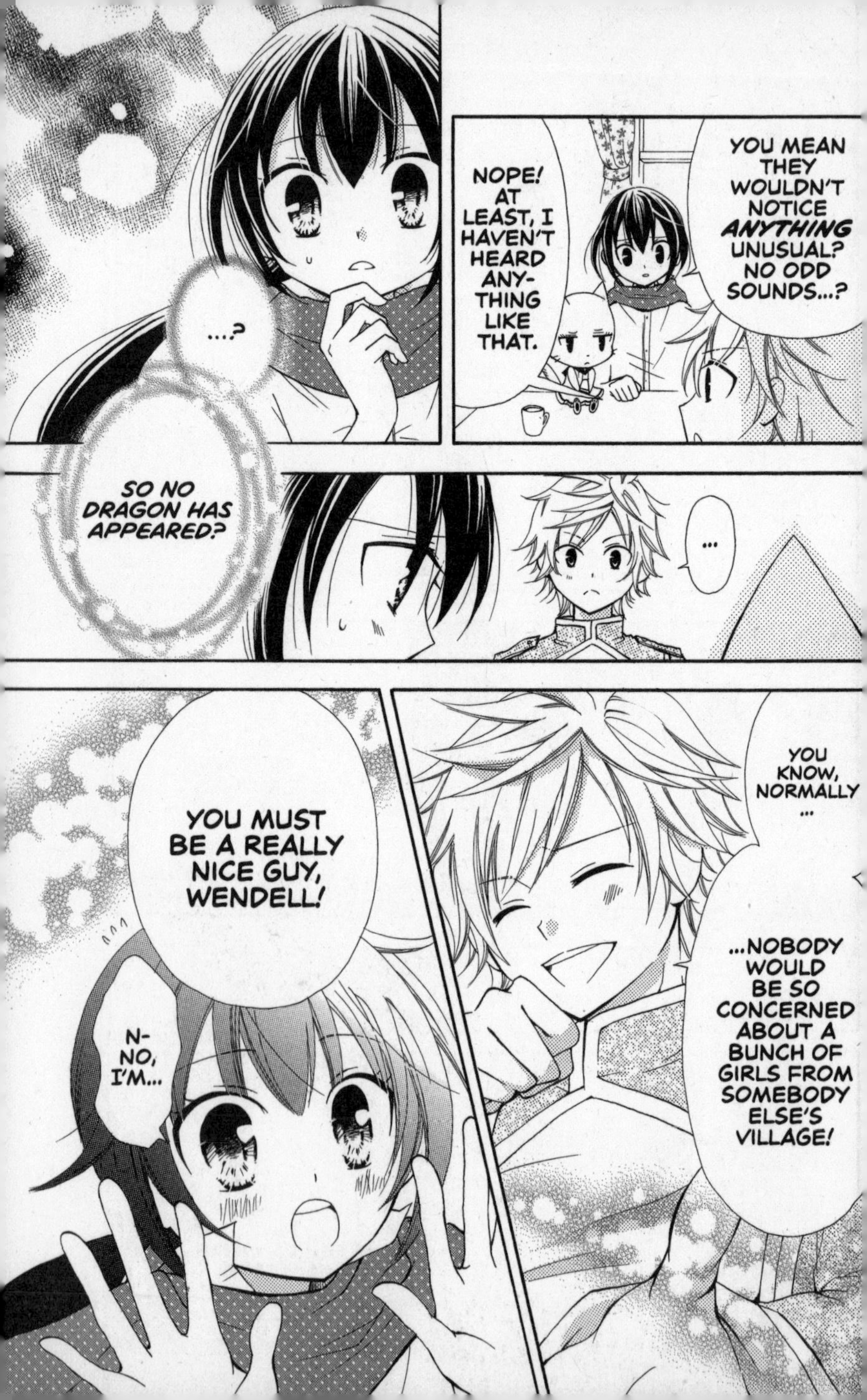

YOU MEAN THEY WOULDN'T NOTICE *ANYTHING* UNUSUAL? NO ODD SOUNDS...?
NOPE! AT LEAST, I HAVEN'T HEARD ANY-THING LIKE THAT.
...?
SO NO DRAGON HAS APPEARED?
...
YOU KNOW, NORMALLY...
...NOBODY WOULD BE SO CONCERNED ABOUT A BUNCH OF GIRLS FROM SOMEBODY ELSE'S VILLAGE!
YOU MUST BE A REALLY NICE GUY, WENDELL!
N-NO, I'M...

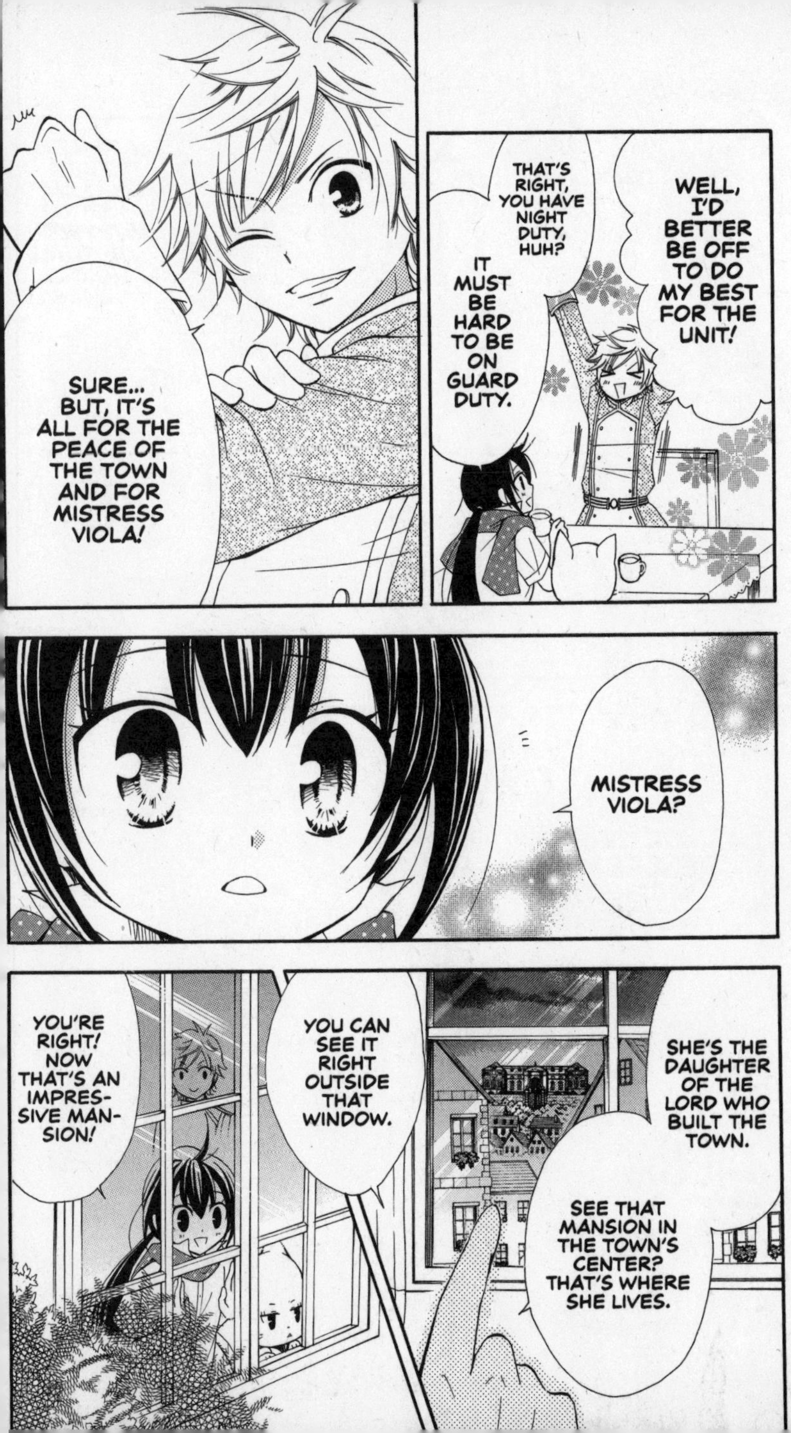
WELL, I'D BETTER BE OFF TO DO MY BEST FOR THE UNIT!
THAT'S RIGHT, YOU HAVE NIGHT DUTY, HUH?
IT MUST BE HARD TO BE ON GUARD DUTY.
SURE... BUT, IT'S ALL FOR THE PEACE OF THE TOWN AND FOR MISTRESS VIOLA!
MISTRESS VIOLA?
SHE'S THE DAUGHTER OF THE LORD WHO BUILT THE TOWN.
SEE THAT MANSION IN THE TOWN'S CENTER? THAT'S WHERE SHE LIVES.
YOU CAN SEE IT RIGHT OUTSIDE THAT WINDOW.
YOU'RE RIGHT! NOW THAT'S AN IMPRESSIVE MAN-SION!

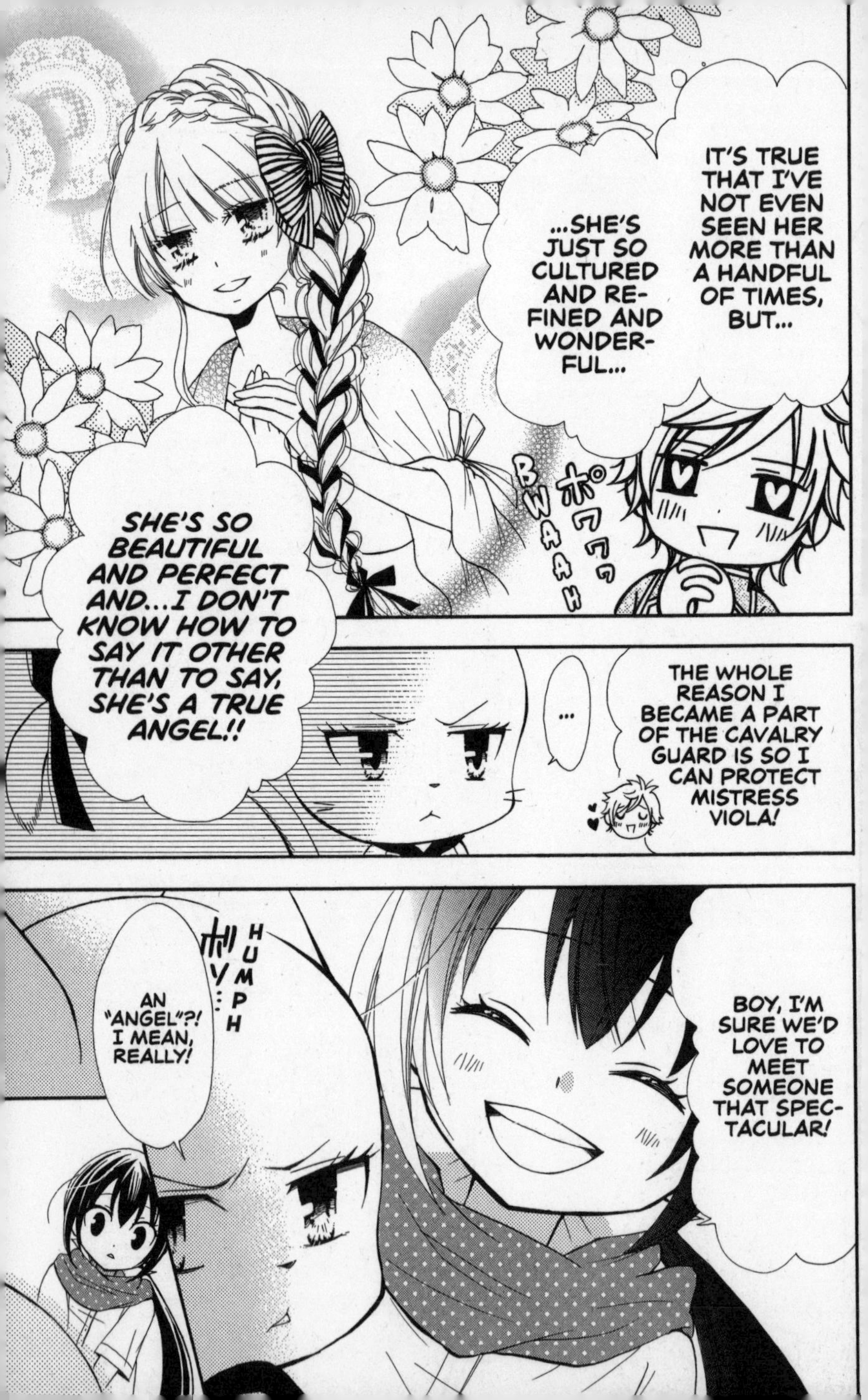
IT'S TRUE THAT I'VE NOT EVEN SEEN HER MORE THAN A HANDFUL OF TIMES, BUT...
...SHE'S JUST SO CULTURED AND RE-FINED AND WONDER-FUL...
ポワワワ
BWAAAH
SHE'S SO BEAUTIFUL AND PERFECT AND...I DON'T KNOW HOW TO SAY IT OTHER THAN TO SAY, SHE'S A TRUE ANGEL!!
THE WHOLE REASON I BECAME A PART OF THE CAVALRY GUARD IS SO I CAN PROTECT MISTRESS VIOLA!
...
BOY, I'M SURE WE'D LOVE TO MEET SOMEONE THAT SPEC-TACULAR!
HUMPH
AN "ANGEL"?! I MEAN, REALLY!

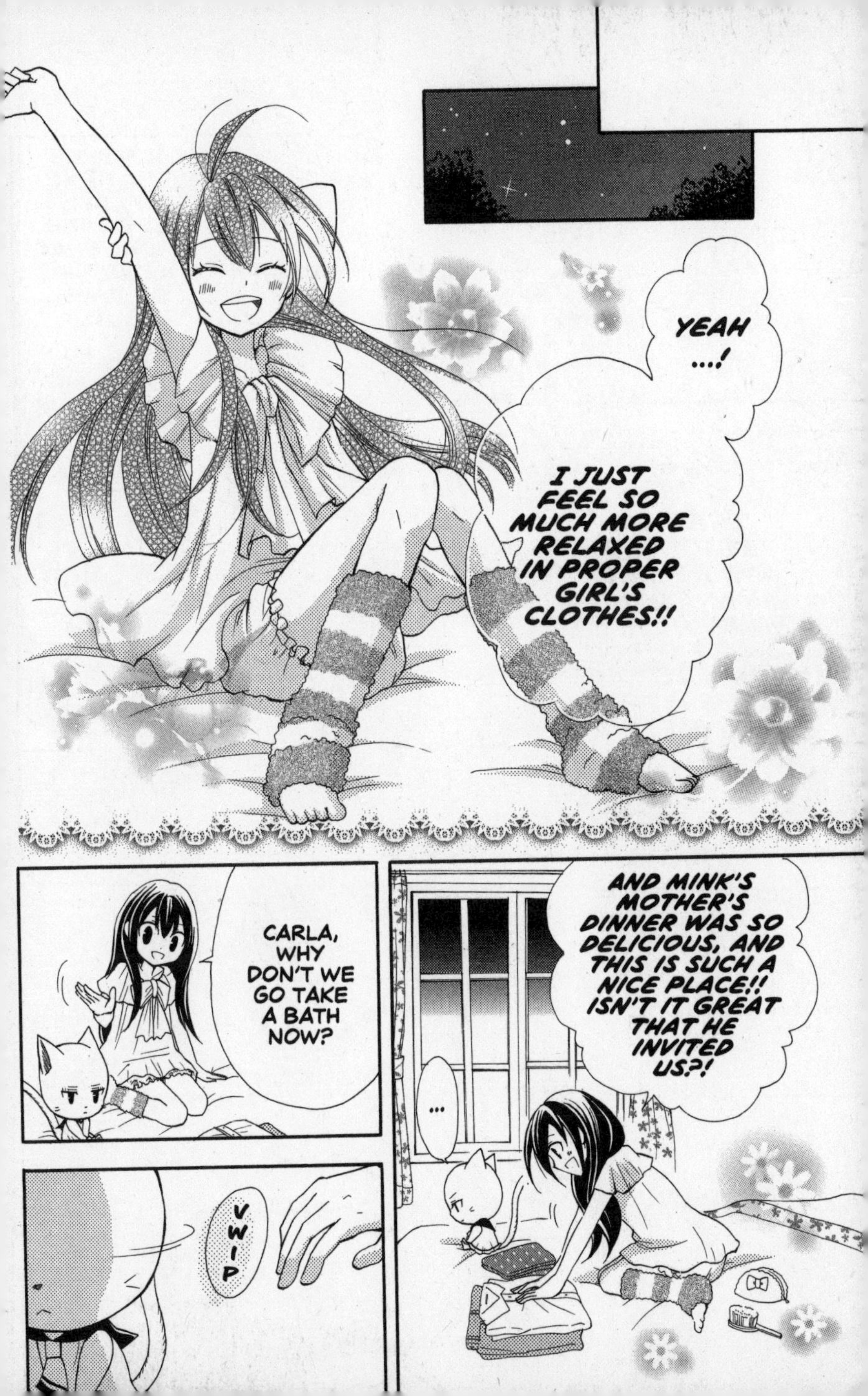
YEAH ...!
I JUST FEEL SO MUCH MORE RELAXED IN PROPER GIRL'S CLOTHES!!
AND MINK'S MOTHER'S DINNER WAS SO DELICIOUS, AND THIS IS SUCH A NICE PLACE!! ISN'T IT GREAT THAT HE INVITED US?!
...
CARLA, WHY DON'T WE GO TAKE A BATH NOW?
VWIP

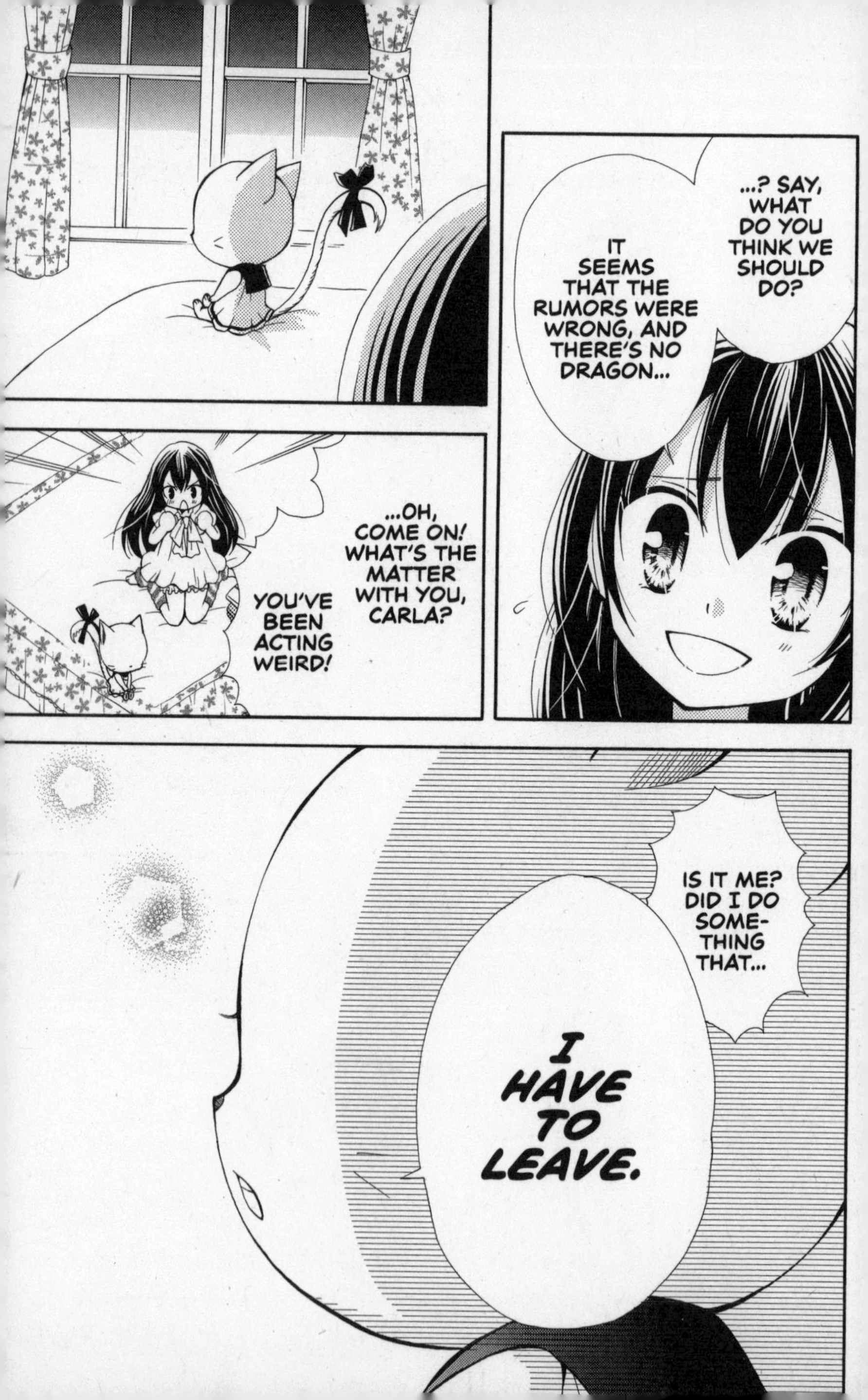
...? SAY, WHAT DO YOU THINK WE SHOULD DO?
IT SEEMS THAT THE RUMORS WERE WRONG, AND THERE'S NO DRAGON...
...OH, COME ON! WHAT'S THE MATTER WITH YOU, CARLA?
YOU'VE BEEN ACTING WEIRD!
IS IT ME? DID I DO SOME-THING THAT...
I HAVE TO LEAVE.

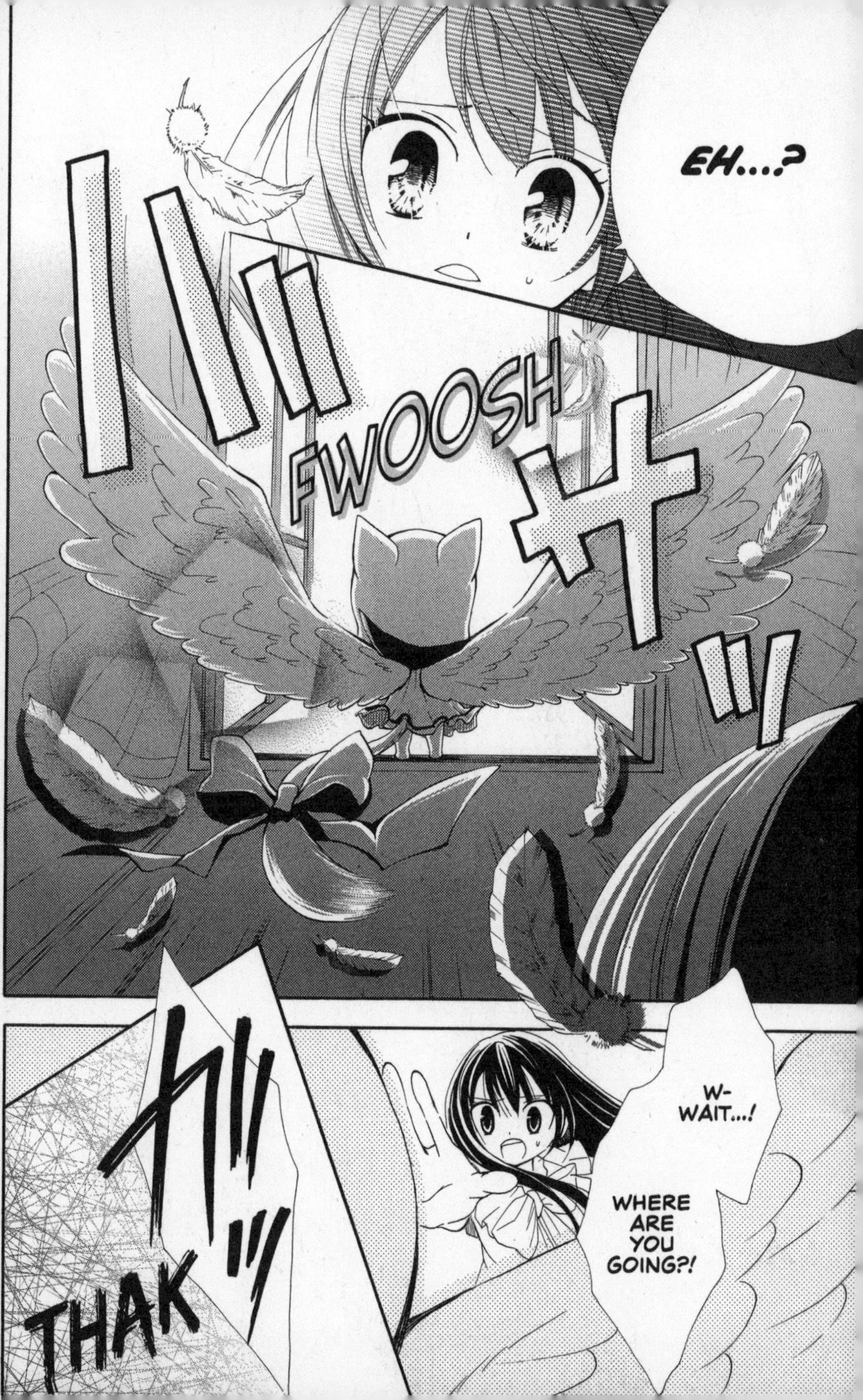
EH...?
FWOOSH
W-WAIT...!
WHERE ARE YOU GOING?!
THAK

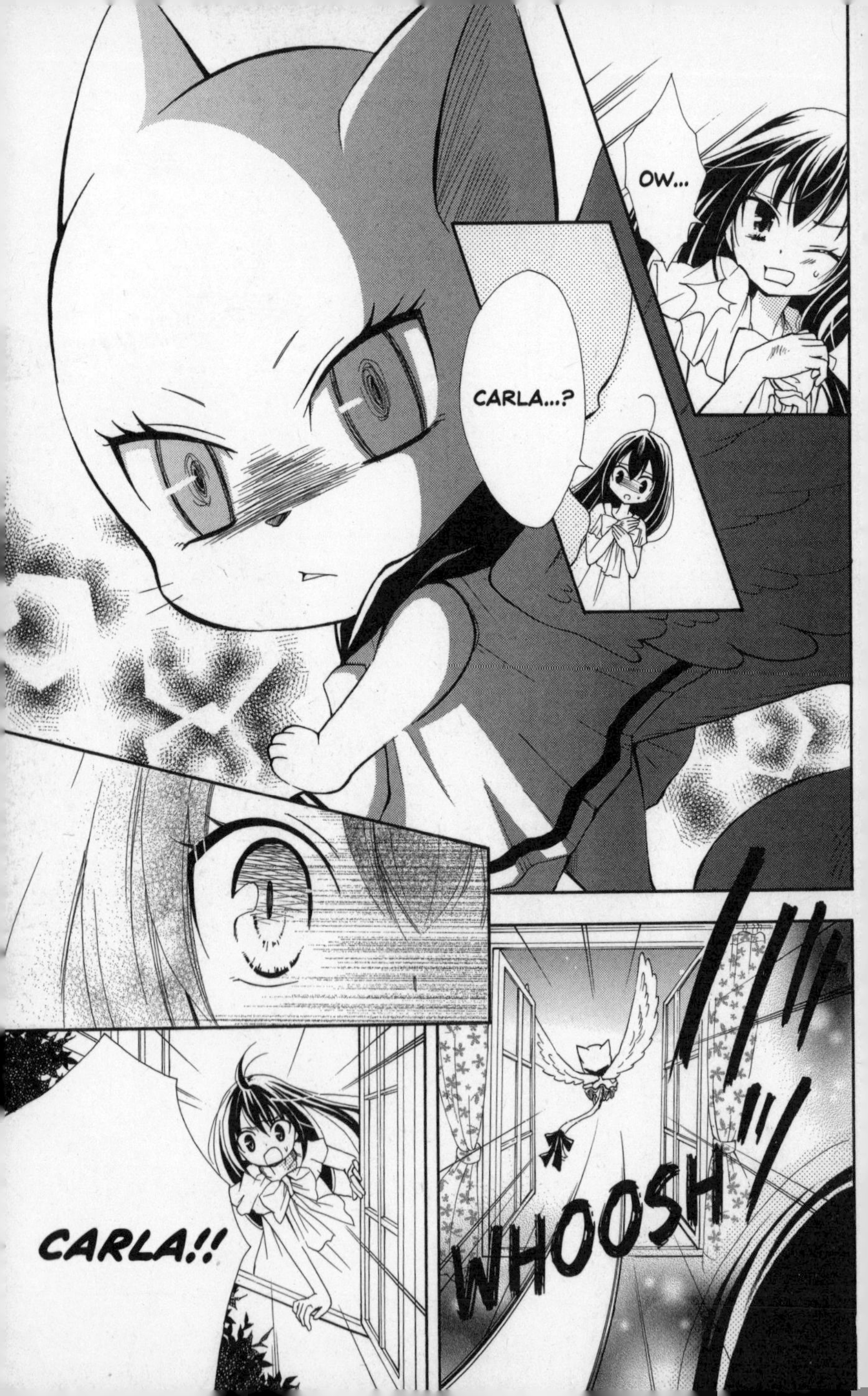
OW...
CARLA...?
WHOOSH
CARLA!!

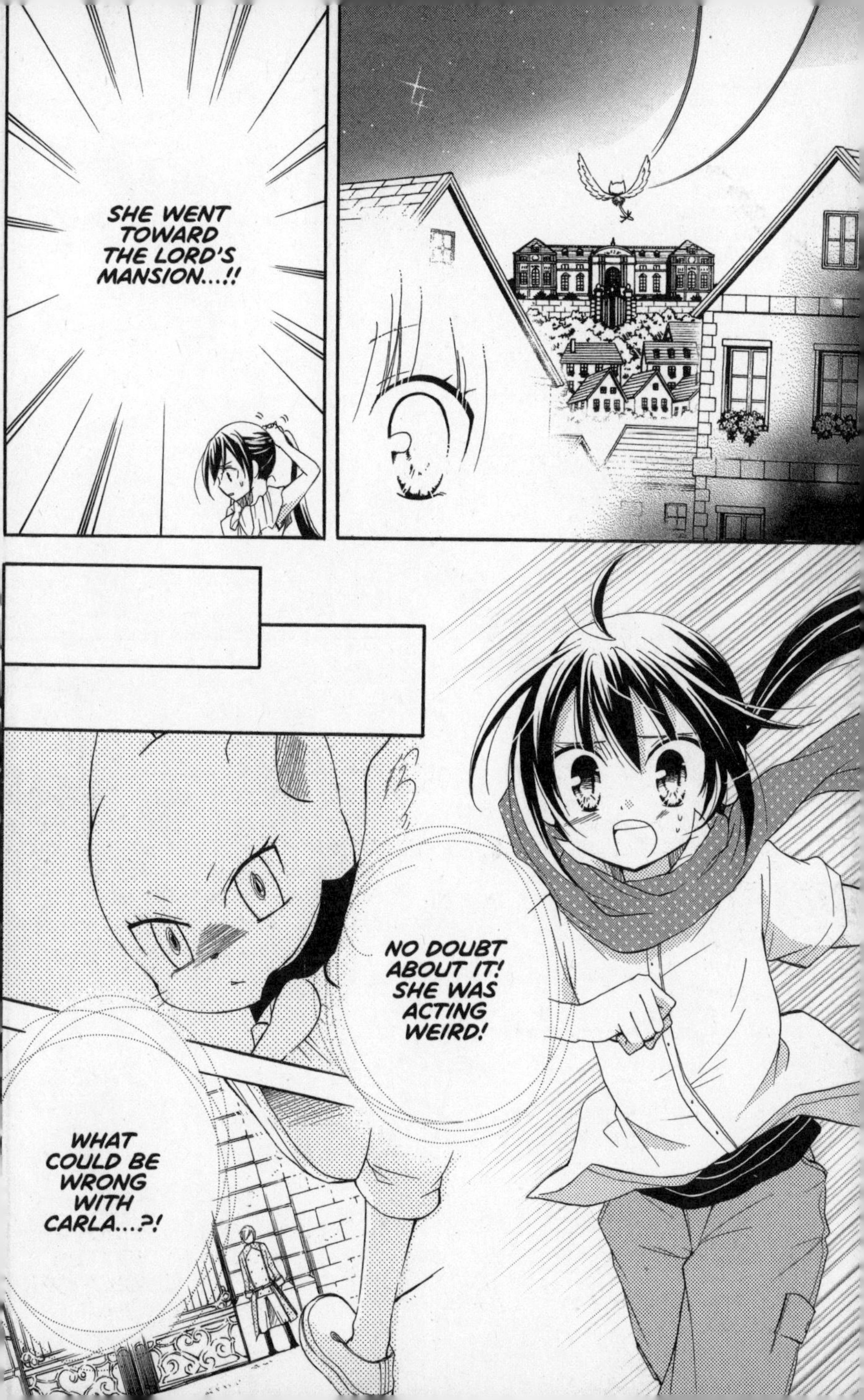
SHE WENT TOWARD THE LORD'S MANSION...!!
NO DOUBT ABOUT IT! SHE WAS ACTING WEIRD!
WHAT COULD BE WRONG WITH CARLA...?!

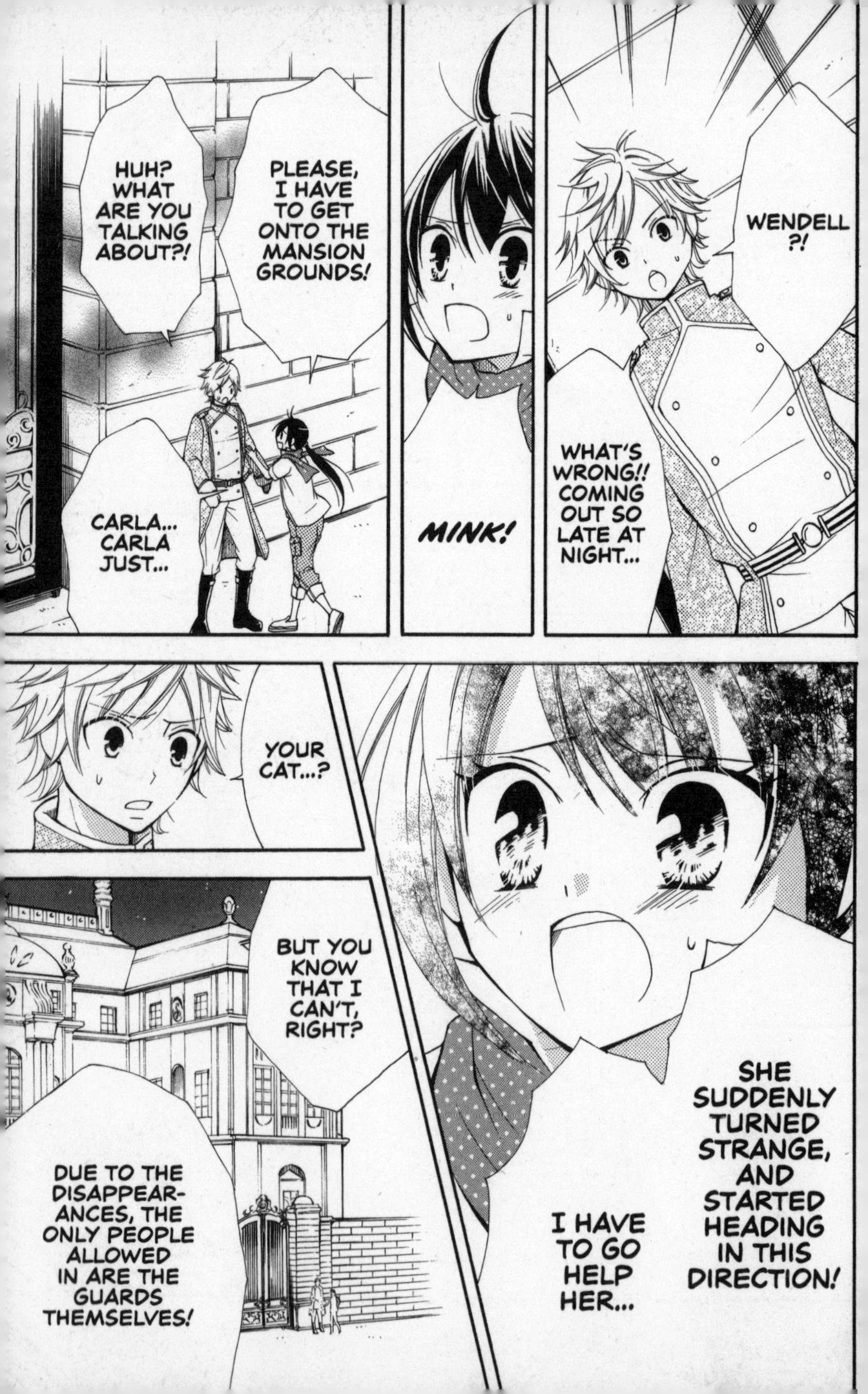
WENDELL ?!
WHAT'S WRONG!! COMING OUT SO LATE AT NIGHT...
MINK!
PLEASE, I HAVE TO GET ONTO THE MANSION GROUNDS!
HUH? WHAT ARE YOU TALKING ABOUT?!
CARLA... CARLA JUST...
SHE SUDDENLY TURNED STRANGE, AND STARTED HEADING IN THIS DIRECTION!
I HAVE TO GO HELP HER...
YOUR CAT...?
BUT YOU KNOW THAT I CAN'T, RIGHT?
DUE TO THE DISAPPEAR-ANCES, THE ONLY PEOPLE ALLOWED IN ARE THE GUARDS THEMSELVES!

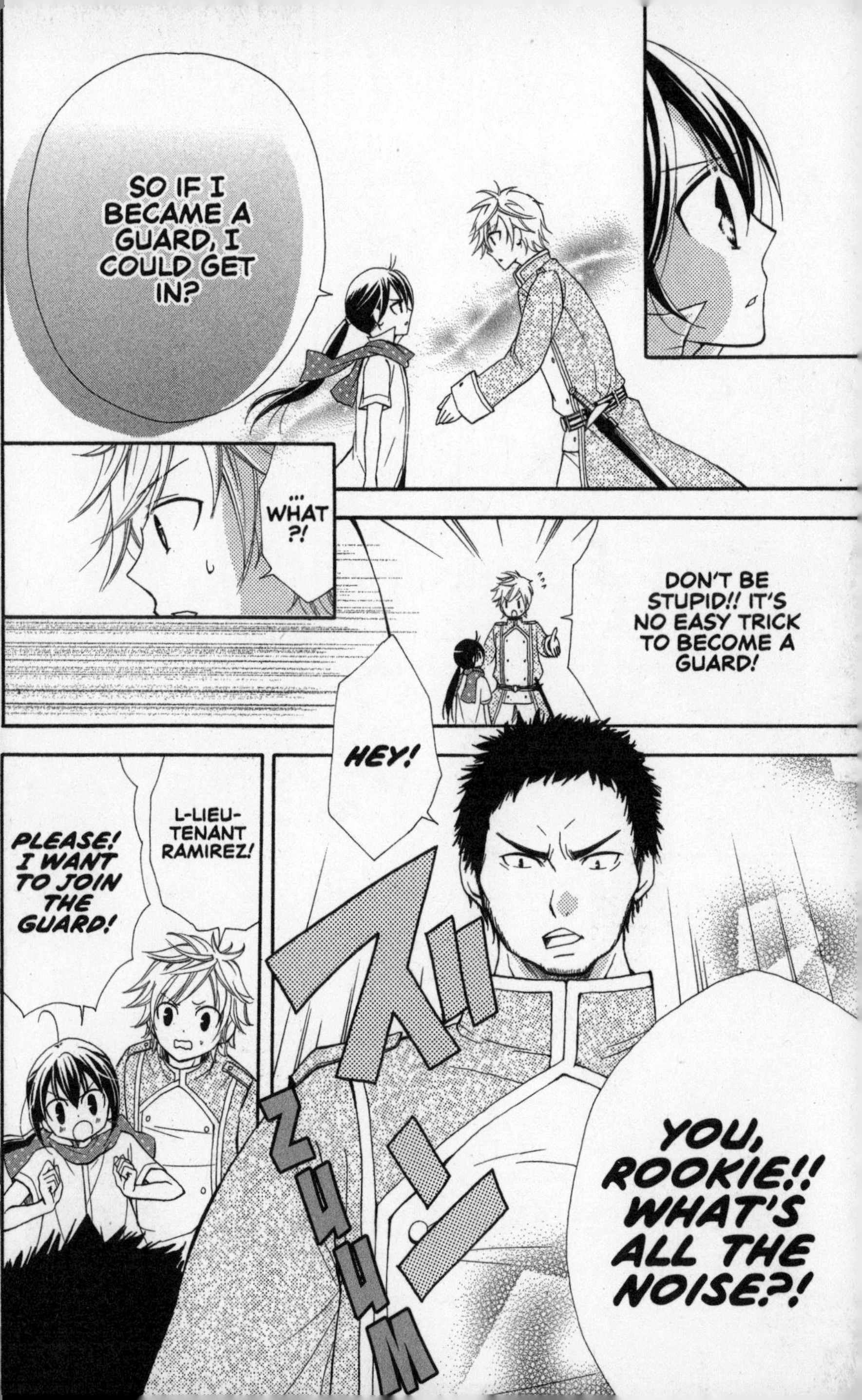
SO IF I BECAME A GUARD, I COULD GET IN?
...WHAT?!
DON'T BE STUPID!! IT'S NO EASY TRICK TO BECOME A GUARD!
HEY!
YOU, ROOKIE!! WHAT'S ALL THE NOISE?!
ZUUUM
L-LIEU-TENANT RAMIREZ!
PLEASE! I WANT TO JOIN THE GUARD!

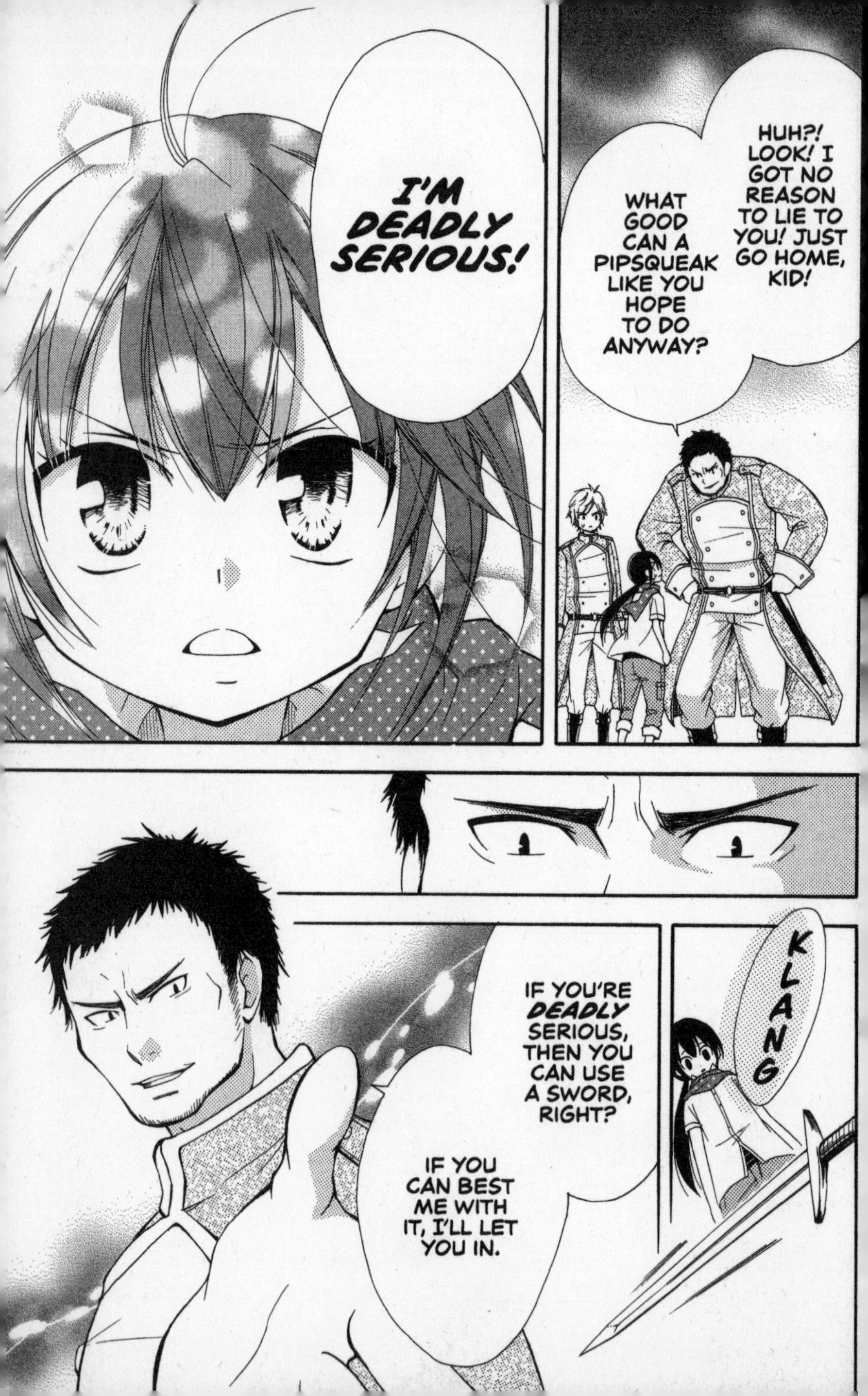
HUH?! LOOK! I GOT NO REASON TO LIE TO YOU! JUST GO HOME, KID!
WHAT GOOD CAN A PIPSQUEAK LIKE YOU HOPE TO DO ANYWAY?
I'M DEADLY SERIOUS!
KLANG
IF YOU'RE *DEADLY* SERIOUS, THEN YOU CAN USE A SWORD, RIGHT?
IF YOU CAN BEST ME WITH IT, I'LL LET YOU IN.

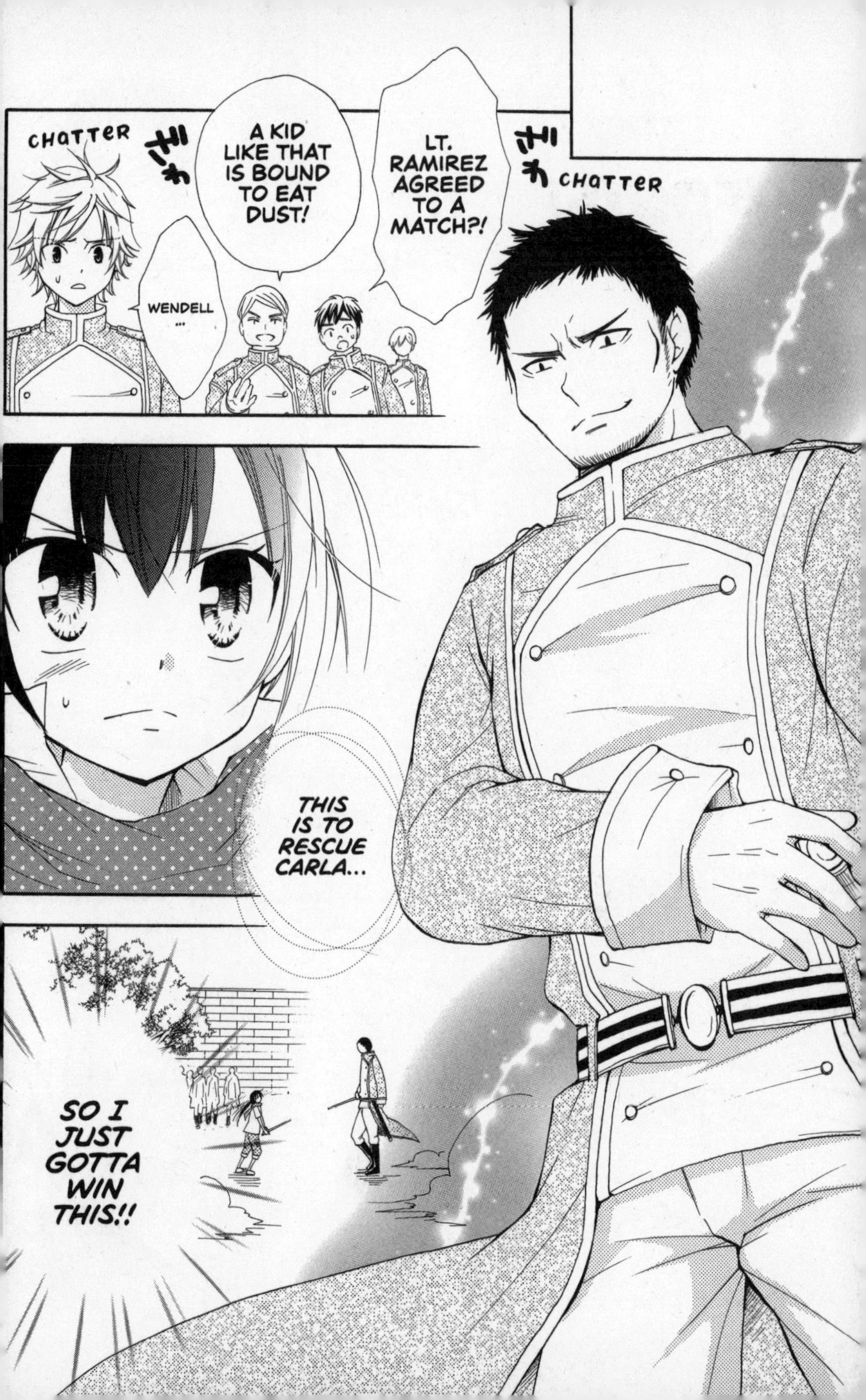
ざわ
CHATTER
LT. RAMIREZ AGREED TO A MATCH?!
A KID LIKE THAT IS BOUND TO EAT DUST!
ざわ
CHATTER
WENDELL ...
THIS IS TO RESCUE CARLA...
SO I JUST GOTTA WIN THIS!!

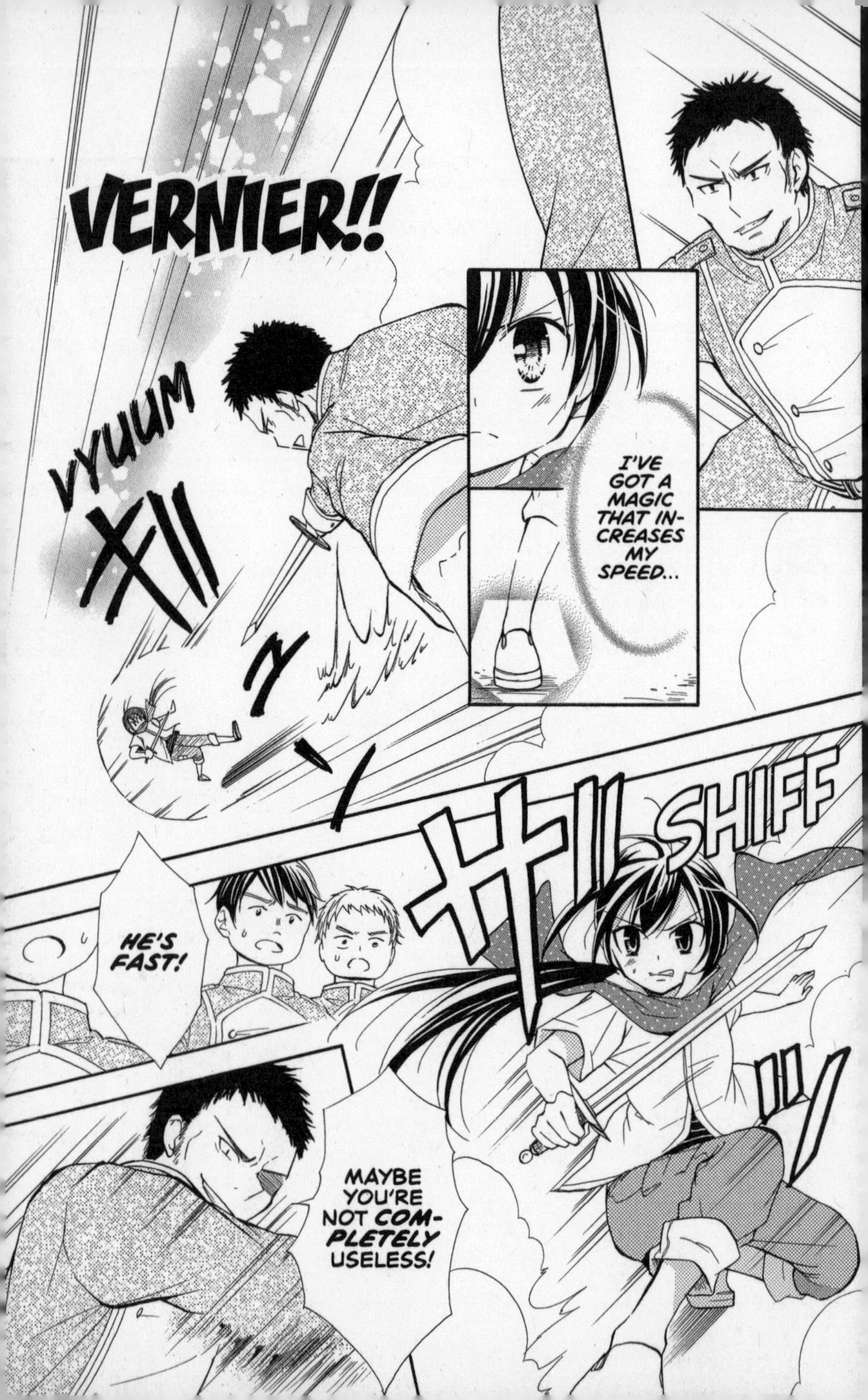
I'VE GOT A MAGIC THAT IN-CREASES MY SPEED...
VERNIER!!
VYUUM
SHIFF
HE'S FAST!
MAYBE YOU'RE NOT *COMPLETELY* USELESS!

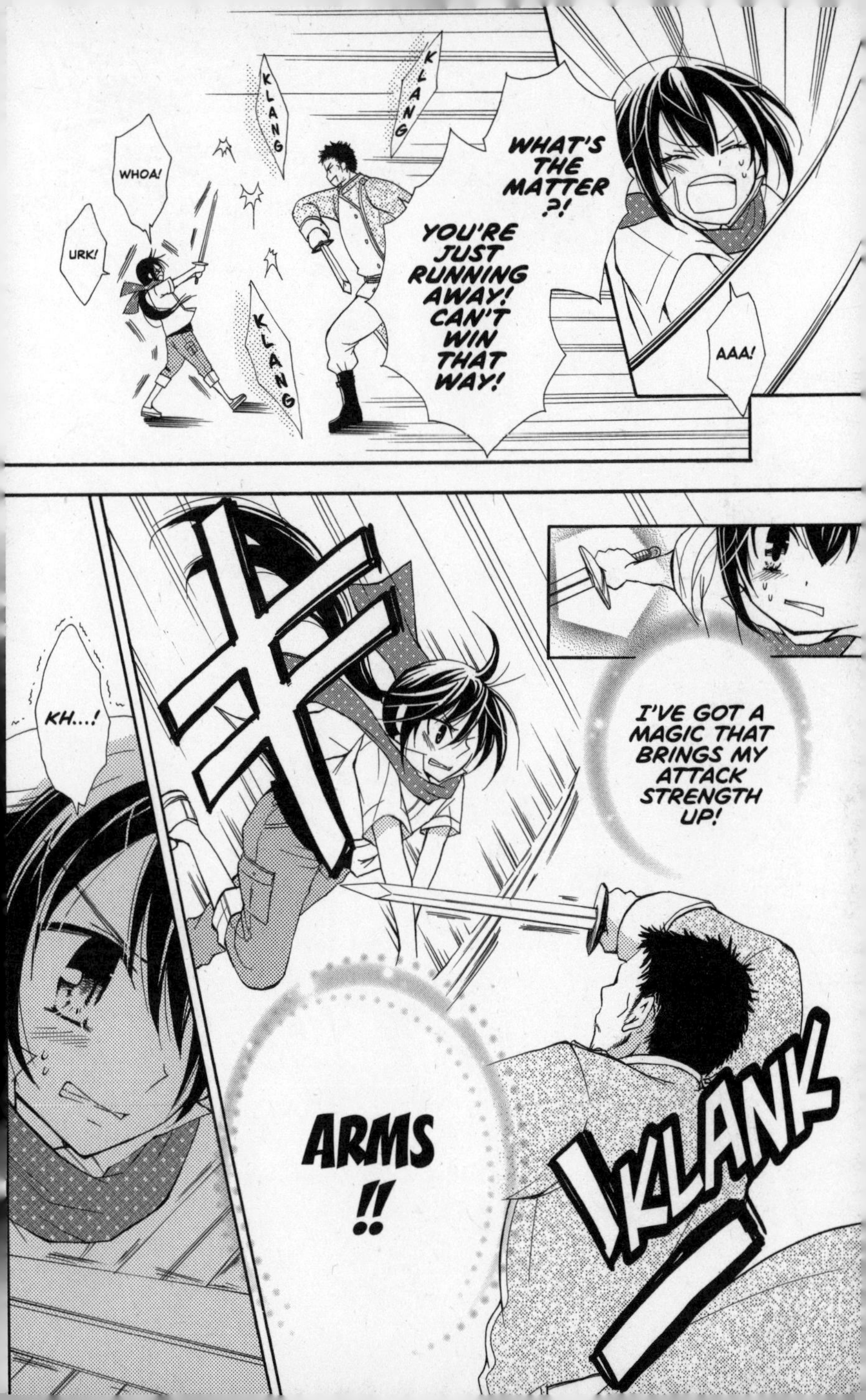
WHAT'S THE MATTER ?!
YOU'RE JUST RUNNING AWAY! CAN'T WIN THAT WAY!
AAA!
KLANG
KLANG
KLANG
WHOA!
URK!
I'VE GOT A MAGIC THAT BRINGS MY ATTACK STRENGTH UP!
ARMS!!
KLANK
KH...!

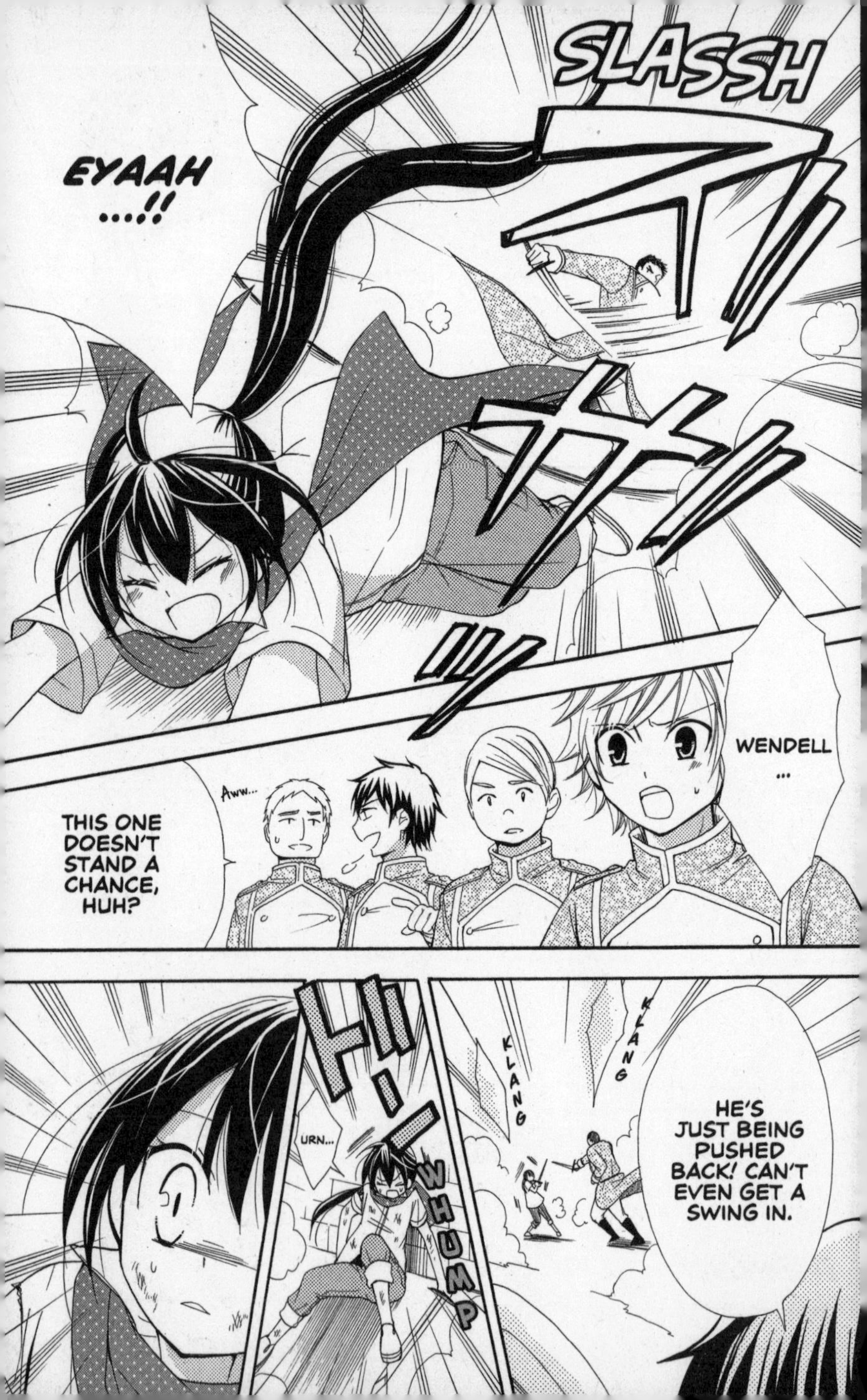
SLASSH
EYAAH ...!!
WENDELL ...
Aww...
THIS ONE DOESN'T STAND A CHANCE, HUH?
HE'S JUST BEING PUSHED BACK! CAN'T EVEN GET A SWING IN.
KLANG
KLANG
URN...
WHUMP

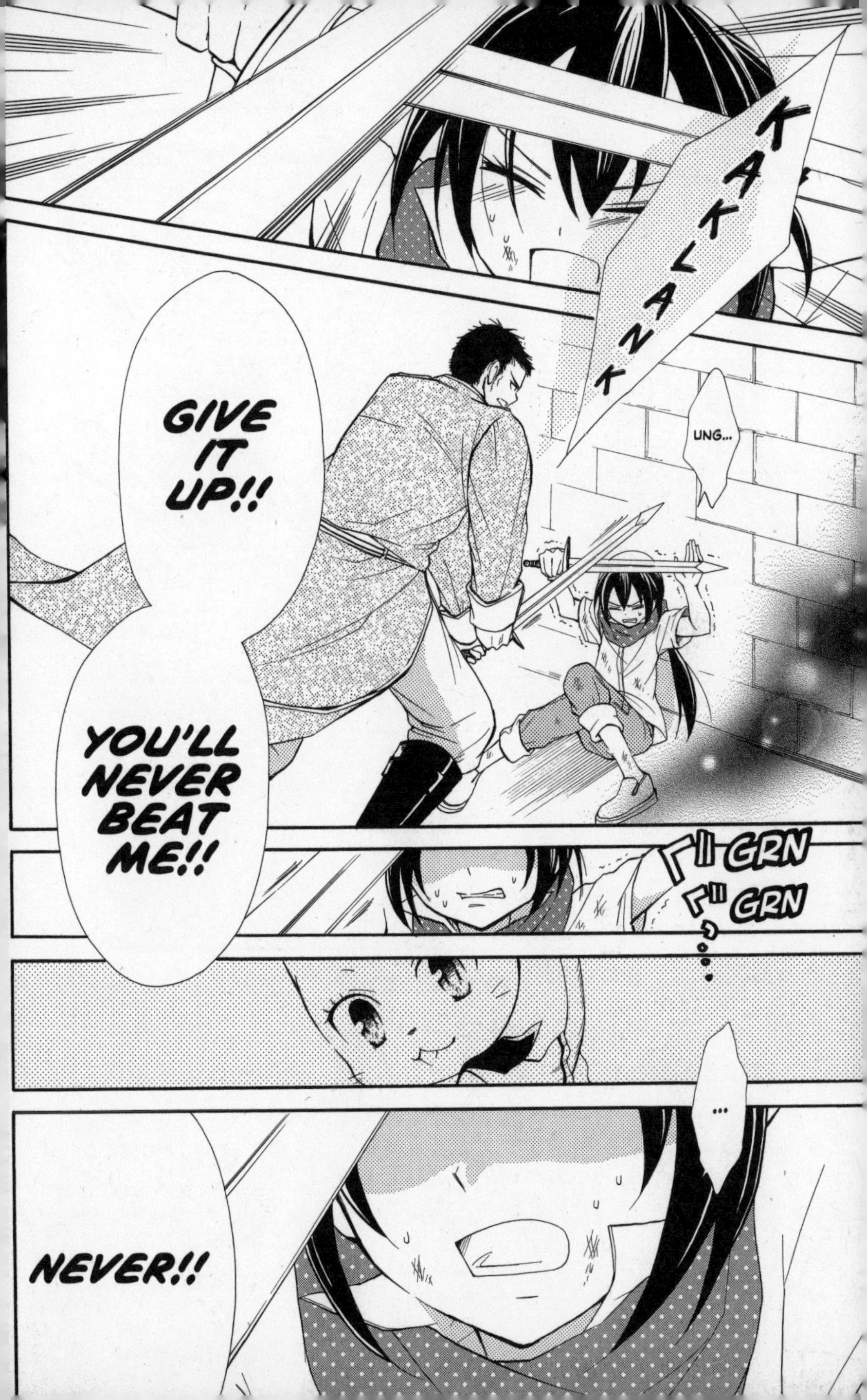
KAKLANK
UNG...
GIVE IT UP!!
GRN
GRN
YOU'LL NEVER BEAT ME!!
...
NEVER!!

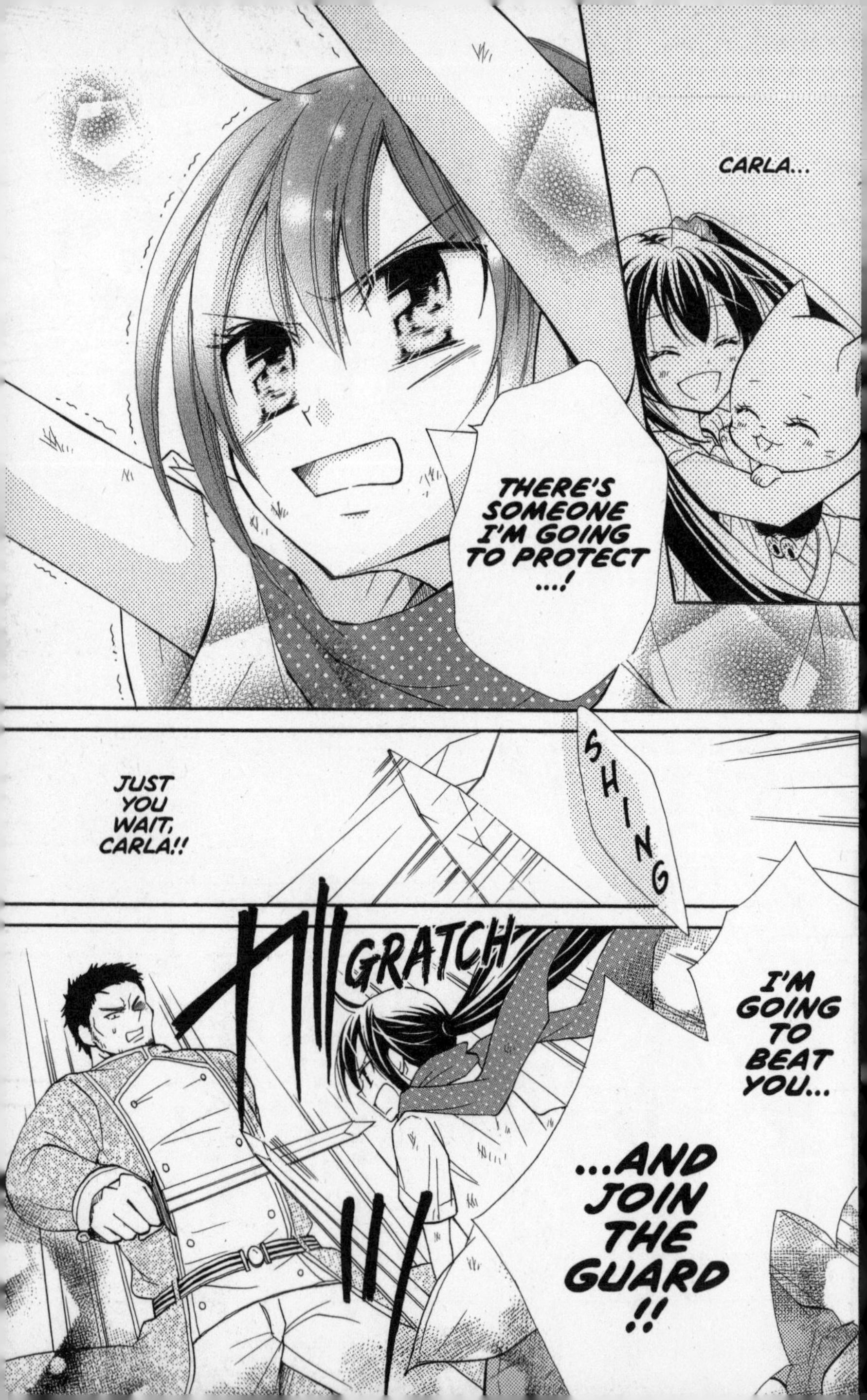
CARLA...
THERE'S SOMEONE I'M GOING TO PROTECT ...!
SHING
JUST YOU WAIT, CARLA!!
I'M GOING TO BEAT YOU...
...AND JOIN THE GUARD!!
GRATCH

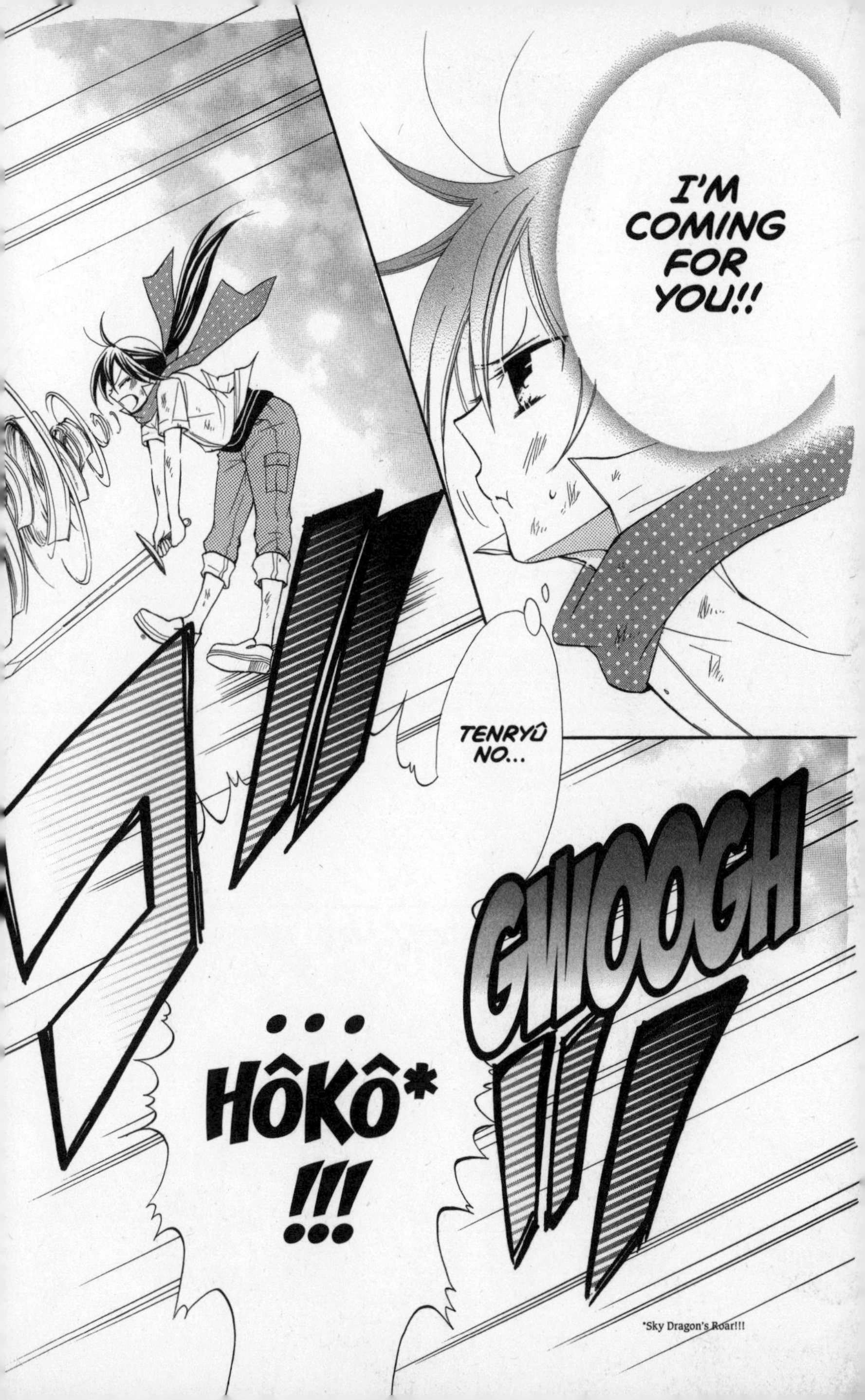
I'M COMING FOR YOU!!
TENRYÛ NO...
GWOOGH
...HÔKÔ* !!!

*Sky Dragon's Roar!!!

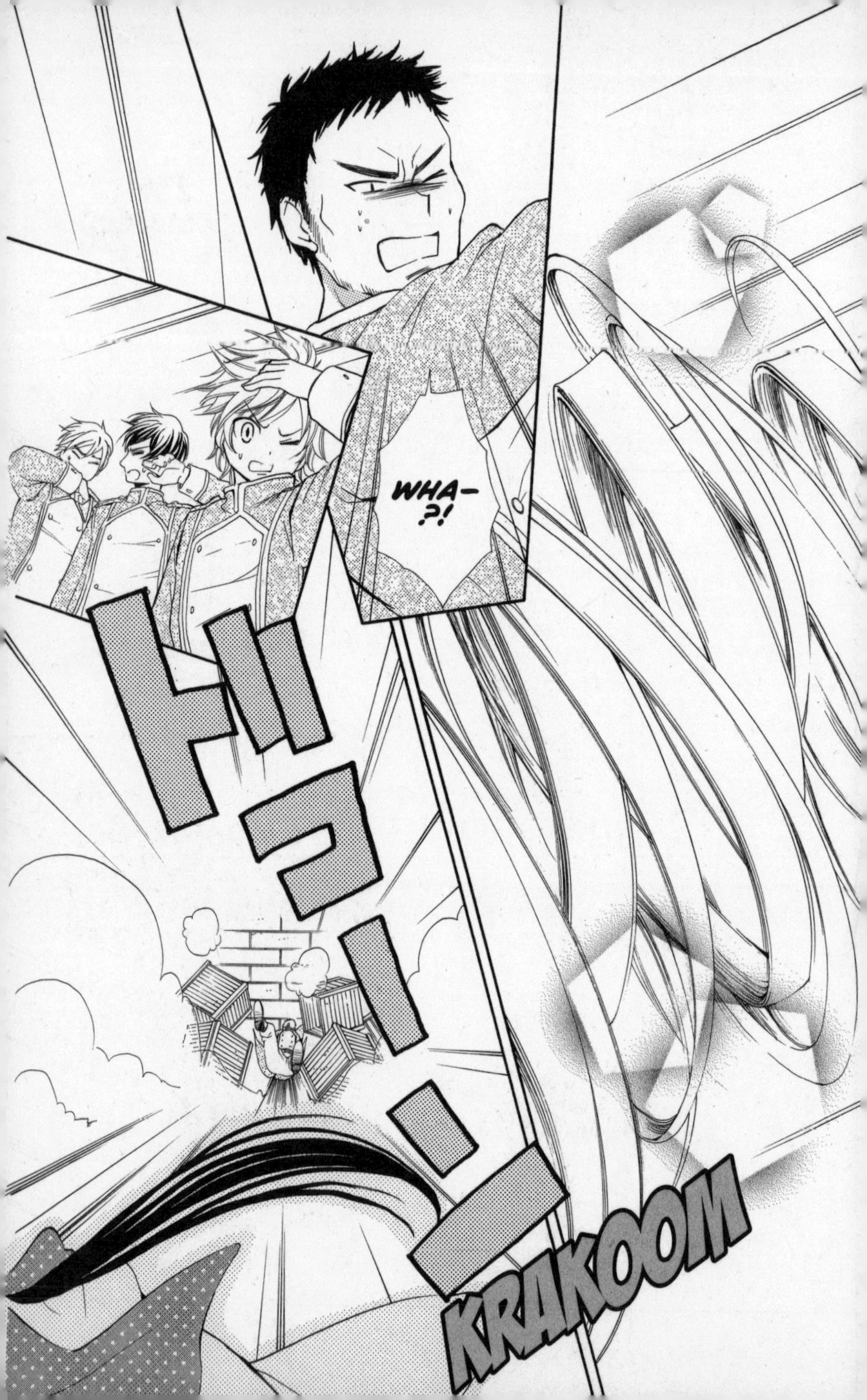
WHA-
?!
KRAKOOM

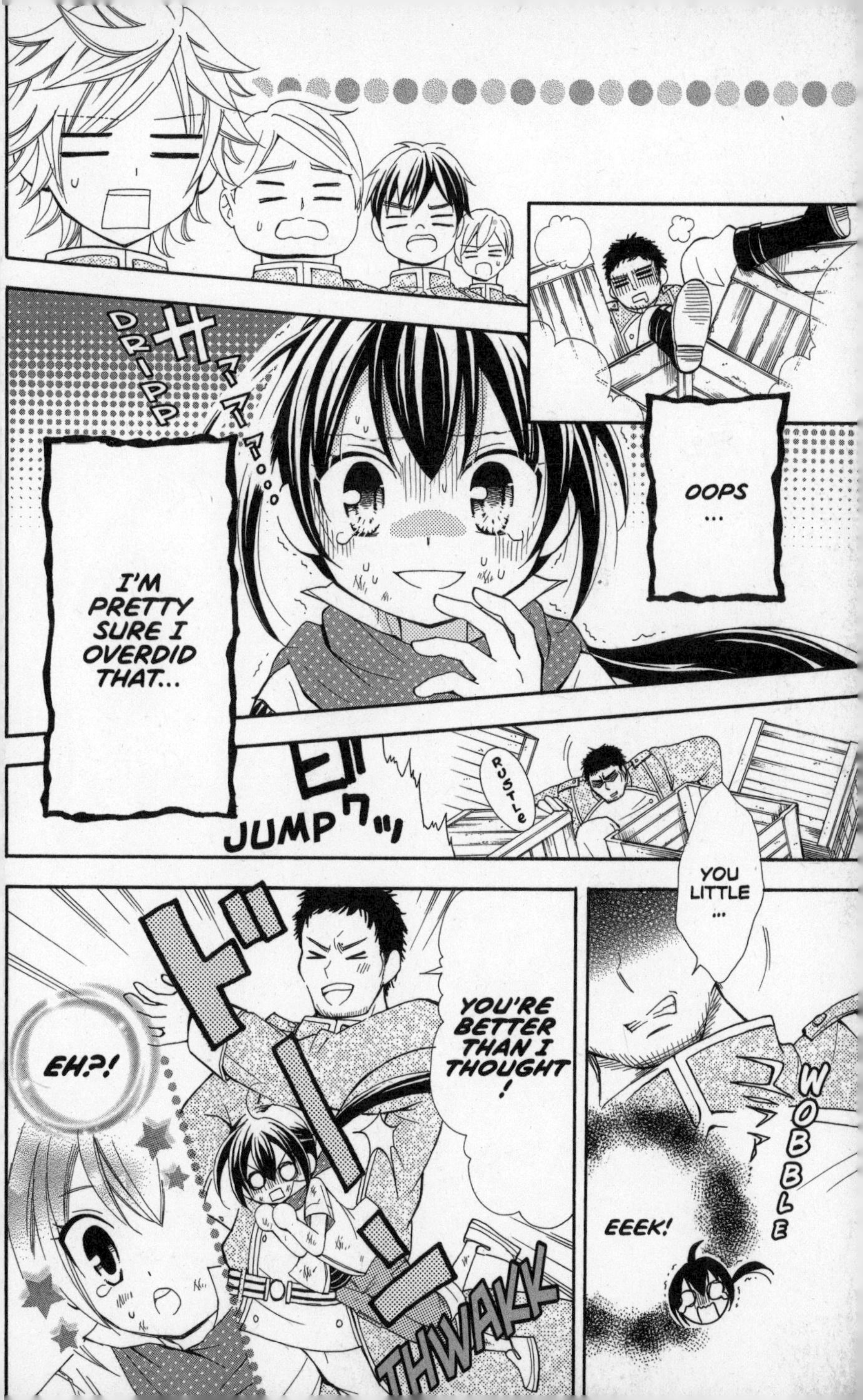
OOPS ...
DRIPP
I'M PRETTY SURE I OVERDID THAT...
RUSTLE
JUMP
YOU LITTLE ...
WOBBLE
EEEK!
THWAKK
YOU'RE BETTER THAN I THOUGHT!
EH?!

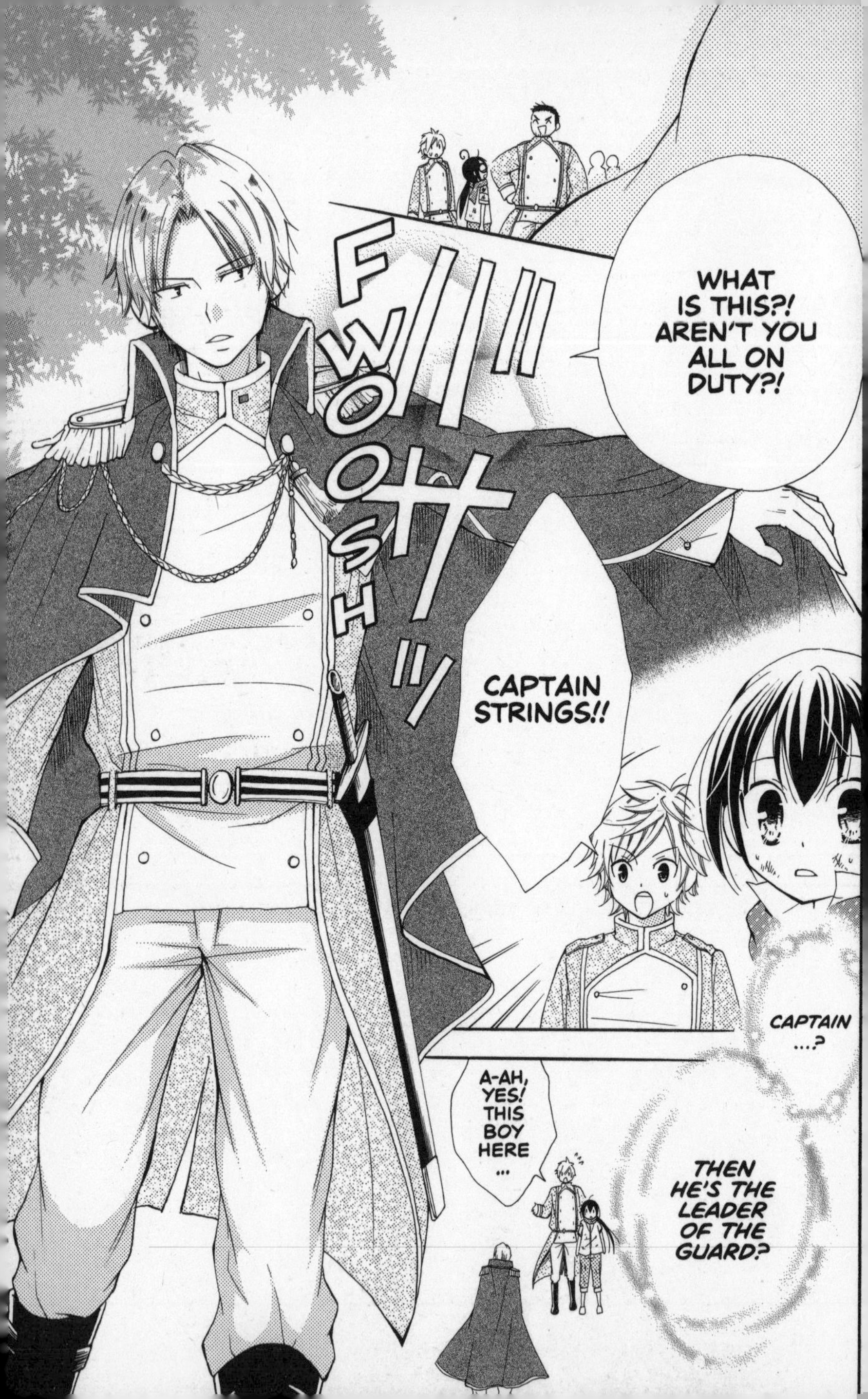
WHAT IS THIS?! AREN'T YOU ALL ON DUTY?!
CAPTAIN STRINGS!!
CAPTAIN ...?
A-AH, YES! THIS BOY HERE ...
THEN HE'S THE LEADER OF THE GUARD?
FWOOSH

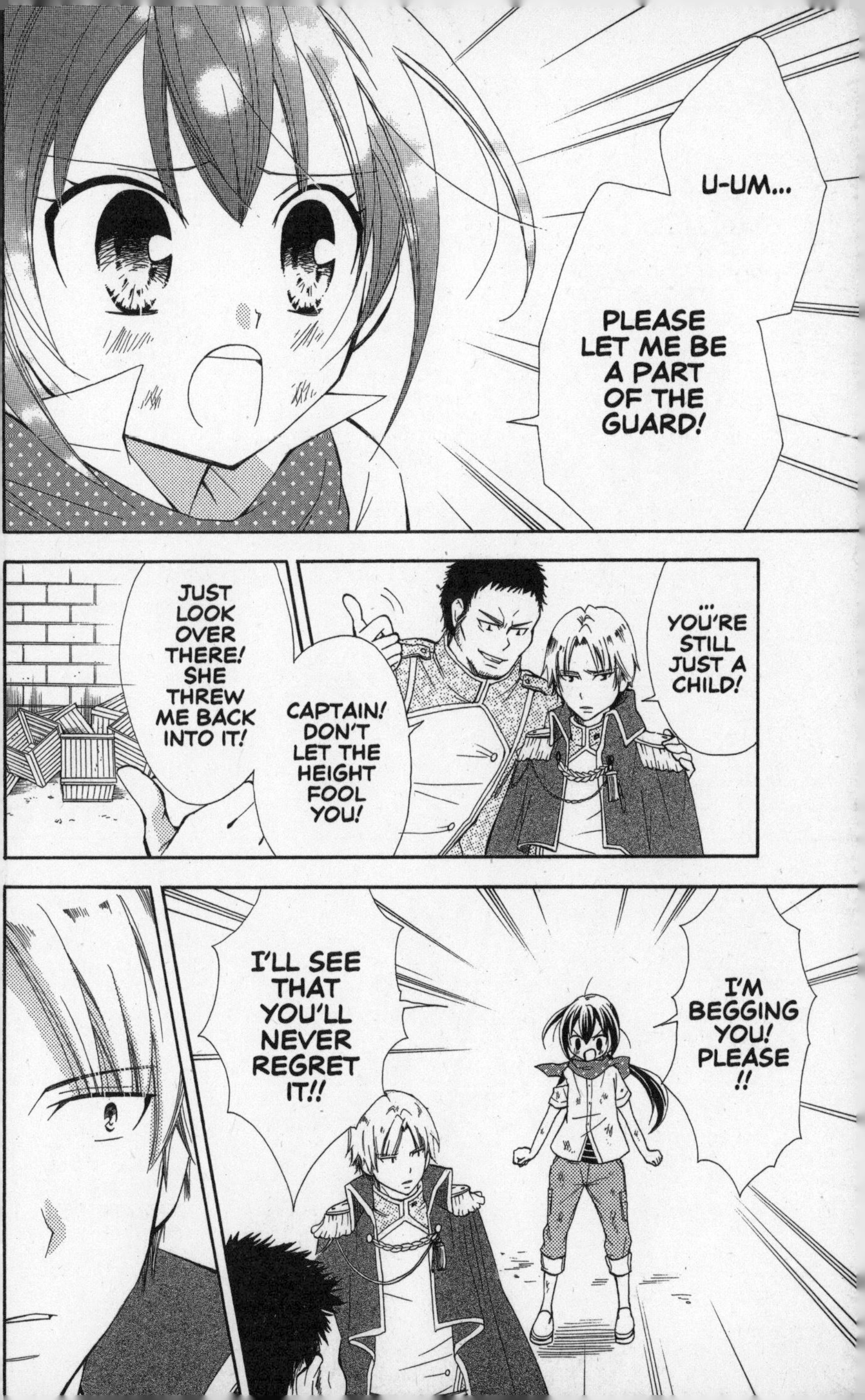
U-UM...
PLEASE LET ME BE A PART OF THE GUARD!
...YOU'RE STILL JUST A CHILD!
CAPTAIN! DON'T LET THE HEIGHT FOOL YOU!
JUST LOOK OVER THERE! SHE THREW ME BACK INTO IT!
I'M BEGGING YOU! PLEASE!!
I'LL SEE THAT YOU'LL NEVER REGRET IT!!

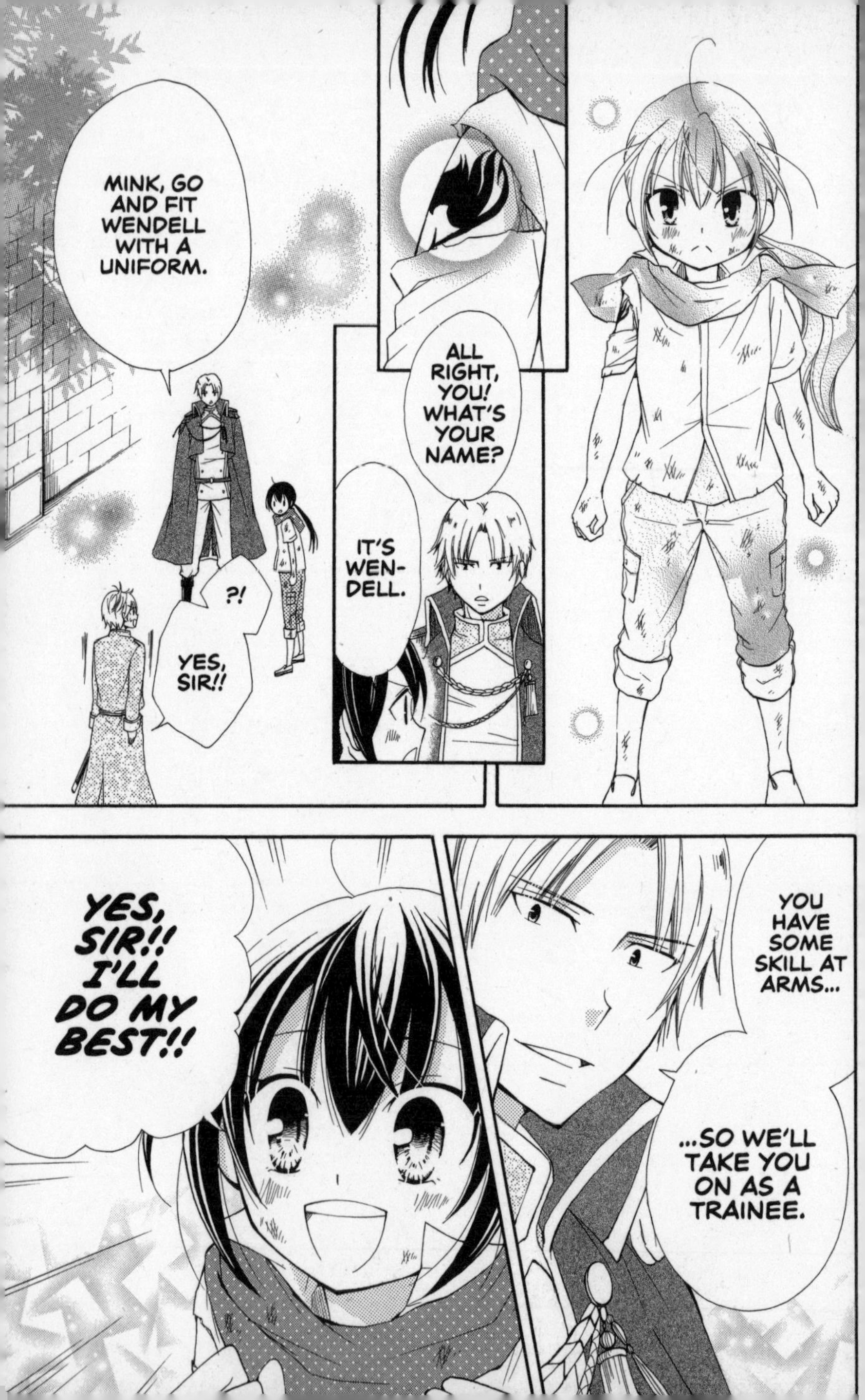
ALL RIGHT, YOU! WHAT'S YOUR NAME?
IT'S WEN-DELL.
MINK, GO AND FIT WENDELL WITH A UNIFORM.
?!
YES, SIR!!
YOU HAVE SOME SKILL AT ARMS...
...SO WE'LL TAKE YOU ON AS A TRAINEE.
YES, SIR!! I'LL DO MY BEST!!

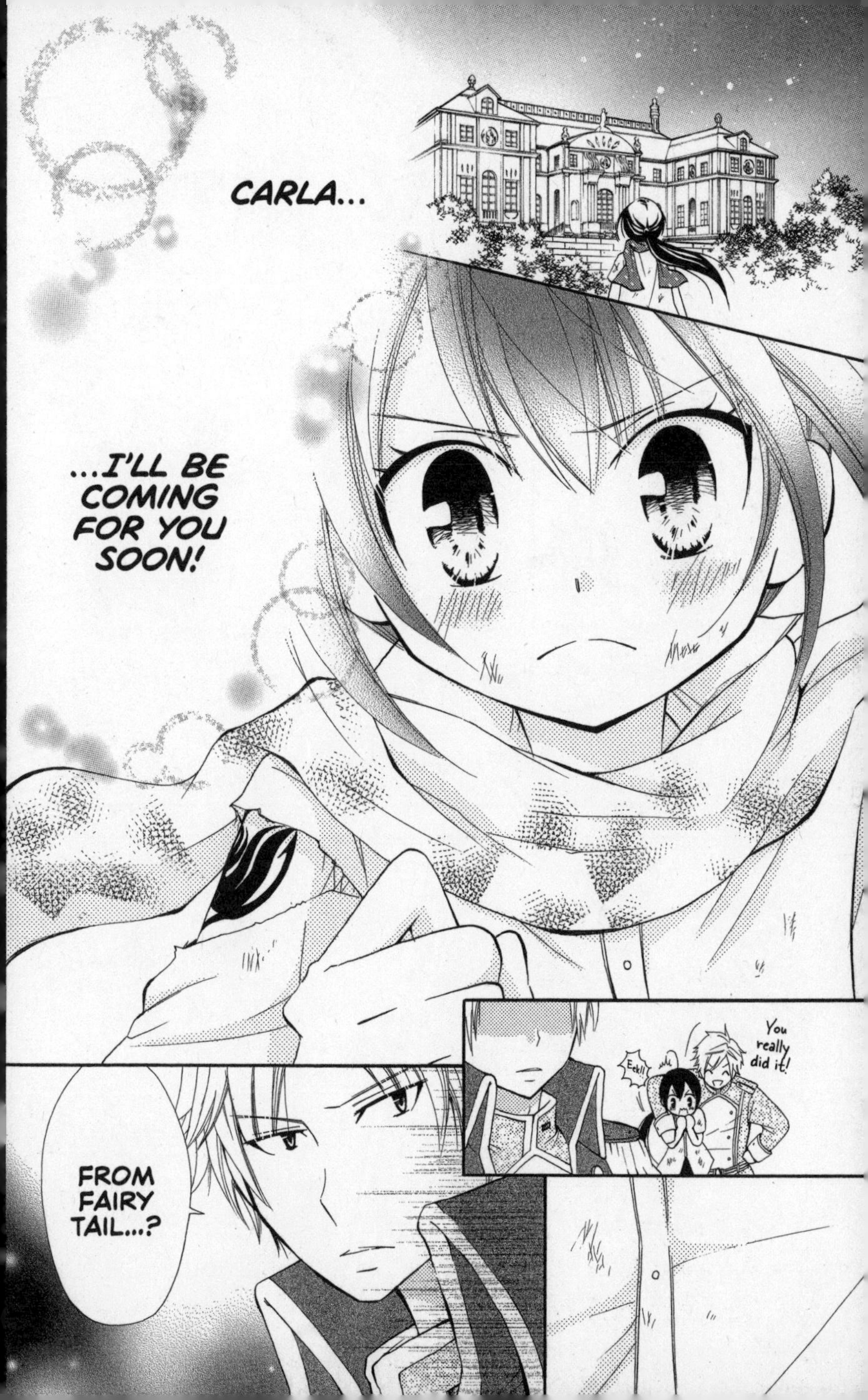
CARLA...
...I'LL BE COMING FOR YOU SOON!
You really did it!
Eek!!
FROM FAIRY TAIL...?

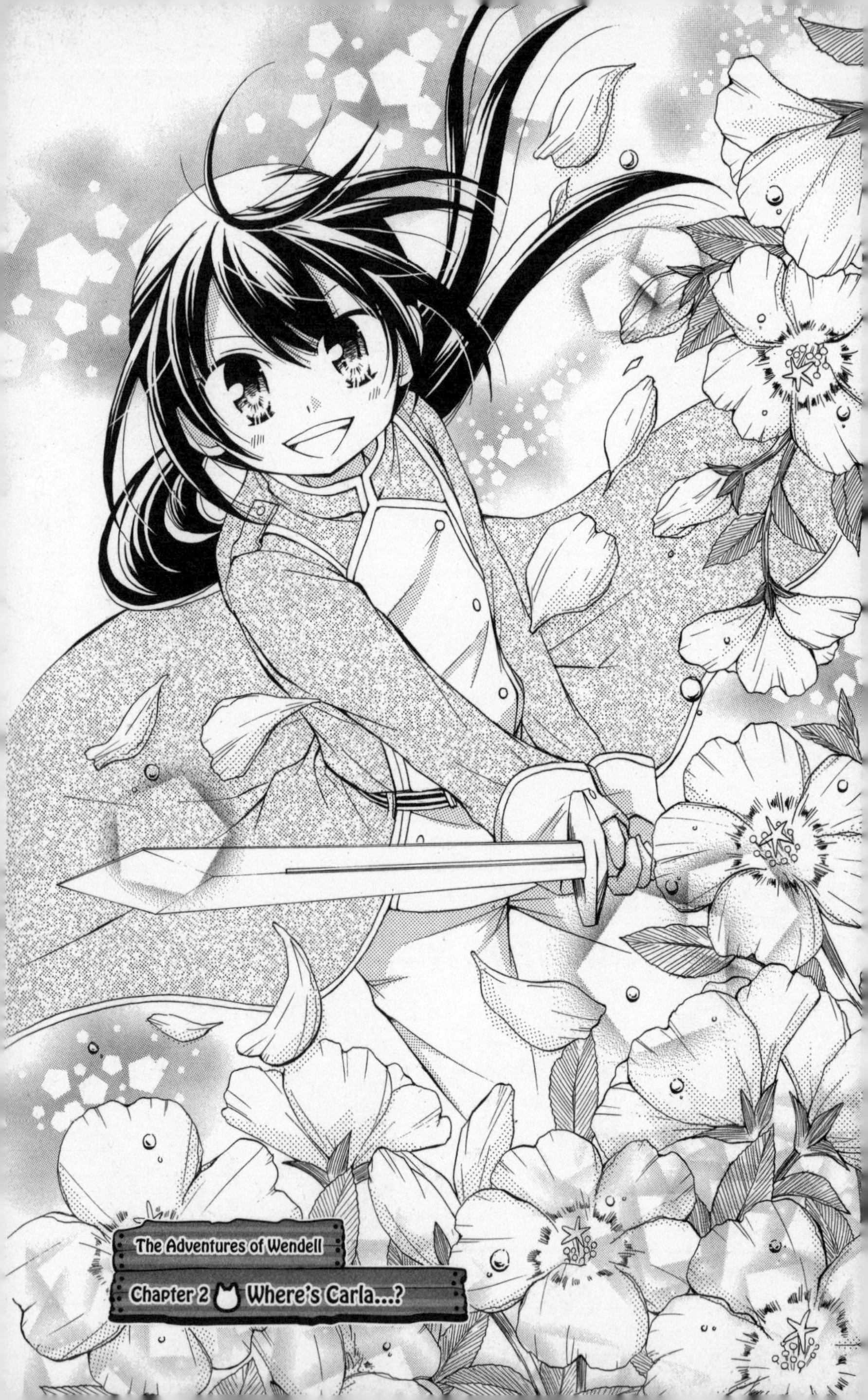
The Adventures of Wendell
Chapter 2 Where's Carla...?

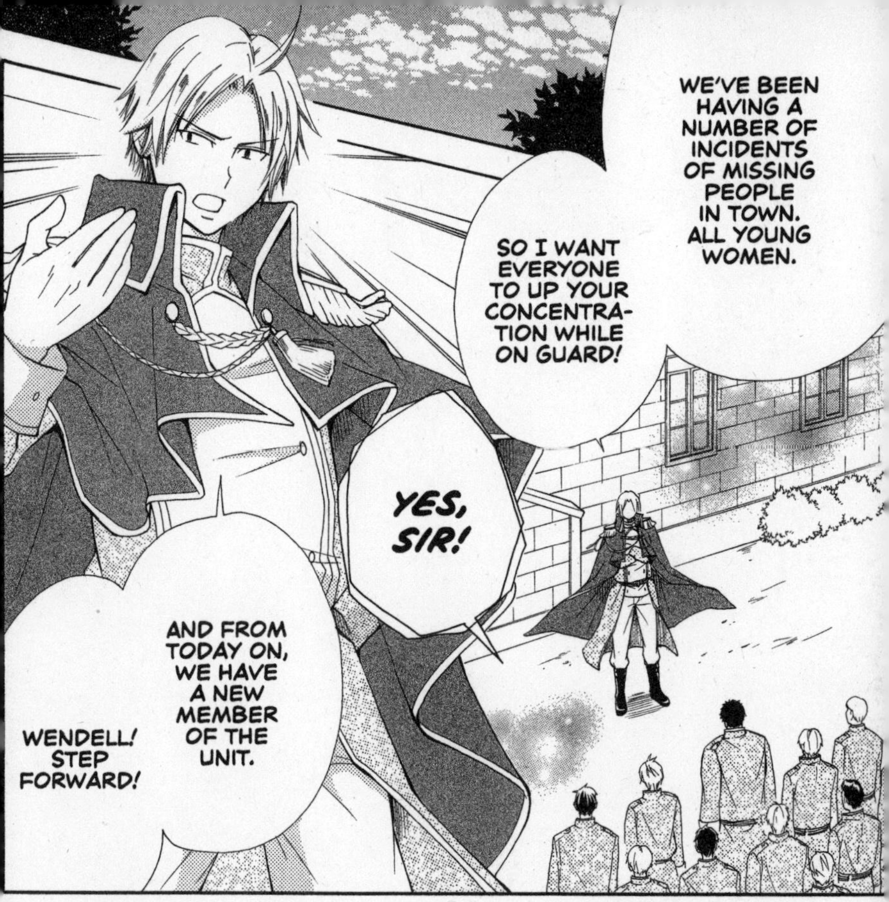
WE'VE BEEN HAVING A NUMBER OF INCIDENTS OF MISSING PEOPLE IN TOWN. ALL YOUNG WOMEN.
SO I WANT EVERYONE TO UP YOUR CONCENTRATION WHILE ON GUARD!
YES, SIR!
AND FROM TODAY ON, WE HAVE A NEW MEMBER OF THE UNIT.
WENDELL! STEP FORWARD!

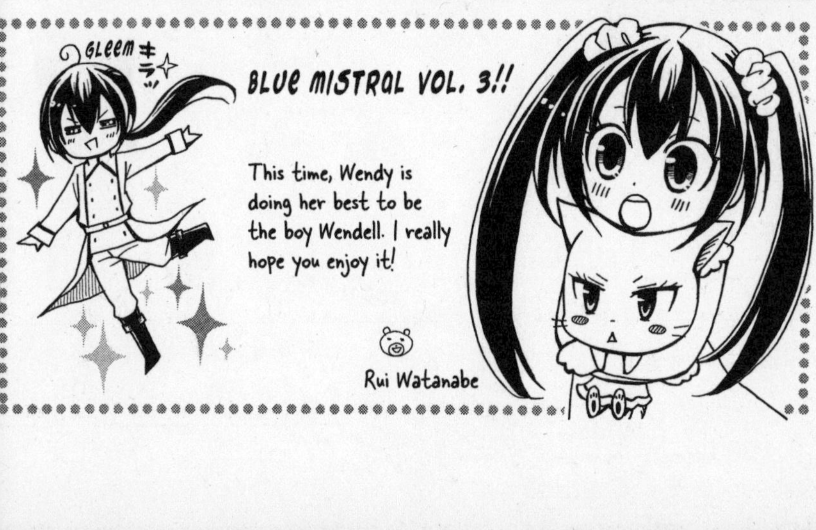
BLUE MISTRAL VOL. 3!!
GLEEM キラッ
This time, Wendy is doing her best to be the boy Wendell. I really hope you enjoy it!
Rui Watanabe

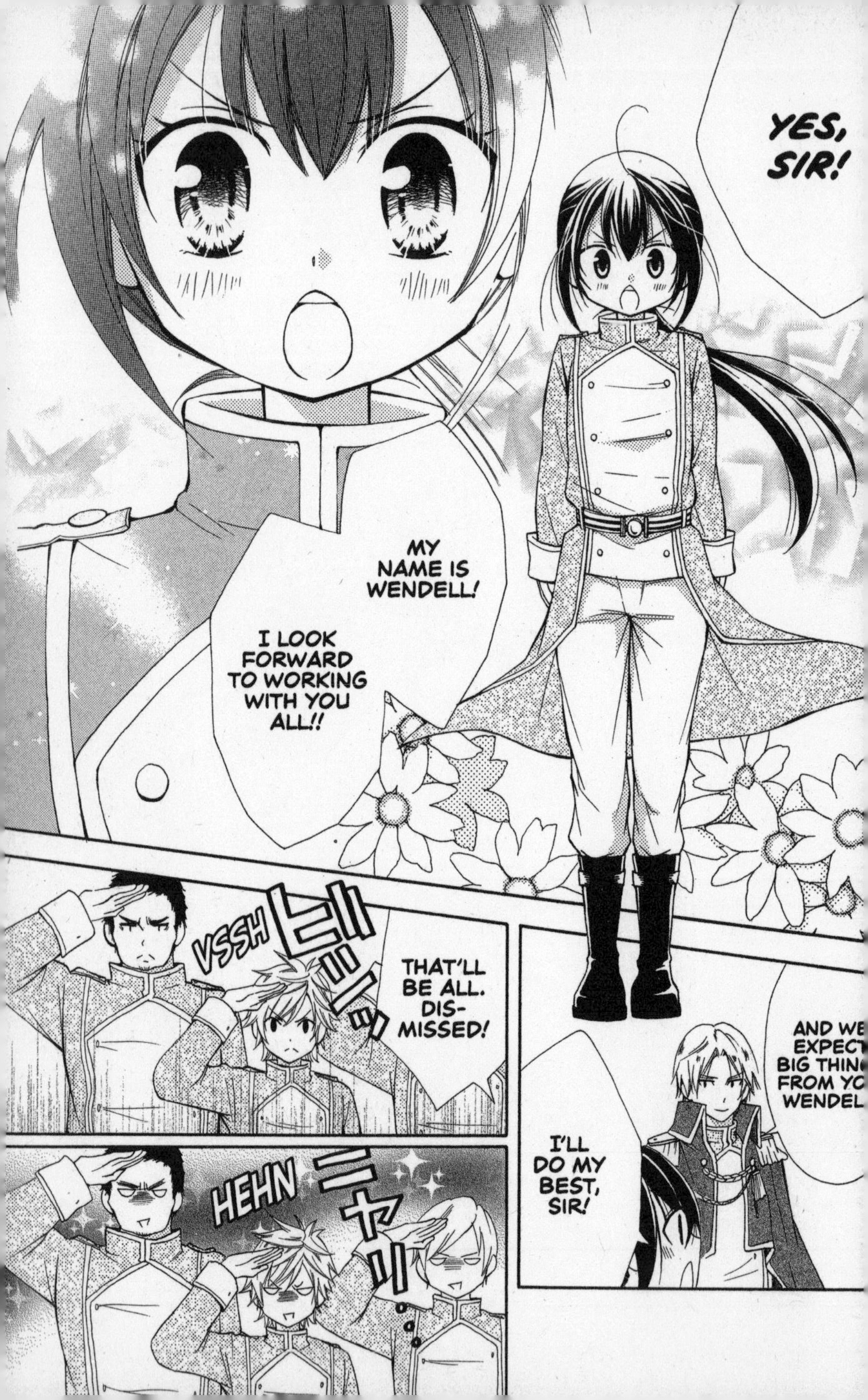
YES, SIR!
MY NAME IS WENDELL!
I LOOK FORWARD TO WORKING WITH YOU ALL!!
AND WE EXPECT BIG THIN FROM YO WENDEL
I'LL DO MY BEST, SIR!
THAT'LL BE ALL. DIS- MISSED!
VSSH
HEHN

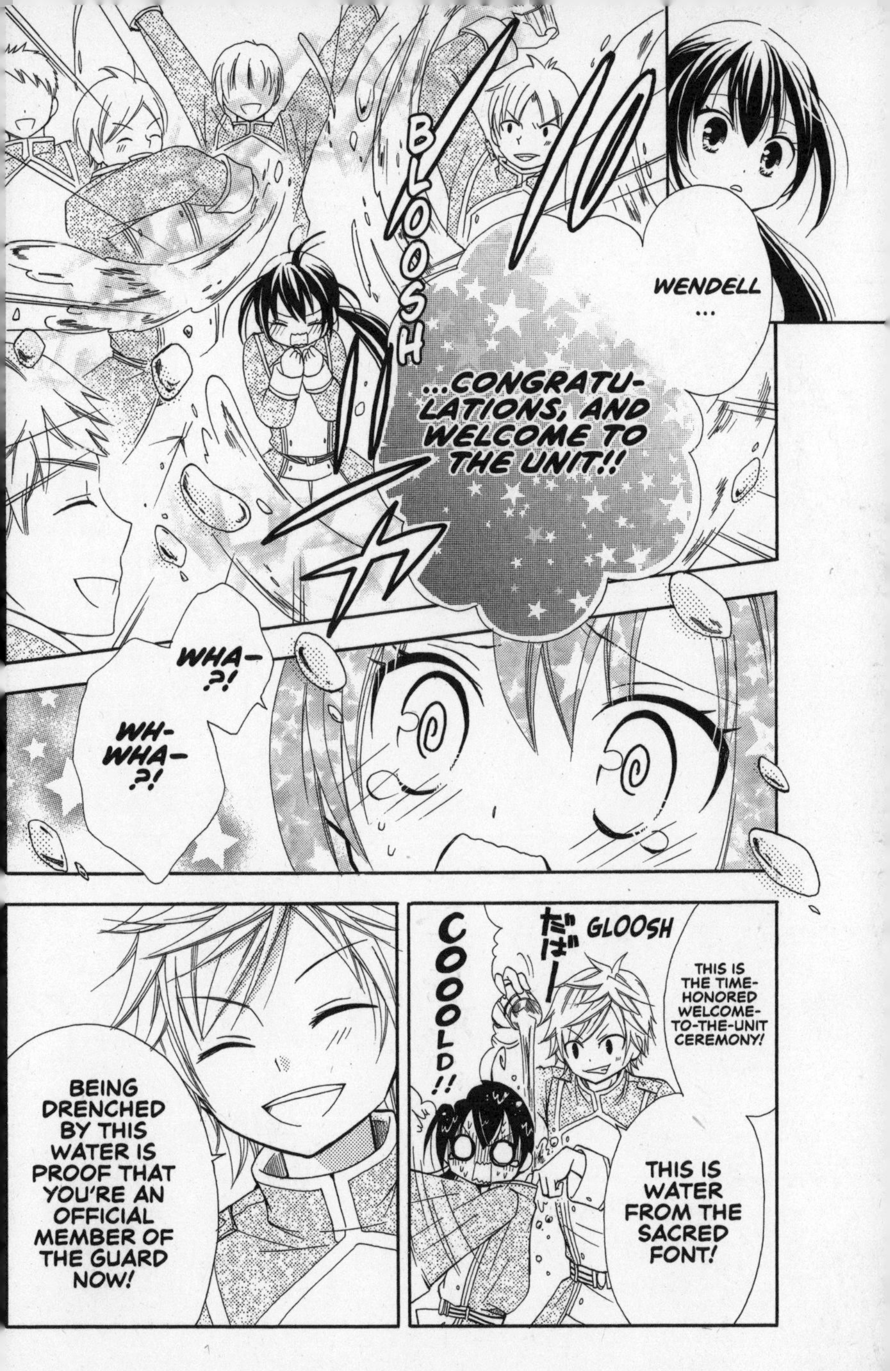
WENDELL ...
BLOOSH
...CONGRATU-LATIONS, AND WELCOME TO THE UNIT!!
WHA-?!
WH-WHA-?!
だばー
GLOOSH
THIS IS THE TIME-HONORED WELCOME-TO-THE-UNIT CEREMONY!
COOOOLD!!
THIS IS WATER FROM THE SACRED FONT!
BEING DRENCHED BY THIS WATER IS PROOF THAT YOU'RE AN OFFICIAL MEMBER OF THE GUARD NOW!

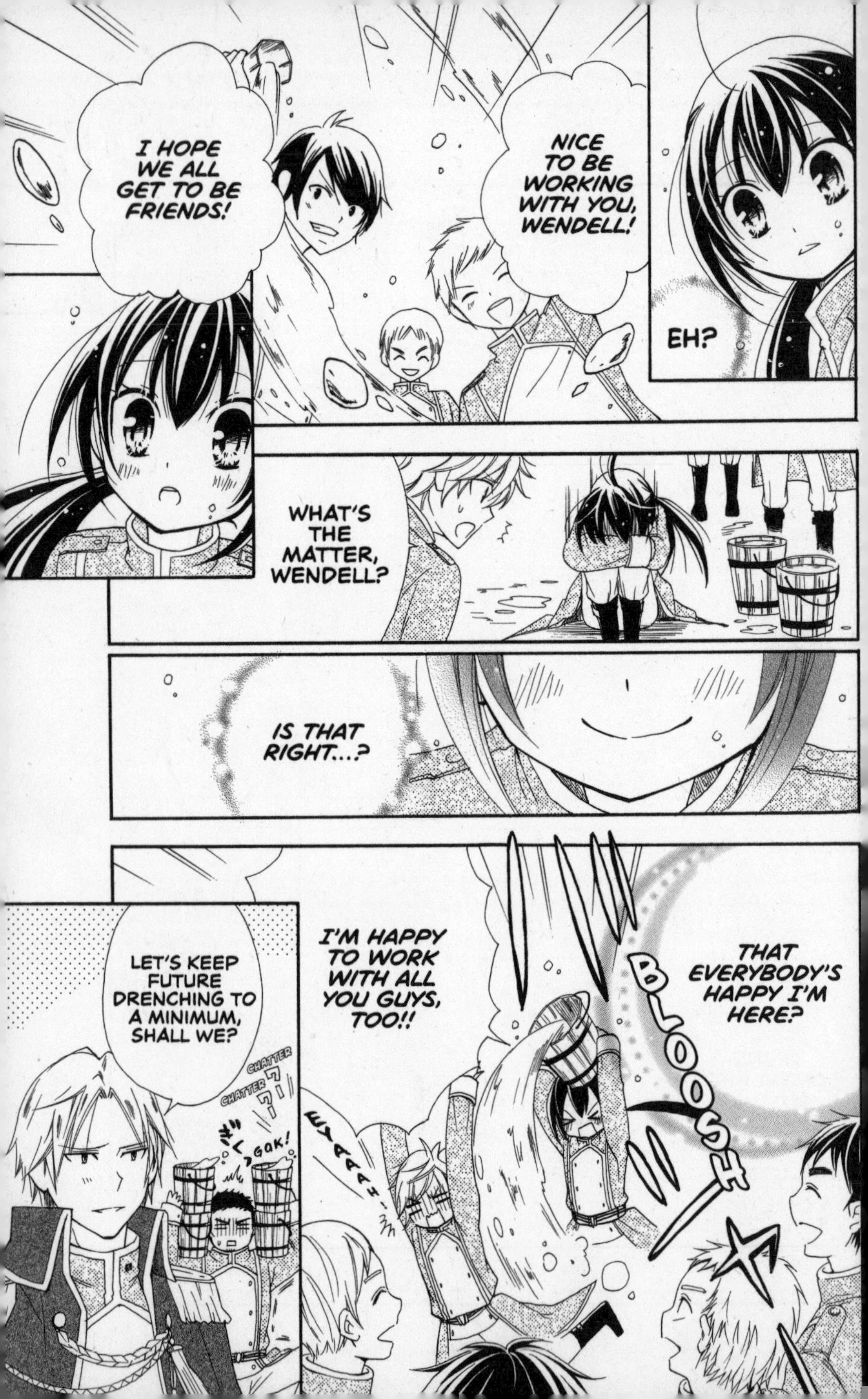
EH?
NICE TO BE WORKING WITH YOU, WENDELL!
I HOPE WE ALL GET TO BE FRIENDS!
WHAT'S THE MATTER, WENDELL?
IS THAT RIGHT...?
THAT EVERYBODY'S HAPPY I'M HERE?
BLOOSH
I'M HAPPY TO WORK WITH ALL YOU GUYS, TOO!!
WYAAAH!
LET'S KEEP FUTURE DRENCHING TO A MINIMUM, SHALL WE?
CHATTER
CHATTER
GAK!

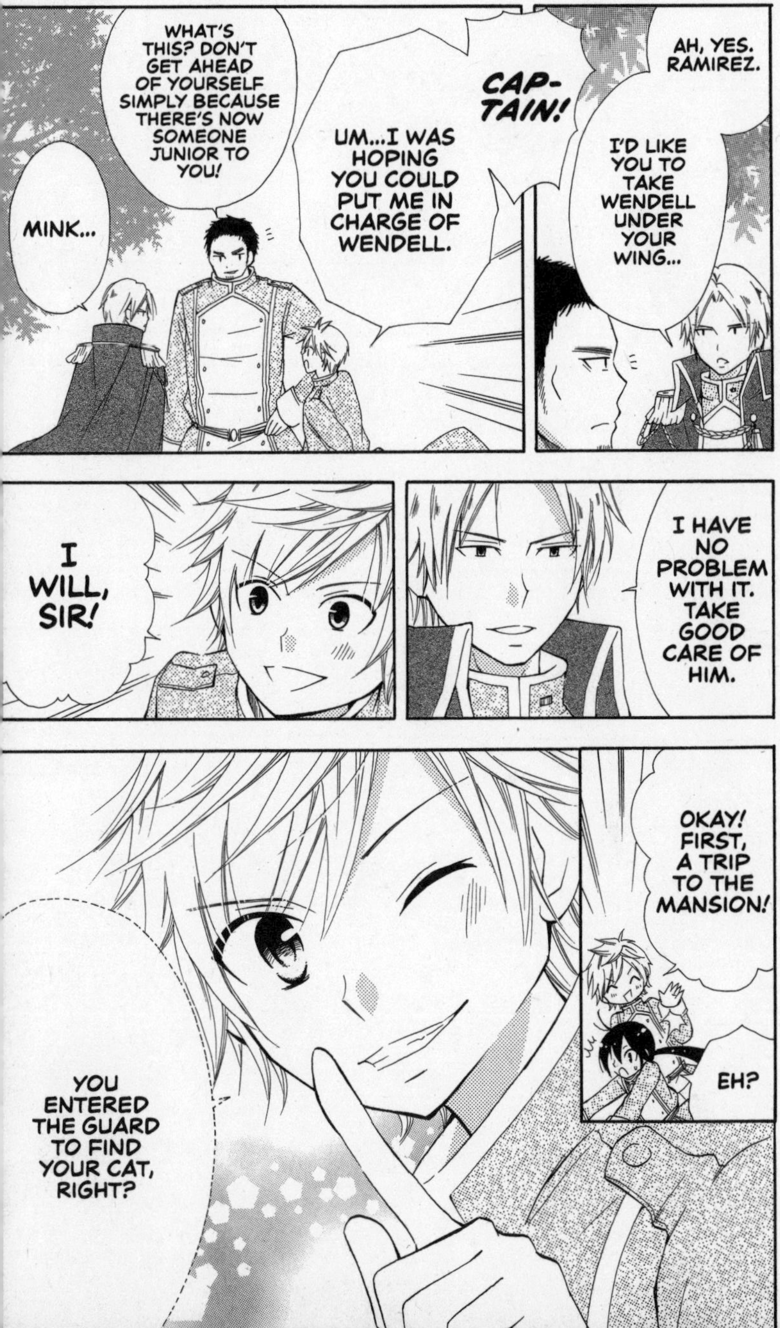
CAP-TAIN!
AH, YES. RAMIREZ.
I'D LIKE YOU TO TAKE WENDELL UNDER YOUR WING...
UM...I WAS HOPING YOU COULD PUT ME IN CHARGE OF WENDELL.
WHAT'S THIS? DON'T GET AHEAD OF YOURSELF SIMPLY BECAUSE THERE'S NOW SOMEONE JUNIOR TO YOU!
MINK...
I HAVE NO PROBLEM WITH IT. TAKE GOOD CARE OF HIM.
I WILL, SIR!
OKAY! FIRST, A TRIP TO THE MANSION!
EH?
YOU ENTERED THE GUARD TO FIND YOUR CAT, RIGHT?

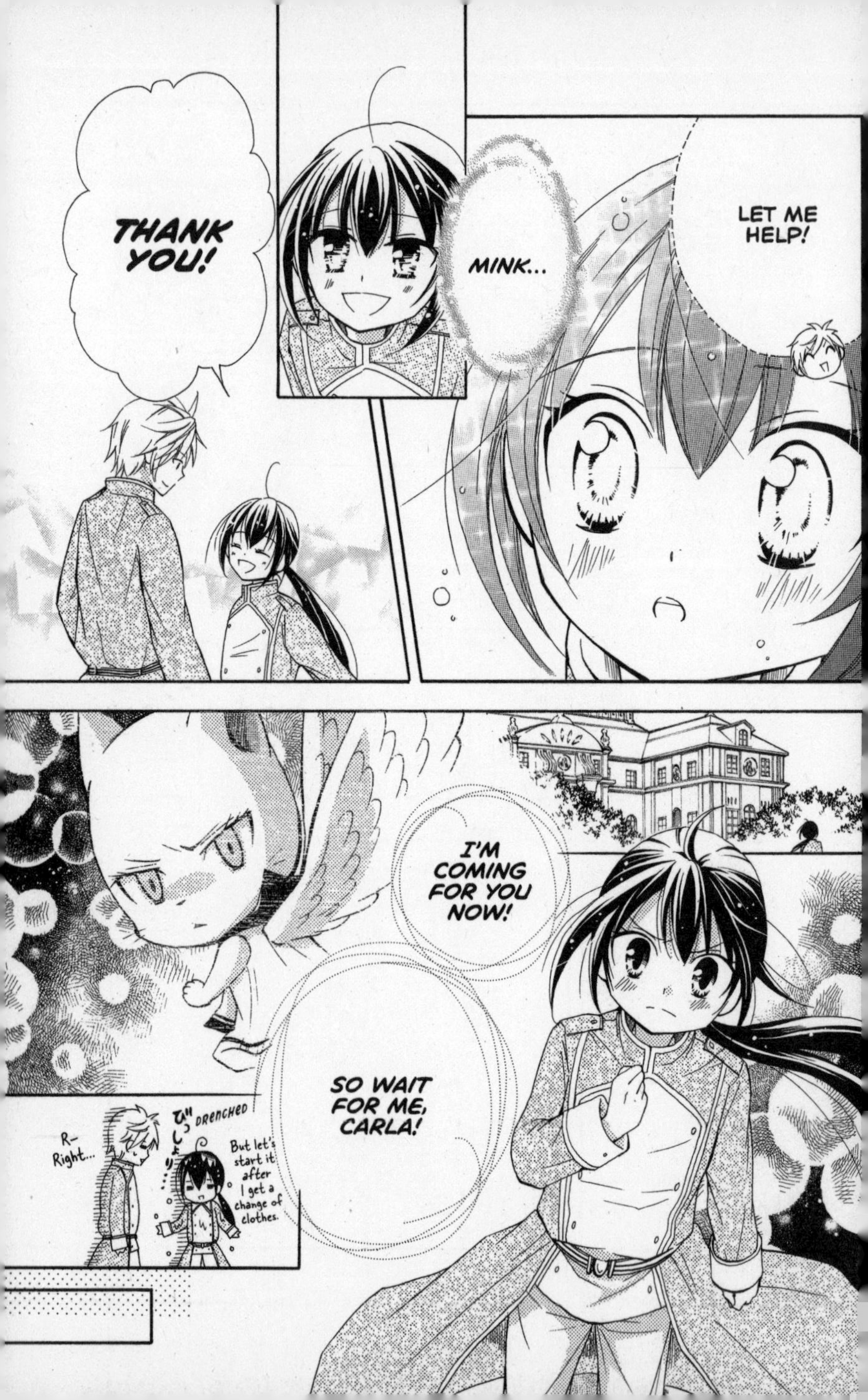
LET ME HELP!
MINK...
THANK YOU!
I'M COMING FOR YOU NOW!
SO WAIT FOR ME, CARLA!
びっしょり…
DRENCHED
But let's start it after I get a change of clothes.
R- Right...

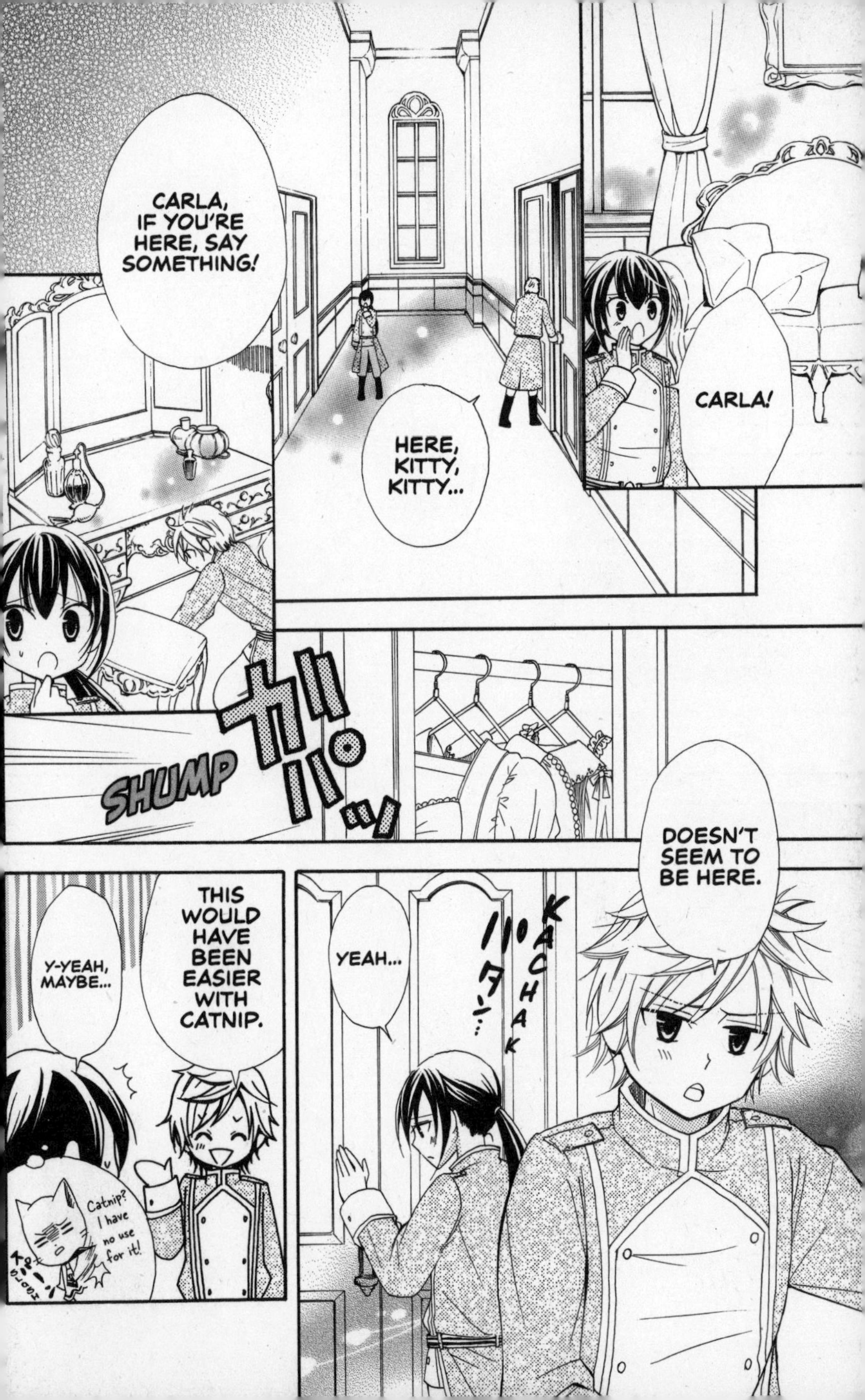
CARLA!
CARLA, IF YOU'RE HERE, SAY SOMETHING!
HERE, KITTY, KITTY...
カパッ
SHUMP
DOESN'T SEEM TO BE HERE.
パタン…
KACHAK
YEAH...
THIS WOULD HAVE BEEN EASIER WITH CATNIP.
Y-YEAH, MAYBE...
Catnip? I have no use for it!

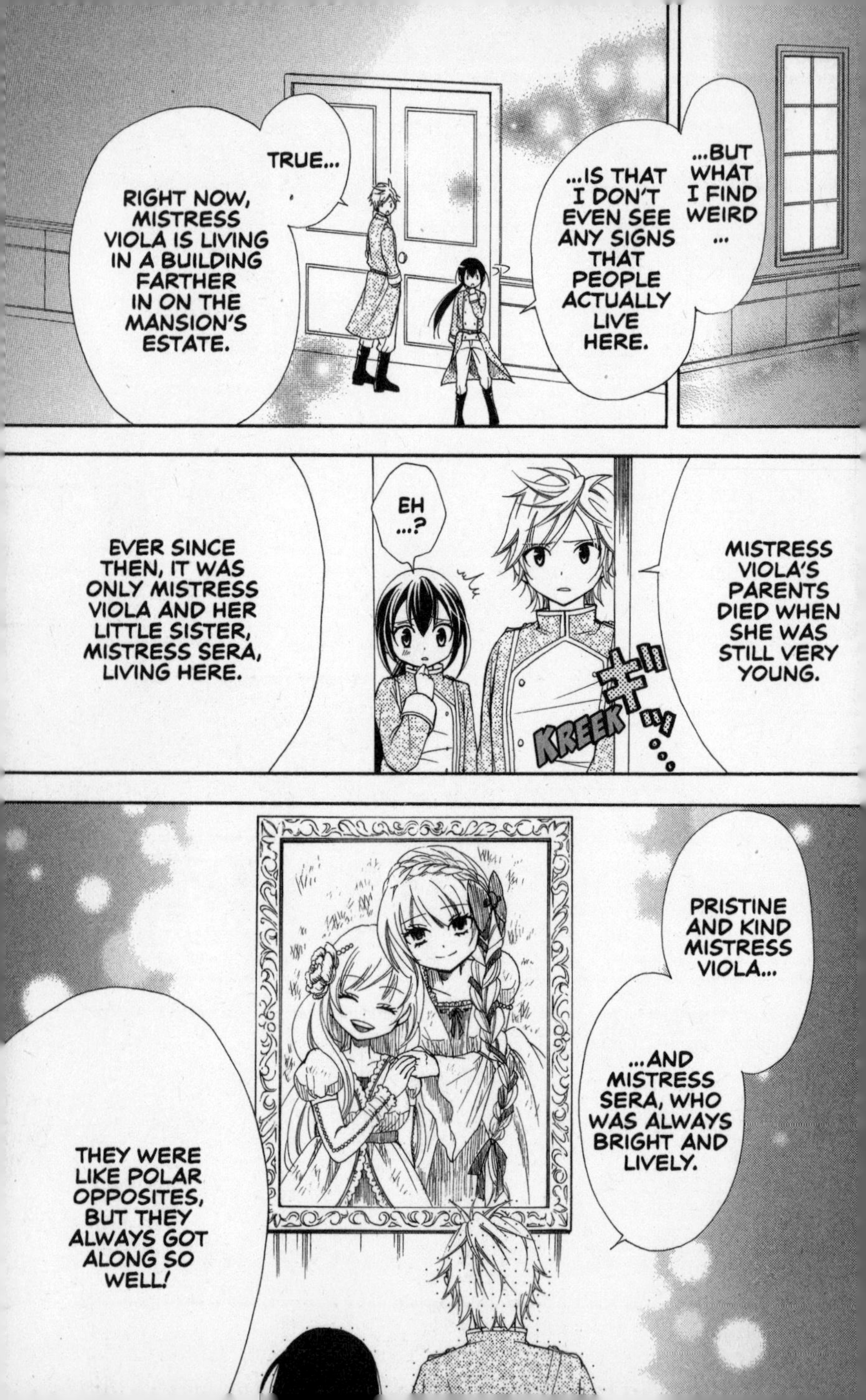
...BUT WHAT I FIND WEIRD...
...IS THAT I DON'T EVEN SEE ANY SIGNS THAT PEOPLE ACTUALLY LIVE HERE.
TRUE...
RIGHT NOW, MISTRESS VIOLA IS LIVING IN A BUILDING FARTHER IN ON THE MANSION'S ESTATE.
MISTRESS VIOLA'S PARENTS DIED WHEN SHE WAS STILL VERY YOUNG.
KREEK
EH ...?
EVER SINCE THEN, IT WAS ONLY MISTRESS VIOLA AND HER LITTLE SISTER, MISTRESS SERA, LIVING HERE.
PRISTINE AND KIND MISTRESS VIOLA...
...AND MISTRESS SERA, WHO WAS ALWAYS BRIGHT AND LIVELY.
THEY WERE LIKE POLAR OPPOSITES, BUT THEY ALWAYS GOT ALONG SO WELL!

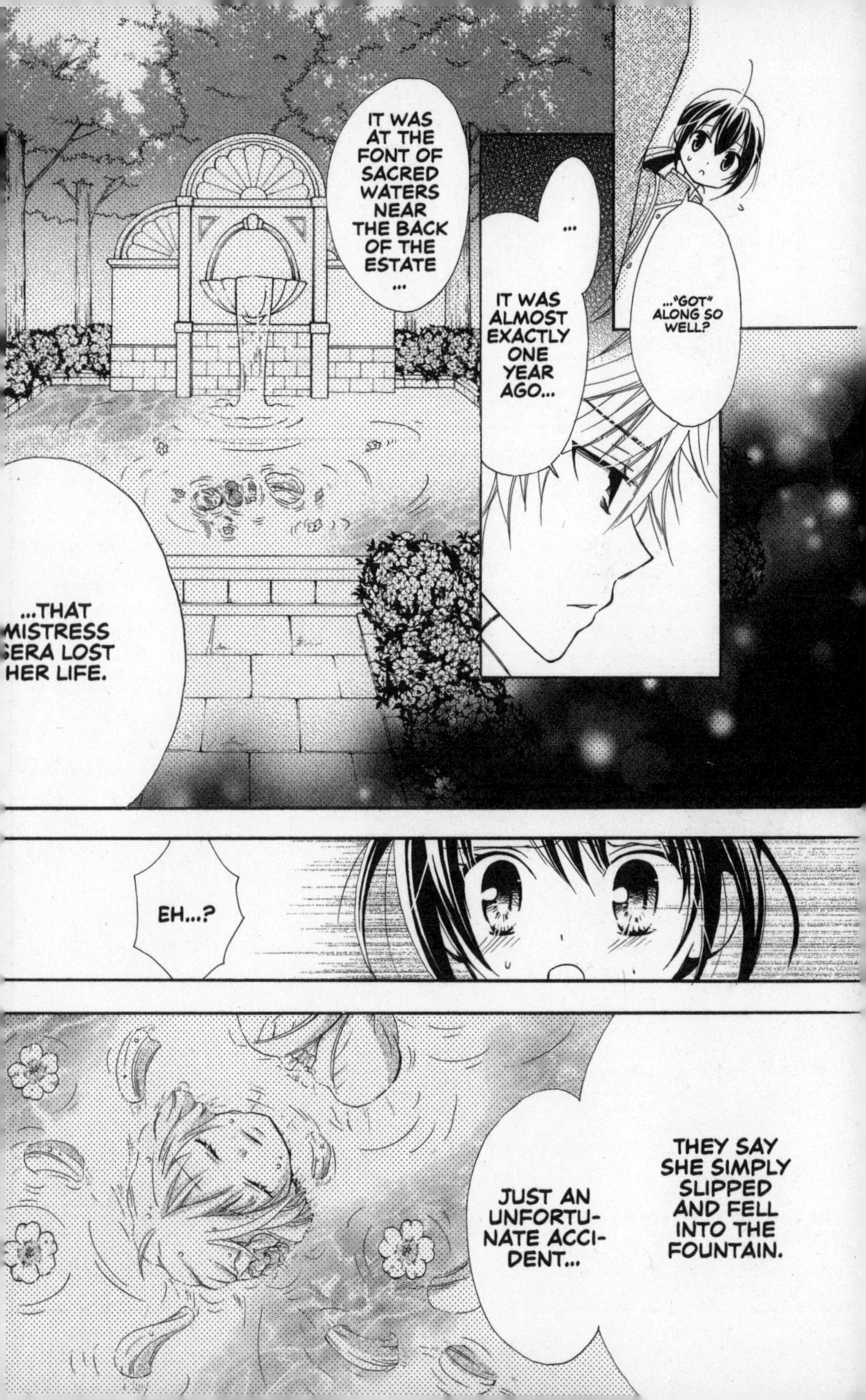
..."GOT" ALONG SO WELL?
...
IT WAS ALMOST EXACTLY ONE YEAR AGO...
IT WAS AT THE FONT OF SACRED WATERS NEAR THE BACK OF THE ESTATE ...
...THAT MISTRESS SERA LOST HER LIFE.
EH...?
THEY SAY SHE SIMPLY SLIPPED AND FELL INTO THE FOUNTAIN.
JUST AN UNFORTUNATE ACCIDENT...

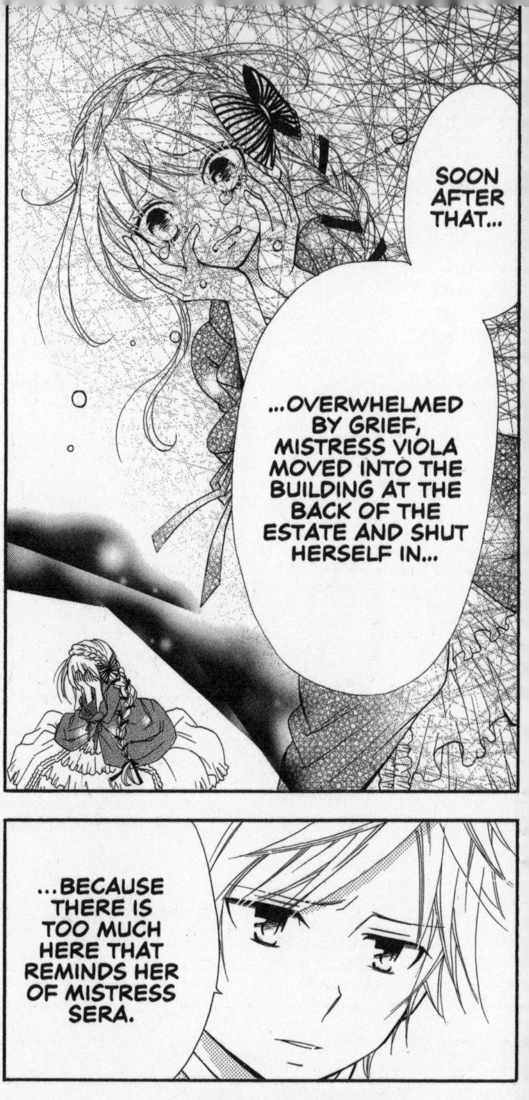
SOON AFTER THAT...
...OVERWHELMED BY GRIEF, MISTRESS VIOLA MOVED INTO THE BUILDING AT THE BACK OF THE ESTATE AND SHUT HERSELF IN...
...BECAUSE THERE IS TOO MUCH HERE THAT REMINDS HER OF MISTRESS SERA.
IS THAT WHAT HAP-PENED ...?
WHAT A TRAGIC PAST...

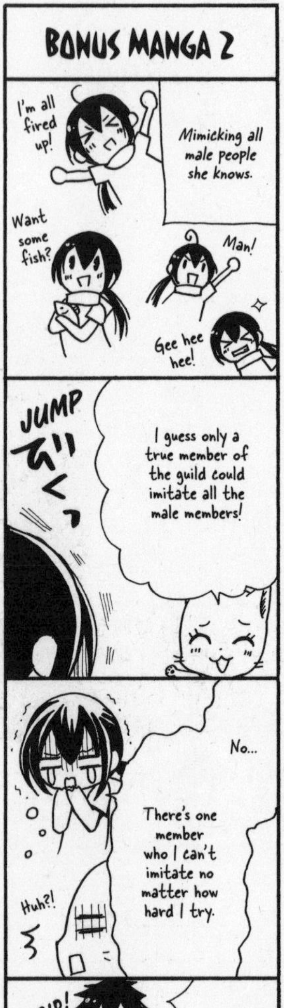
BONUS MANGA 2
Mimicking all male people she knows.
I'm all fired up!
Man!
Want some fish?
Gee hee hee!
I guess only a true member of the guild could imitate all the male members!
JUMP
No...
There's one member who I can't imitate no matter how hard I try.
Huh?!
Don't worry about it, Wendy! You don't need to imitate him!!
STRIP!
Or to put it another way, don't you dare even try!!

The un-imitatable man.

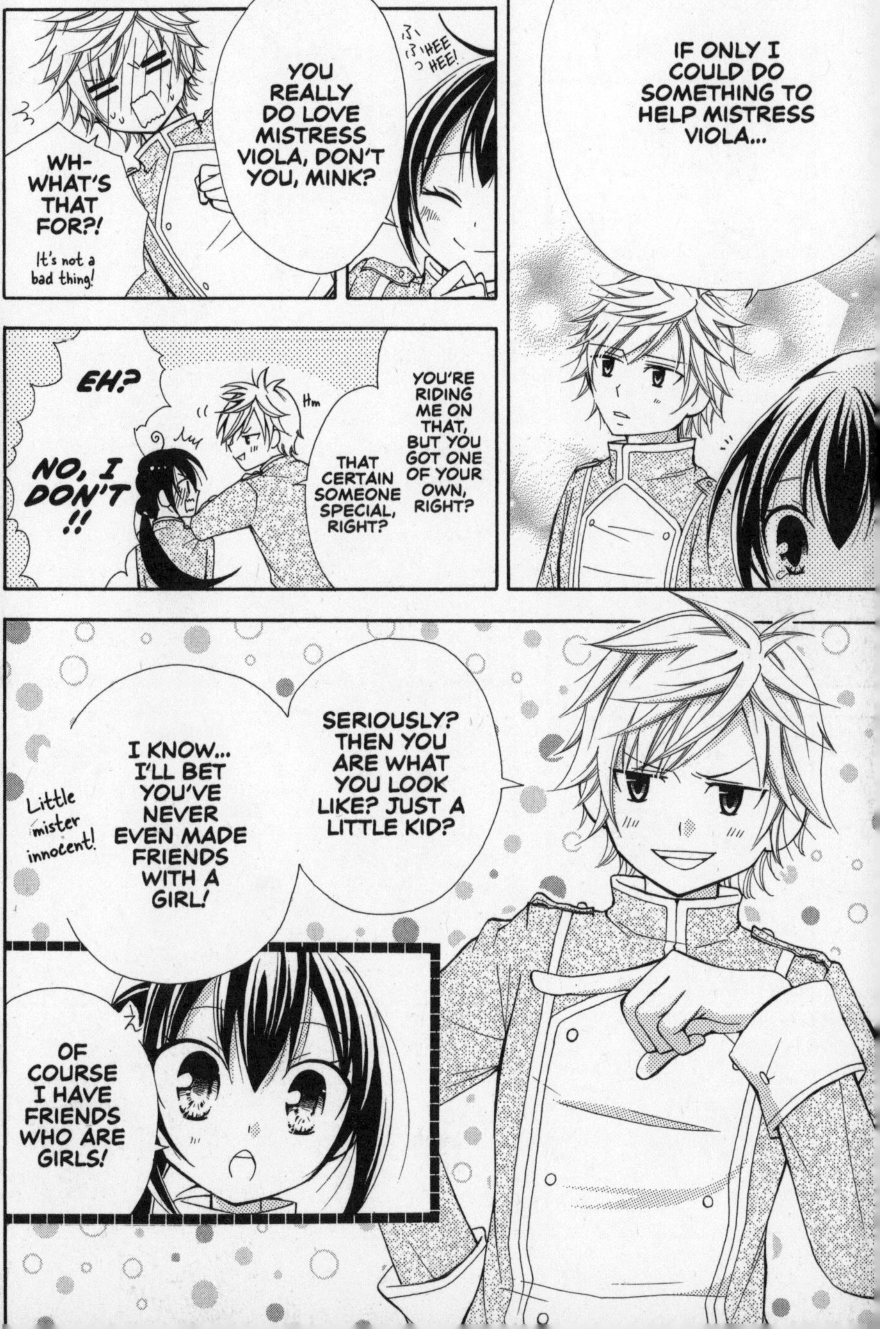
IF ONLY I COULD DO SOMETHING TO HELP MISTRESS VIOLA...
ふふ HEE HEE!
YOU REALLY DO LOVE MISTRESS VIOLA, DON'T YOU, MINK?
WH-WHAT'S THAT FOR?!
It's not a bad thing!
YOU'RE RIDING ME ON THAT, BUT YOU GOT ONE OF YOUR OWN, RIGHT?
THAT CERTAIN SOMEONE SPECIAL, RIGHT?
Hm
EH?
NO, I DON'T!!
SERIOUSLY? THEN YOU ARE WHAT YOU LOOK LIKE? JUST A LITTLE KID?
I KNOW... I'LL BET YOU'VE NEVER EVEN MADE FRIENDS WITH A GIRL!
Little mister innocent!
OF COURSE I HAVE FRIENDS WHO ARE GIRLS!

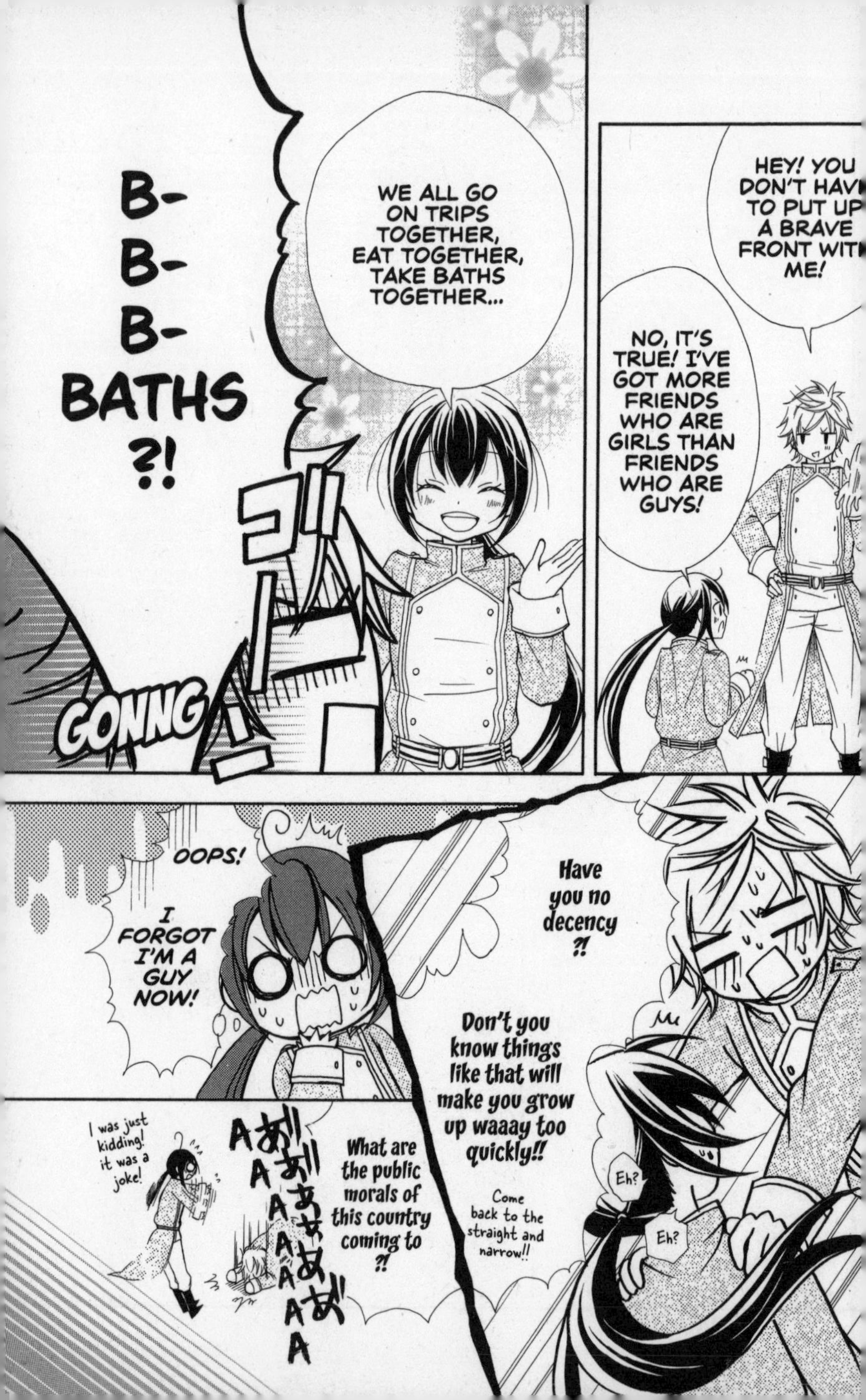

HEY! YOU DON'T HAV TO PUT UP A BRAVE FRONT WIT ME!
NO, IT'S TRUE! I'VE GOT MORE FRIENDS WHO ARE GIRLS THAN FRIENDS WHO ARE GUYS!
WE ALL GO ON TRIPS TOGETHER, EAT TOGETHER, TAKE BATHS TOGETHER...
B- B- B- BATHS ?!
GONNG
Have you no decency ?!
Don't you know things like that will make you grow up waaay too quickly!!
Come back to the straight and narrow!!
Eh?
Eh?
OOPS!
I FORGOT I'M A GUY NOW!
What are the public morals of this country coming to ?!
AAAAAAAA
I was just kidding! it was a joke!

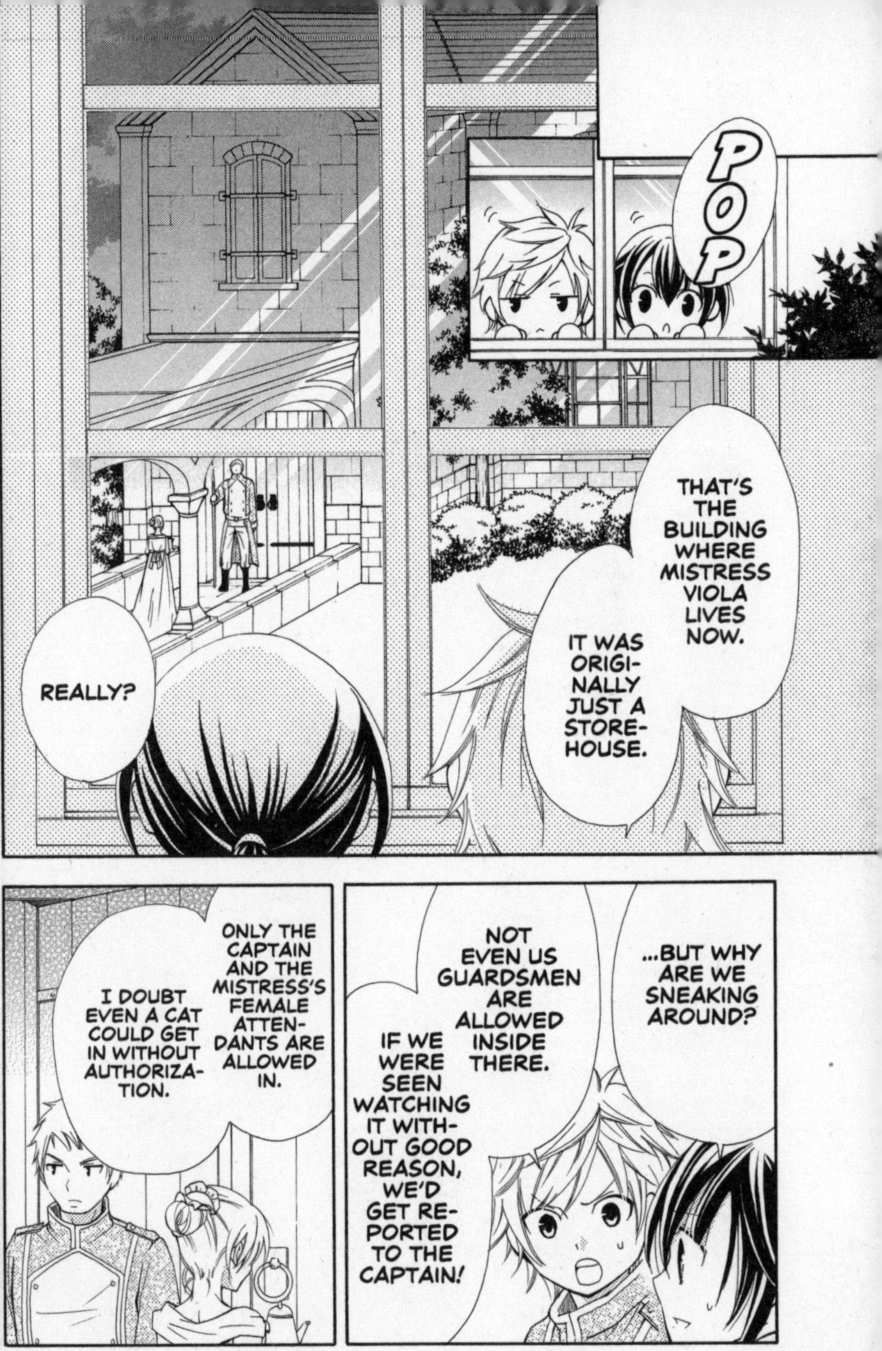
POP
THAT'S THE BUILDING WHERE MISTRESS VIOLA LIVES NOW.
IT WAS ORIGINALLY JUST A STOREHOUSE.
REALLY?
...BUT WHY ARE WE SNEAKING AROUND?
NOT EVEN US GUARDSMEN ARE ALLOWED INSIDE THERE.
IF WE WERE SEEN WATCHING IT WITHOUT GOOD REASON, WE'D GET REPORTED TO THE CAPTAIN!
ONLY THE CAPTAIN AND THE MISTRESS'S FEMALE ATTENDANTS ARE ALLOWED IN.
I DOUBT EVEN A CAT COULD GET IN WITHOUT AUTHORIZATION.

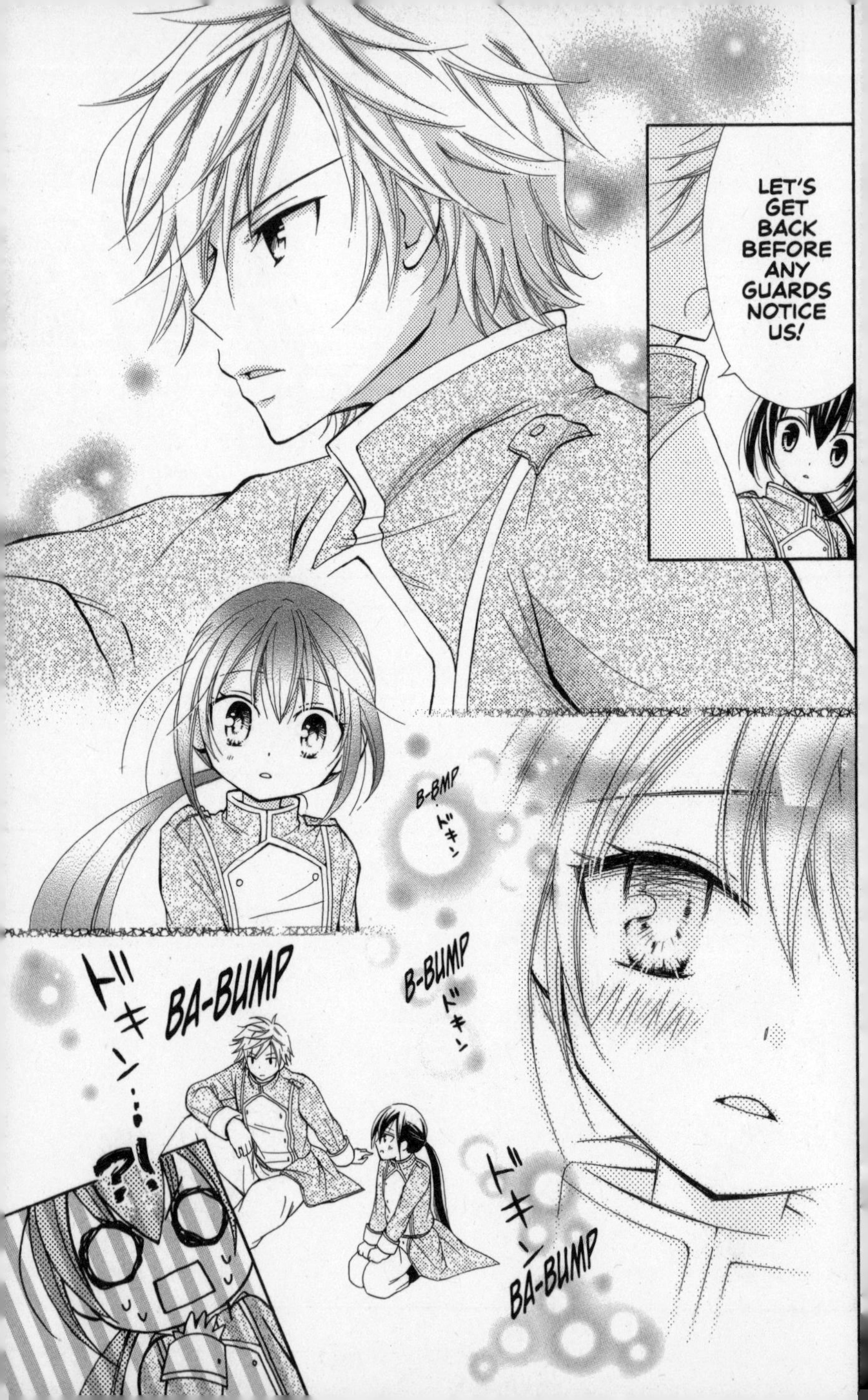
LET'S GET BACK BEFORE ANY GUARDS NOTICE US!
B-BMP ドキン
ドキン BA-BUMP
B-BUMP ドキン
ドキン…!? BA-BUMP

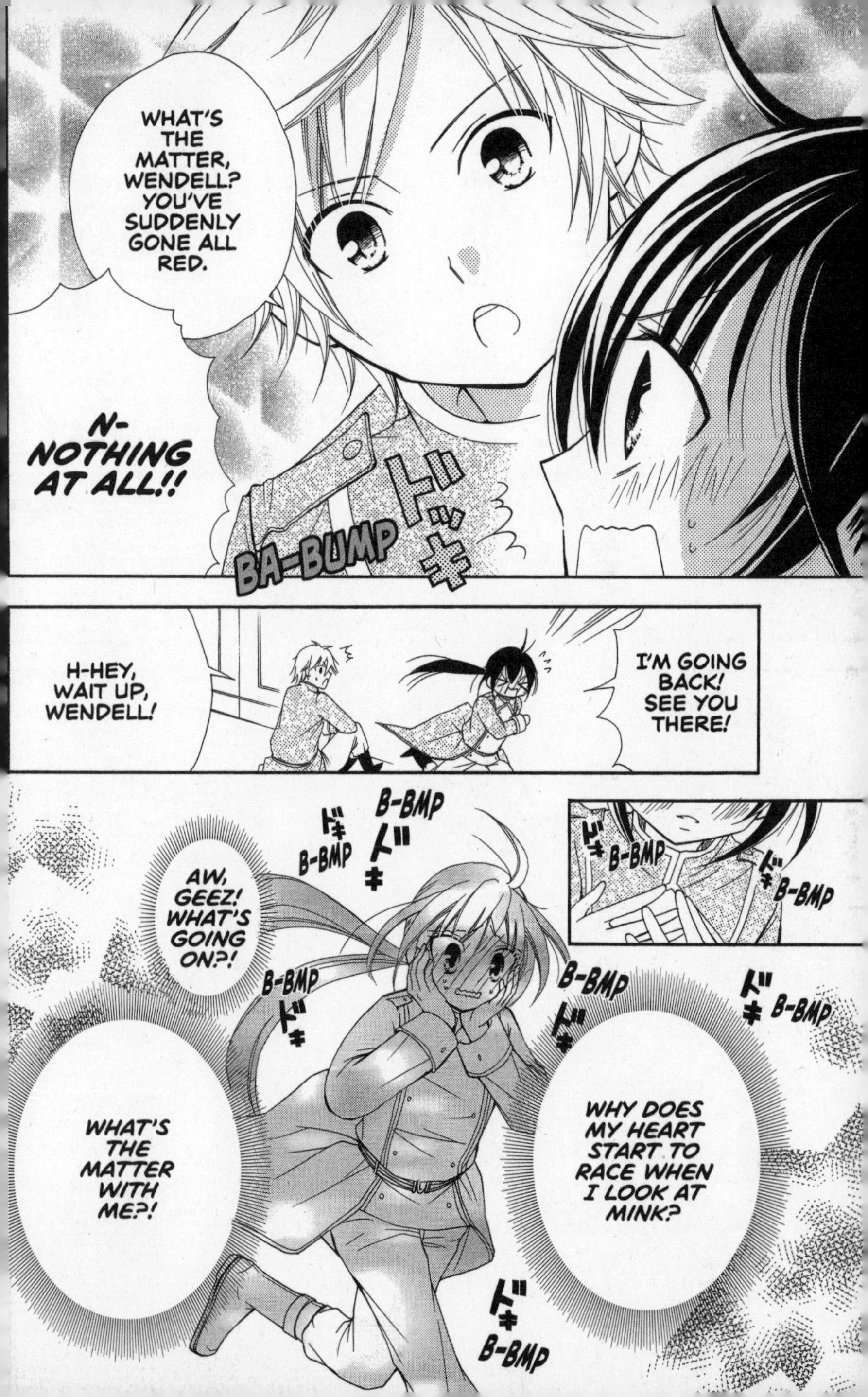
WHAT'S THE MATTER, WENDELL? YOU'VE SUDDENLY GONE ALL RED.
N-NOTHING AT ALL!!
ドッキ
BA-BUMP
I'M GOING BACK! SEE YOU THERE!
H-HEY, WAIT UP, WENDELL!
ドキ B-BMP
ドキ B-BMP
ドキ B-BMP
B-BMP ドキ
ドキ B-BMP
AW, GEEZ! WHAT'S GOING ON?!
B-BMP ドキ
WHY DOES MY HEART START TO RACE WHEN I LOOK AT MINK?
B-BMP ドキ
WHAT'S THE MATTER WITH ME?!
ドキ B-BMP

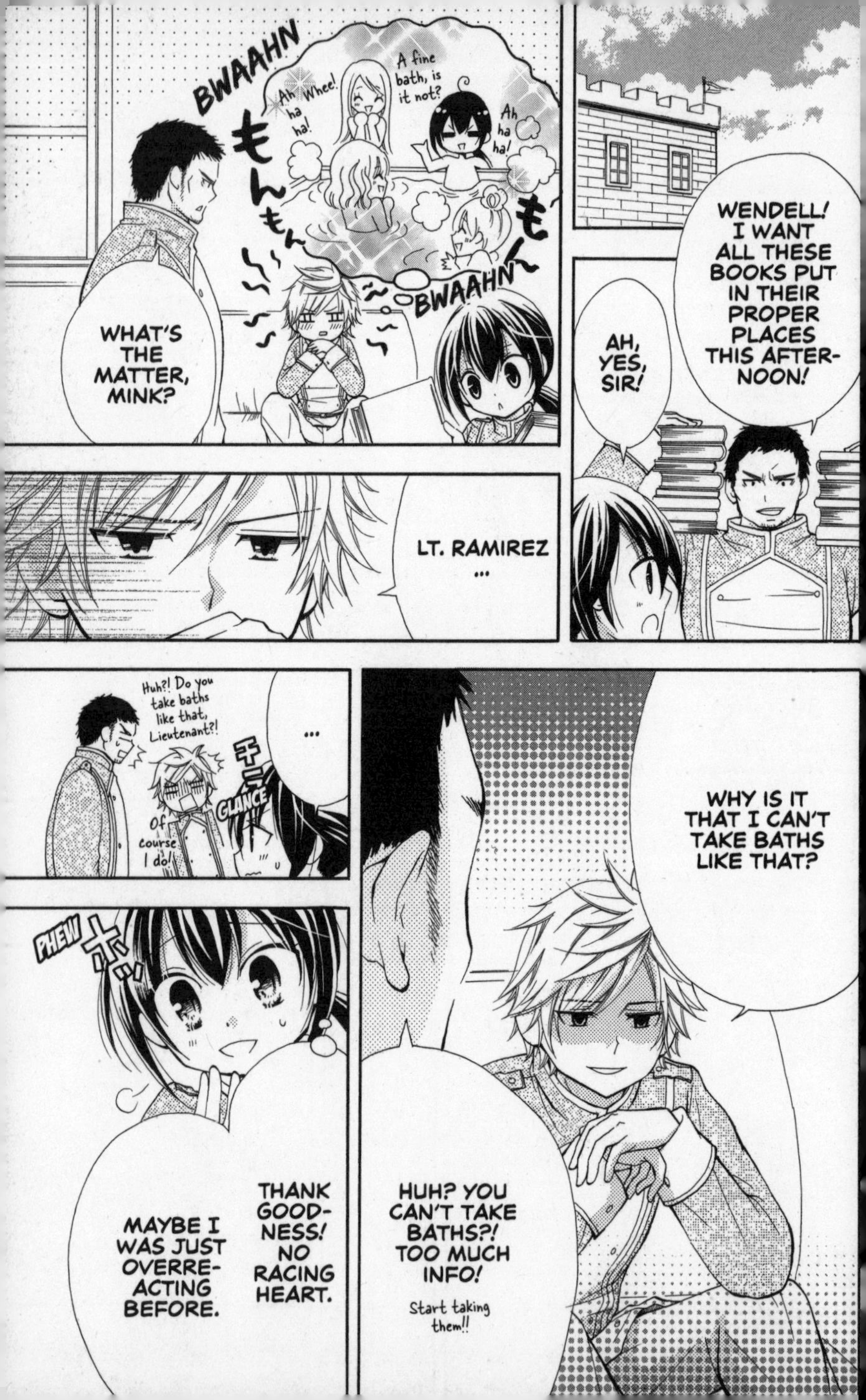
WENDELL! I WANT ALL THESE BOOKS PUT IN THEIR PROPER PLACES THIS AFTER-NOON!
AH, YES, SIR!
BWAAHN
A fine bath, is it not?
Whee!
Ah ha ha!
Ah ha ha!
もんもん
もん
BWAAHN
WHAT'S THE MATTER, MINK?
LT. RAMIREZ ...
WHY IS IT THAT I CAN'T TAKE BATHS LIKE THAT?
HUH? YOU CAN'T TAKE BATHS?! TOO MUCH INFO!
Start taking them!!
Huh?! Do you take baths like that, Lieutenant?!
...
GLANCE
Of course I do!
PHEW
THANK GOOD-NESS! NO RACING HEART.
MAYBE I WAS JUST OVERRE-ACTING BEFORE.

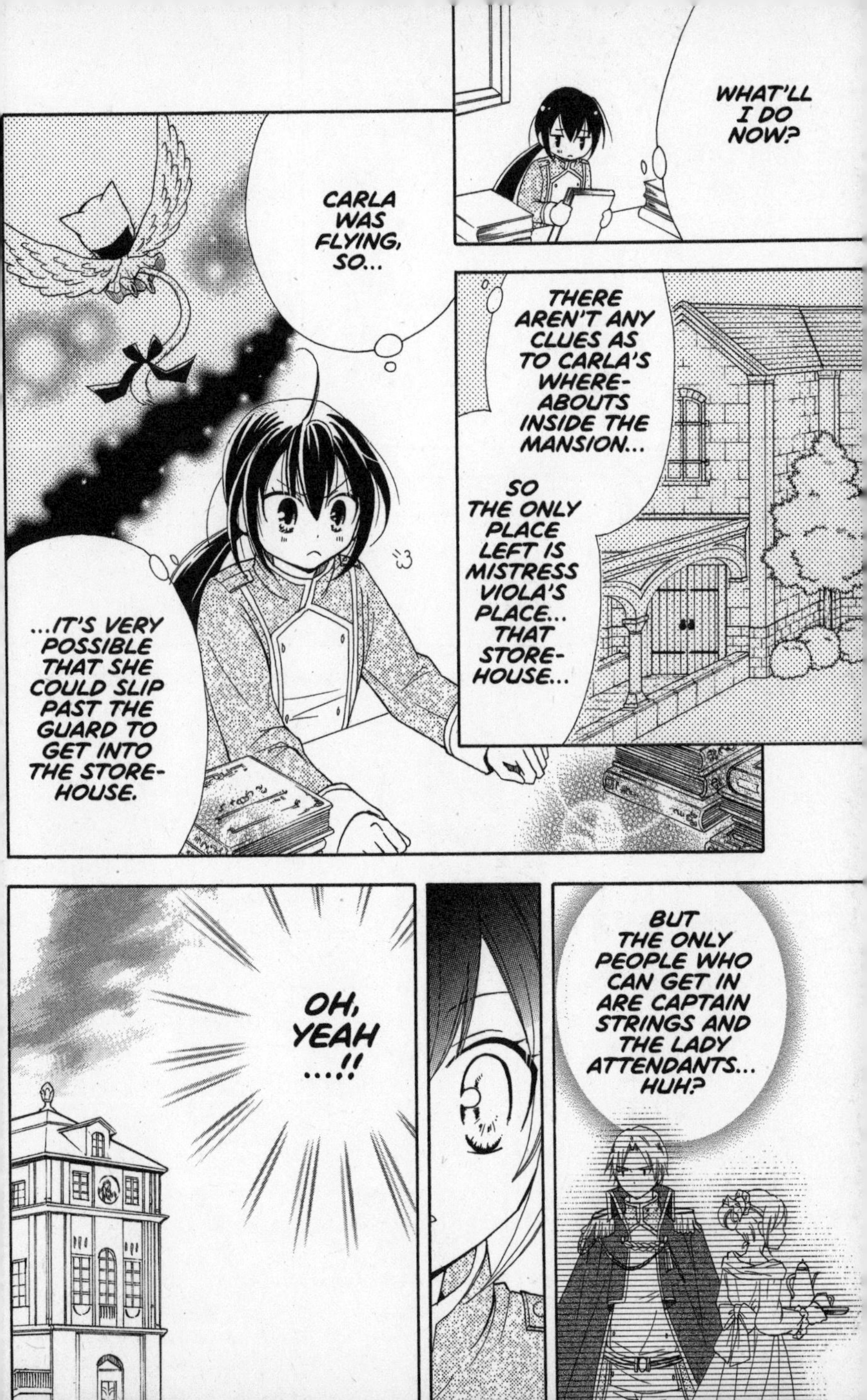
WHAT'LL I DO NOW?
THERE AREN'T ANY CLUES AS TO CARLA'S WHERE-ABOUTS INSIDE THE MANSION...
SO THE ONLY PLACE LEFT IS MISTRESS VIOLA'S PLACE... THAT STORE-HOUSE...
CARLA WAS FLYING, SO...
...IT'S VERY POSSIBLE THAT SHE COULD SLIP PAST THE GUARD TO GET INTO THE STORE-HOUSE.
BUT THE ONLY PEOPLE WHO CAN GET IN ARE CAPTAIN STRINGS AND THE LADY ATTENDANTS... HUH?
OH, YEAH ...!!

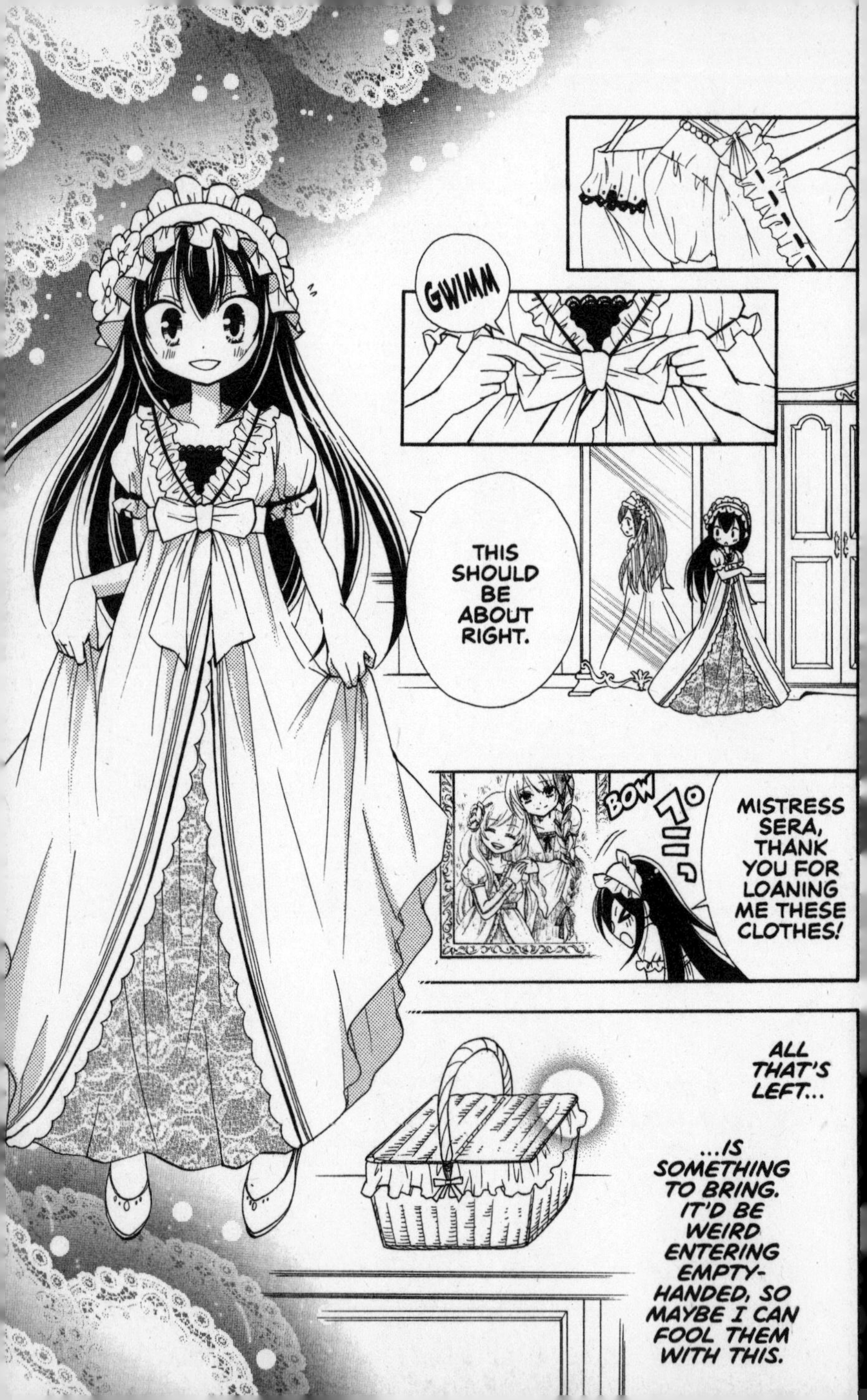
GWIMM
THIS SHOULD BE ABOUT RIGHT.
MISTRESS SERA, THANK YOU FOR LOANING ME THESE CLOTHES!
BOW
ALL THAT'S LEFT...
...IS SOMETHING TO BRING. IT'D BE WEIRD ENTERING EMPTY-HANDED, SO MAYBE I CAN FOOL THEM WITH THIS.

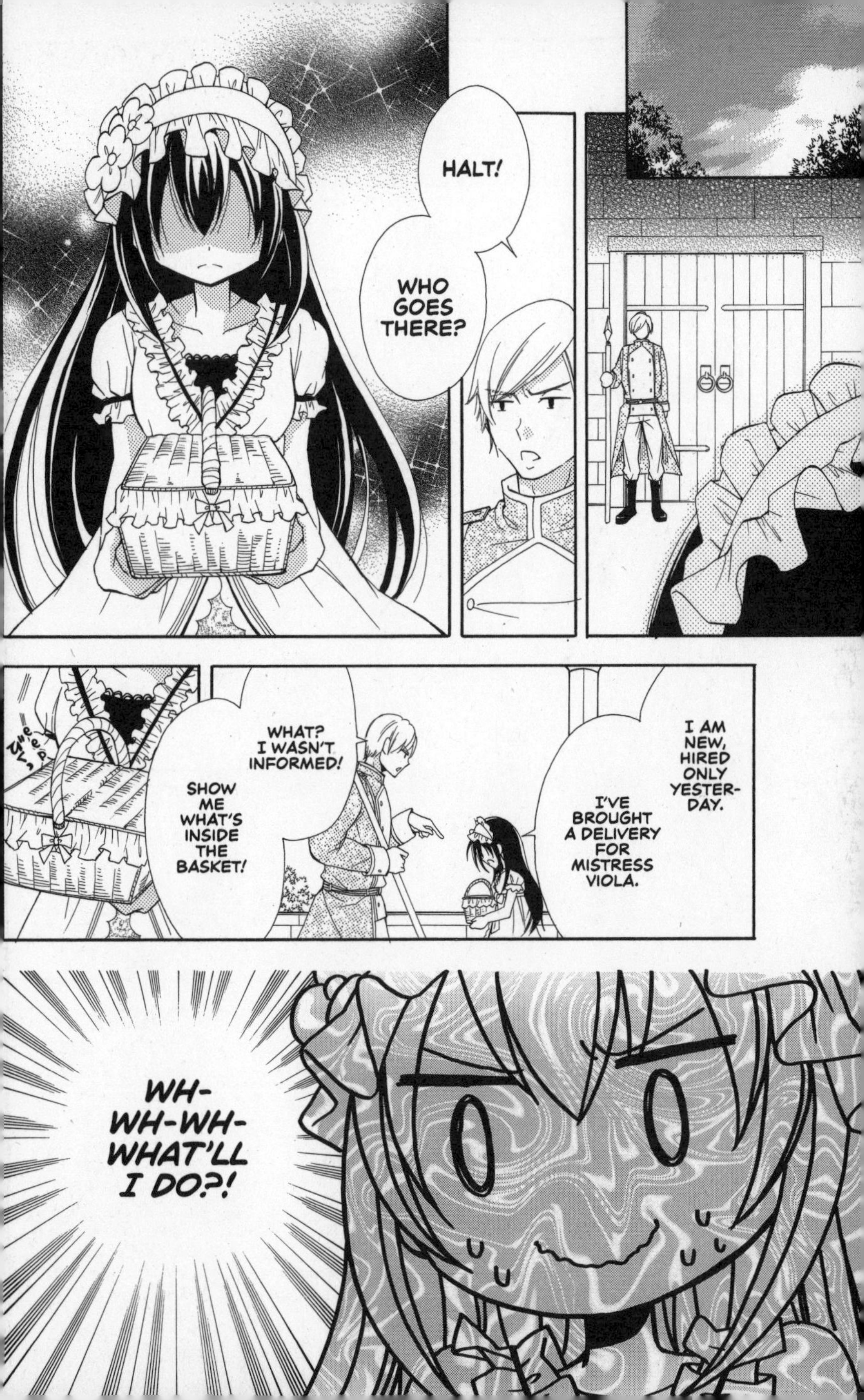
HALT!
WHO GOES THERE?
I AM NEW, HIRED ONLY YESTER-DAY.
I'VE BROUGHT A DELIVERY FOR MISTRESS VIOLA.
WHAT? I WASN'T INFORMED!
SHOW ME WHAT'S INSIDE THE BASKET!
WH-WH-WH-WHAT'LL I DO?!

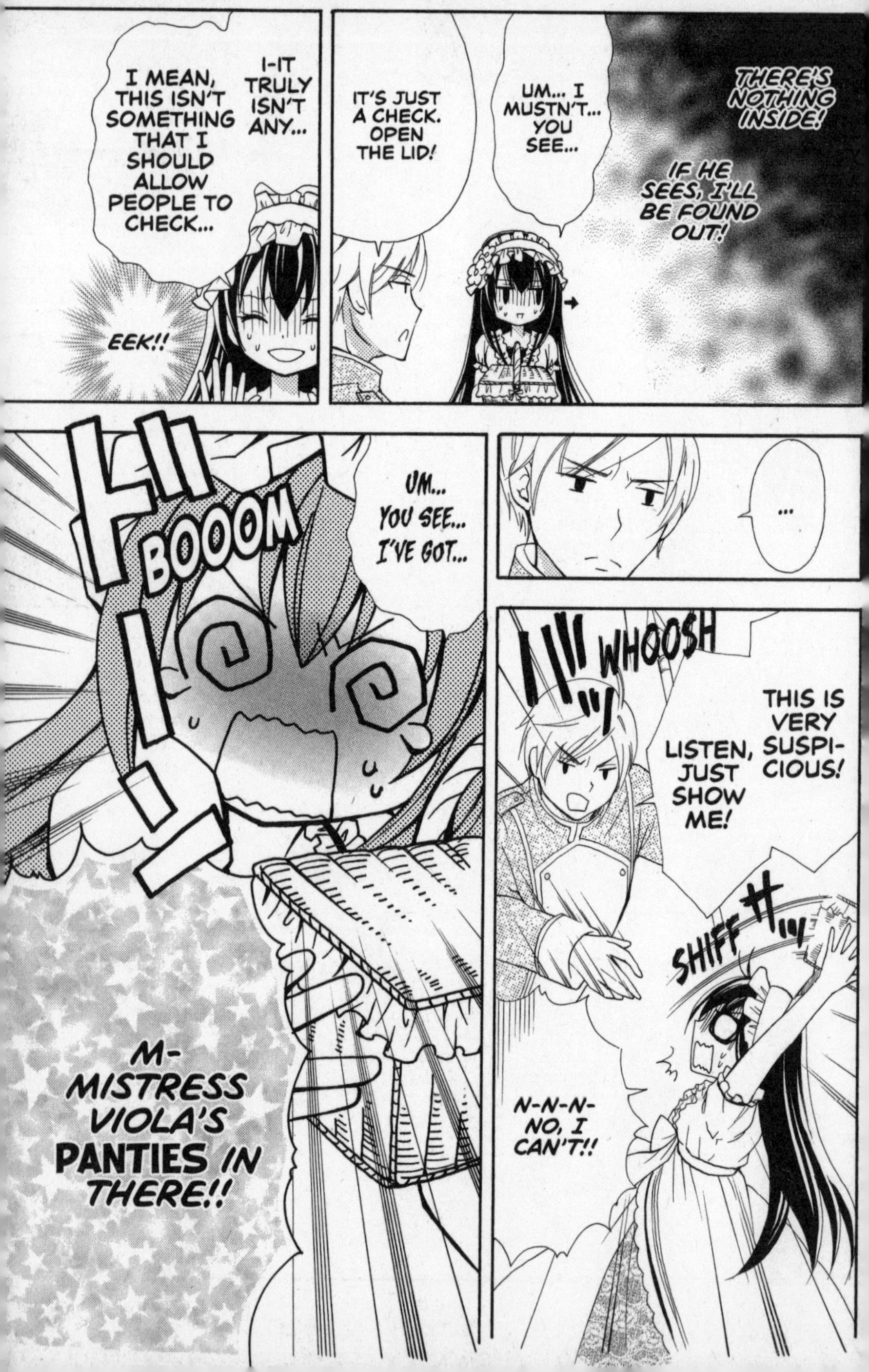
THERE'S NOTHING INSIDE!
IF HE SEES, I'LL BE FOUND OUT!
UM... I MUSTN'T... YOU SEE...
IT'S JUST A CHECK. OPEN THE LID!
I-IT TRULY ISN'T ANY...
I MEAN, THIS ISN'T SOMETHING THAT I SHOULD ALLOW PEOPLE TO CHECK...
EEK!!
...
WHOOSH
THIS IS VERY SUSPICIOUS!
LISTEN, JUST SHOW ME!
SHIFF
N-N-N-NO, I CAN'T!!
BOOOM
UM... YOU SEE... I'VE GOT...
M-MISTRESS VIOLA'S PANTIES IN THERE!!

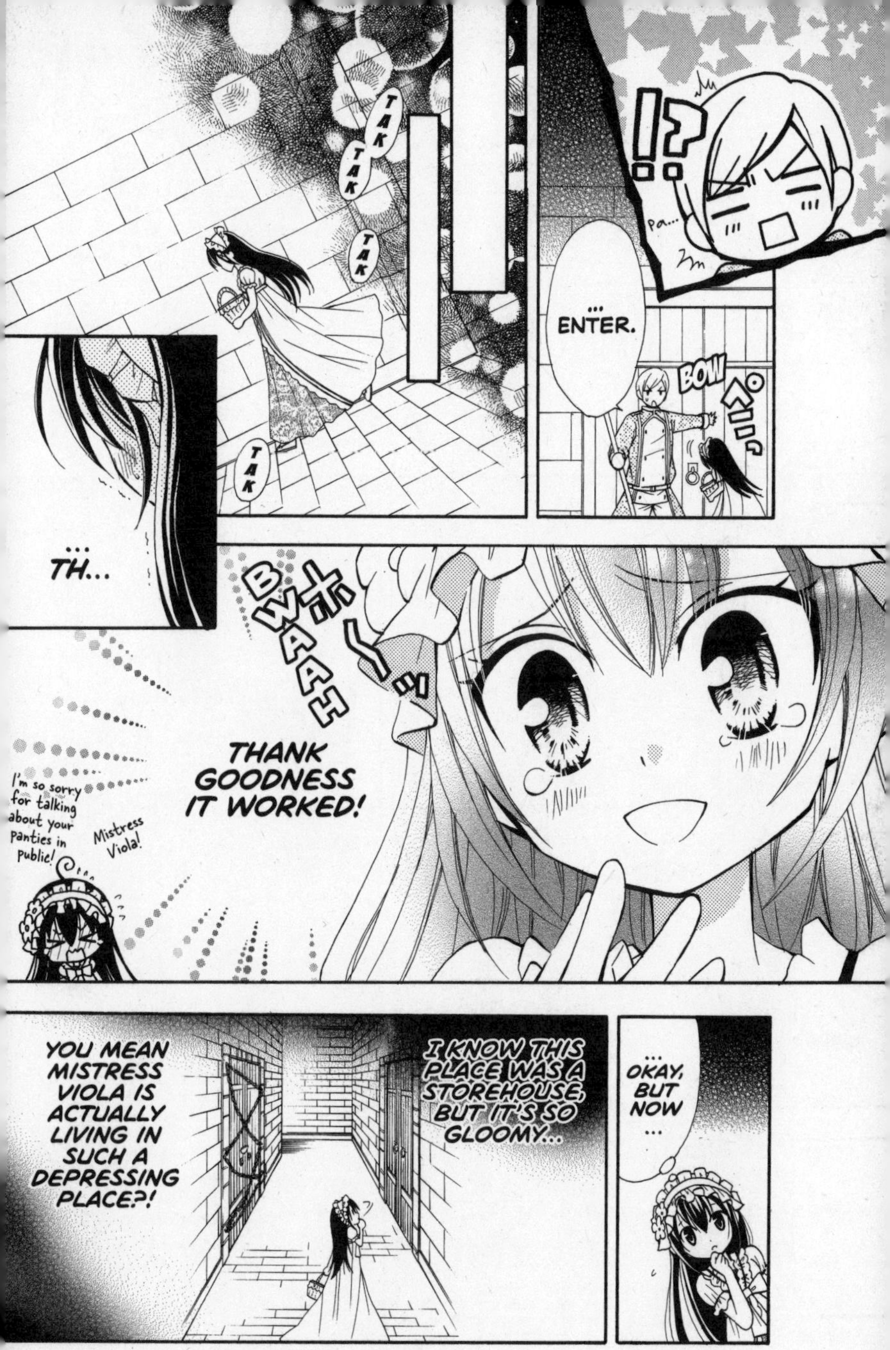
!?
Pa...
...ENTER.
BOW
TAK TAK TAK
TAK TAK
TAK
...TH...
BWAAAH
THANK GOODNESS IT WORKED!
I'm so sorry for talking about your panties in public!
Mistress Viola!
...OKAY, BUT NOW...
I KNOW THIS PLACE WAS A STOREHOUSE, BUT IT'S SO GLOOMY...
YOU MEAN MISTRESS VIOLA IS ACTUALLY LIVING IN SUCH A DEPRESSING PLACE?!

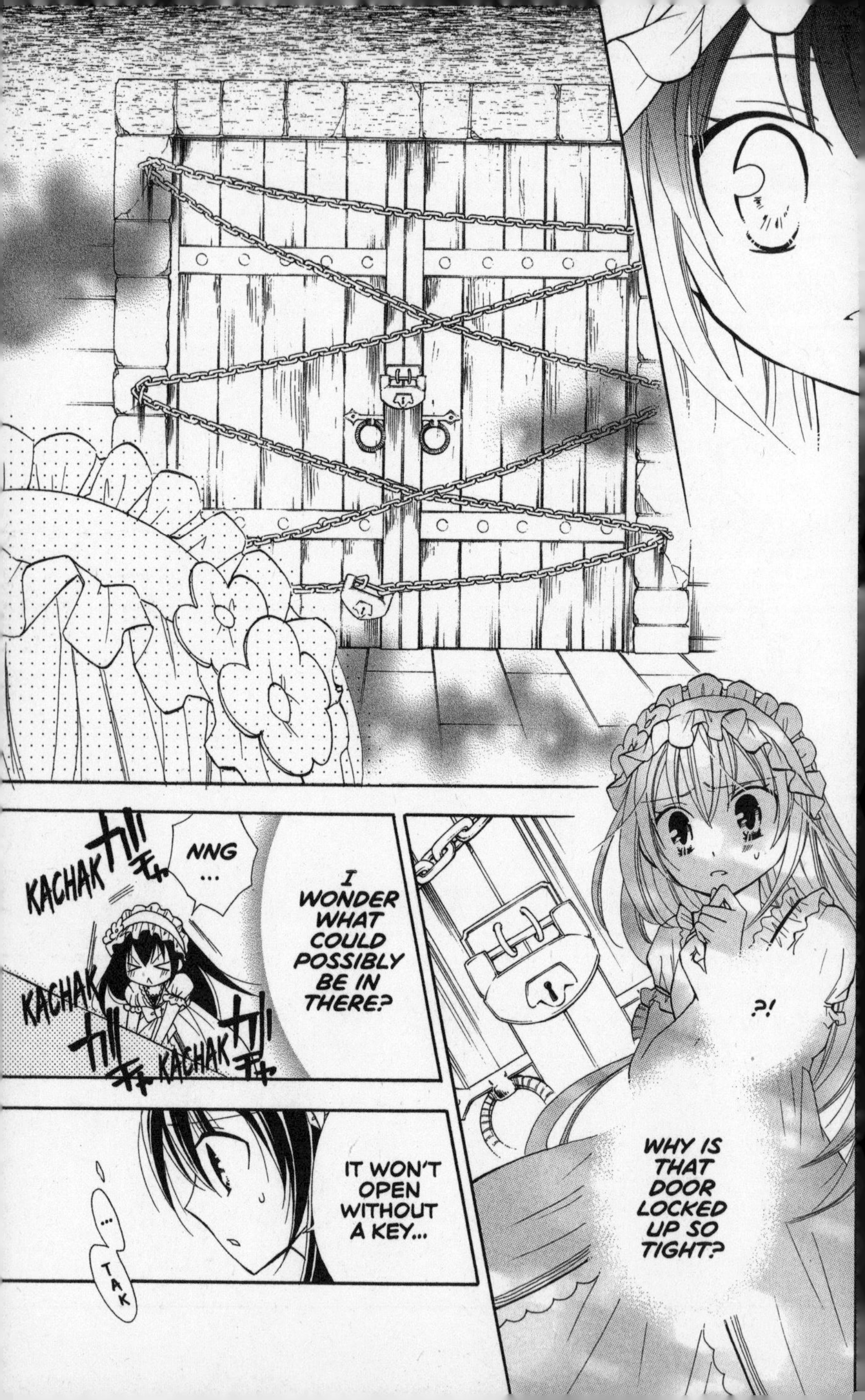
?!
WHY IS THAT DOOR LOCKED UP SO TIGHT?
I WONDER WHAT COULD POSSIBLY BE IN THERE?
NNG ...
KACHAK
KACHAK
KACHAK
IT WON'T OPEN WITHOUT A KEY...
...
TAK

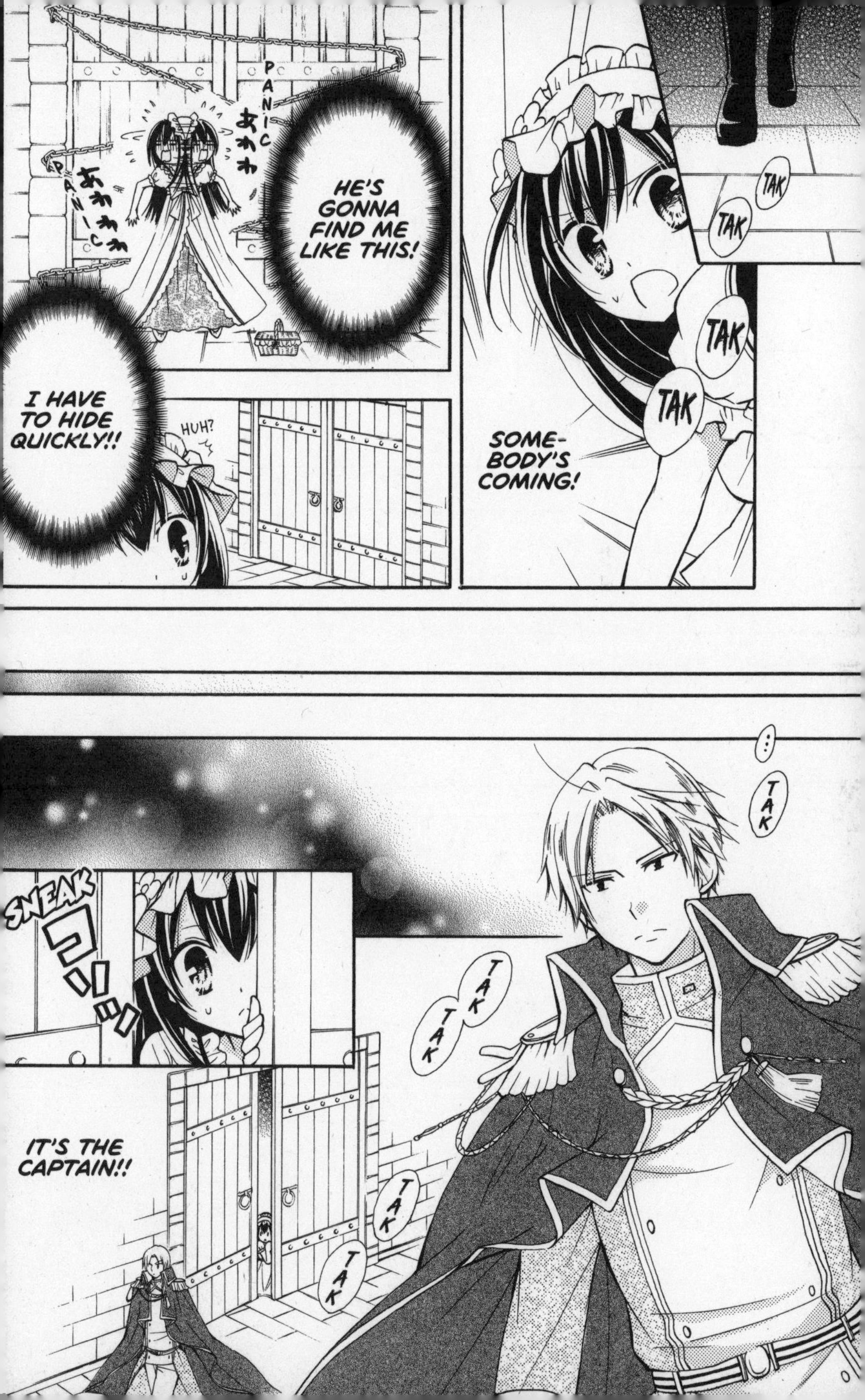
TAK
TAK
TAK
TAK
SOME-BODY'S COMING!
PANIC
あわわ
PANIC
あわわわ
HE'S GONNA FIND ME LIKE THIS!
I HAVE TO HIDE QUICKLY!!
HUH?
...
TAK
TAK TAK
SNEAK
IT'S THE CAPTAIN!!
TAK TAK

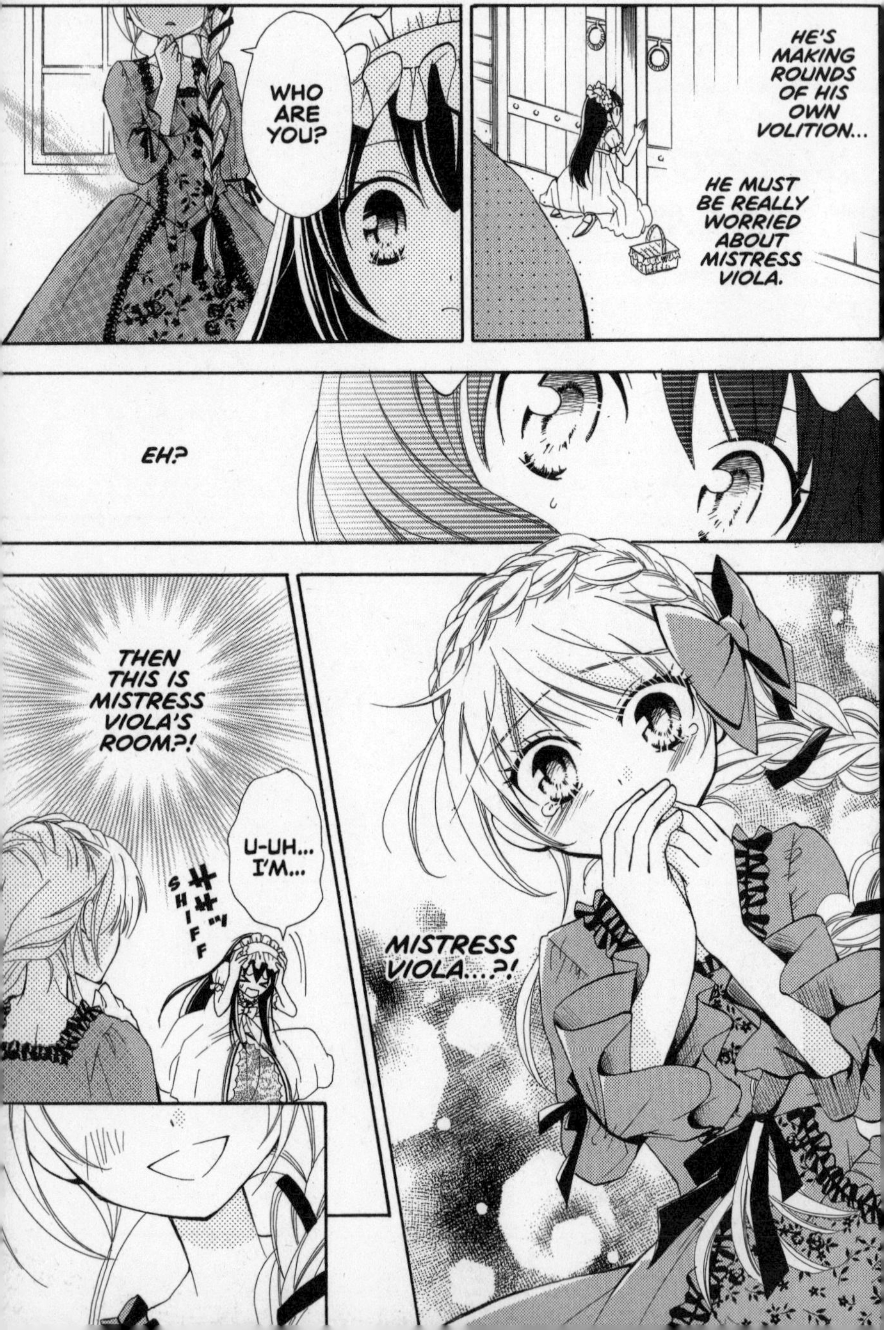
HE'S MAKING ROUNDS OF HIS OWN VOLITION...
HE MUST BE REALLY WORRIED ABOUT MISTRESS VIOLA.
WHO ARE YOU?
EH?
MISTRESS VIOLA...?!
THEN THIS IS MISTRESS VIOLA'S ROOM?!
U-UH... I'M...
SHIFF

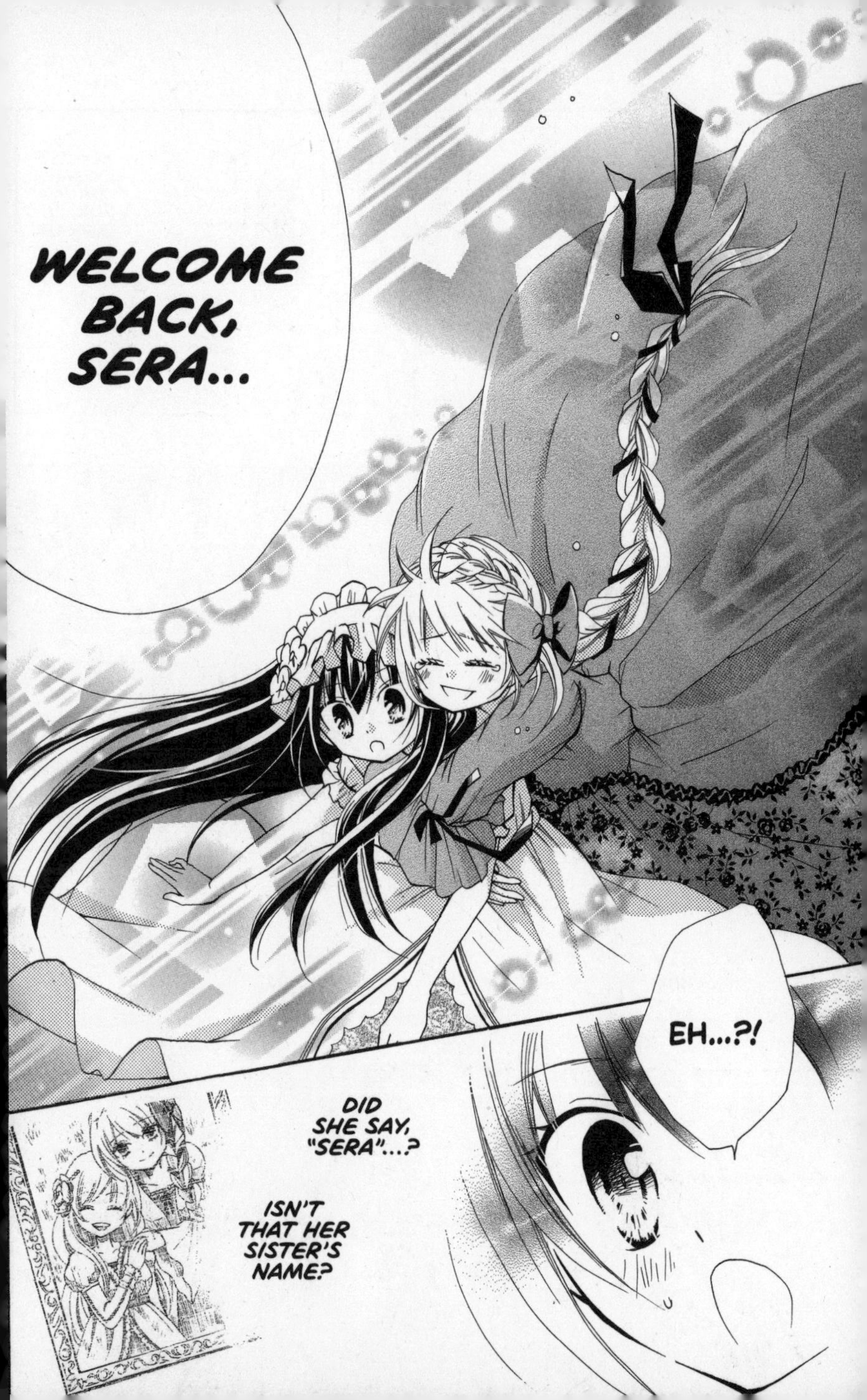
WELCOME BACK, SERA...
EH...?!
DID SHE SAY, "SERA"...?
ISN'T THAT HER SISTER'S NAME?

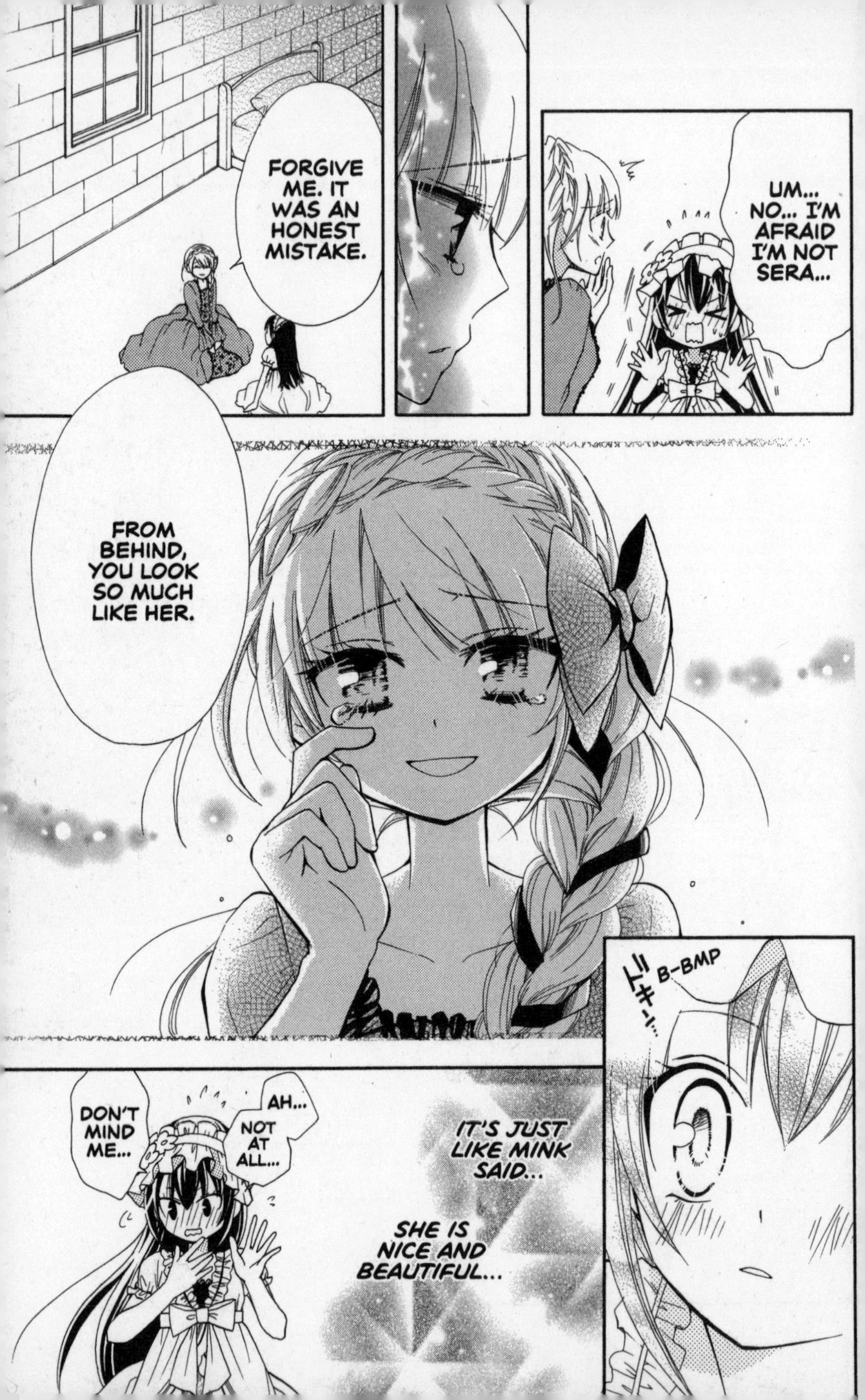
UM... NO... I'M AFRAID I'M NOT SERA...
FORGIVE ME. IT WAS AN HONEST MISTAKE.
FROM BEHIND, YOU LOOK SO MUCH LIKE HER.
B-BMP
IT'S JUST LIKE MINK SAID...
SHE IS NICE AND BEAUTIFUL...
AH... NOT AT ALL...
DON'T MIND ME...

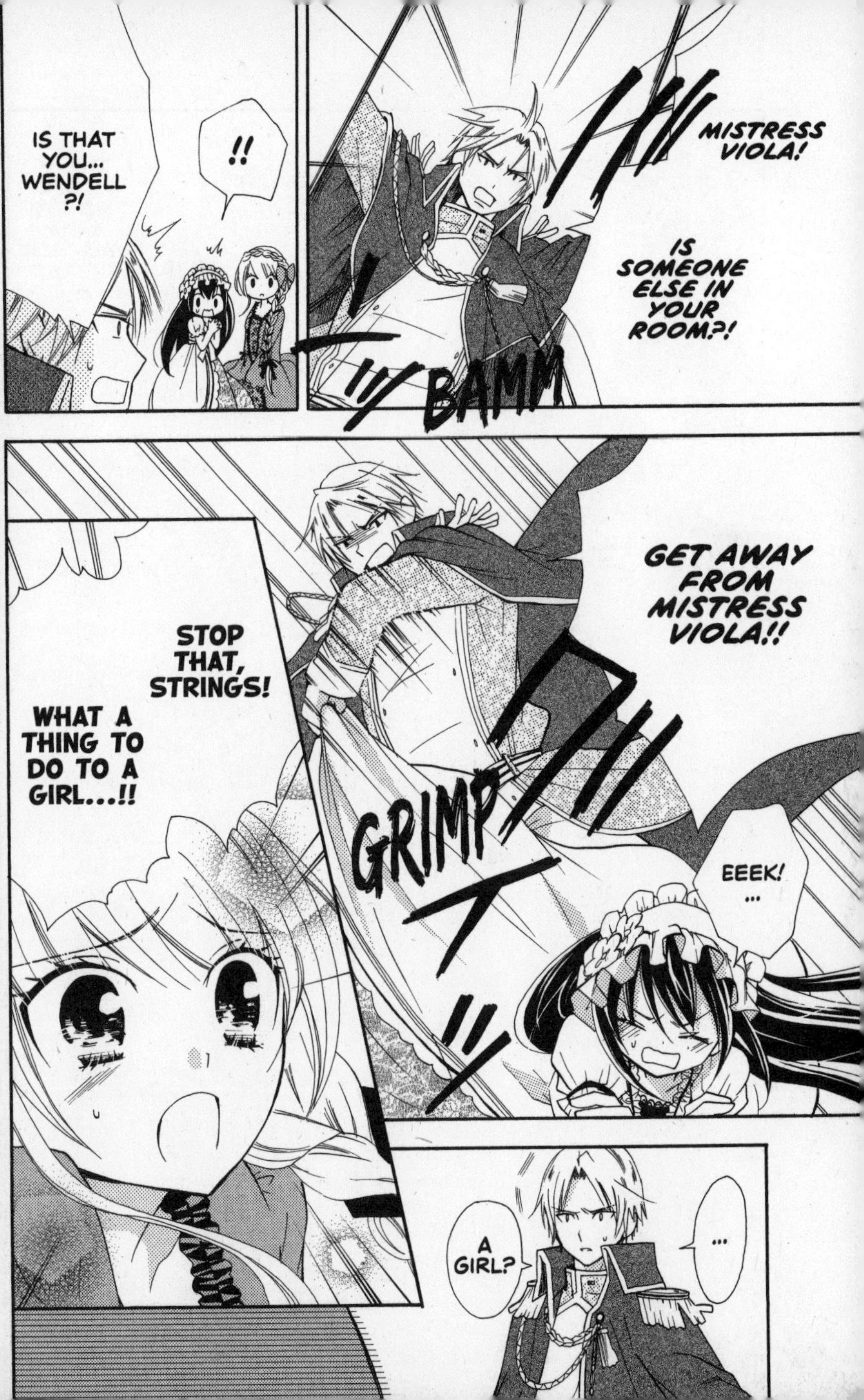
MISTRESS VIOLA!
IS SOMEONE ELSE IN YOUR ROOM?!
BAMM
!!
IS THAT YOU... WENDELL ?!
GET AWAY FROM MISTRESS VIOLA!!
GRIMP
EEEK! ...
STOP THAT, STRINGS!
WHAT A THING TO DO TO A GIRL...!!
...
A GIRL?

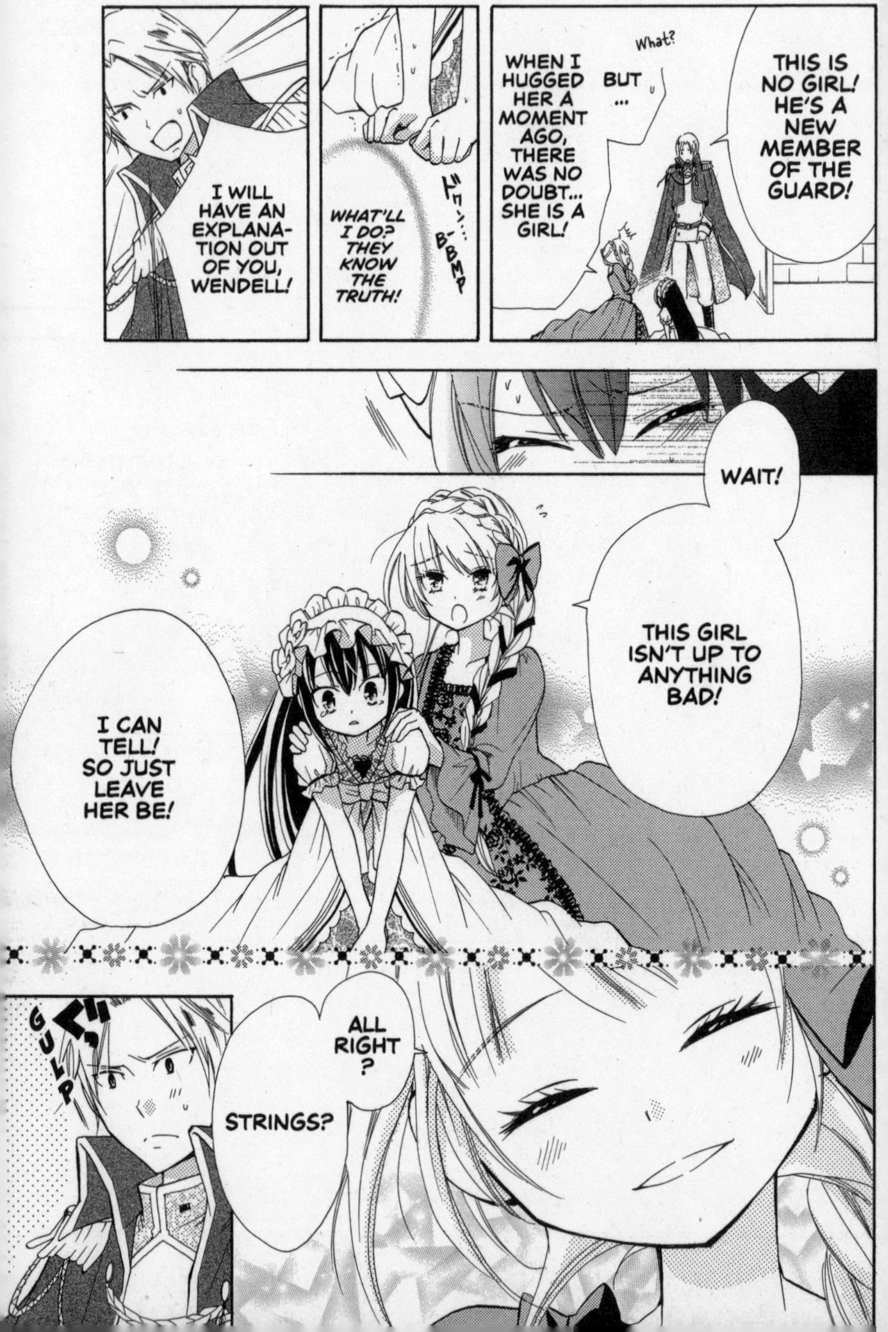
THIS IS NO GIRL! HE'S A NEW MEMBER OF THE GUARD!
What?
BUT ...
WHEN I HUGGED HER A MOMENT AGO, THERE WAS NO DOUBT... SHE IS A GIRL!
WHAT'LL I DO? THEY KNOW THE TRUTH!
B-BMP
I WILL HAVE AN EXPLANATION OUT OF YOU, WENDELL!
WAIT!
THIS GIRL ISN'T UP TO ANYTHING BAD!
I CAN TELL! SO JUST LEAVE HER BE!
ALL RIGHT?
STRINGS?
GULP

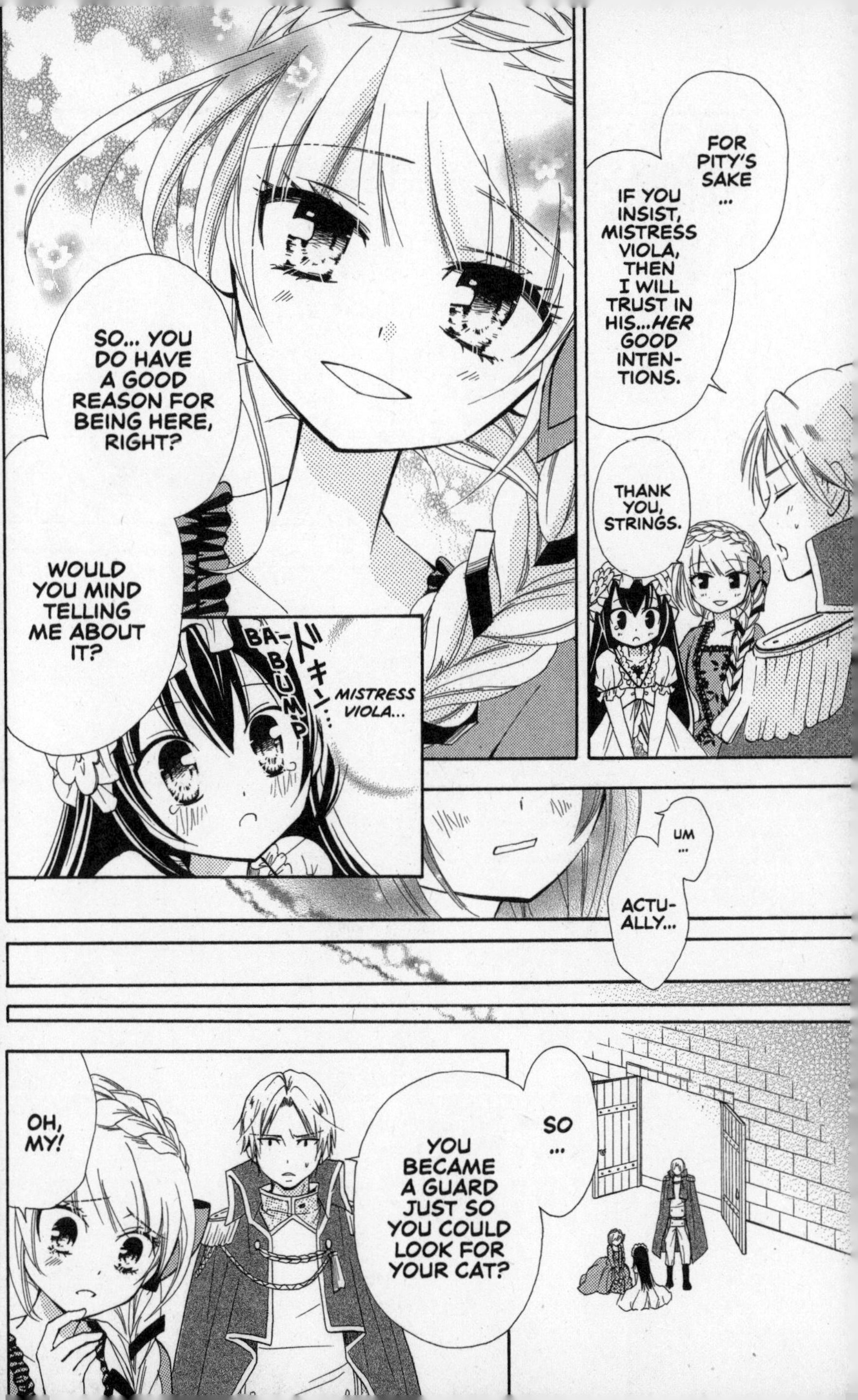
FOR PITY'S SAKE...
IF YOU INSIST, MISTRESS VIOLA, THEN I WILL TRUST IN HIS...*HER* GOOD INTENTIONS.
THANK YOU, STRINGS.
SO... YOU DO HAVE A GOOD REASON FOR BEING HERE, RIGHT?
WOULD YOU MIND TELLING ME ABOUT IT?
UM...
ACTUALLY...
BA-BUMP
ドキン…
MISTRESS VIOLA...
SO...
YOU BECAME A GUARD JUST SO YOU COULD LOOK FOR YOUR CAT?
OH, MY!

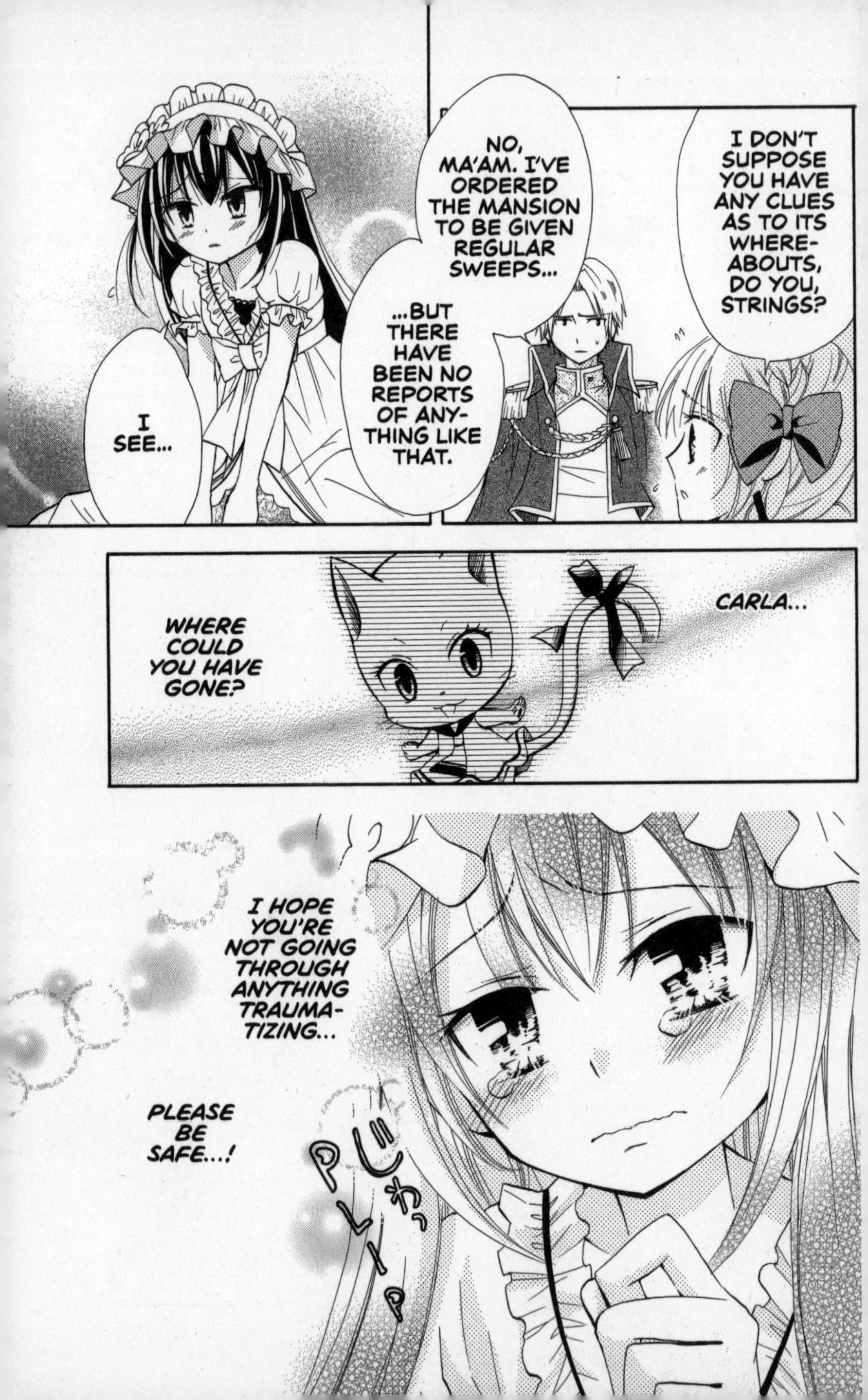
I DON'T SUPPOSE YOU HAVE ANY CLUES AS TO ITS WHERE-ABOUTS, DO YOU, STRINGS?
NO, MA'AM. I'VE ORDERED THE MANSION TO BE GIVEN REGULAR SWEEPS...
...BUT THERE HAVE BEEN NO REPORTS OF ANY-THING LIKE THAT.
I SEE...
CARLA...
WHERE COULD YOU HAVE GONE?
I HOPE YOU'RE NOT GOING THROUGH ANYTHING TRAUMA-TIZING...
PLEASE BE SAFE...!

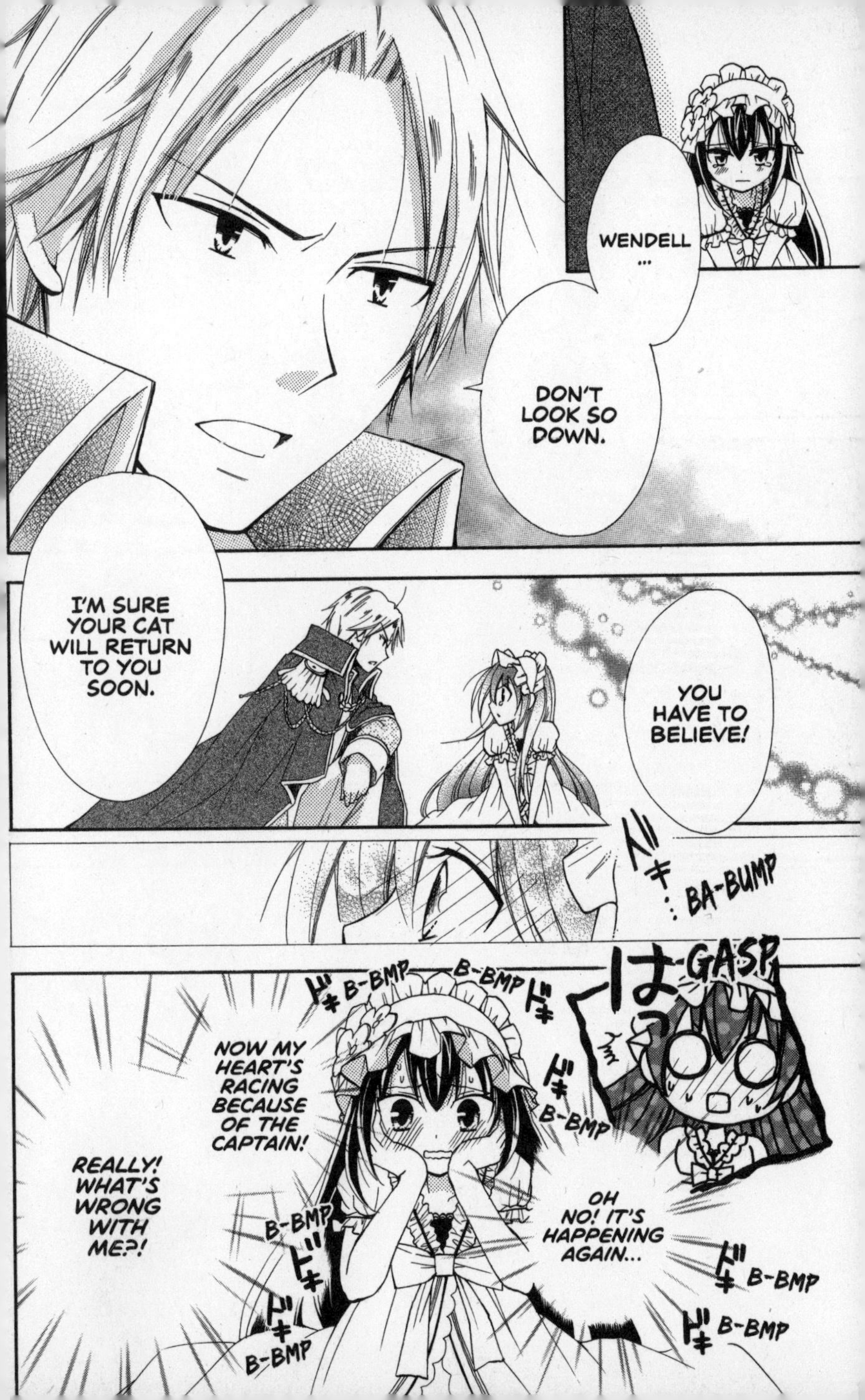

WENDELL ...
DON'T LOOK SO DOWN.
I'M SURE YOUR CAT WILL RETURN TO YOU SOON.
YOU HAVE TO BELIEVE!
ドキ... BA-BUMP
はっ GASP
B-BMP ドキ
ドキ B-BMP
ドキ B-BMP
NOW MY HEART'S RACING BECAUSE OF THE CAPTAIN!
OH NO! IT'S HAPPENING AGAIN...
ドキ B-BMP
ドキ B-BMP
B-BMP ドキ
ドキ B-BMP
REALLY! WHAT'S WRONG WITH ME?!

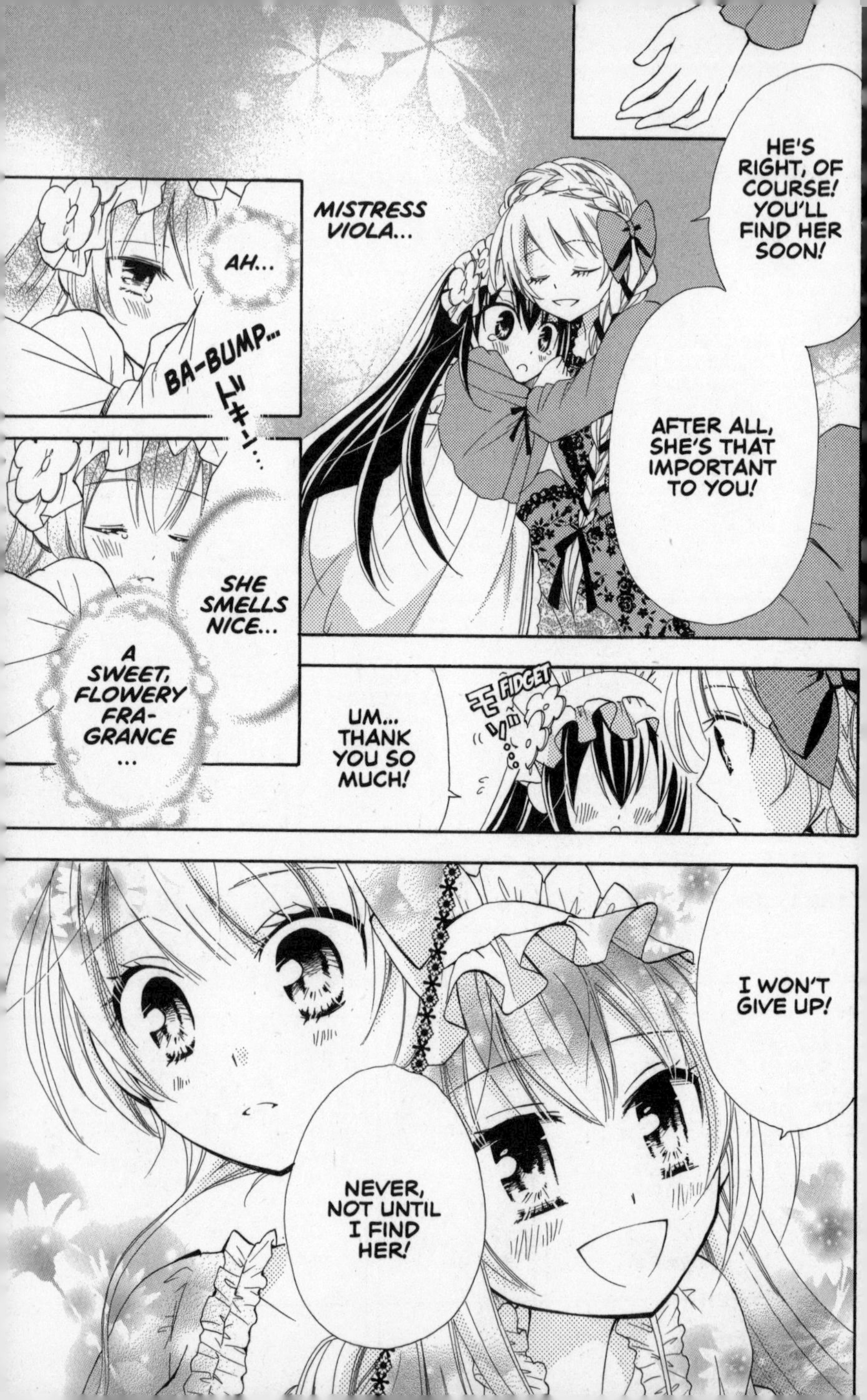
HE'S RIGHT, OF COURSE! YOU'LL FIND HER SOON!
AFTER ALL, SHE'S THAT IMPORTANT TO YOU!
MISTRESS VIOLA...
AH...
BA-BUMP...
ドキーン...
SHE SMELLS NICE...
A SWEET, FLOWERY FRA-GRANCE...
FIDGET
UM... THANK YOU SO MUCH!
I WON'T GIVE UP!
NEVER, NOT UNTIL I FIND HER!

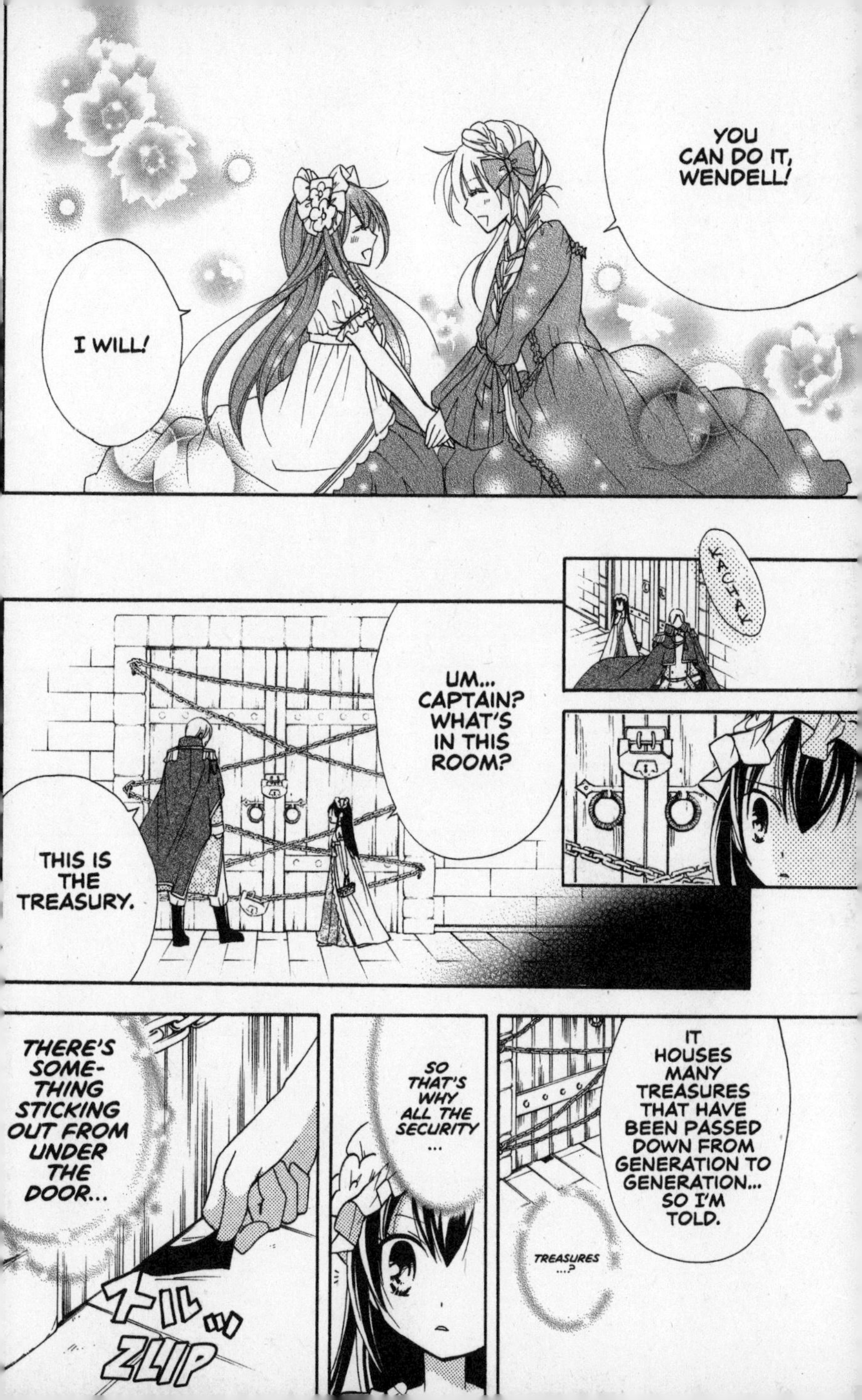
YOU CAN DO IT, WENDELL!
I WILL!
KACHAK
UM... CAPTAIN? WHAT'S IN THIS ROOM?
THIS IS THE TREASURY.
IT HOUSES MANY TREASURES THAT HAVE BEEN PASSED DOWN FROM GENERATION TO GENERATION... SO I'M TOLD.
TREASURES ...?
SO THAT'S WHY ALL THE SECURITY ...
THERE'S SOME-THING STICKING OUT FROM UNDER THE DOOR...
ZLIP

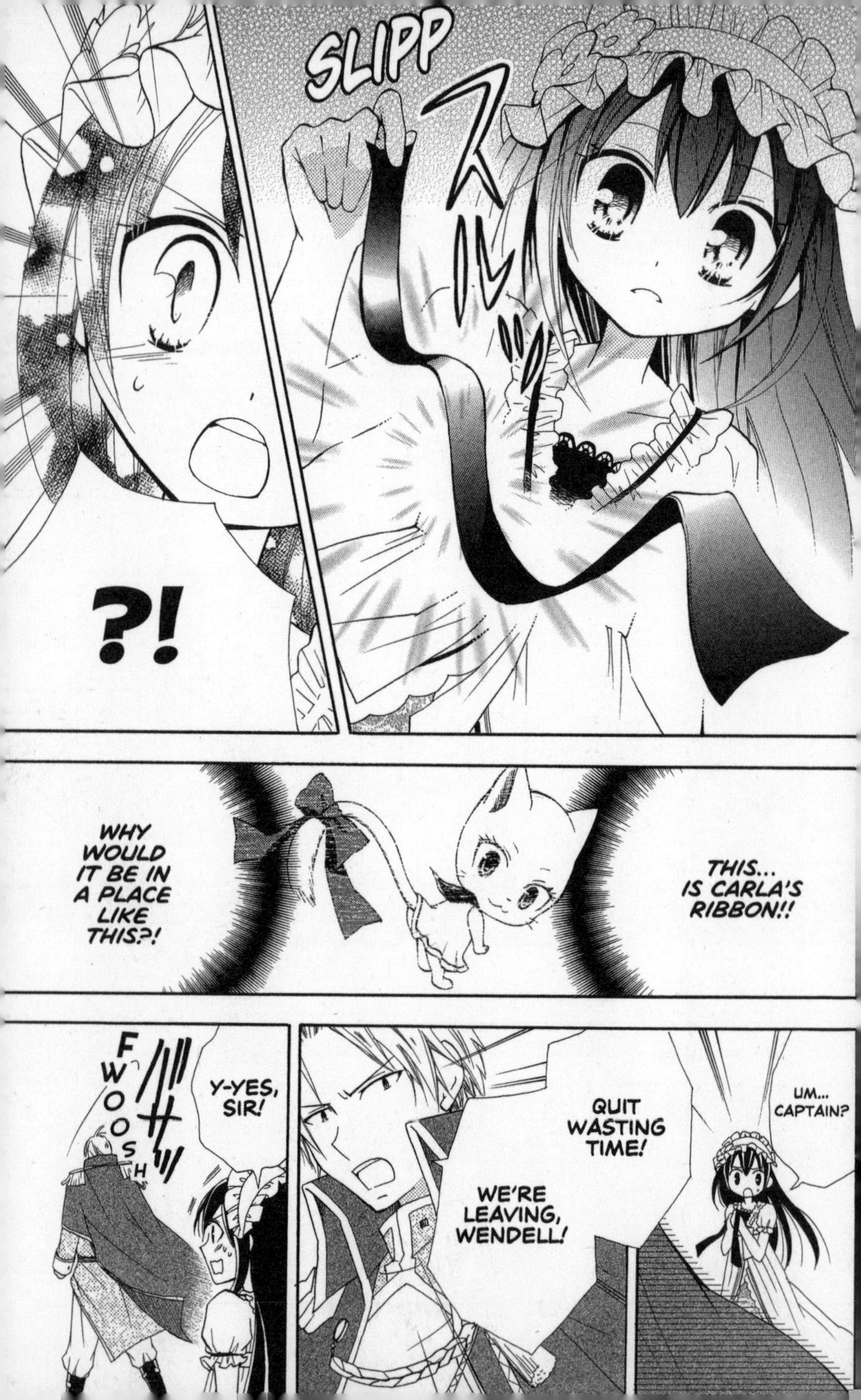

SLIPP
?!
THIS... IS CARLA'S RIBBON!!
WHY WOULD IT BE IN A PLACE LIKE THIS?!
UM... CAPTAIN?
QUIT WASTING TIME!
WE'RE LEAVING, WENDELL!
Y-YES, SIR!
FWOOSH

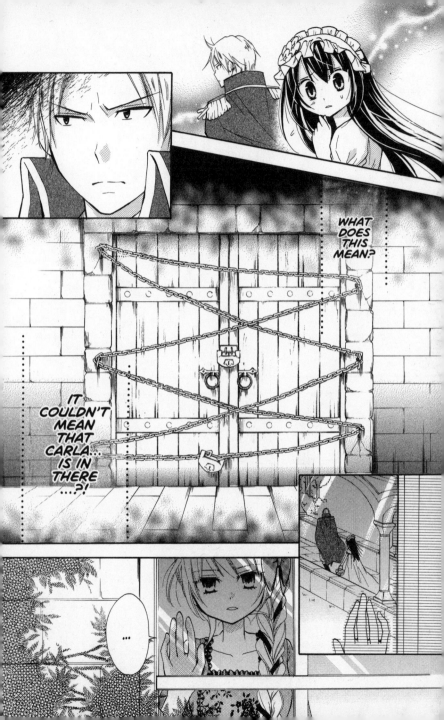

WHAT DOES THIS MEAN?

IT COULDN'T MEAN THAT CARLA... IS IN THERE ...?!

...

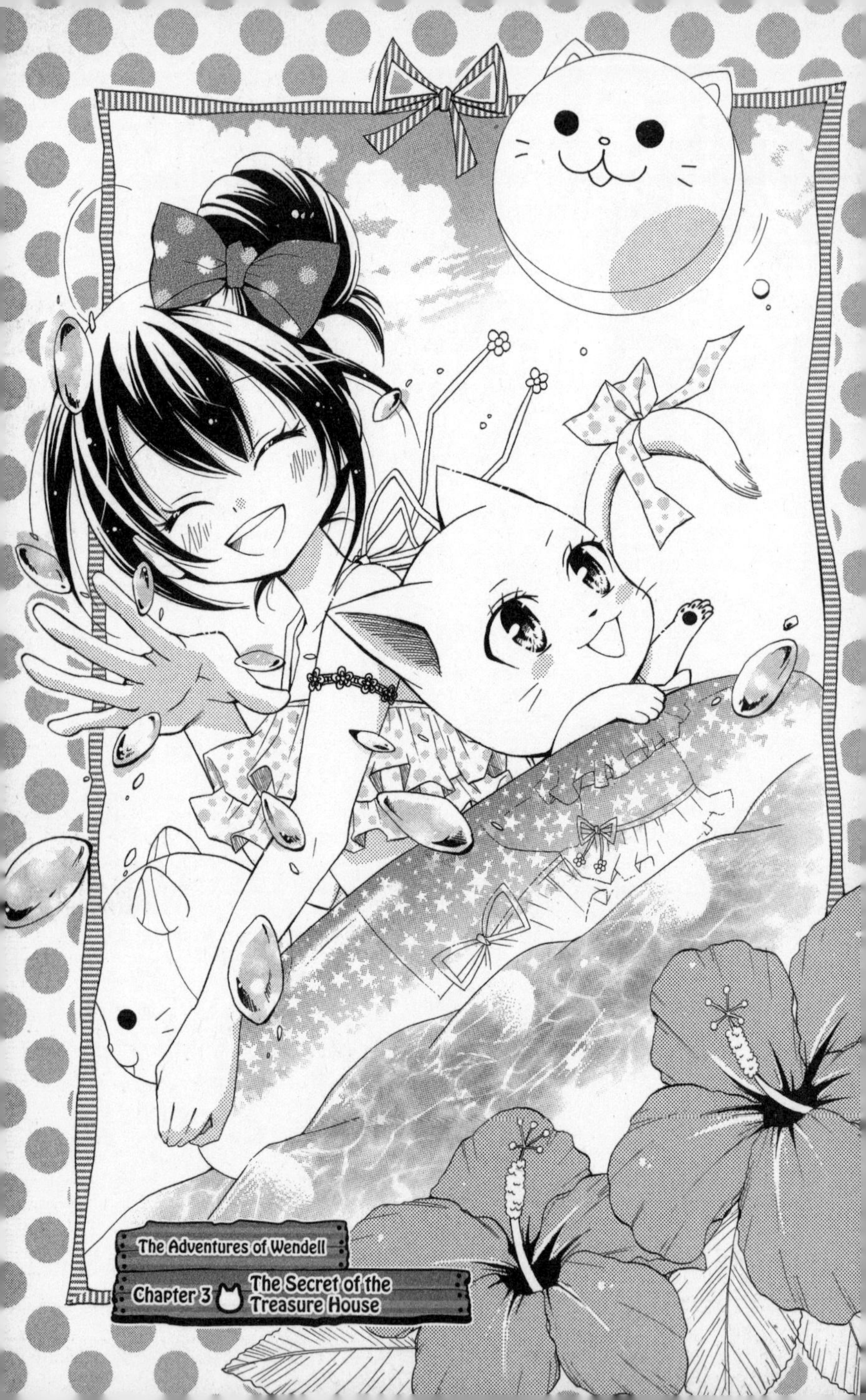

The Adventures of Wendell
Chapter 3
The Secret of the Treasure House

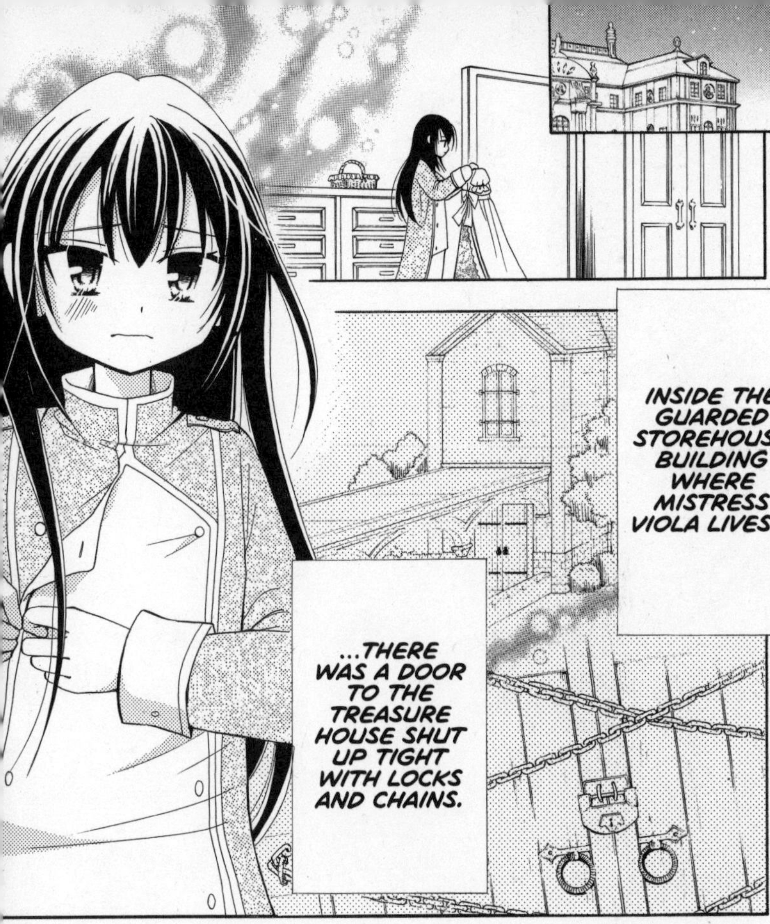
INSIDE THE GUARDED STOREHOUSE BUILDING WHERE MISTRESS VIOLA LIVES...
...THERE WAS A DOOR TO THE TREASURE HOUSE SHUT UP TIGHT WITH LOCKS AND CHAINS.

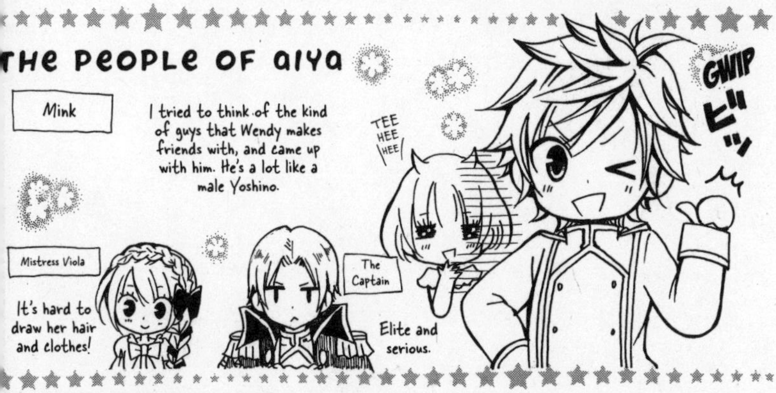
The People of aiya
Mink
I tried to think of the kind of guys that Wendy makes friends with, and came up with him. He's a lot like a male Yoshino.
GWIP
TEE HEE HEE
Mistress Viola
It's hard to draw her hair and clothes!
The Captain
Elite and serious.

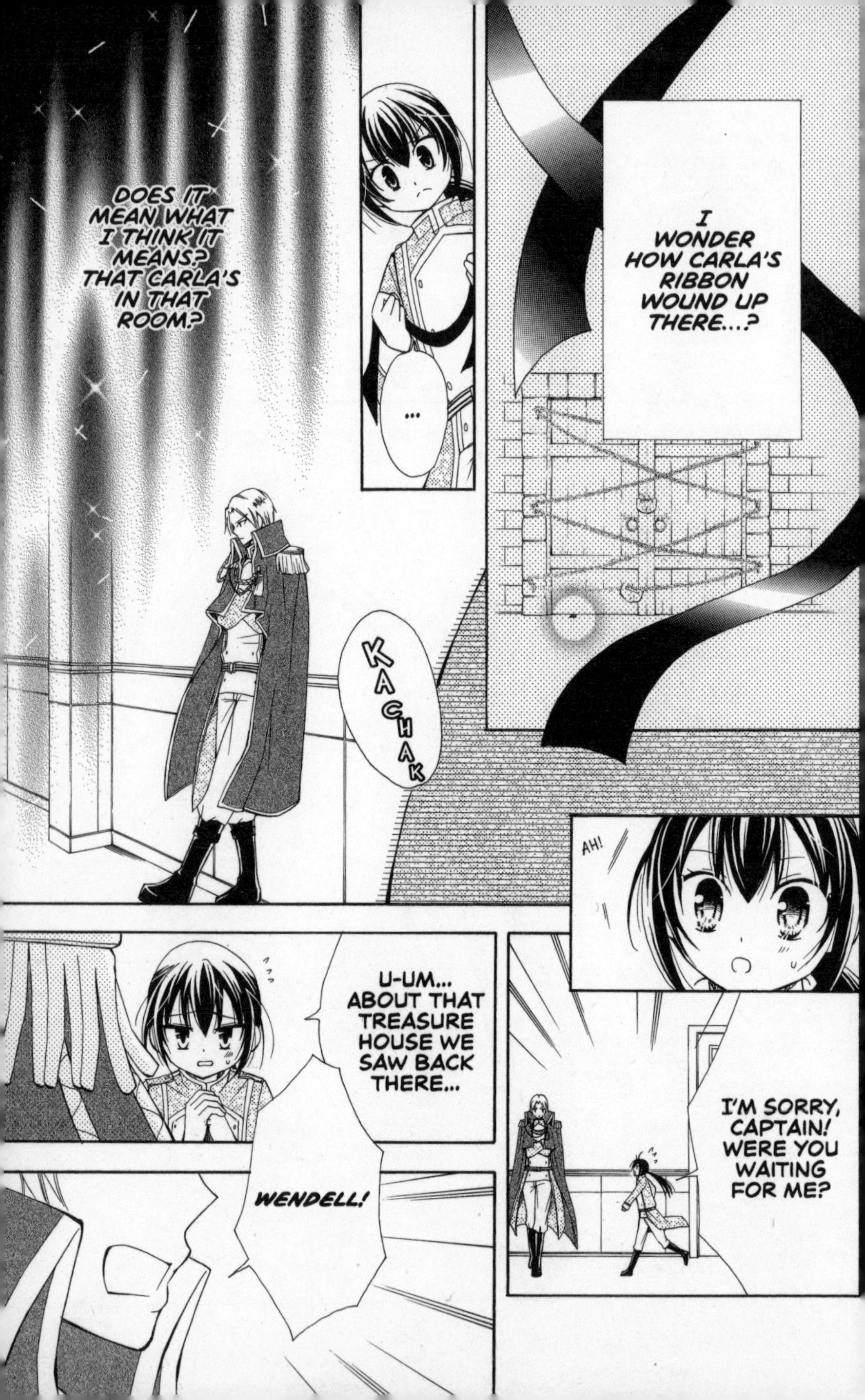
I WONDER HOW CARLA'S RIBBON WOUND UP THERE...?
...
DOES IT MEAN WHAT I THINK IT MEANS? THAT CARLA'S IN THAT ROOM?
KACHAK
AH!
I'M SORRY, CAPTAIN! WERE YOU WAITING FOR ME?
U-UM... ABOUT THAT TREASURE HOUSE WE SAW BACK THERE...
WENDELL!

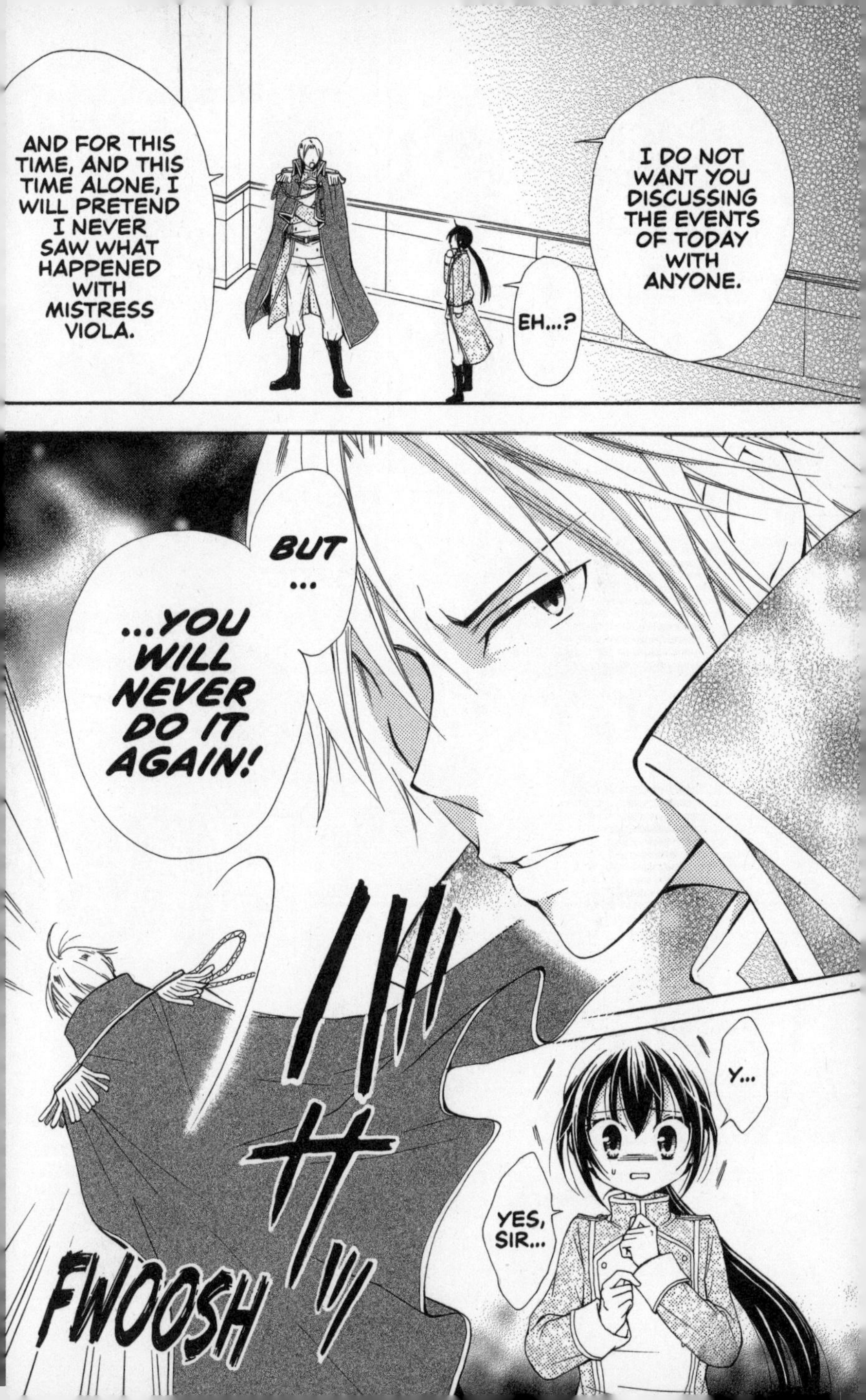
I DO NOT WANT YOU DISCUSSING THE EVENTS OF TODAY WITH ANYONE.
EH...?
AND FOR THIS TIME, AND THIS TIME ALONE, I WILL PRETEND I NEVER SAW WHAT HAPPENED WITH MISTRESS VIOLA.
BUT ...
...YOU WILL NEVER DO IT AGAIN!
Y...
YES, SIR...
FWOOSH

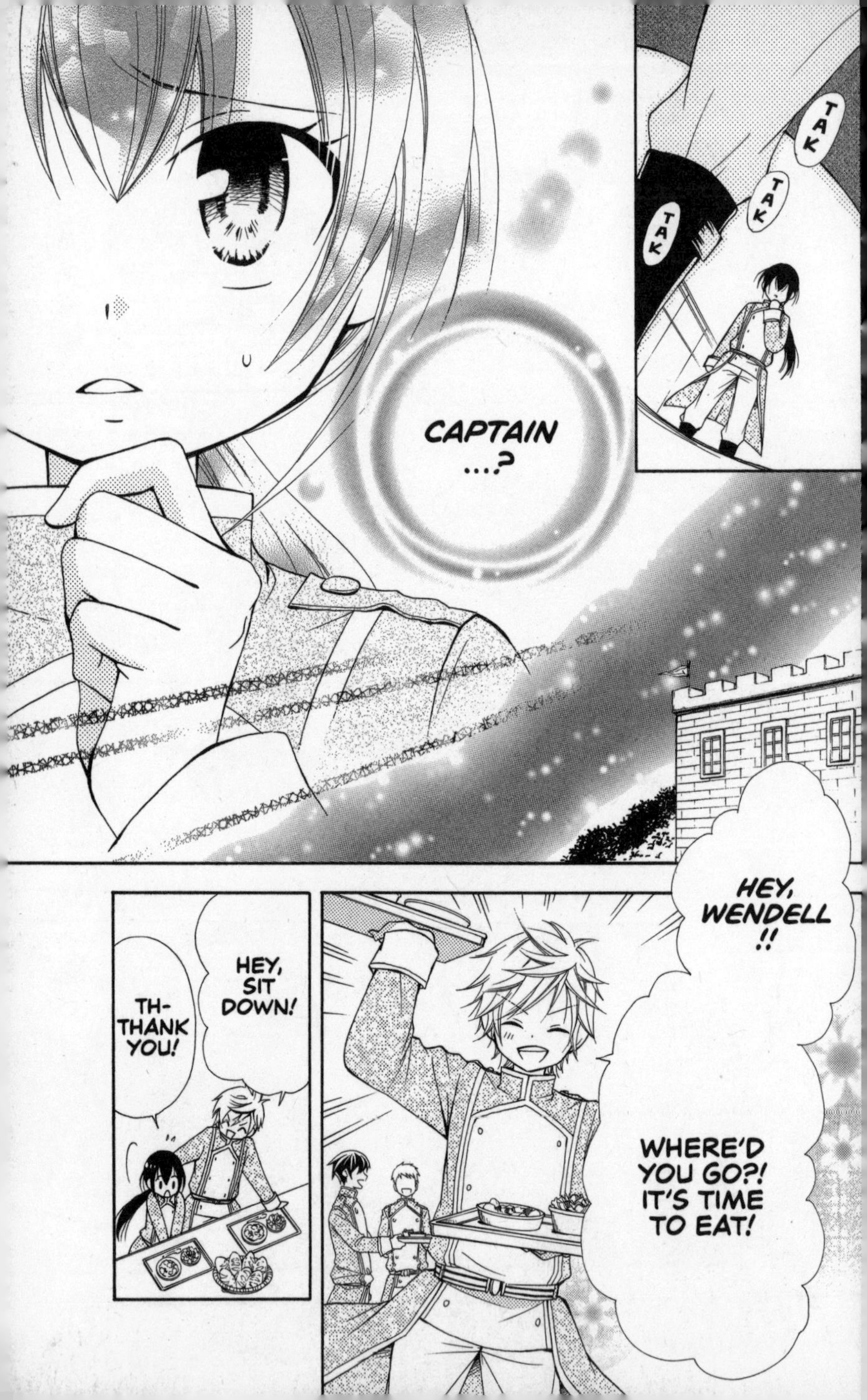
TAK
TAK
TAK
CAPTAIN ...?
HEY, WENDELL !!
WHERE'D YOU GO?! IT'S TIME TO EAT!
HEY, SIT DOWN!
TH-THANK YOU!

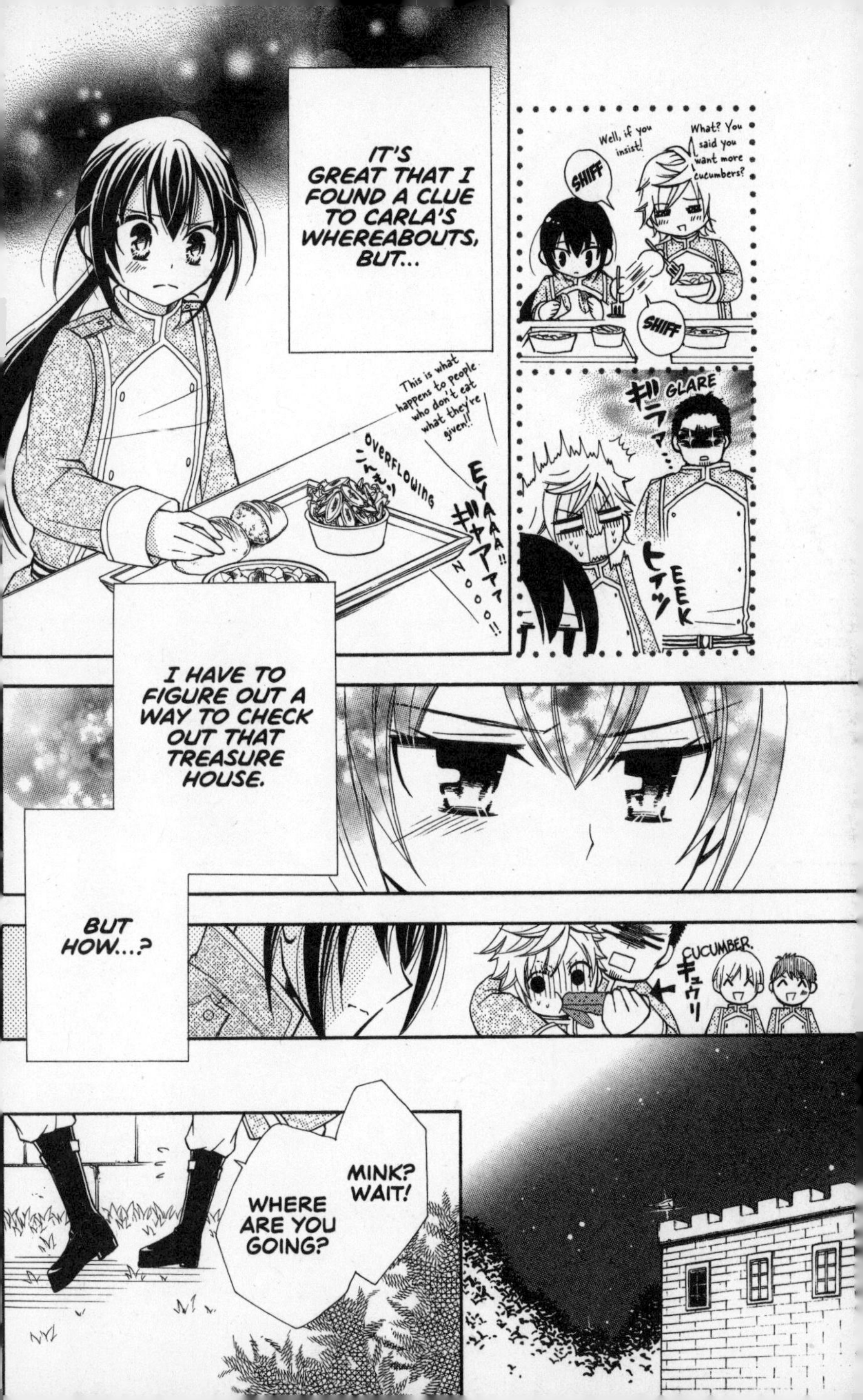

What? You said you want more cucumbers?
Well, if you insist!
SHIFF
SHIFF
ギラァ GLARE
ヒィッ EEK
IT'S GREAT THAT I FOUND A CLUE TO CARLA'S WHEREABOUTS, BUT...
This is what happens to people who don't eat what they're given!!
こんもり OVERFLOWING
ギャアァァ EYAAA!! NOOOO!!
I HAVE TO FIGURE OUT A WAY TO CHECK OUT THAT TREASURE HOUSE.
BUT HOW...?
キュウリ CUCUMBER.
MINK? WAIT!
WHERE ARE YOU GOING?

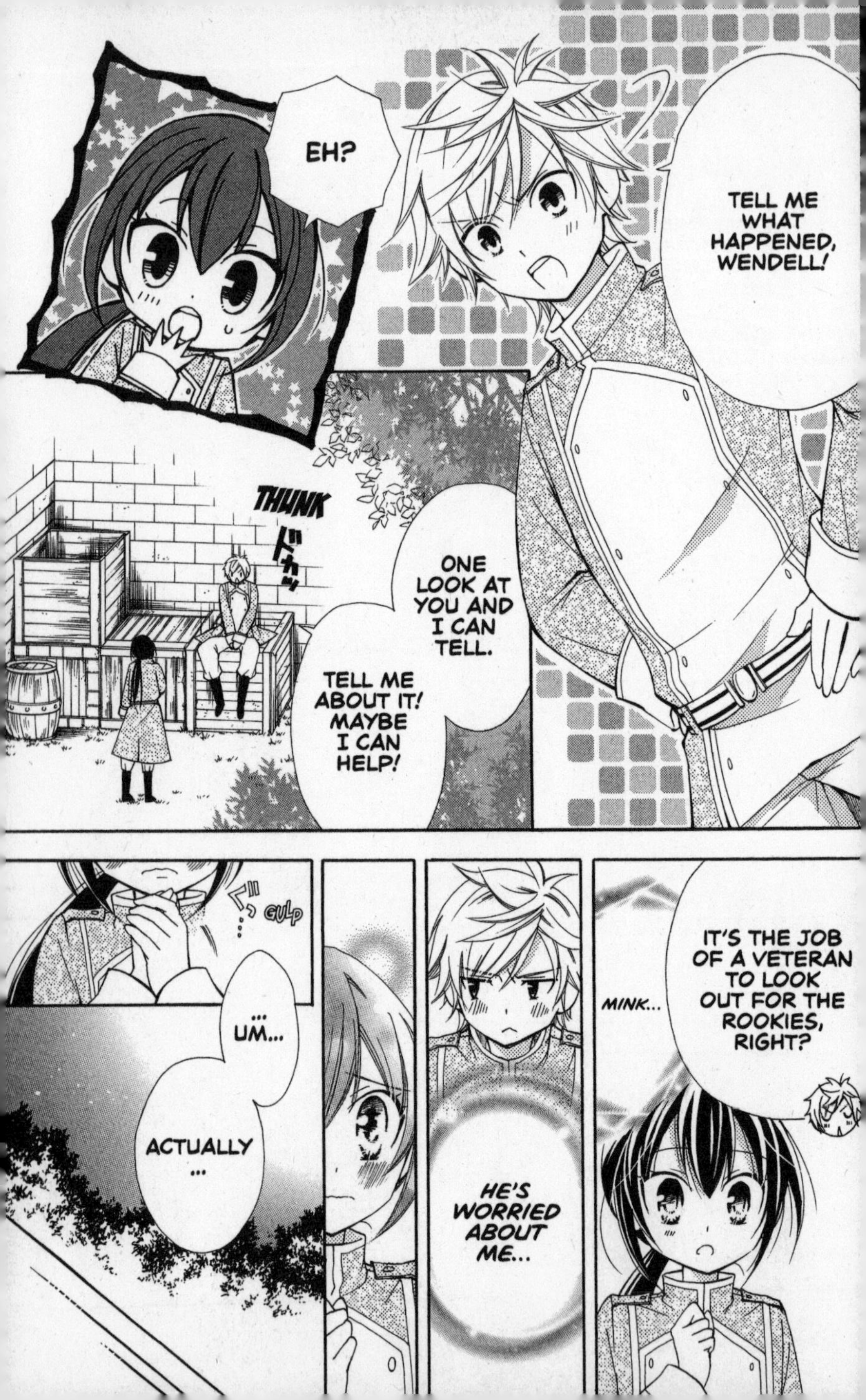
TELL ME WHAT HAPPENED, WENDELL!
EH?
THUNK
ONE LOOK AT YOU AND I CAN TELL.
TELL ME ABOUT IT! MAYBE I CAN HELP!
IT'S THE JOB OF A VETERAN TO LOOK OUT FOR THE ROOKIES, RIGHT?
MINK...
HE'S WORRIED ABOUT ME...
GULP
... UM...
ACTUALLY ...

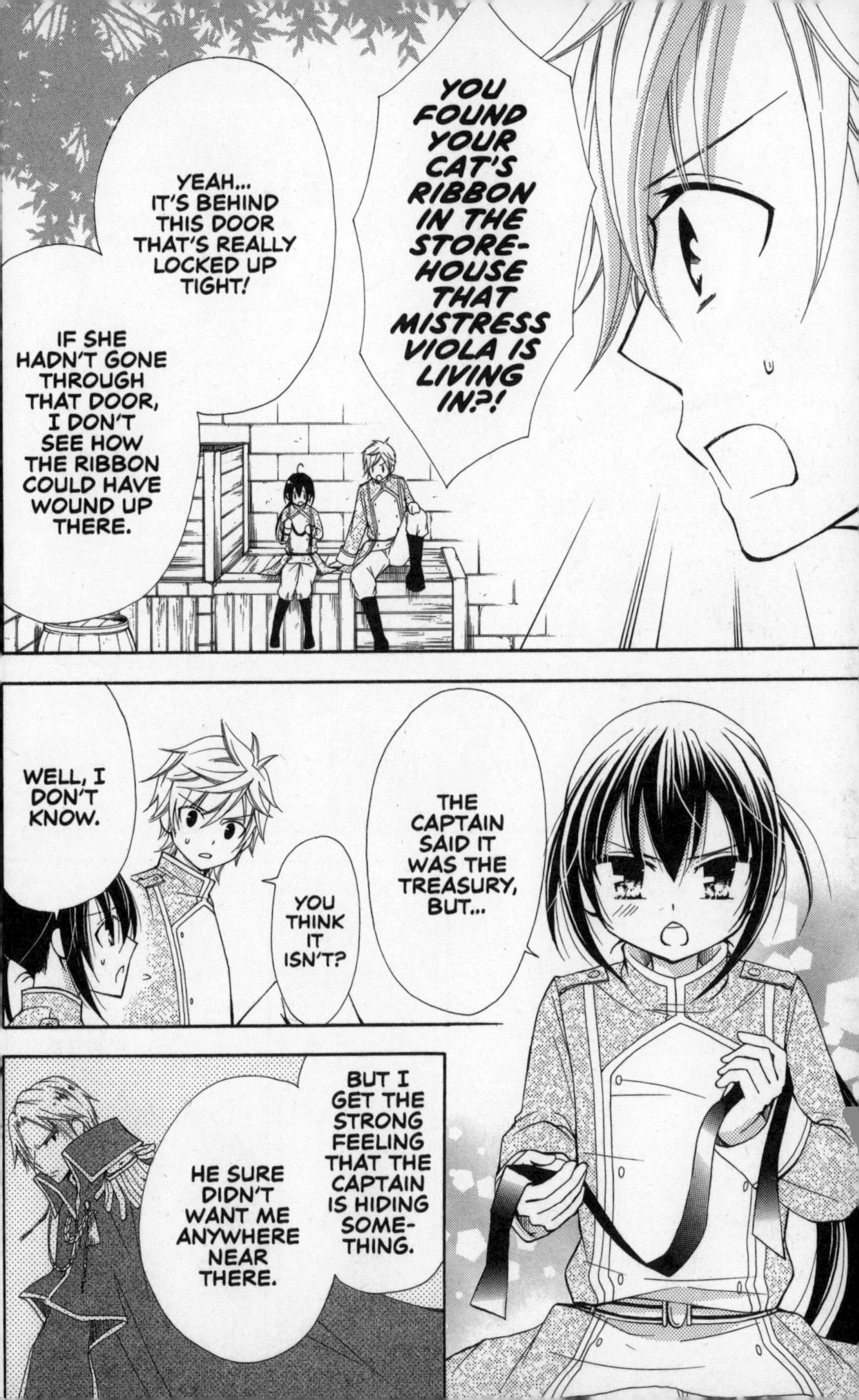
YOU FOUND YOUR CAT'S RIBBON IN THE STOREHOUSE THAT MISTRESS VIOLA IS LIVING IN?!
YEAH... IT'S BEHIND THIS DOOR THAT'S REALLY LOCKED UP TIGHT!
IF SHE HADN'T GONE THROUGH THAT DOOR, I DON'T SEE HOW THE RIBBON COULD HAVE WOUND UP THERE.
THE CAPTAIN SAID IT WAS THE TREASURY, BUT...
YOU THINK IT ISN'T?
WELL, I DON'T KNOW.
BUT I GET THE STRONG FEELING THAT THE CAPTAIN IS HIDING SOMETHING.
HE SURE DIDN'T WANT ME ANYWHERE NEAR THERE.

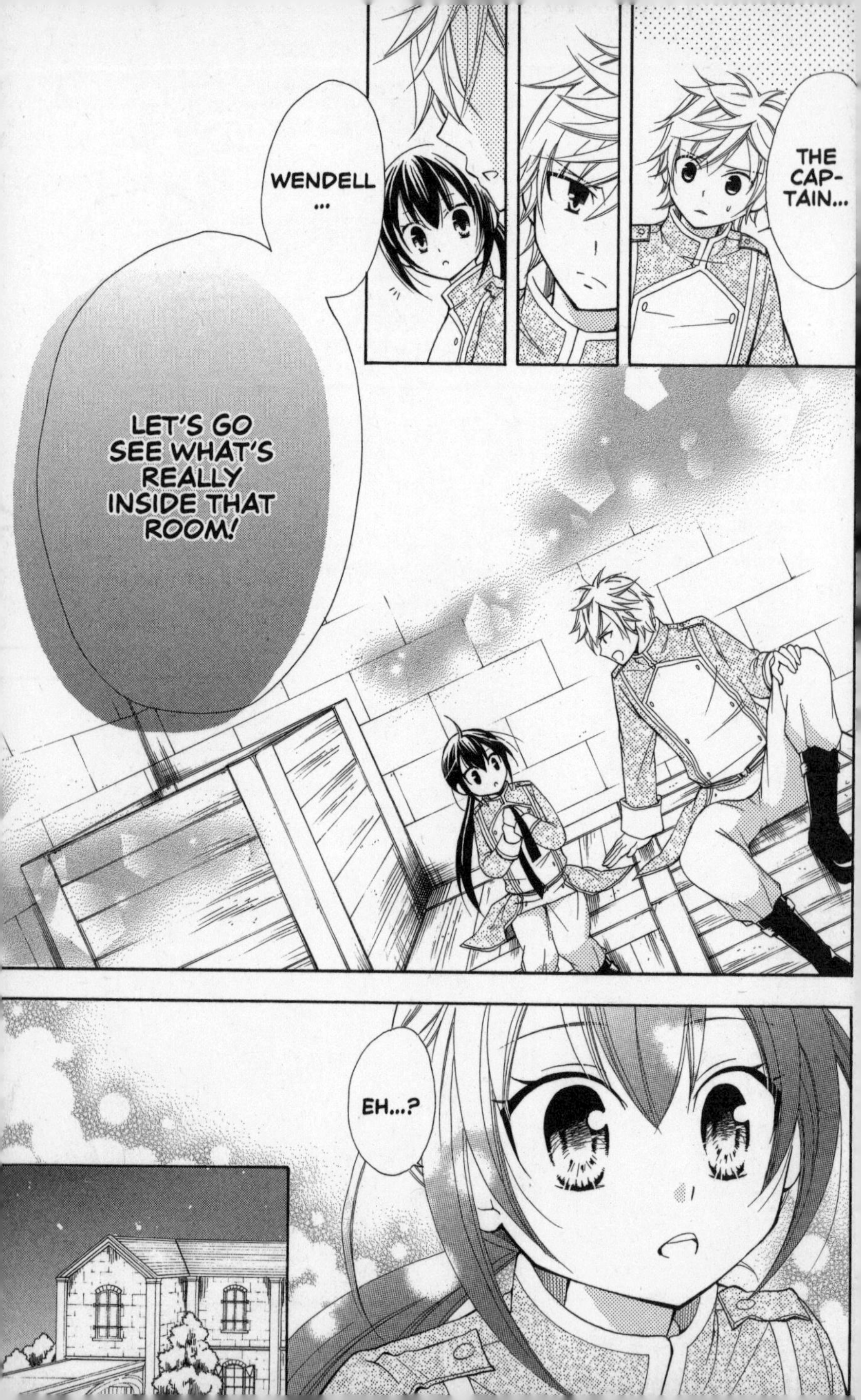
THE CAP-TAIN...
WENDELL ...
LET'S GO SEE WHAT'S REALLY INSIDE THAT ROOM!
EH...?

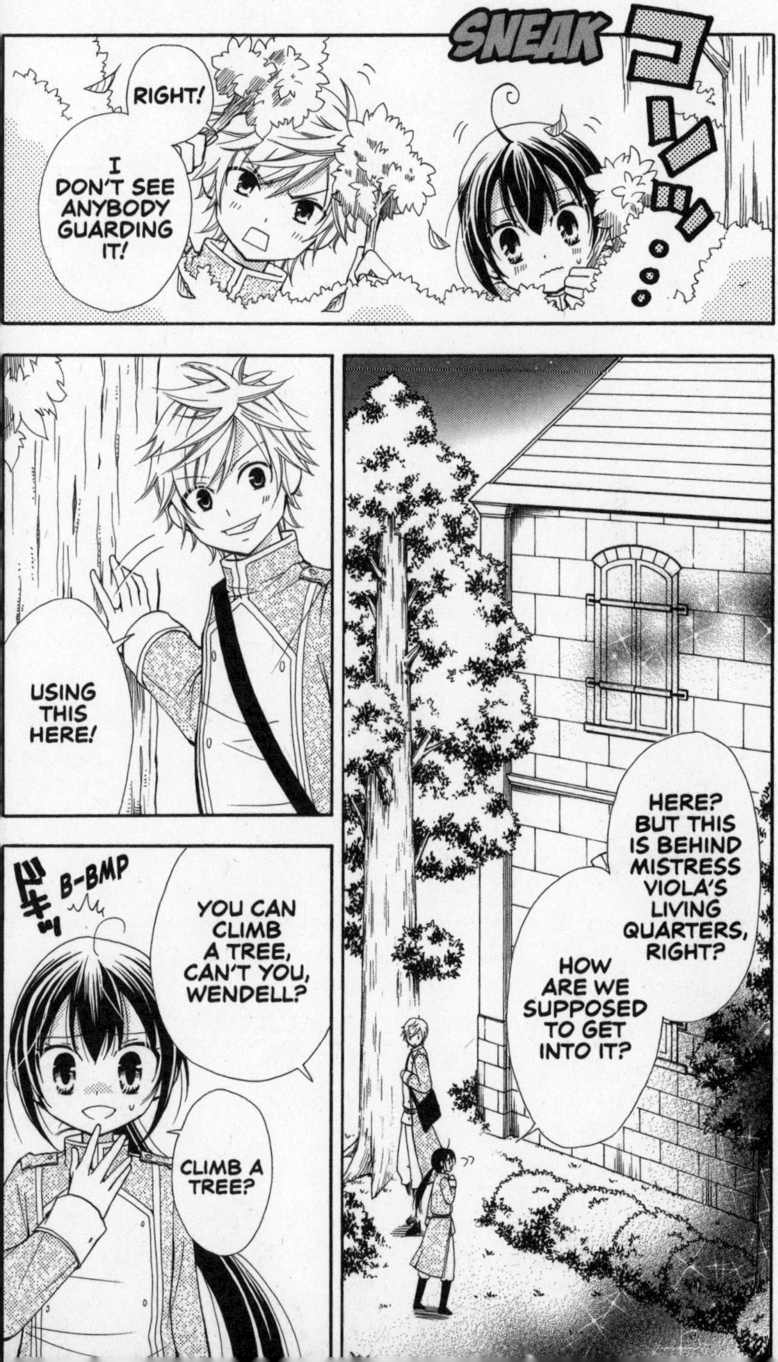
SNEAK
RIGHT!
I DON'T SEE ANYBODY GUARDING IT!
HERE? BUT THIS IS BEHIND MISTRESS VIOLA'S LIVING QUARTERS, RIGHT?
HOW ARE WE SUPPOSED TO GET INTO IT?
USING THIS HERE!
YOU CAN CLIMB A TREE, CAN'T YOU, WENDELL?
B-BMP
CLIMB A TREE?

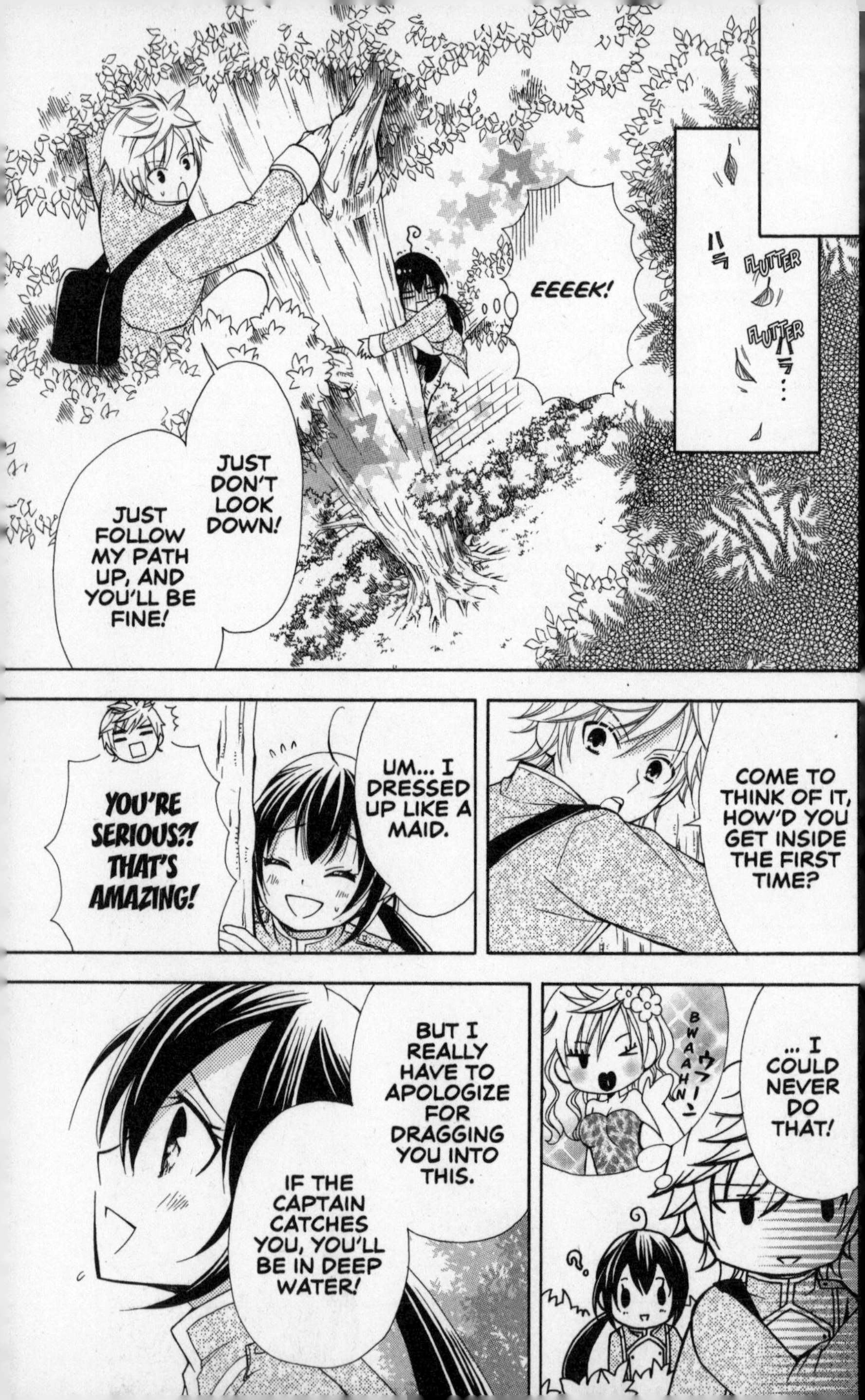
FLUTTER
FLUTTER
EEEEK!
JUST DON'T LOOK DOWN!
JUST FOLLOW MY PATH UP, AND YOU'LL BE FINE!
COME TO THINK OF IT, HOW'D YOU GET INSIDE THE FIRST TIME?
UM... I DRESSED UP LIKE A MAID.
YOU'RE SERIOUS?! THAT'S AMAZING!
... I COULD NEVER DO THAT!
BWAAHN
BUT I REALLY HAVE TO APOLOGIZE FOR DRAGGING YOU INTO THIS.
IF THE CAPTAIN CATCHES YOU, YOU'LL BE IN DEEP WATER!

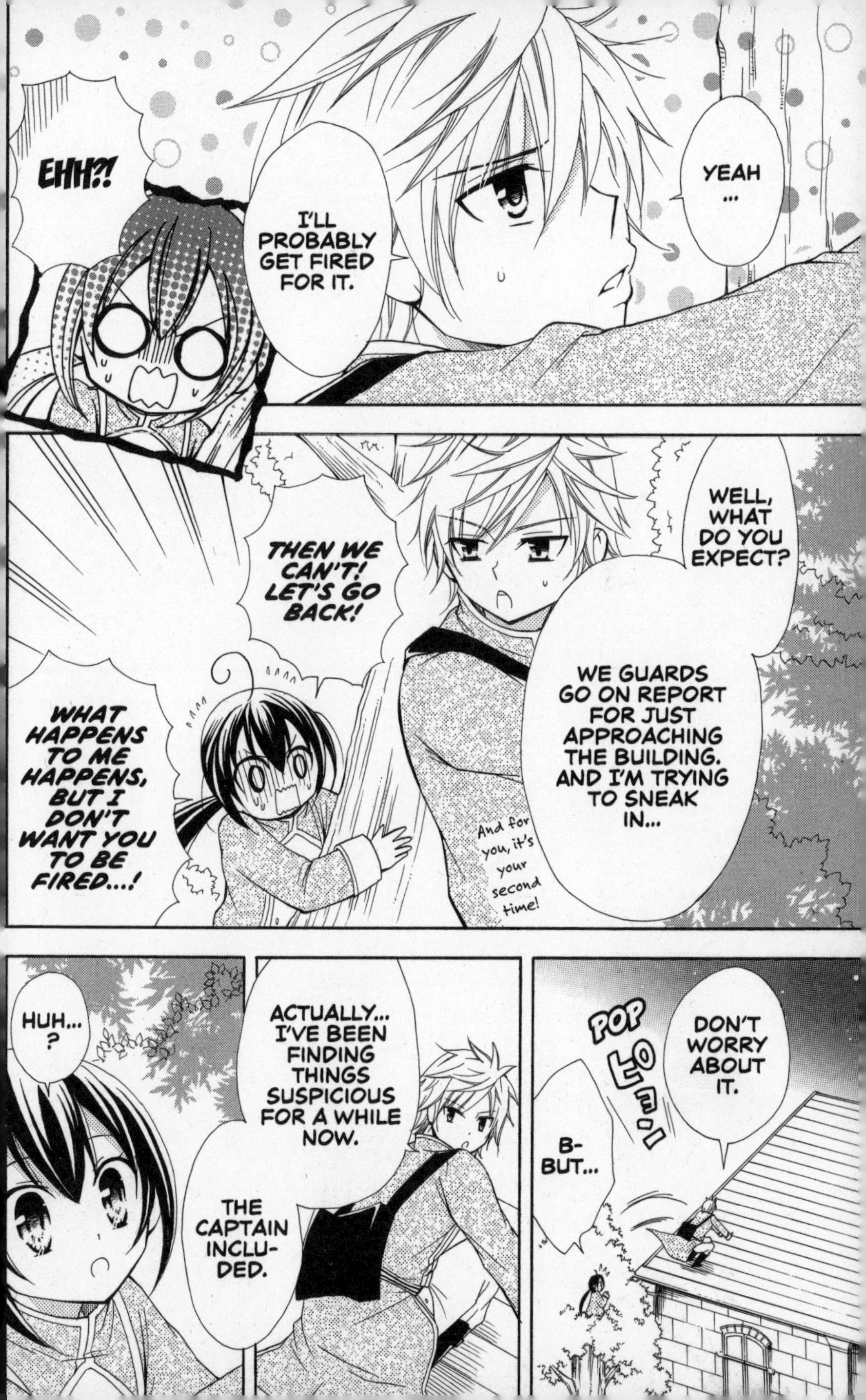
YEAH ...
I'LL PROBABLY GET FIRED FOR IT.
EHH?!
WELL, WHAT DO YOU EXPECT?
WE GUARDS GO ON REPORT FOR JUST APPROACHING THE BUILDING. AND I'M TRYING TO SNEAK IN...
And for you, it's your second time!
THEN WE CAN'T! LET'S GO BACK!
WHAT HAPPENS TO ME HAPPENS, BUT I DON'T WANT YOU TO BE FIRED...!
DON'T WORRY ABOUT IT.
POP
B-BUT...
ACTUALLY... I'VE BEEN FINDING THINGS SUSPICIOUS FOR A WHILE NOW.
THE CAPTAIN INCLUDED.
HUH... ?

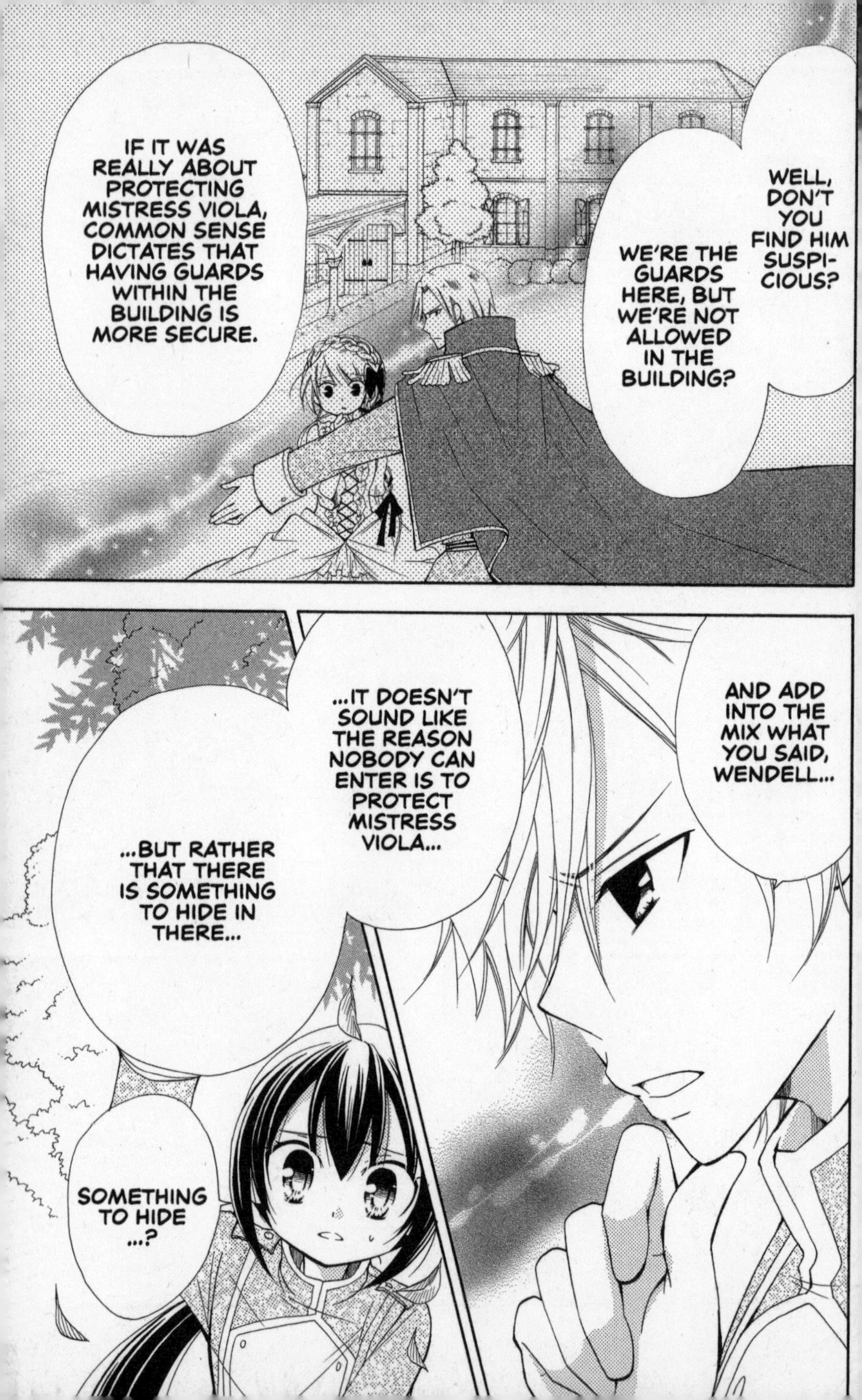
WELL, DON'T YOU FIND HIM SUSPICIOUS?
WE'RE THE GUARDS HERE, BUT WE'RE NOT ALLOWED IN THE BUILDING?
IF IT WAS REALLY ABOUT PROTECTING MISTRESS VIOLA, COMMON SENSE DICTATES THAT HAVING GUARDS WITHIN THE BUILDING IS MORE SECURE.
AND ADD INTO THE MIX WHAT YOU SAID, WENDELL...
...IT DOESN'T SOUND LIKE THE REASON NOBODY CAN ENTER IS TO PROTECT MISTRESS VIOLA...
...BUT RATHER THAT THERE IS SOMETHING TO HIDE IN THERE...
SOMETHING TO HIDE ...?

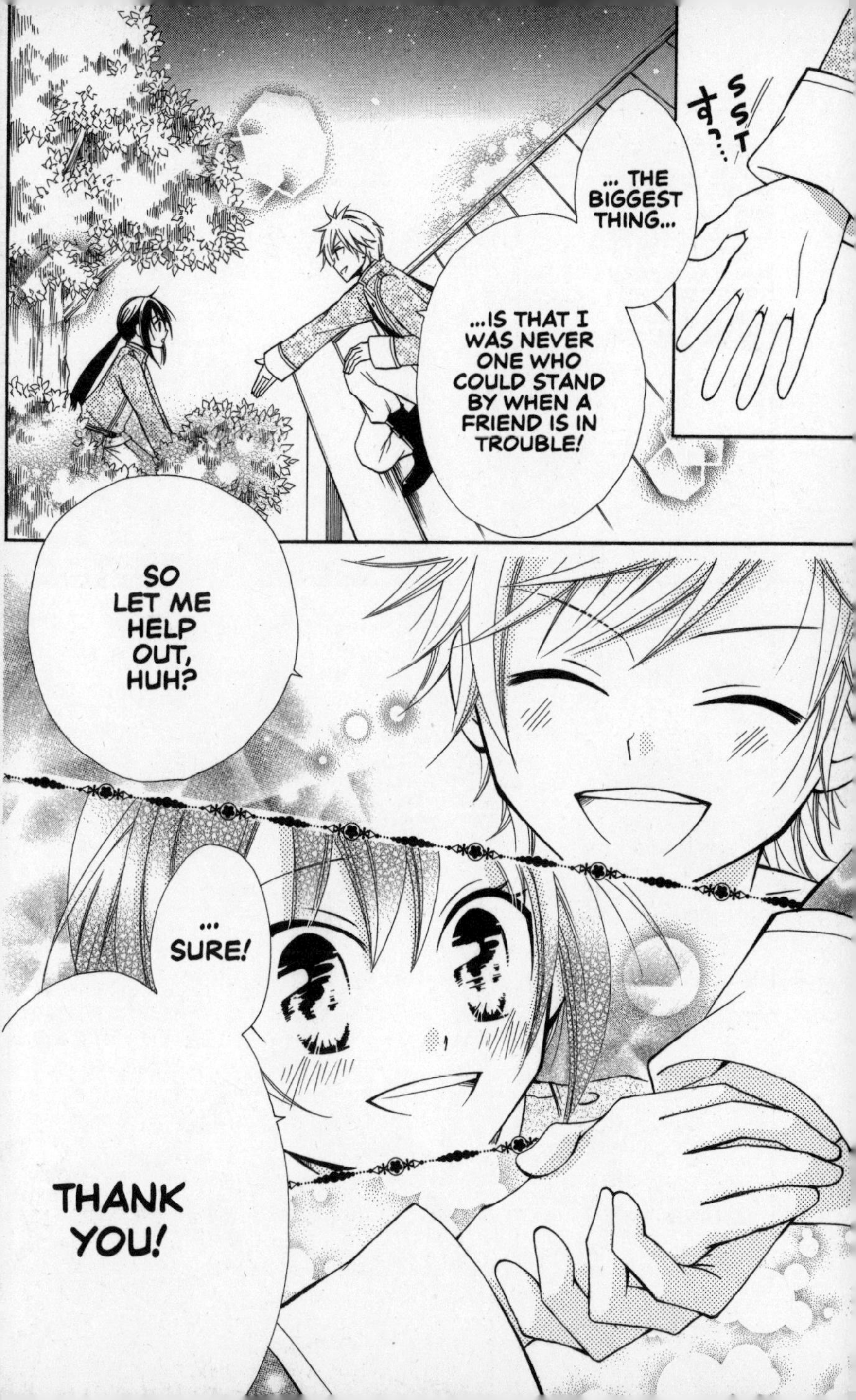
すっ…
SST
... THE BIGGEST THING...
...IS THAT I WAS NEVER ONE WHO COULD STAND BY WHEN A FRIEND IS IN TROUBLE!
SO LET ME HELP OUT, HUH?
... SURE!
THANK YOU!

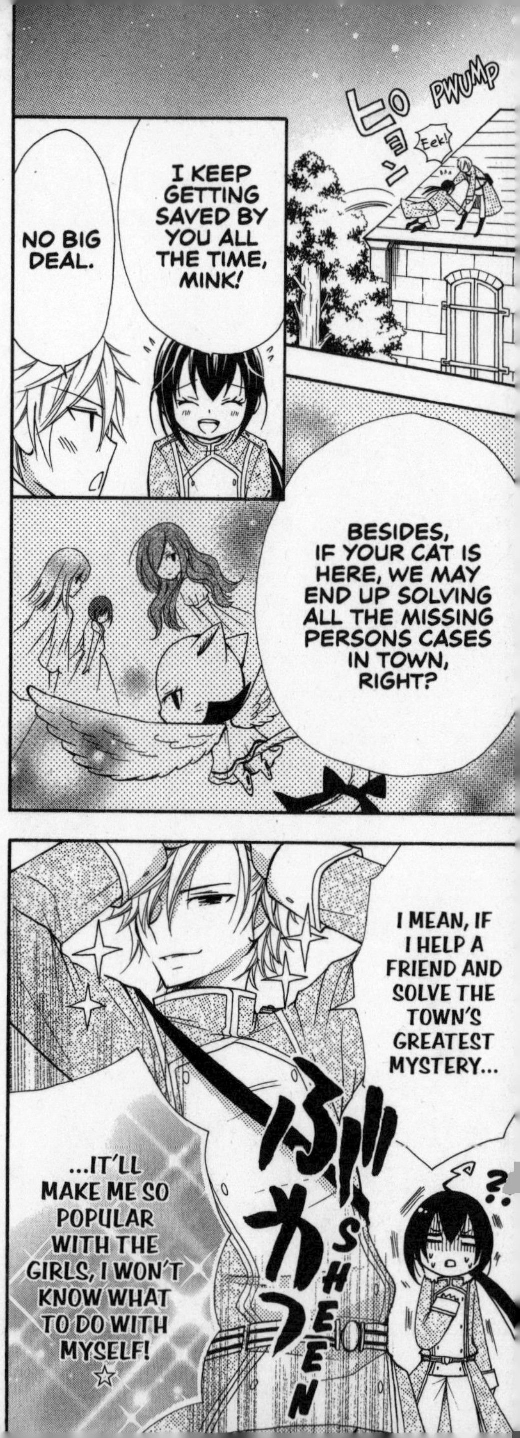
PWUMP
Eek!
I KEEP GETTING SAVED BY YOU ALL THE TIME, MINK!
NO BIG DEAL.
BESIDES, IF YOUR CAT IS HERE, WE MAY END UP SOLVING ALL THE MISSING PERSONS CASES IN TOWN, RIGHT?
I MEAN, IF I HELP A FRIEND AND SOLVE THE TOWN'S GREATEST MYSTERY...
...IT'LL MAKE ME SO POPULAR WITH THE GIRLS, I WON'T KNOW WHAT TO DO WITH MYSELF! ☆
SHEEN

BONUS MANGA 3

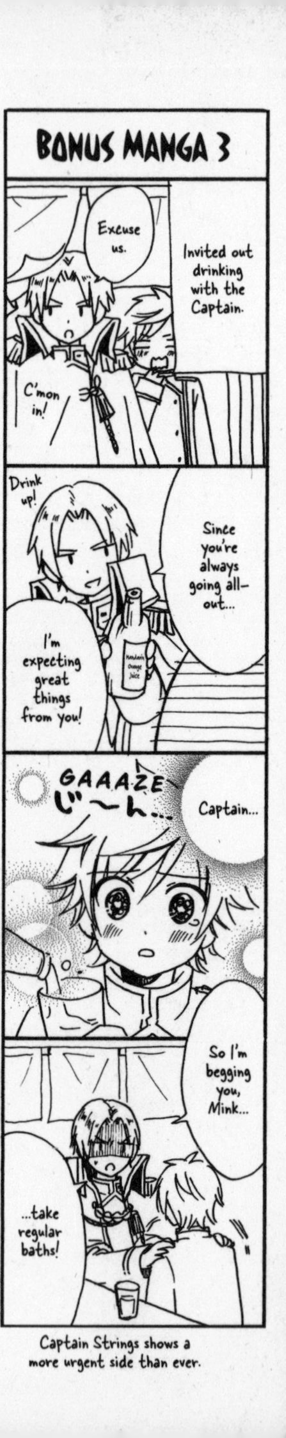
Invited out drinking with the Captain.
Excuse us.
C'mon in!
Drink up!
Since you're always going all-out...
I'm expecting great things from you!
Captain...
GAAAZE
じ〜ん...
So I'm begging you, Mink...
...take regular baths!

Captain Strings shows a more urgent side than ever.

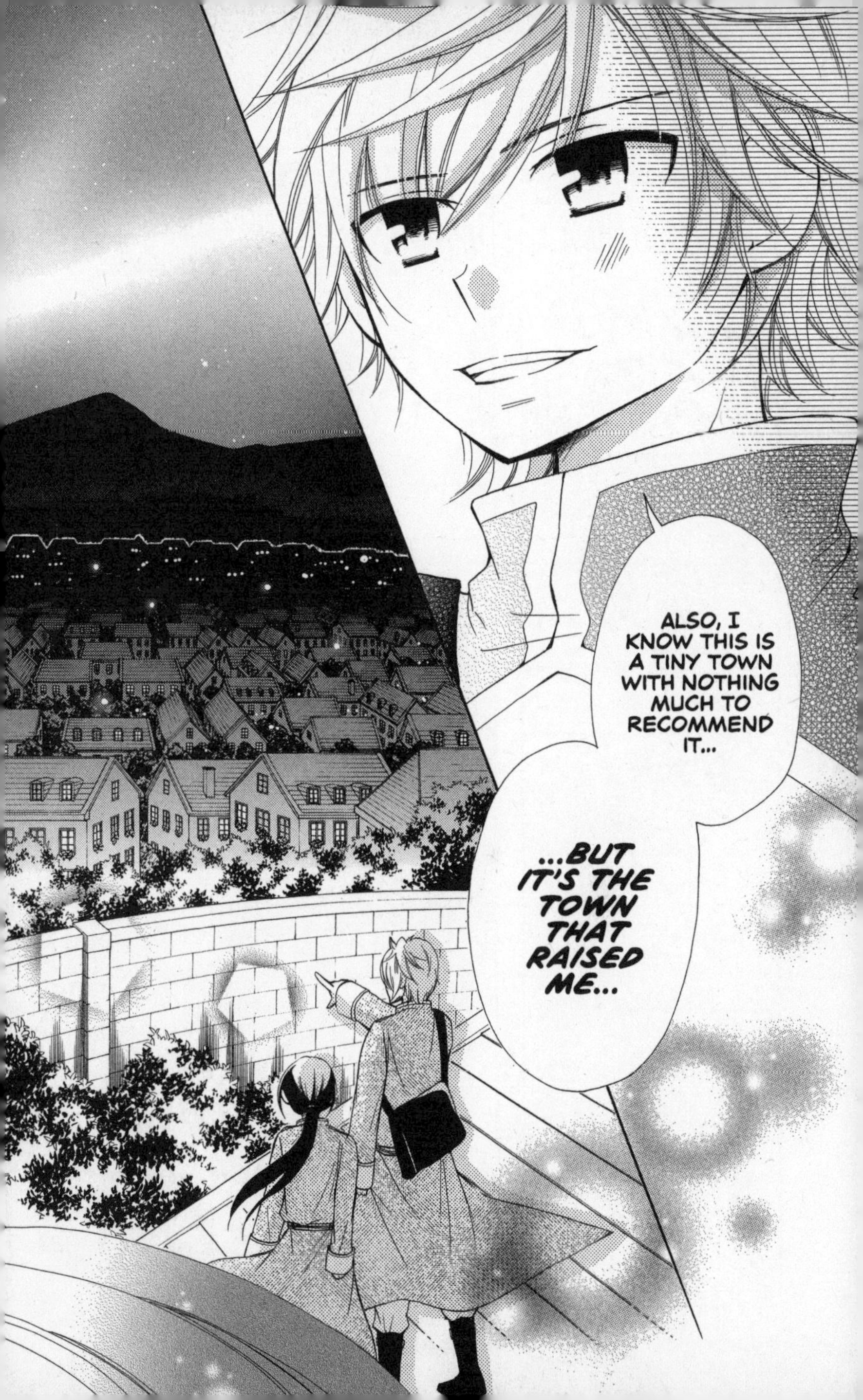
ALSO, I KNOW THIS IS A TINY TOWN WITH NOTHING MUCH TO RECOMMEND IT...
...BUT IT'S THE TOWN THAT RAISED ME...

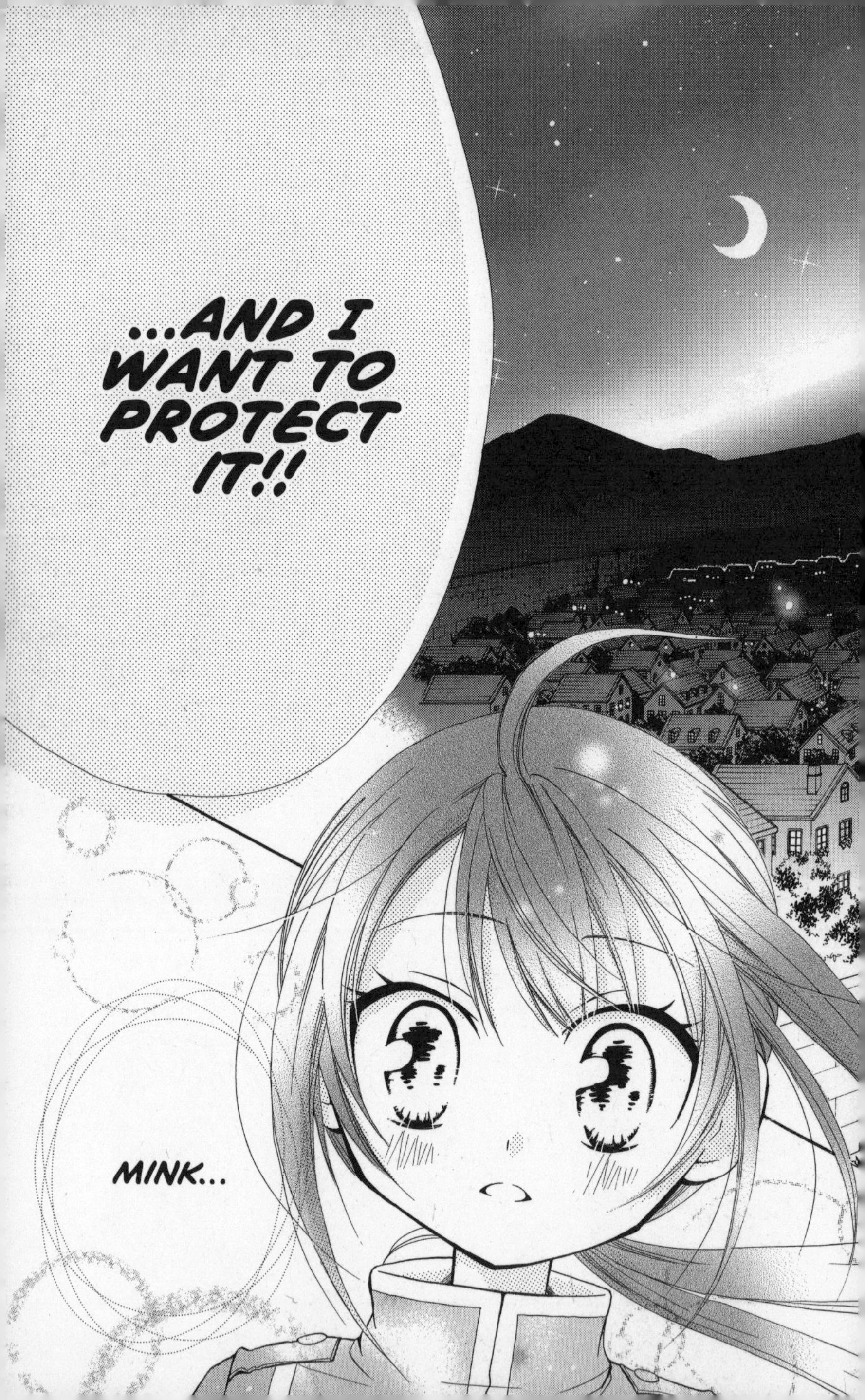
...AND I WANT TO PROTECT IT!!
MINK...

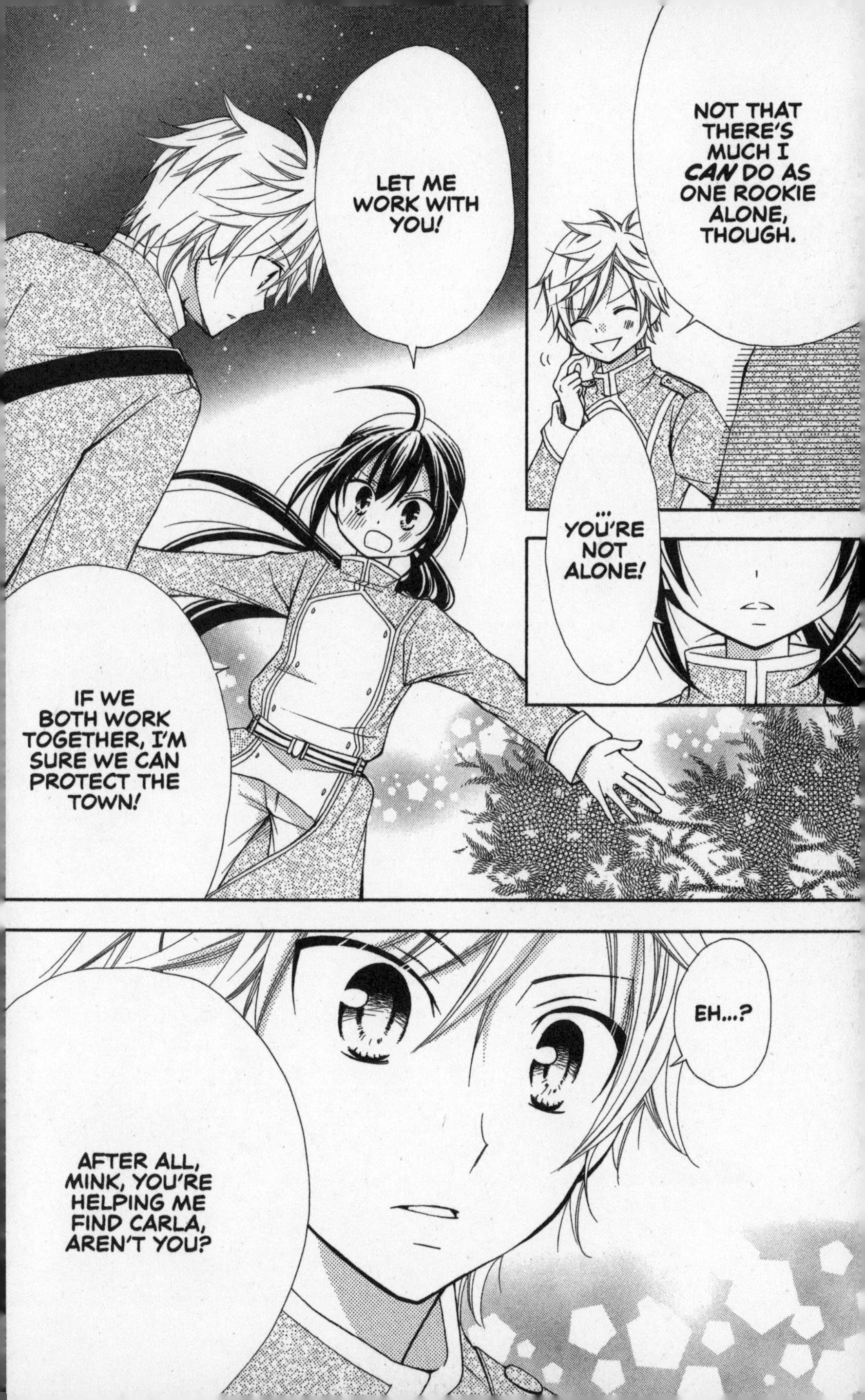
NOT THAT THERE'S MUCH I CAN DO AS ONE ROOKIE ALONE, THOUGH.
...YOU'RE NOT ALONE!
LET ME WORK WITH YOU!
IF WE BOTH WORK TOGETHER, I'M SURE WE CAN PROTECT THE TOWN!
EH...?
AFTER ALL, MINK, YOU'RE HELPING ME FIND CARLA, AREN'T YOU?

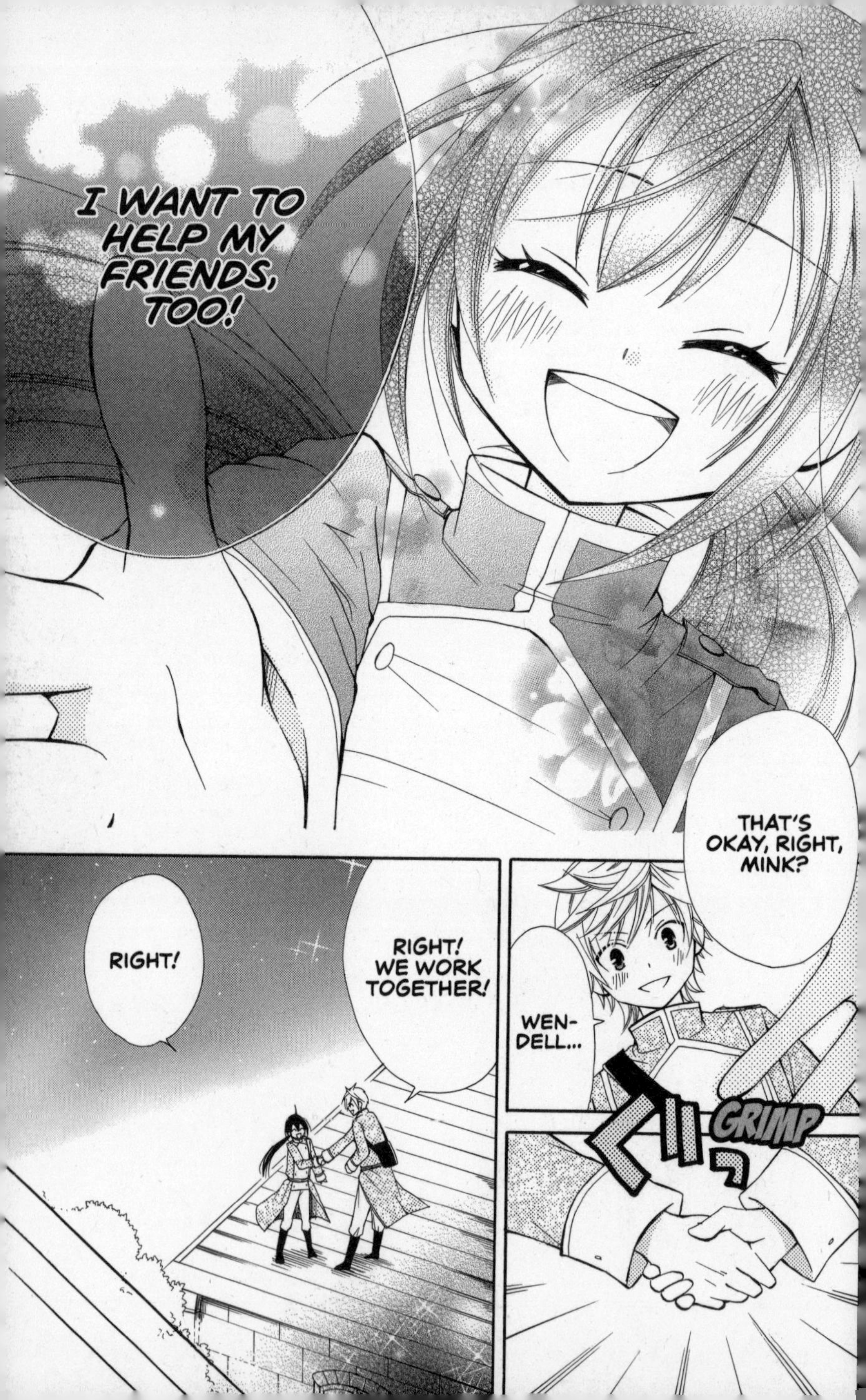
I WANT TO HELP MY FRIENDS, TOO!
THAT'S OKAY, RIGHT, MINK?
WEN-DELL...
GRIMP
RIGHT! WE WORK TOGETHER!
RIGHT!

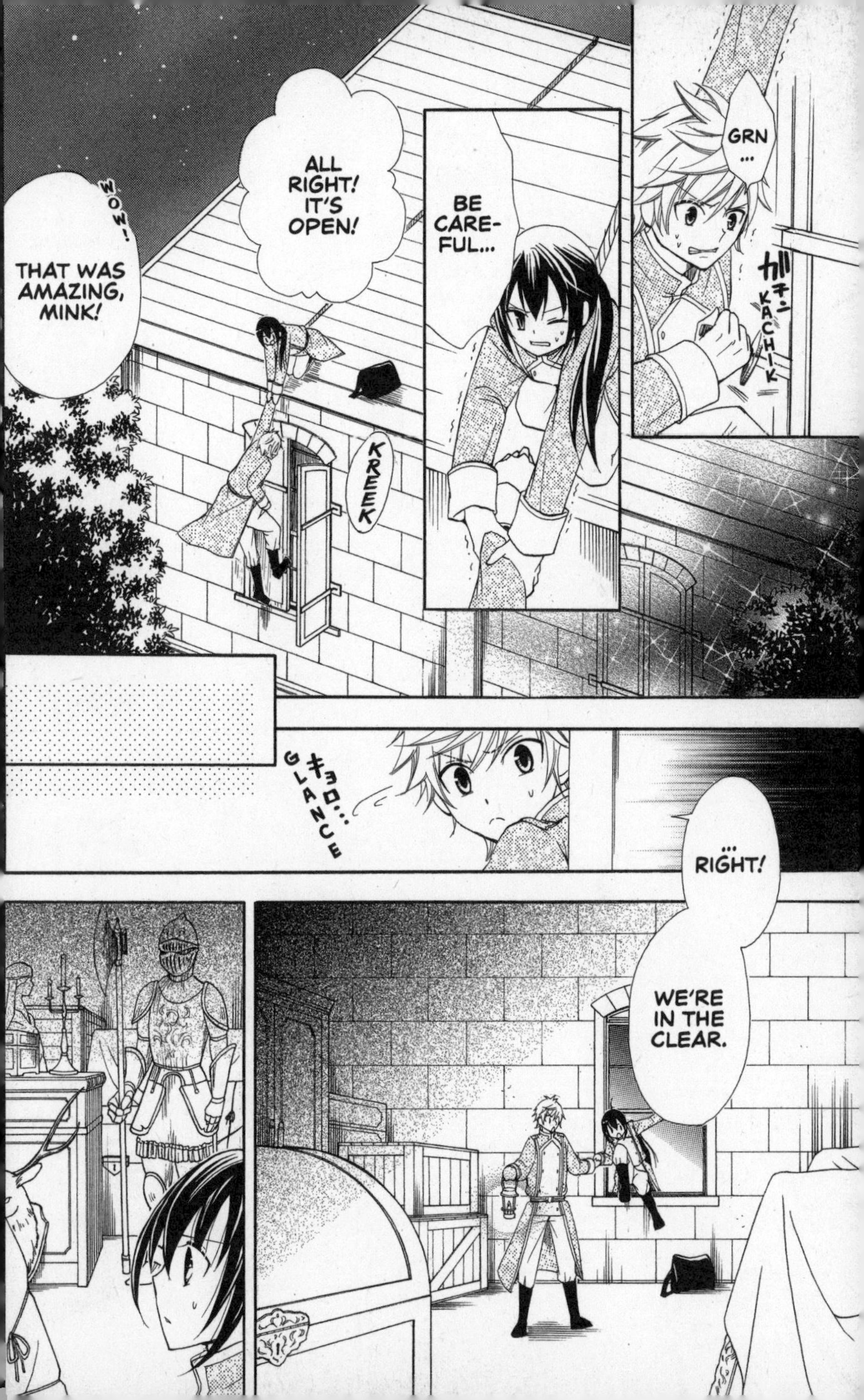
GRN...
カチン KACHIK
BE CAREFUL...
ALL RIGHT! IT'S OPEN!
WOW! THAT WAS AMAZING, MINK!
KREEK
...RIGHT!
キョロ... GLANCE
WE'RE IN THE CLEAR.

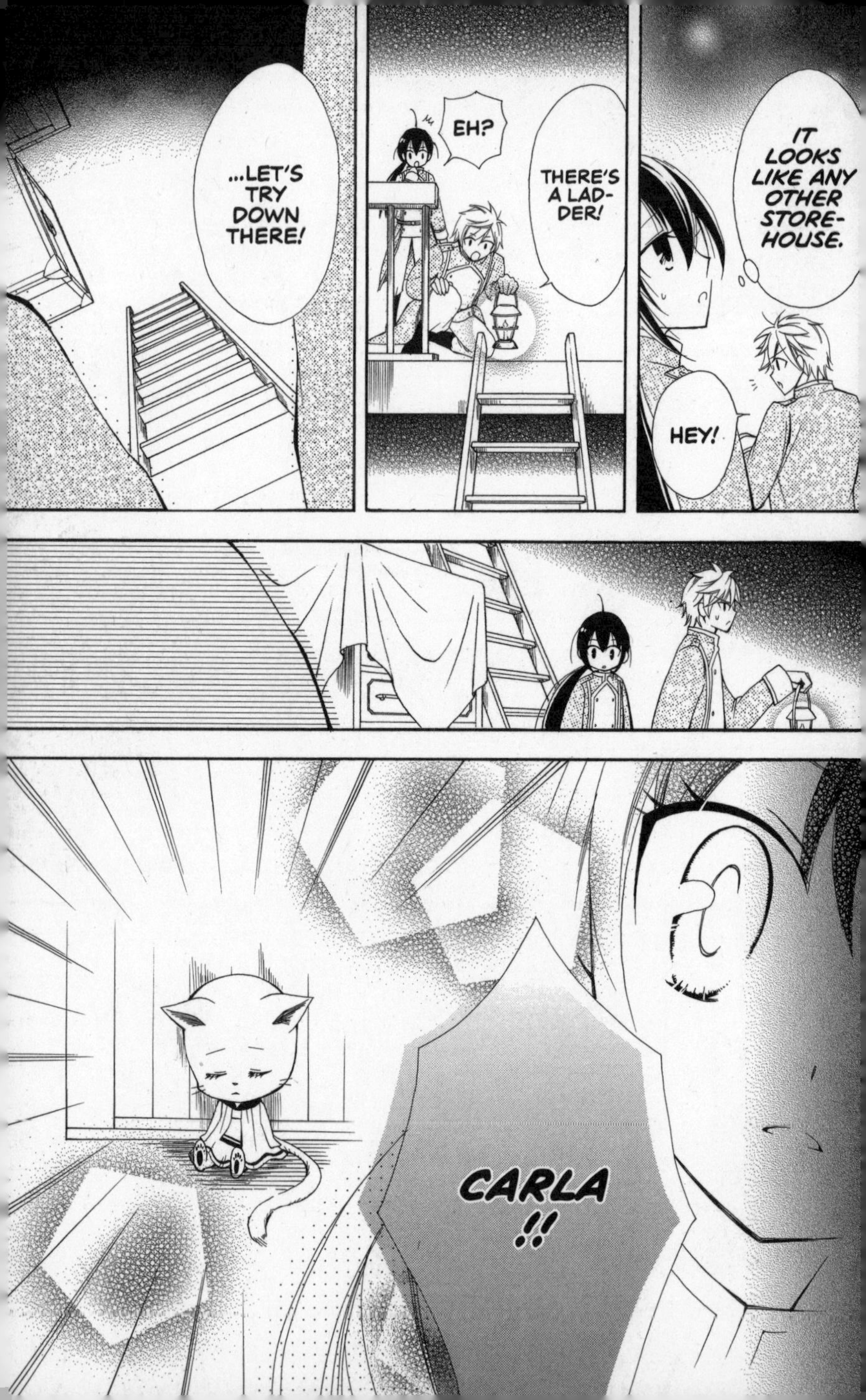
IT LOOKS LIKE ANY OTHER STORE-HOUSE.
HEY!
THERE'S A LAD-DER!
EH?
...LET'S TRY DOWN THERE!
CARLA !!

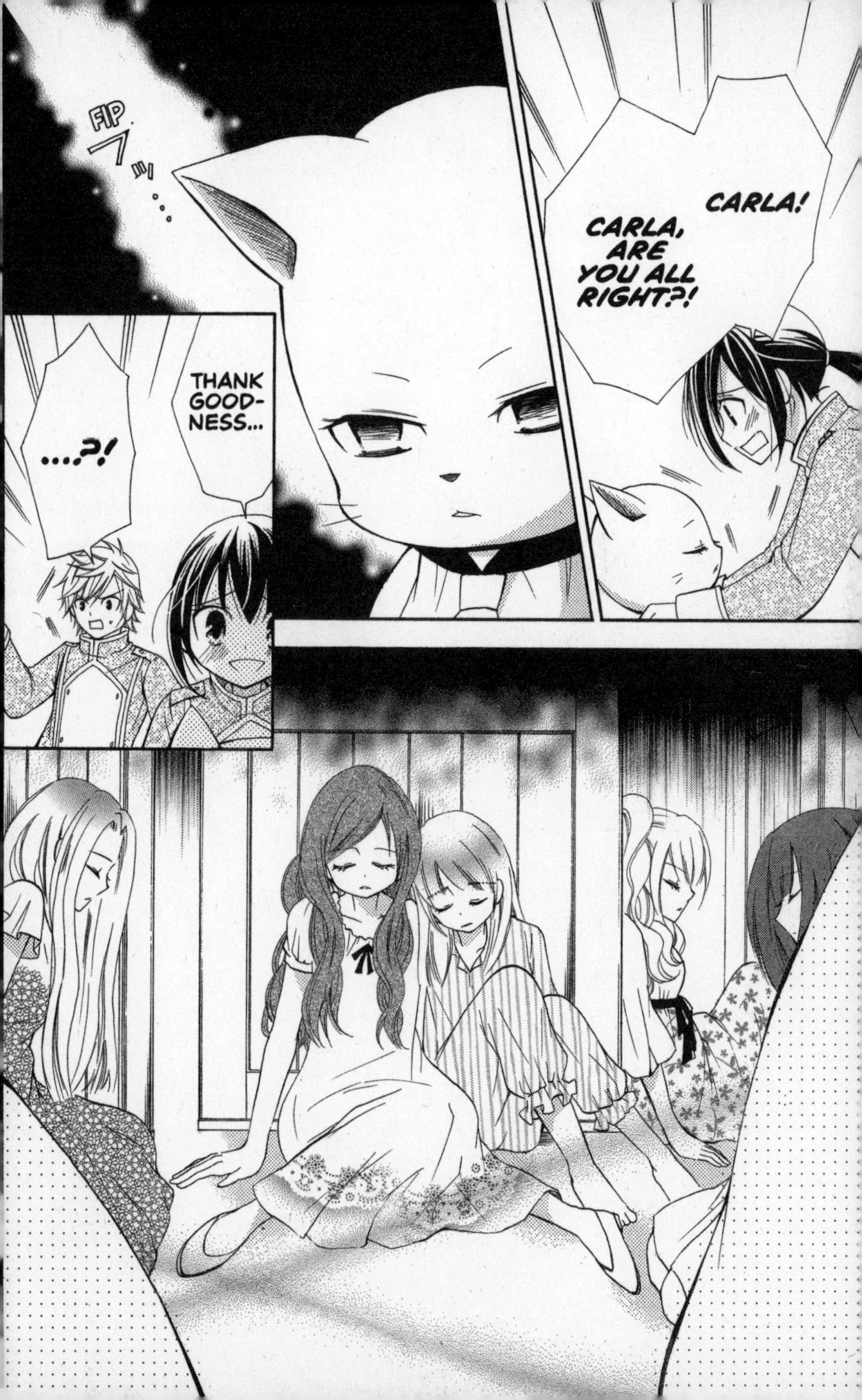
CARLA!
CARLA, ARE YOU ALL RIGHT?!
FIP
THANK GOOD-NESS...
...?!

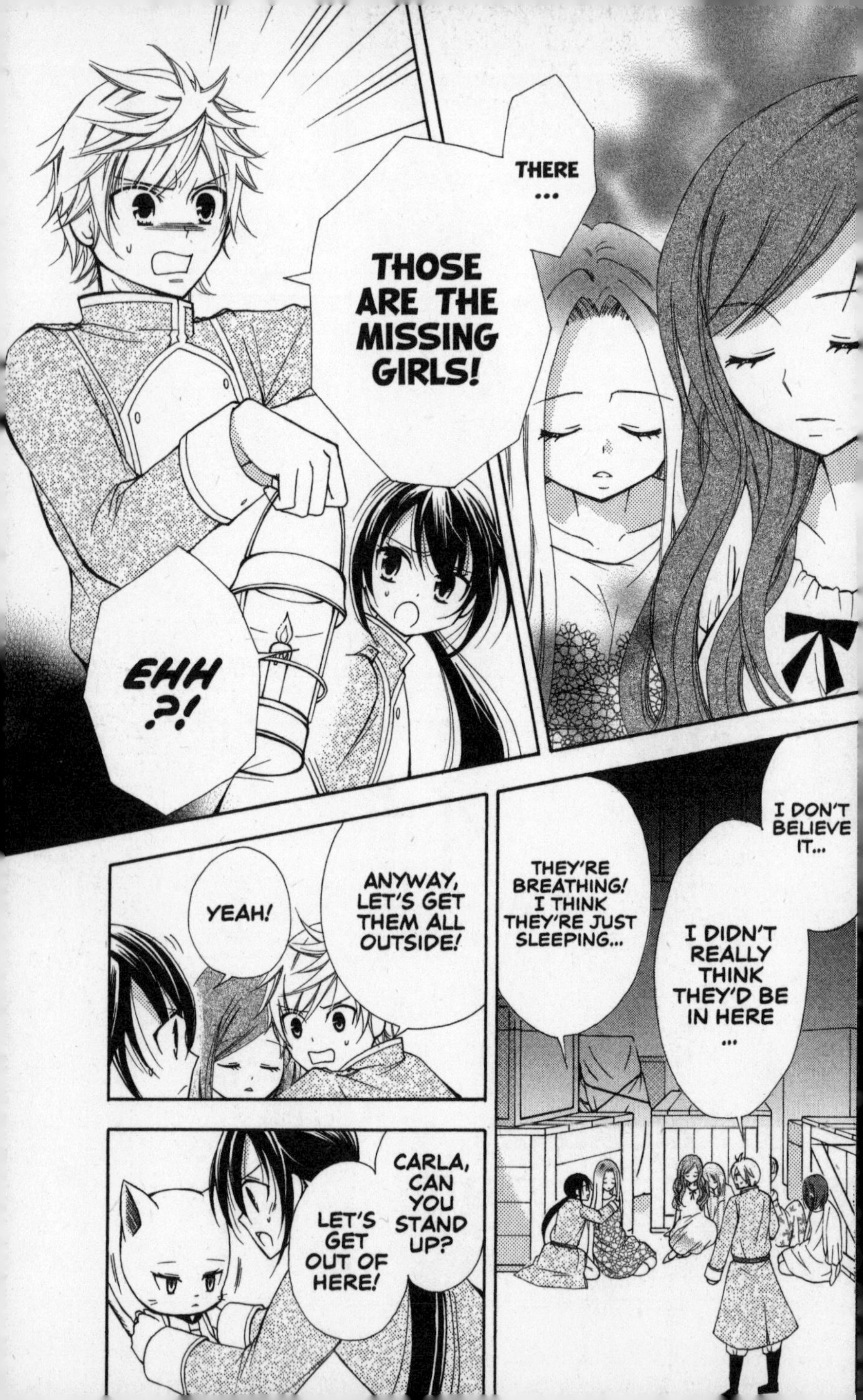
THERE ...
THOSE ARE THE MISSING GIRLS!
EHH ?!
I DON'T BELIEVE IT...
I DIDN'T REALLY THINK THEY'D BE IN HERE ...
THEY'RE BREATHING! I THINK THEY'RE JUST SLEEPING...
ANYWAY, LET'S GET THEM ALL OUTSIDE!
YEAH!
CARLA, CAN YOU STAND UP?
LET'S GET OUT OF HERE!

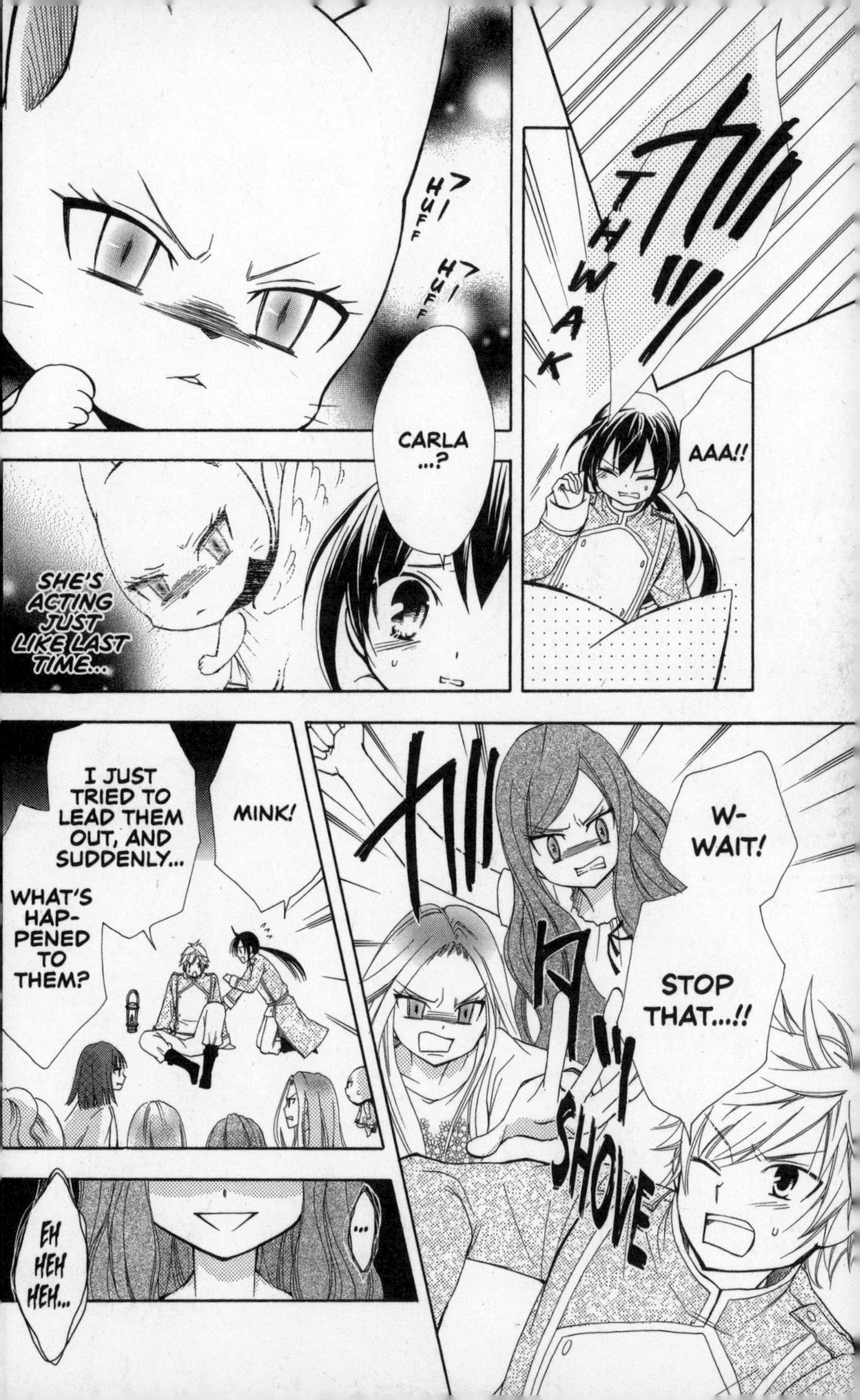
THWAK
AAA!!
HUFF HUFF
CARLA ...?
SHE'S ACTING JUST LIKE LAST TIME...
W-WAIT!
STOP THAT...!!
SHOVE
MINK!
I JUST TRIED TO LEAD THEM OUT, AND SUDDENLY...
WHAT'S HAP-PENED TO THEM?
...
EH HEH HEH...

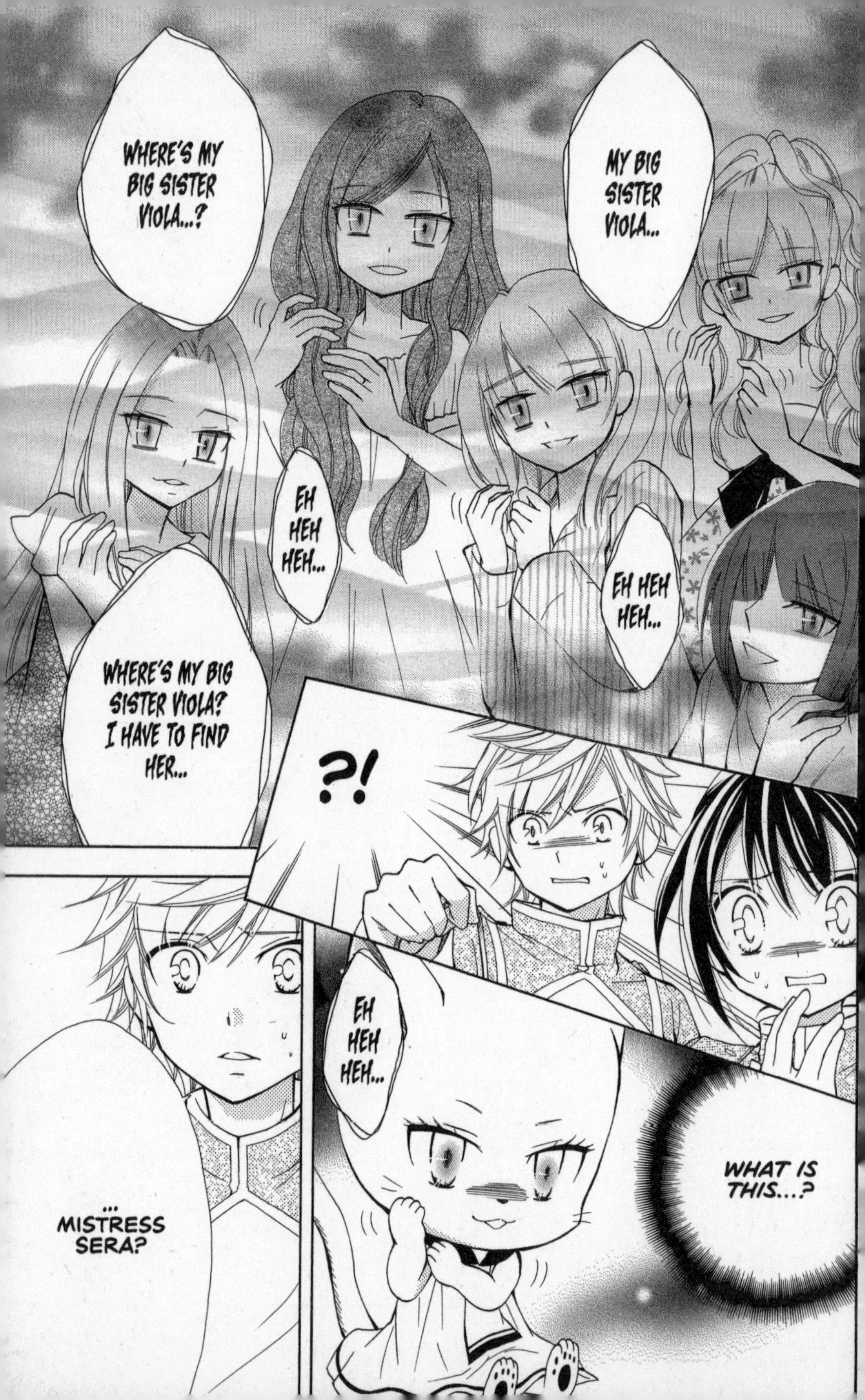
MY BIG SISTER VIOLA...
WHERE'S MY BIG SISTER VIOLA...?
EH HEH HEH...
EH HEH HEH...
WHERE'S MY BIG SISTER VIOLA? I HAVE TO FIND HER...
?!
EH HEH HEH...
WHAT IS THIS...?
...MISTRESS SERA?

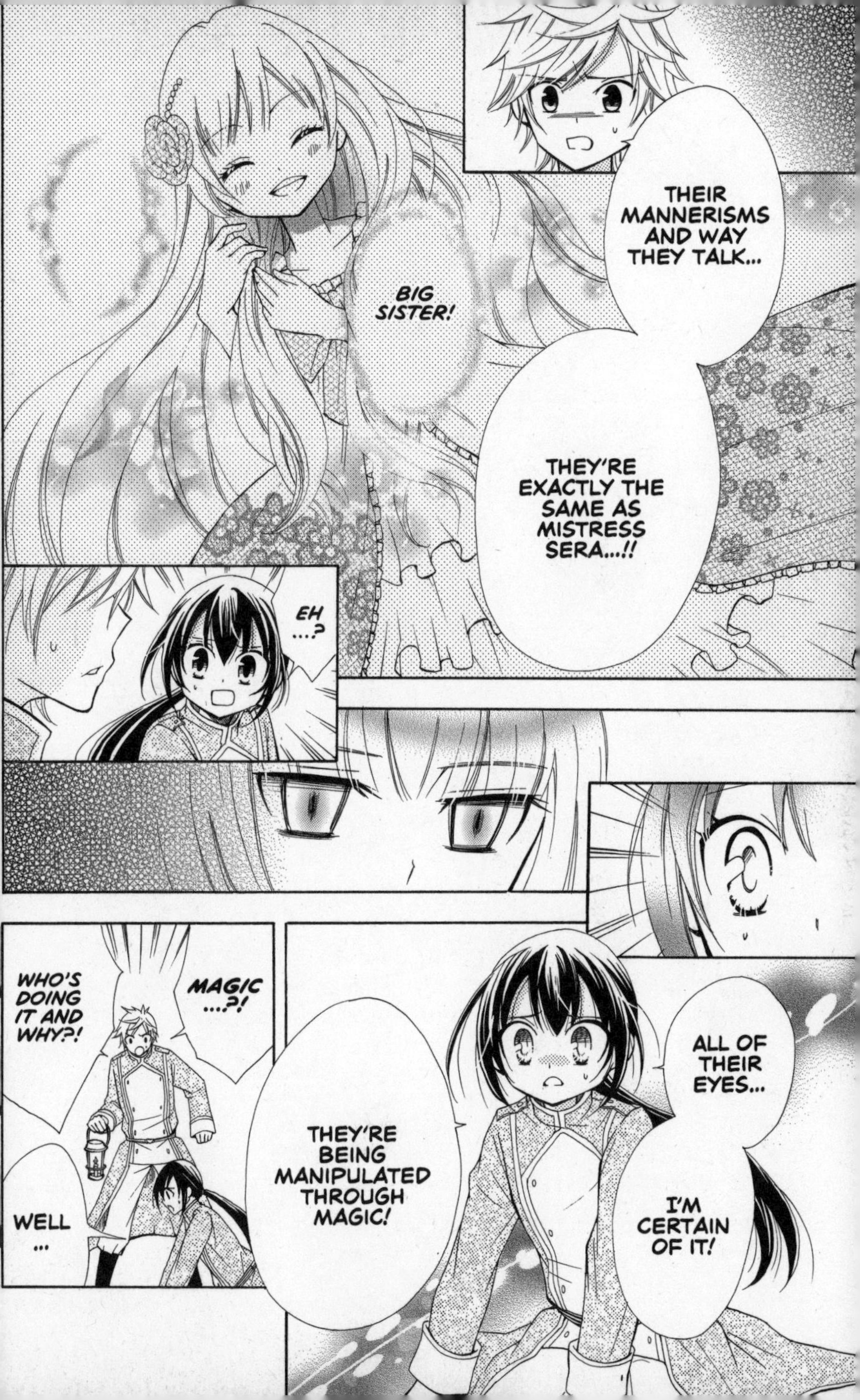

THEIR MANNERISMS AND WAY THEY TALK...
BIG SISTER!
THEY'RE EXACTLY THE SAME AS MISTRESS SERA...!!
EH ...?
ALL OF THEIR EYES...
I'M CERTAIN OF IT!
THEY'RE BEING MANIPULATED THROUGH MAGIC!
MAGIC ...?!
WHO'S DOING IT AND WHY?!
WELL ...

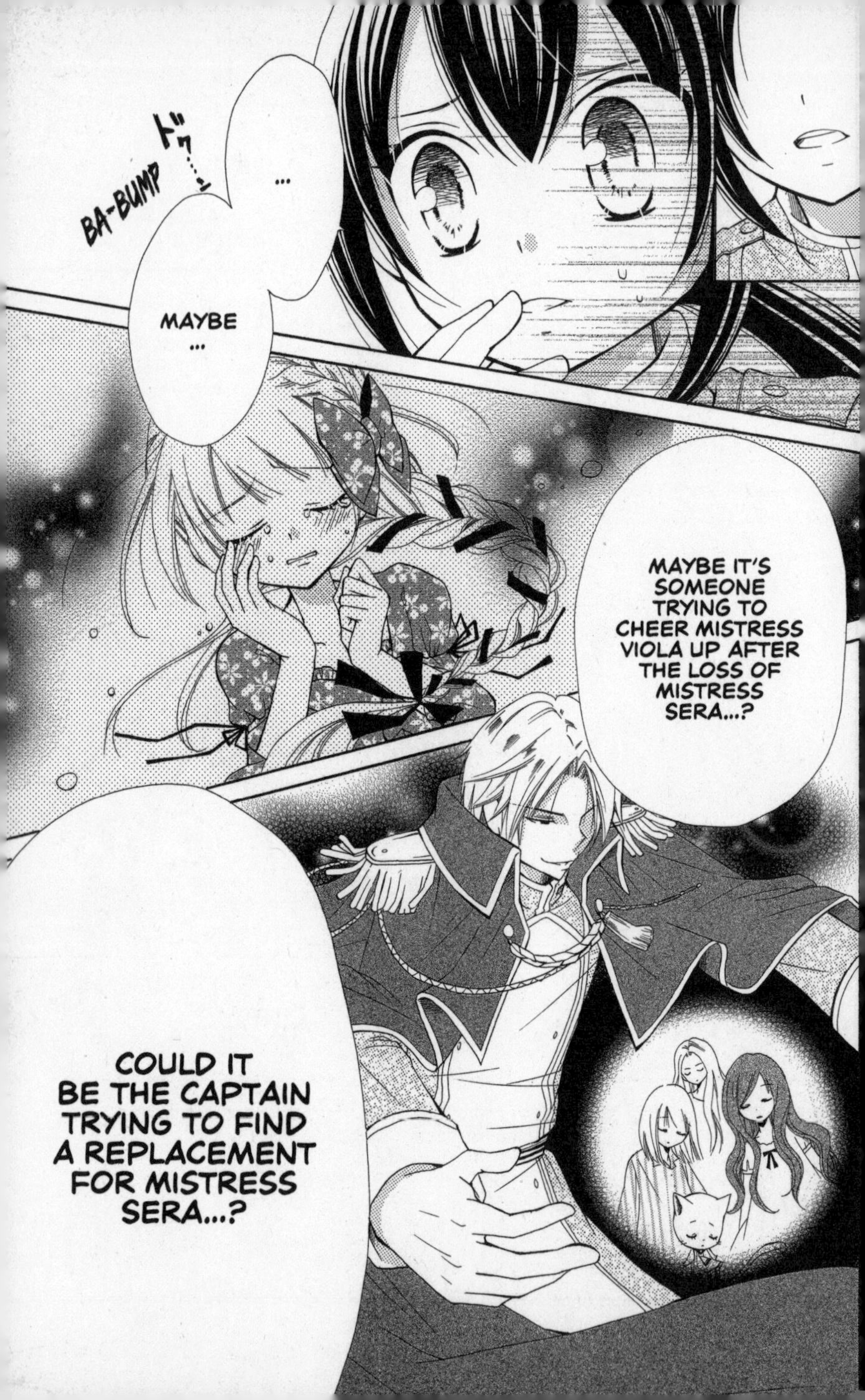
...
BA-BUMP
MAYBE ...
MAYBE IT'S SOMEONE TRYING TO CHEER MISTRESS VIOLA UP AFTER THE LOSS OF MISTRESS SERA...?
COULD IT BE THE CAPTAIN TRYING TO FIND A REPLACEMENT FOR MISTRESS SERA...?

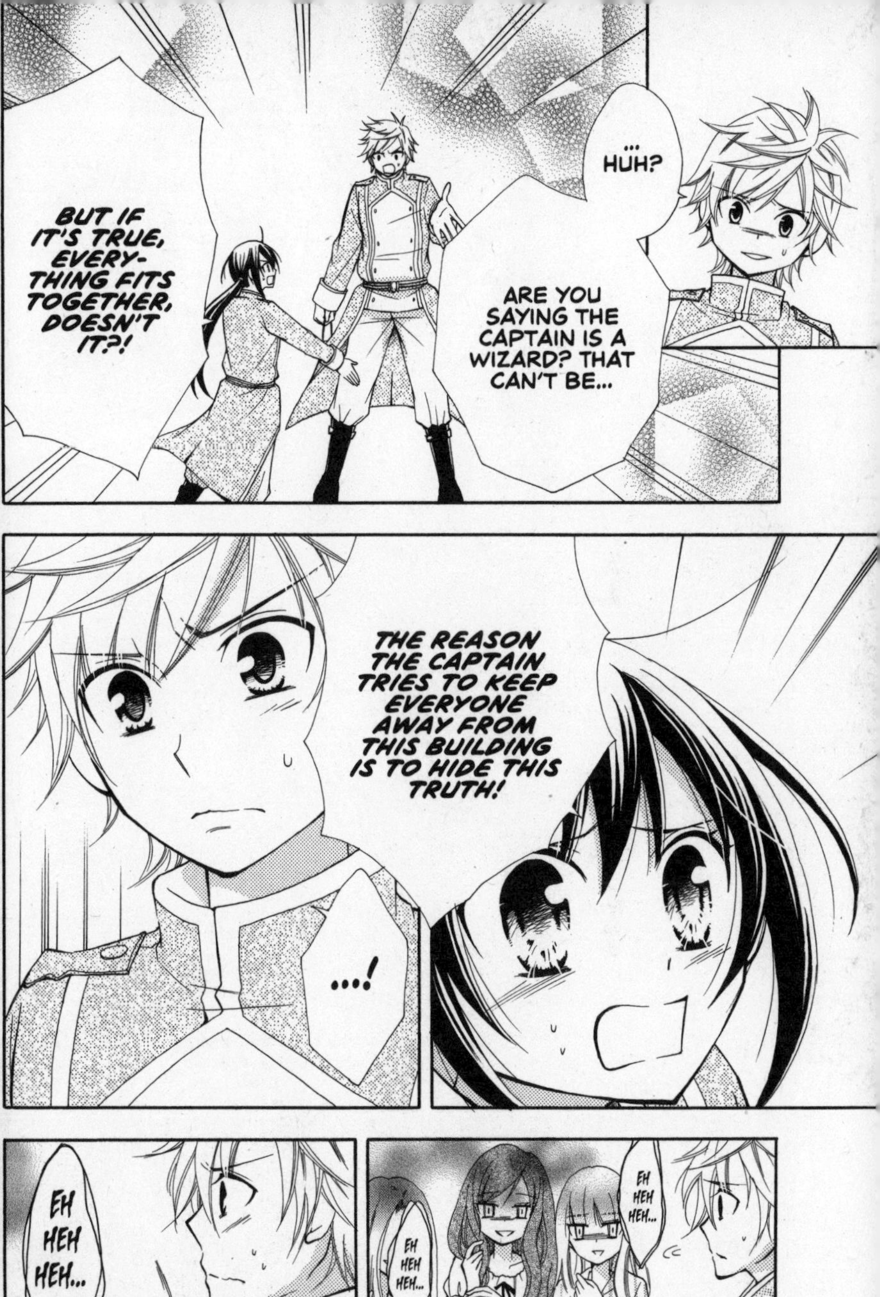
...HUH?
ARE YOU SAYING THE CAPTAIN IS A WIZARD? THAT CAN'T BE...
BUT IF IT'S TRUE, EVERY-THING FITS TOGETHER, DOESN'T IT?!
THE REASON THE CAPTAIN TRIES TO KEEP EVERYONE AWAY FROM THIS BUILDING IS TO HIDE THIS TRUTH!
...!
EH HEH HEH...
EH HEH HEH...
EH HEH HEH...

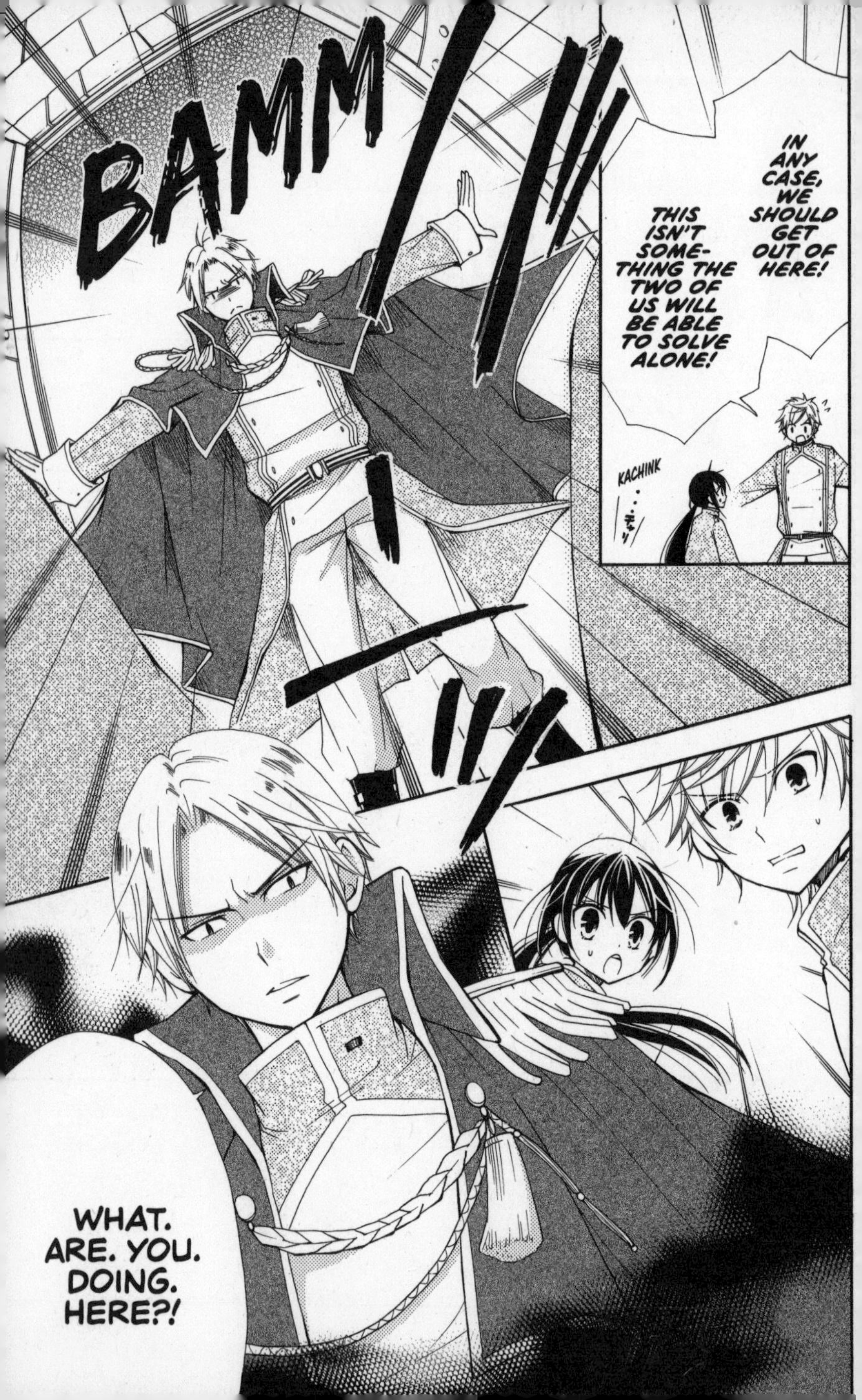
IN ANY CASE, WE SHOULD GET OUT OF HERE!
THIS ISN'T SOME-THING THE TWO OF US WILL BE ABLE TO SOLVE ALONE!
KACHINK
BAMM
WHAT. ARE. YOU. DOING. HERE?!

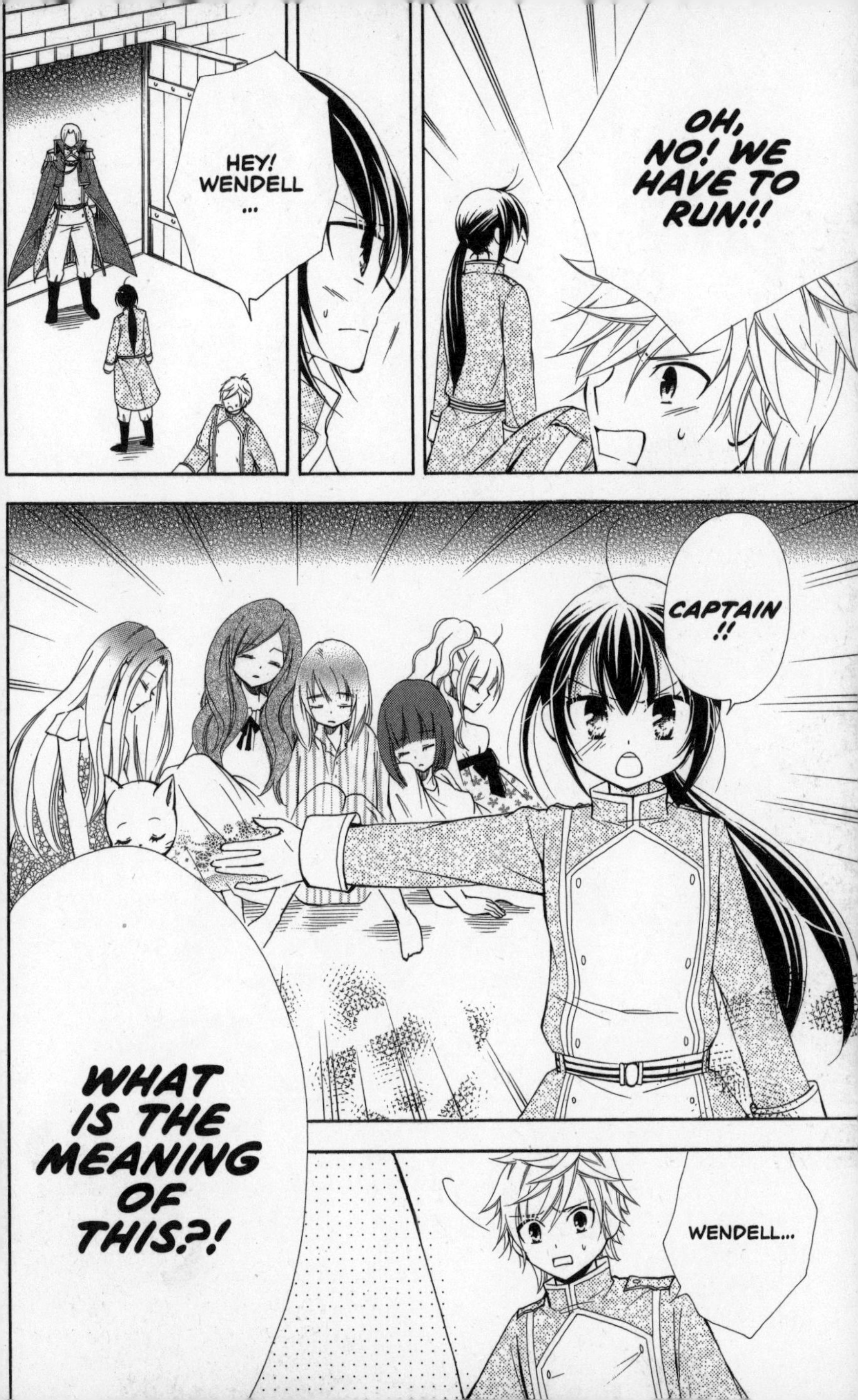
OH, NO! WE HAVE TO RUN!!
HEY! WENDELL ...
CAPTAIN !!
WHAT IS THE MEANING OF THIS?!
WENDELL...

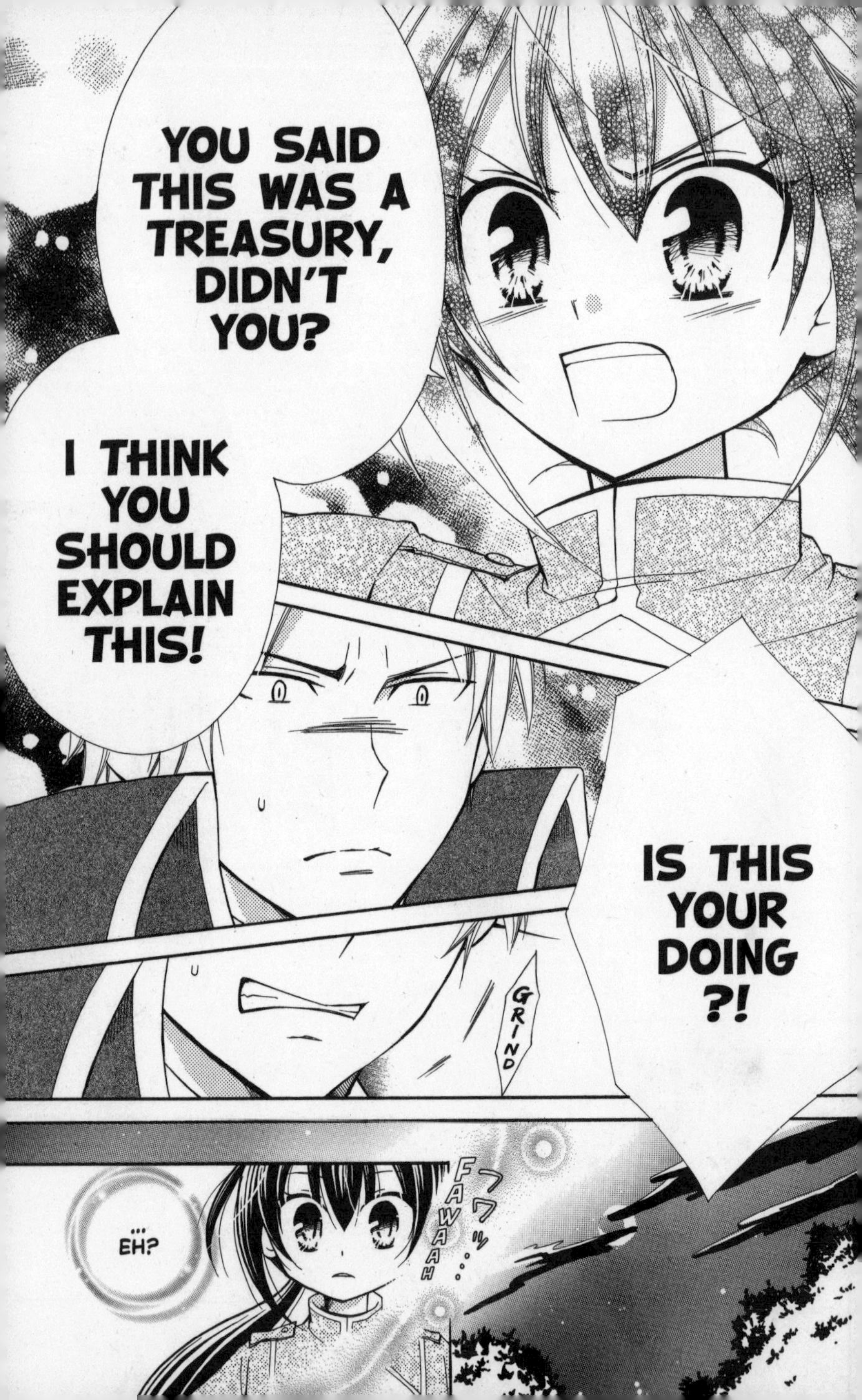
YOU SAID THIS WAS A TREASURY, DIDN'T YOU?
I THINK YOU SHOULD EXPLAIN THIS!
IS THIS YOUR DOING ?!
GRIND
FAWAAAH...
... EH?

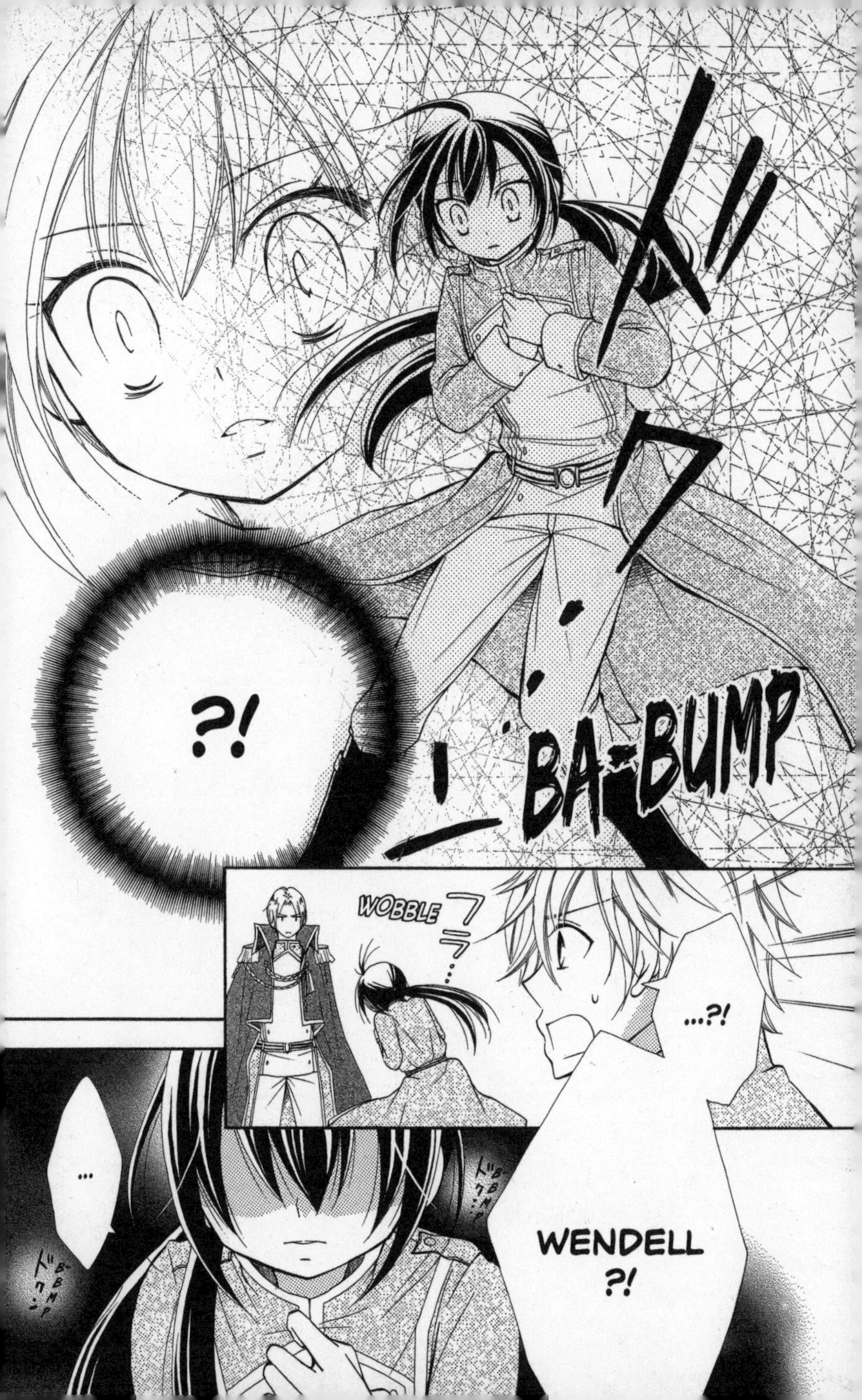
BA-BUMP
?!
WOBBLE
...?!
WENDELL ?!
...

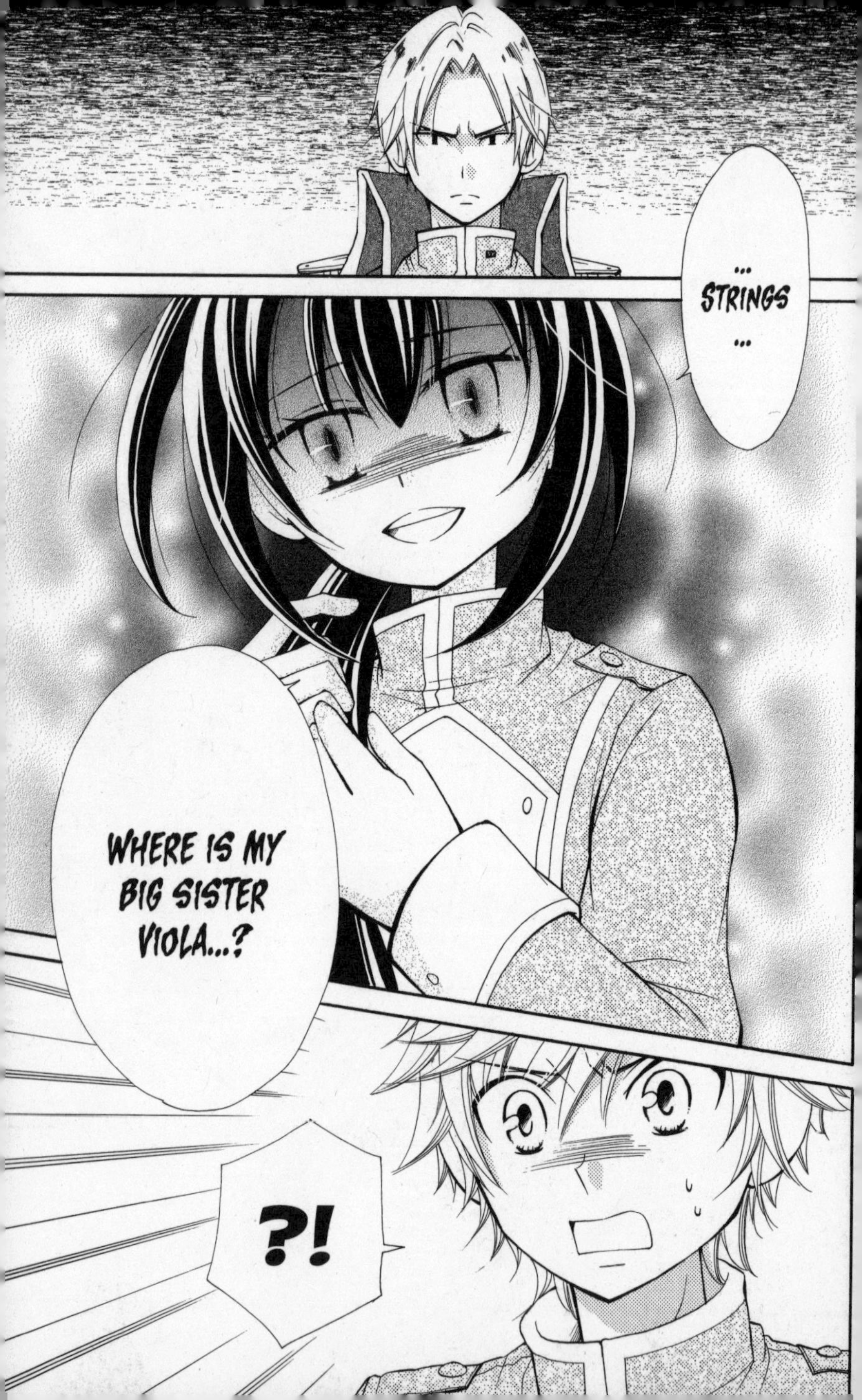
...STRINGS...
WHERE IS MY BIG SISTER VIOLA...?
?!

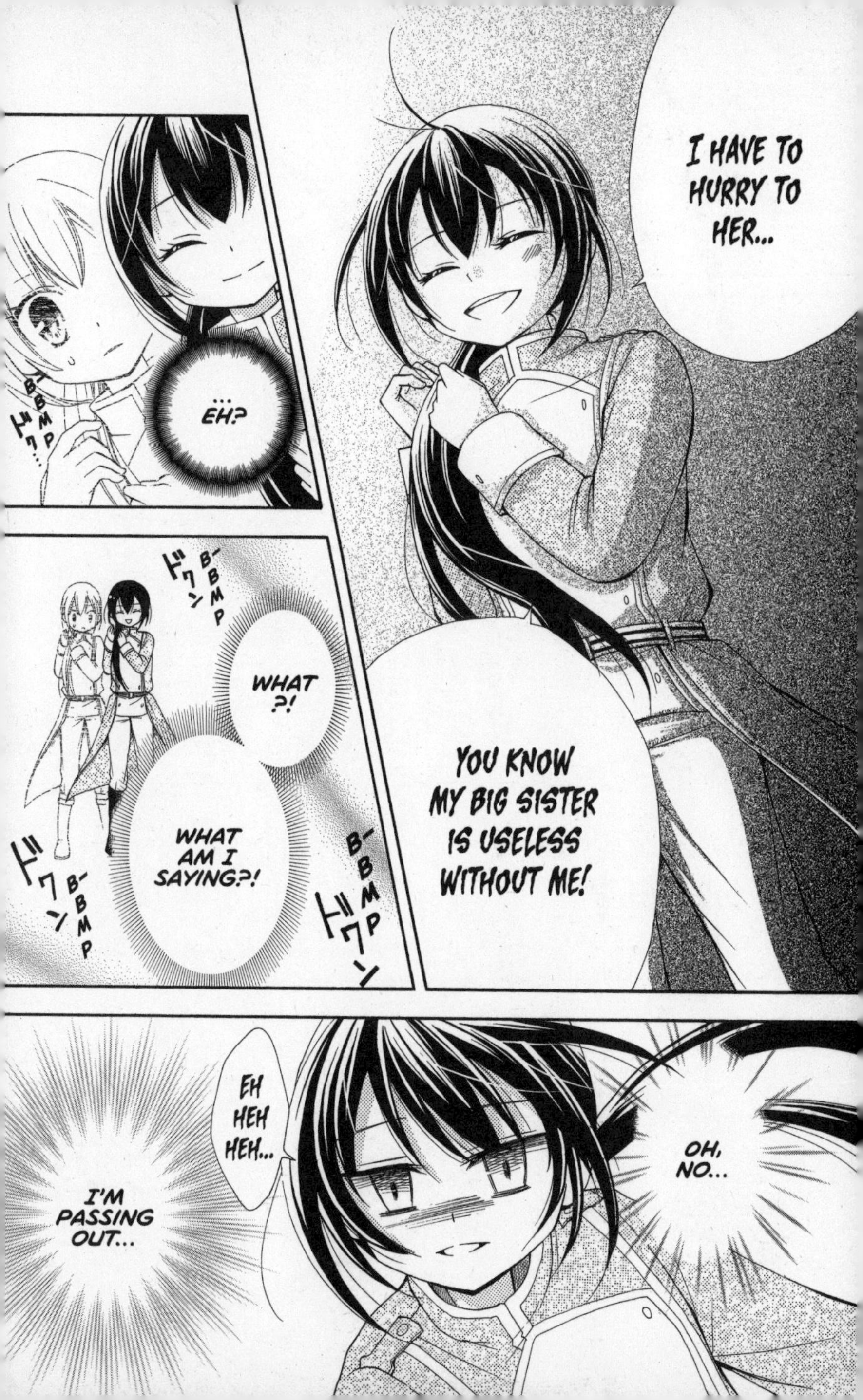

I HAVE TO HURRY TO HER...
YOU KNOW MY BIG SISTER IS USELESS WITHOUT ME!
...EH?
B-BMP
B-BMP
WHAT?!
WHAT AM I SAYING?!
B-BMP
B-BMP
OH, NO...
EH HEH HEH...
I'M PASSING OUT...

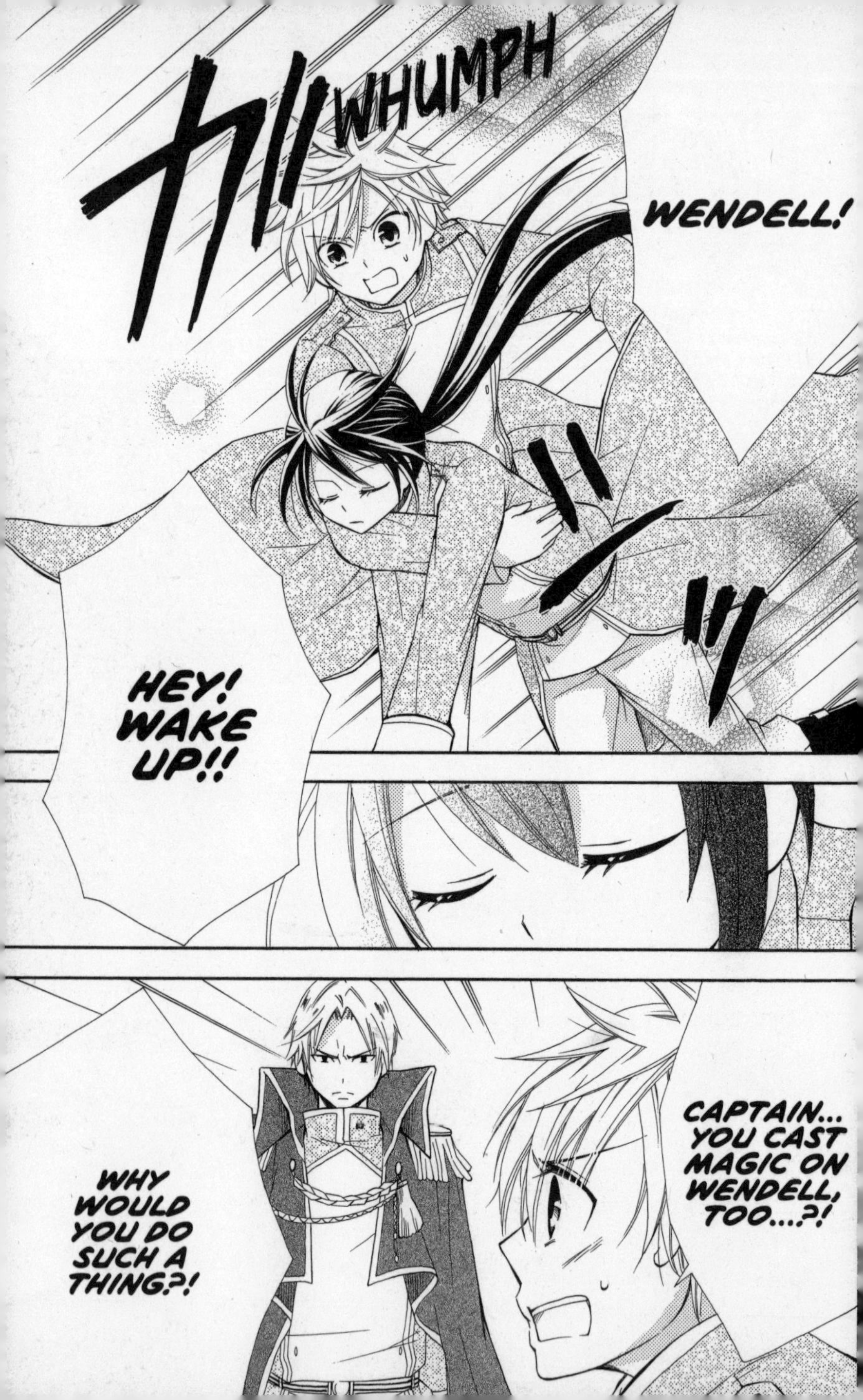
カッ
WHUMPH
WENDELL!
HEY! WAKE UP!!
CAPTAIN... YOU CAST MAGIC ON WENDELL, TOO...?!
WHY WOULD YOU DO SUCH A THING?!

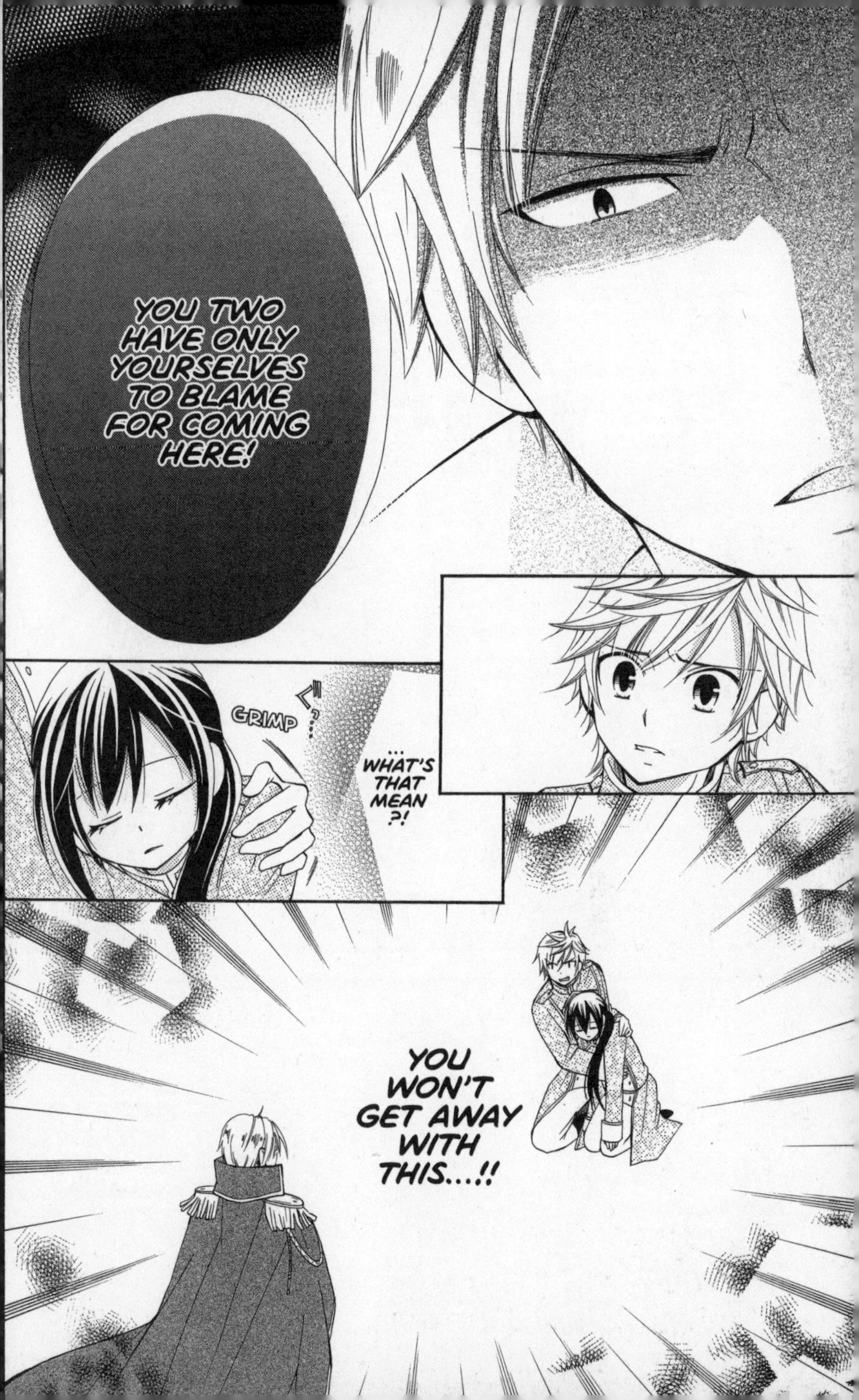
YOU TWO HAVE ONLY YOURSELVES TO BLAME FOR COMING HERE!
...WHAT'S THAT MEAN?!
GRIMP
YOU WON'T GET AWAY WITH THIS...!!

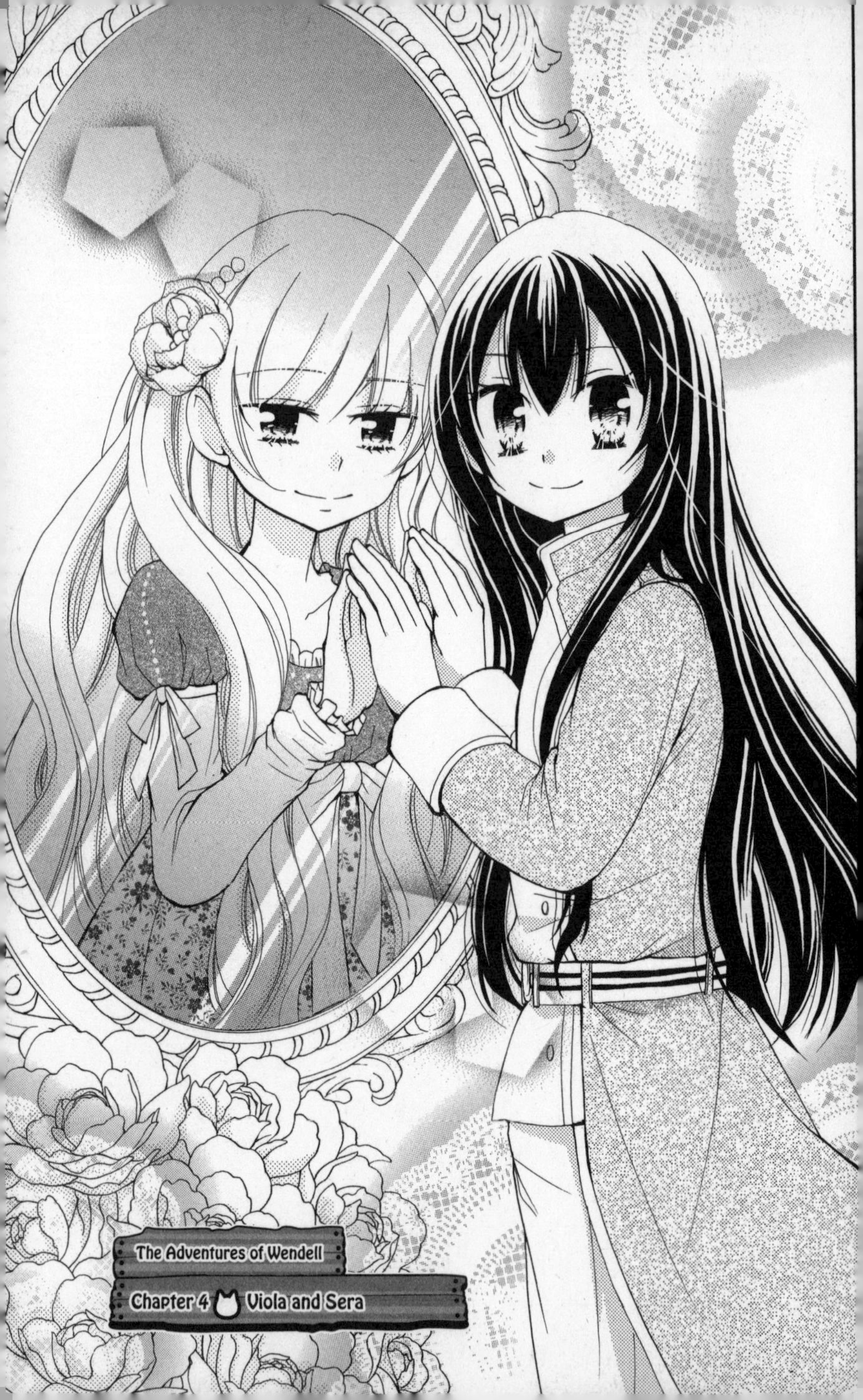
The Adventures of Wendell
Chapter 4 Viola and Sera

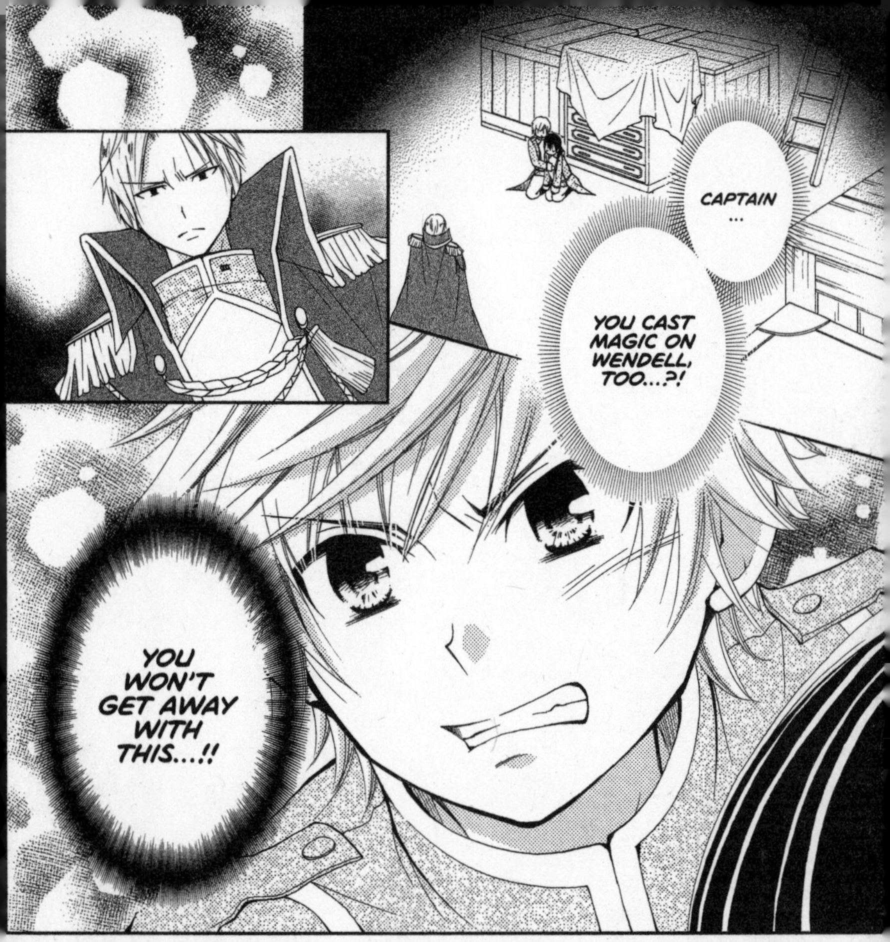
CAPTAIN ...
YOU CAST MAGIC ON WENDELL, TOO...?!
YOU WON'T GET AWAY WITH THIS...!!

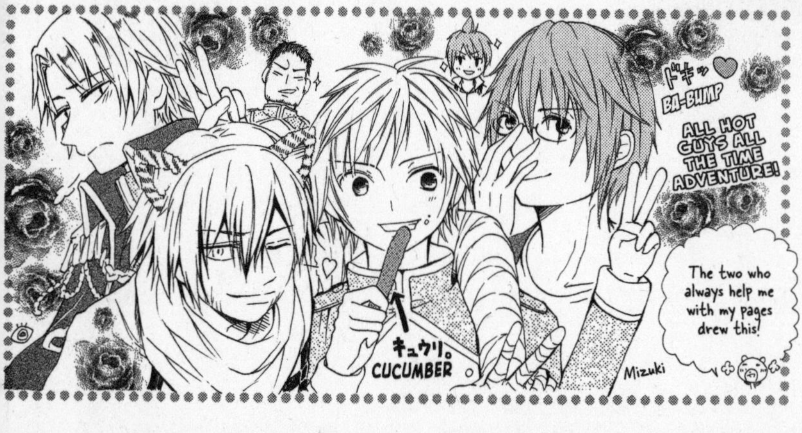
ドキッ
BA-BUMP
ALL HOT GUYS ALL THE TIME ADVENTURE!
The two who always help me with my pages drew this!
Mizuki
キュウリ。
CUCUMBER

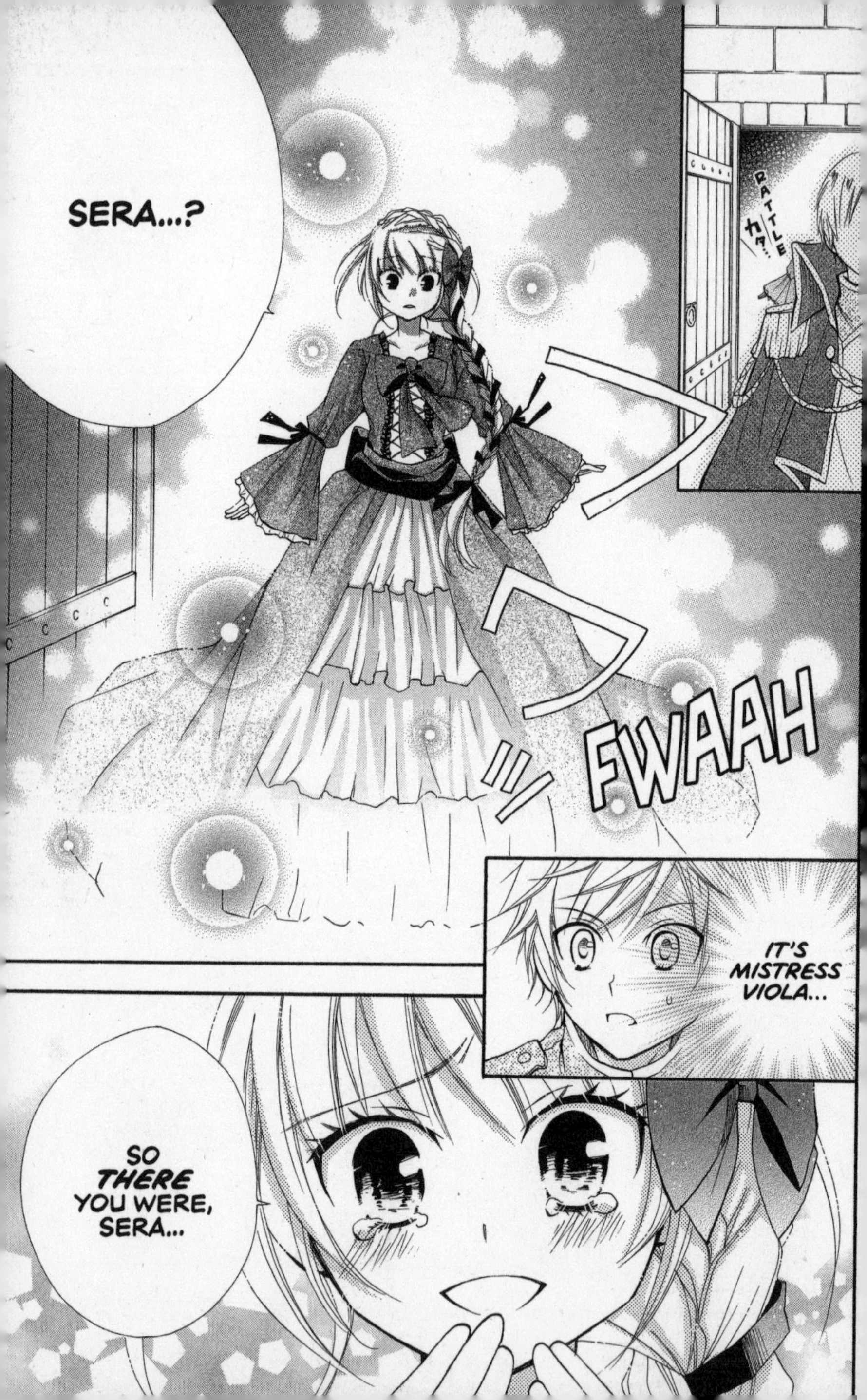
RATTLE
カタ…
SERA...?
FWAAH
IT'S MISTRESS VIOLA...
SO *THERE* YOU WERE, SERA...

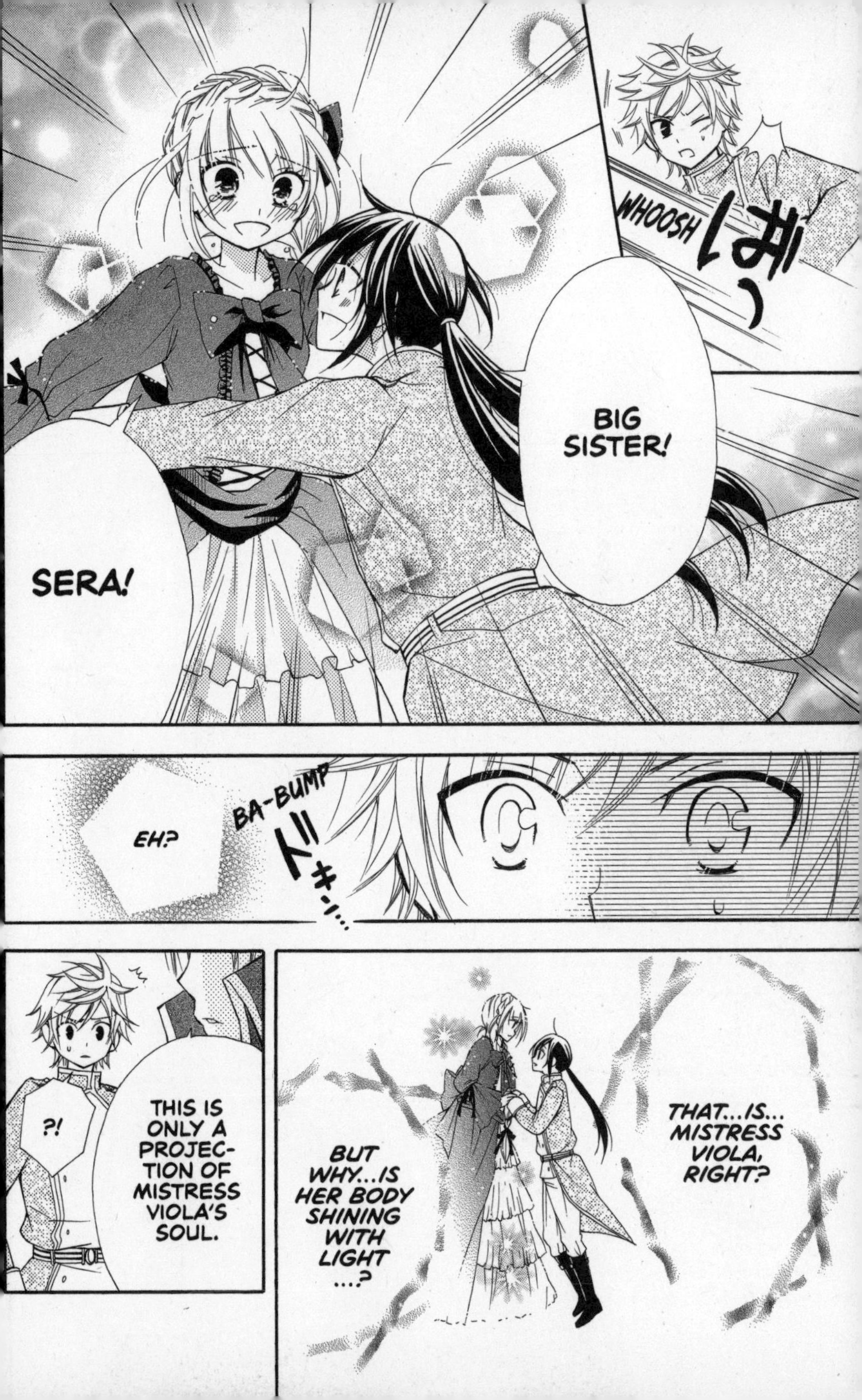
WHOOSH
BIG SISTER!
SERA!
BA-BUMP
EH?
THAT...IS... MISTRESS VIOLA, RIGHT?
BUT WHY...IS HER BODY SHINING WITH LIGHT ...?
THIS IS ONLY A PROJECTION OF MISTRESS VIOLA'S SOUL.
?!

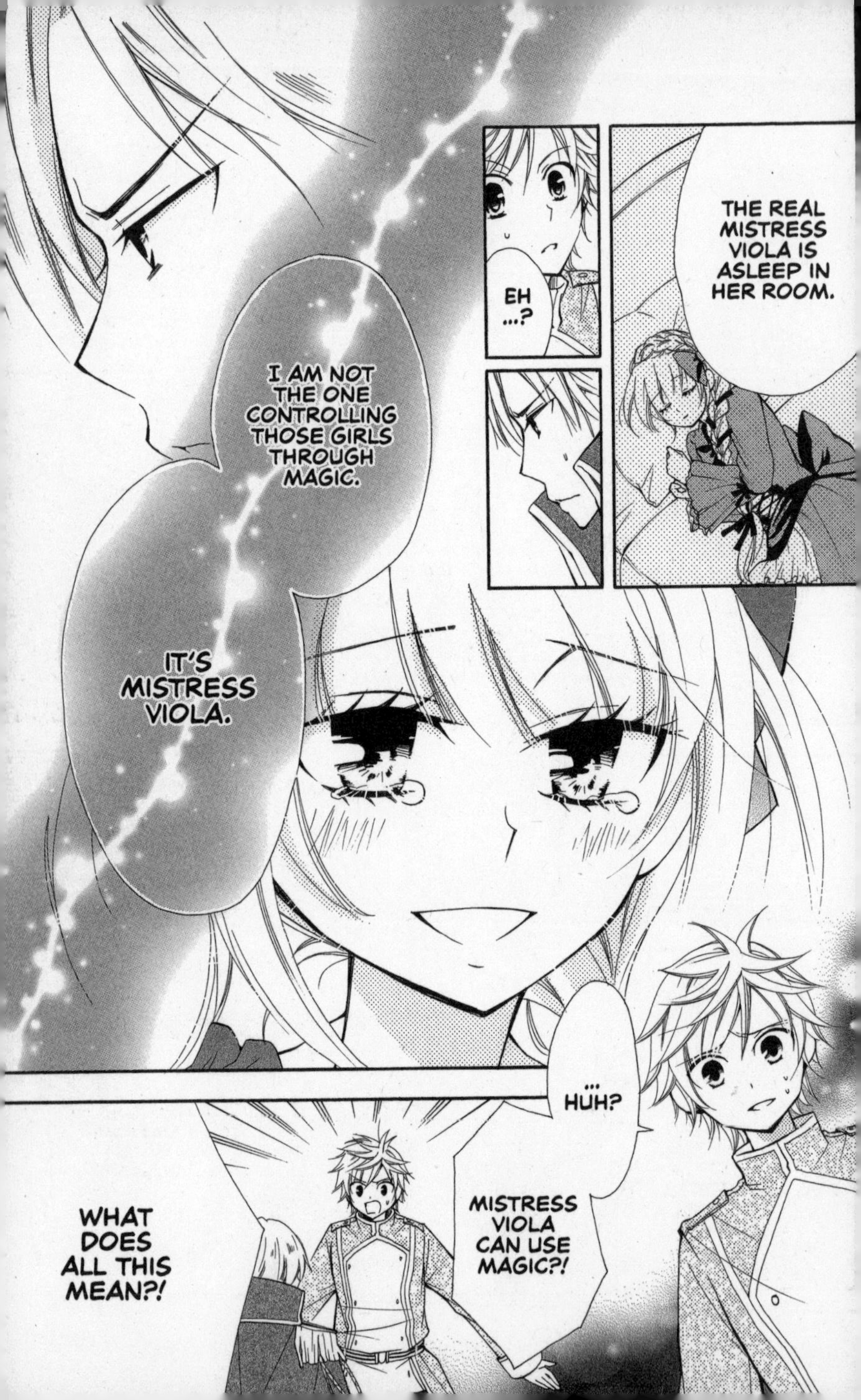
THE REAL MISTRESS VIOLA IS ASLEEP IN HER ROOM.
EH ...?
I AM NOT THE ONE CONTROLLING THOSE GIRLS THROUGH MAGIC.
IT'S MISTRESS VIOLA.
... HUH?
MISTRESS VIOLA CAN USE MAGIC?!
WHAT DOES ALL THIS MEAN?!

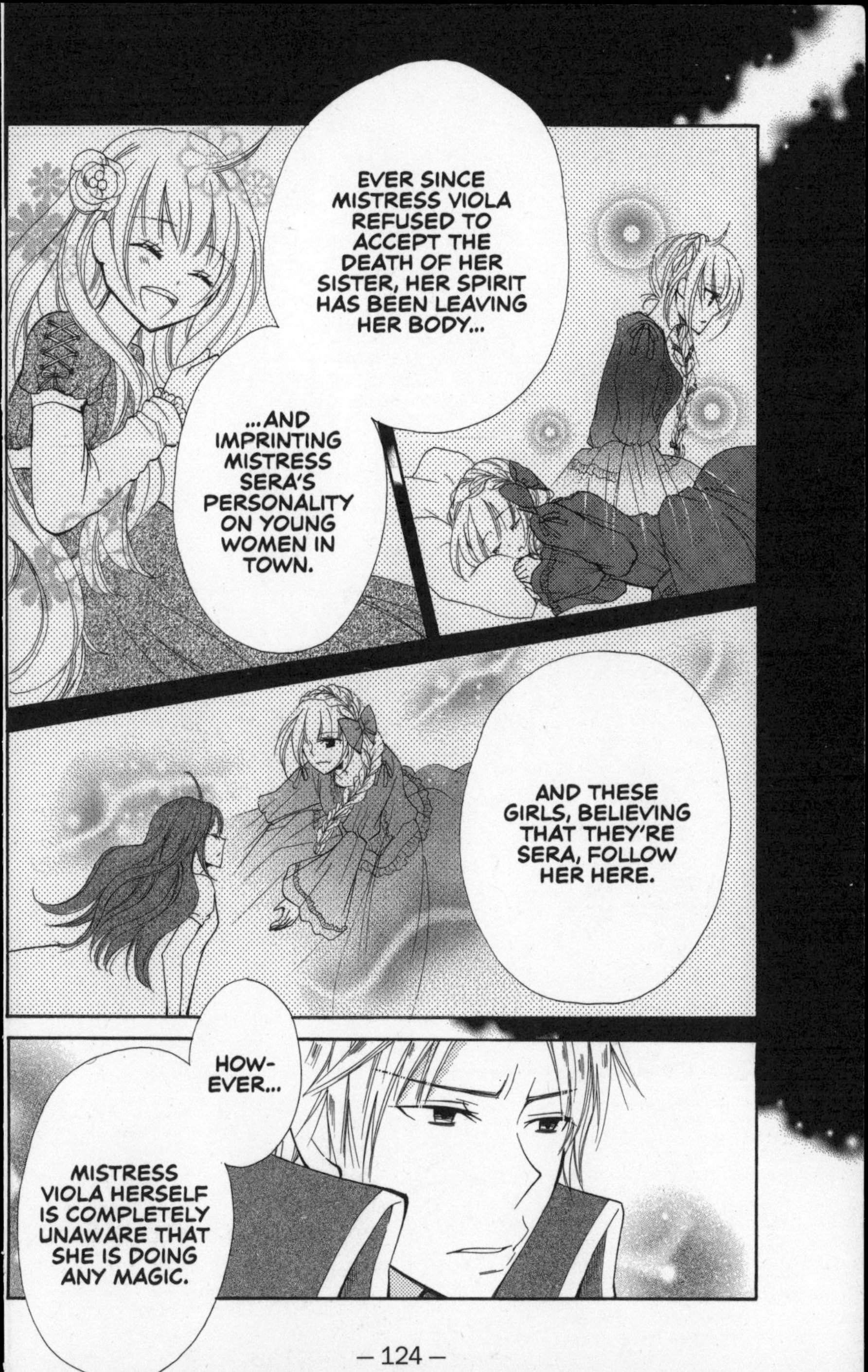
EVER SINCE MISTRESS VIOLA REFUSED TO ACCEPT THE DEATH OF HER SISTER, HER SPIRIT HAS BEEN LEAVING HER BODY...
...AND IMPRINTING MISTRESS SERA'S PERSONALITY ON YOUNG WOMEN IN TOWN.
AND THESE GIRLS, BELIEVING THAT THEY'RE SERA, FOLLOW HER HERE.
HOW-EVER...
MISTRESS VIOLA HERSELF IS COMPLETELY UNAWARE THAT SHE IS DOING ANY MAGIC.

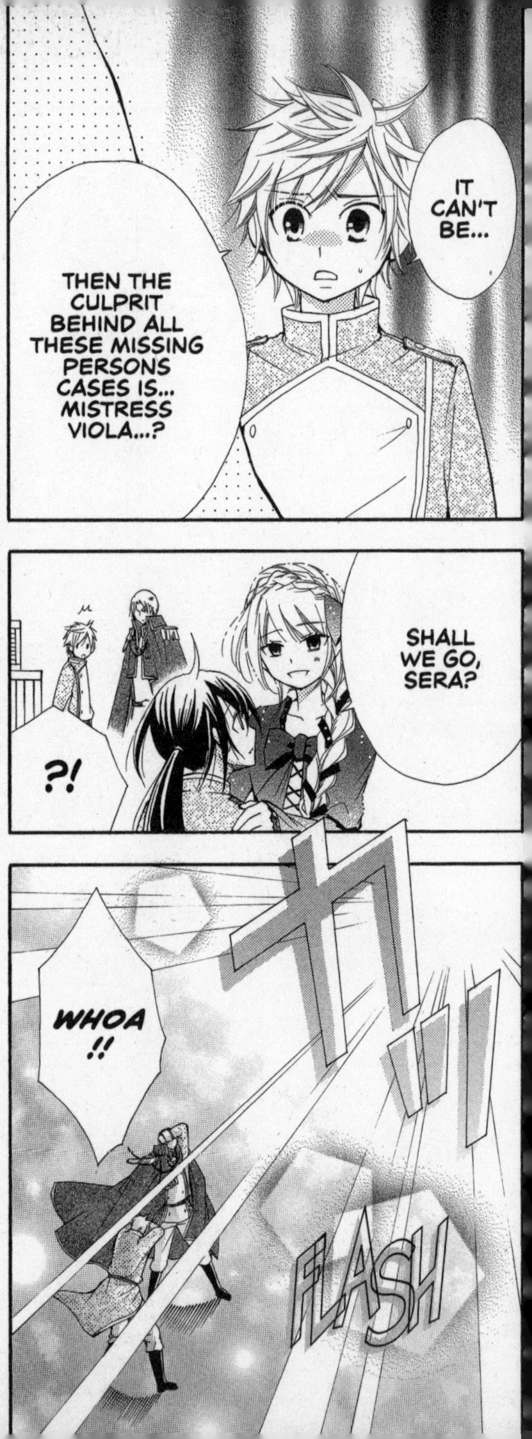
IT CAN'T BE...
THEN THE CULPRIT BEHIND ALL THESE MISSING PERSONS CASES IS... MISTRESS VIOLA...?
SHALL WE GO, SERA?
?!
WHOA !!
FLASH

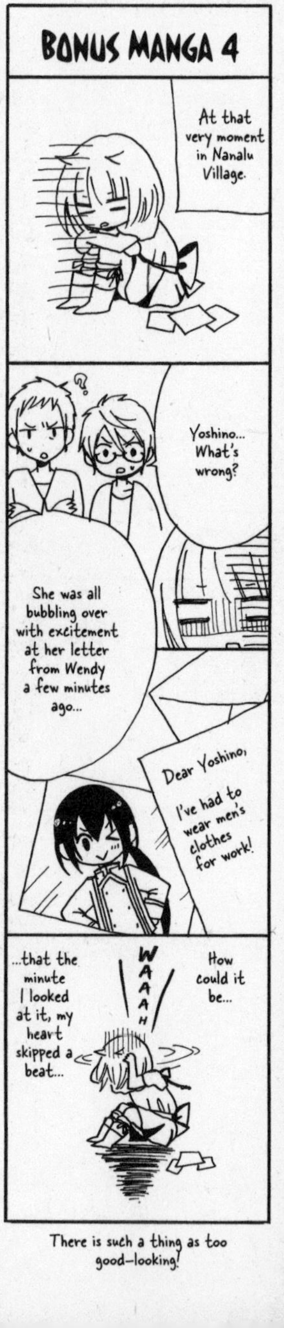
BONUS MANGA 4
At that very moment in Nanalu Village.
Yoshino... What's wrong?
She was all bubbling over with excitement at her letter from Wendy a few minutes ago...
Dear Yoshino, I've had to wear men's clothes for work!
How could it be...
WAAAAH
...that the minute I looked at it, my heart skipped a beat...

There is such a thing as too good-looking!

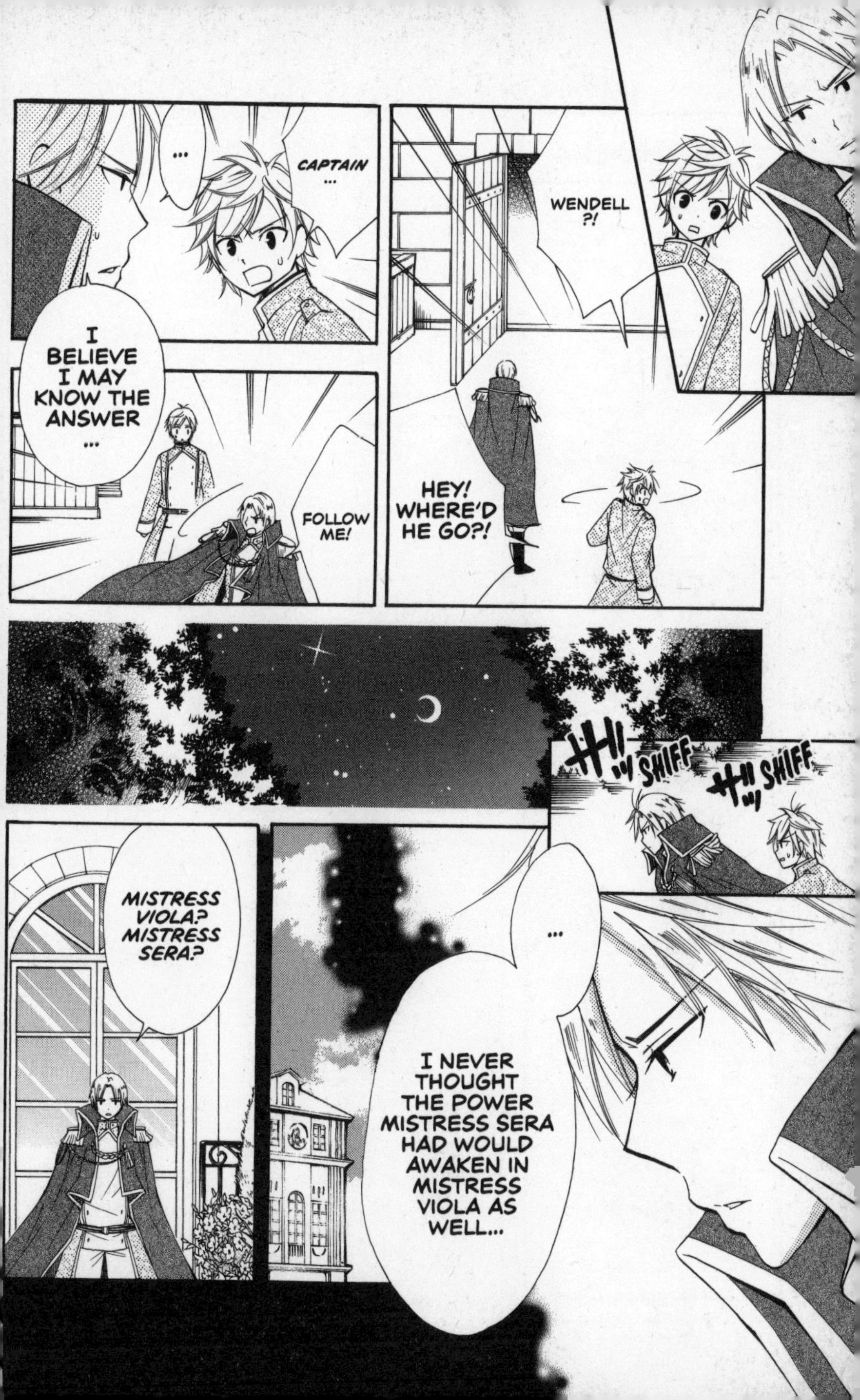
WENDELL ?!
CAPTAIN ...
...
I BELIEVE I MAY KNOW THE ANSWER ...
HEY! WHERE'D HE GO?!
FOLLOW ME!
SHIFF
SHIFF
...
I NEVER THOUGHT THE POWER MISTRESS SERA HAD WOULD AWAKEN IN MISTRESS VIOLA AS WELL...
MISTRESS VIOLA? MISTRESS SERA?

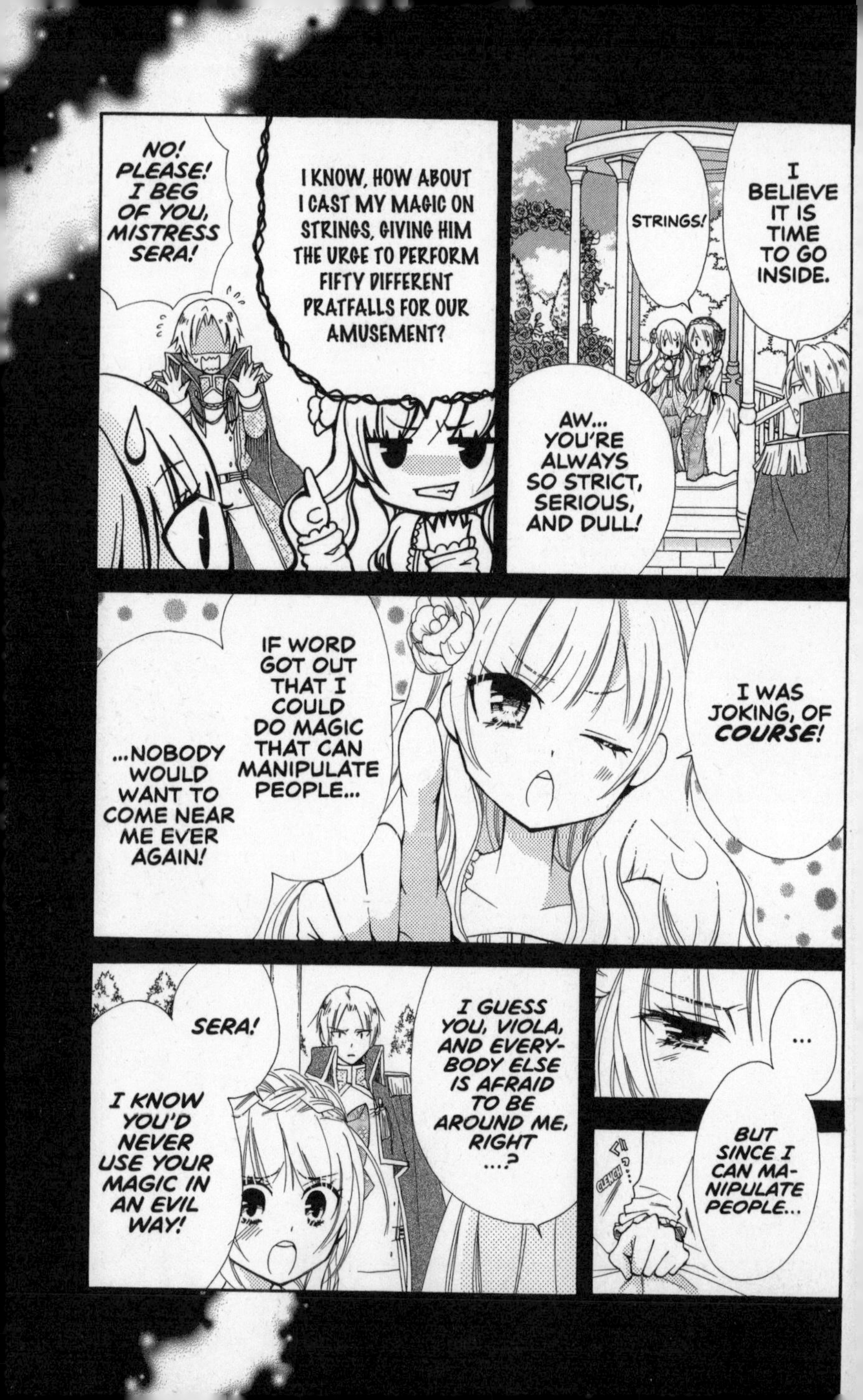
I BELIEVE IT IS TIME TO GO INSIDE.
STRINGS!
AW... YOU'RE ALWAYS SO STRICT, SERIOUS, AND DULL!
I KNOW, HOW ABOUT I CAST MY MAGIC ON STRINGS, GIVING HIM THE URGE TO PERFORM FIFTY DIFFERENT PRATFALLS FOR OUR AMUSEMENT?
NO! PLEASE! I BEG OF YOU, MISTRESS SERA!
I WAS JOKING, OF COURSE!
IF WORD GOT OUT THAT I COULD DO MAGIC THAT CAN MANIPULATE PEOPLE...
...NOBODY WOULD WANT TO COME NEAR ME EVER AGAIN!
...
BUT SINCE I CAN MA-NIPULATE PEOPLE...
CLENCH
I GUESS YOU, VIOLA, AND EVERY-BODY ELSE IS AFRAID TO BE AROUND ME, RIGHT ...?
SERA!
I KNOW YOU'D NEVER USE YOUR MAGIC IN AN EVIL WAY!

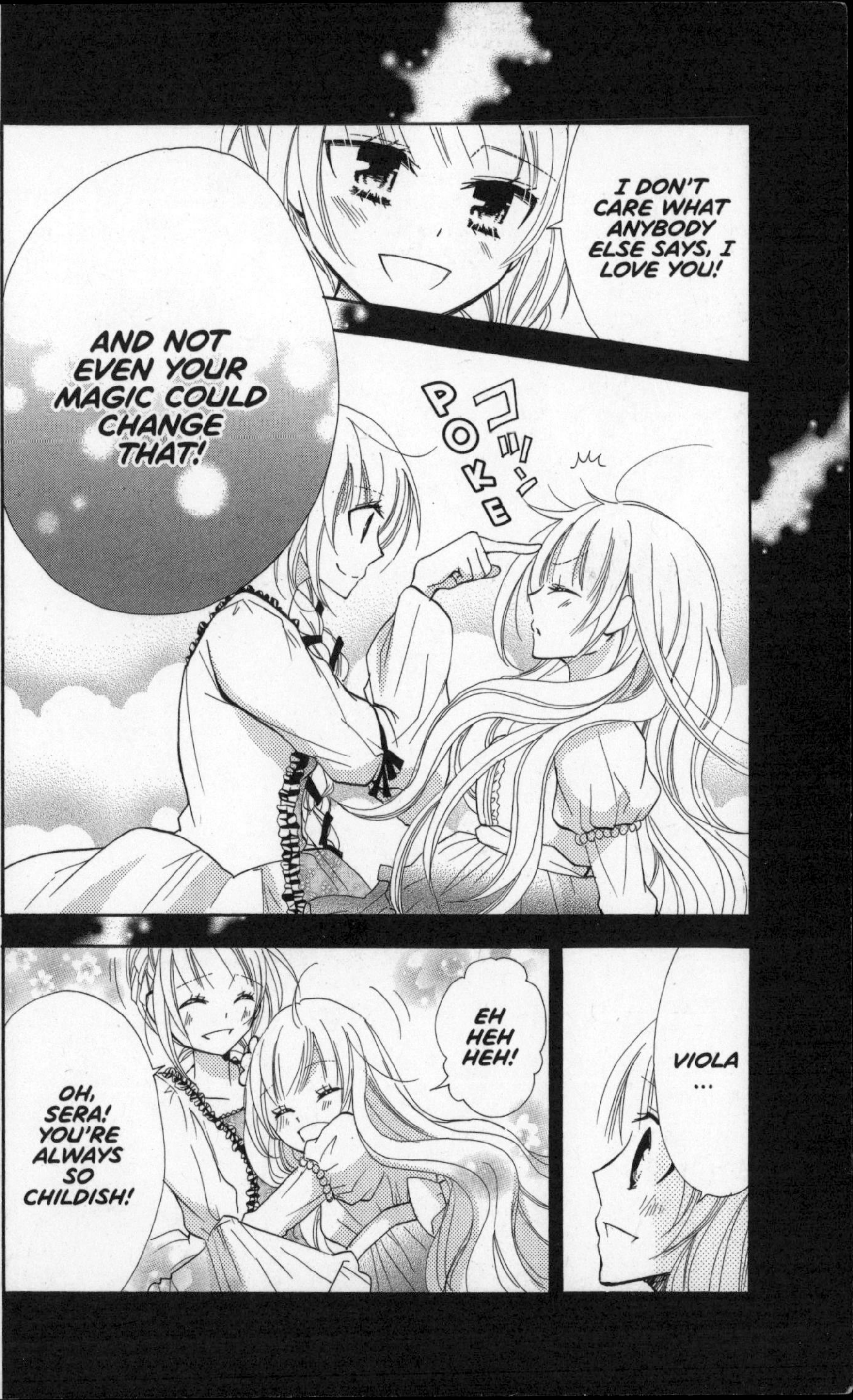
I DON'T CARE WHAT ANYBODY ELSE SAYS, I LOVE YOU!
AND NOT EVEN YOUR MAGIC COULD CHANGE THAT!
POKE
VIOLA ...
EH HEH HEH!
OH, SERA! YOU'RE ALWAYS SO CHILDISH!

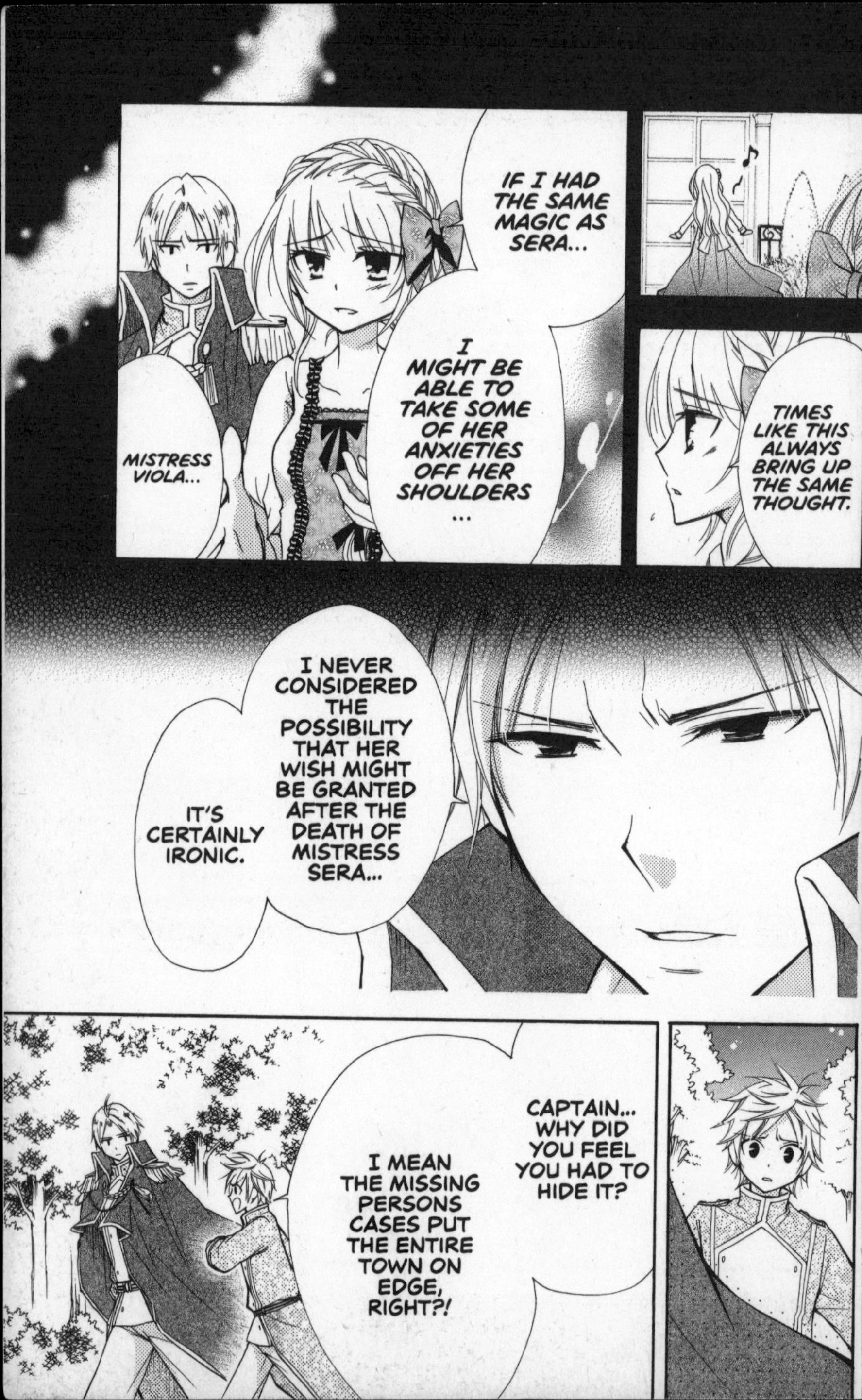
TIMES LIKE THIS ALWAYS BRING UP THE SAME THOUGHT.
IF I HAD THE SAME MAGIC AS SERA...
I MIGHT BE ABLE TO TAKE SOME OF HER ANXIETIES OFF HER SHOULDERS ...
MISTRESS VIOLA...
I NEVER CONSIDERED THE POSSIBILITY THAT HER WISH MIGHT BE GRANTED AFTER THE DEATH OF MISTRESS SERA...
IT'S CERTAINLY IRONIC.
CAPTAIN... WHY DID YOU FEEL YOU HAD TO HIDE IT?
I MEAN THE MISSING PERSONS CASES PUT THE ENTIRE TOWN ON EDGE, RIGHT?!

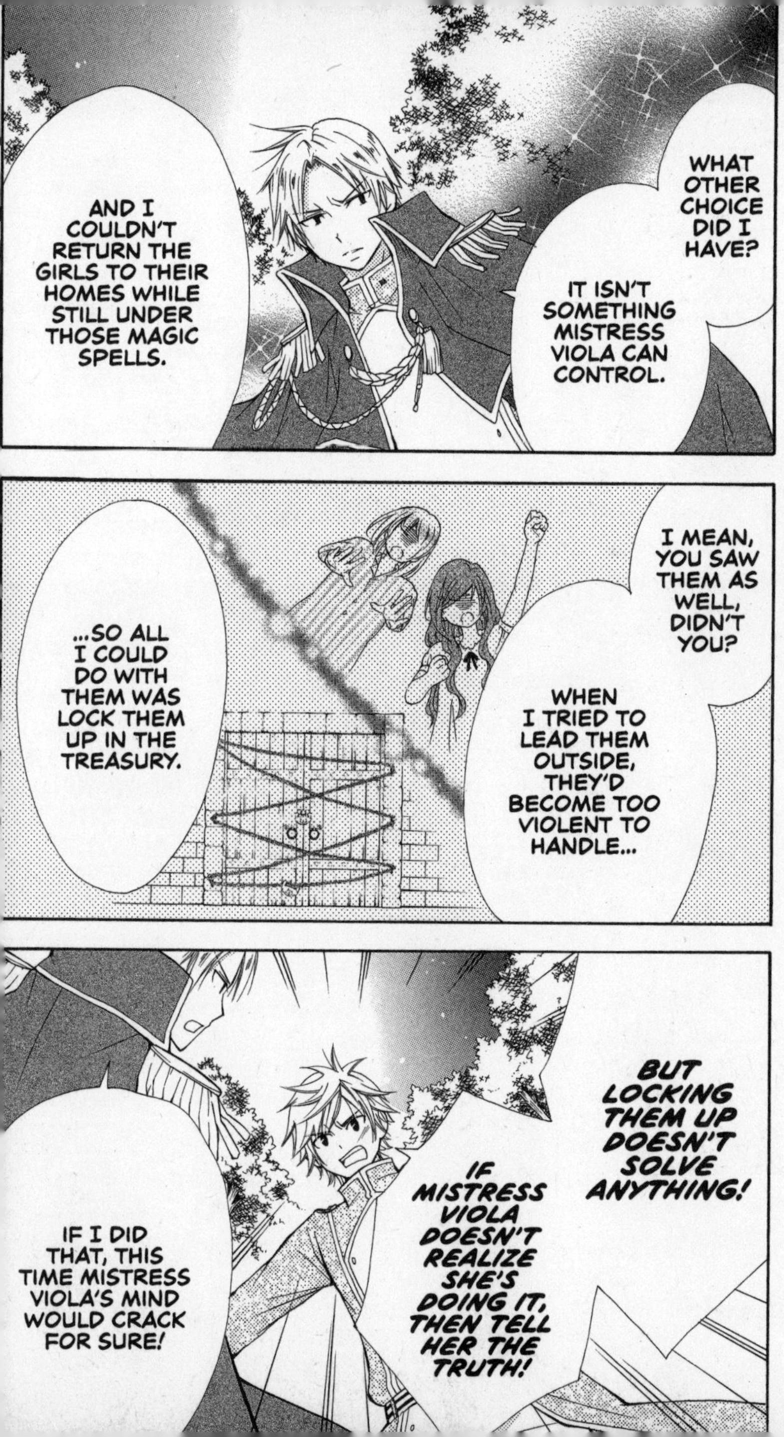
WHAT OTHER CHOICE DID I HAVE?
IT ISN'T SOMETHING MISTRESS VIOLA CAN CONTROL.
AND I COULDN'T RETURN THE GIRLS TO THEIR HOMES WHILE STILL UNDER THOSE MAGIC SPELLS.
I MEAN, YOU SAW THEM AS WELL, DIDN'T YOU?
WHEN I TRIED TO LEAD THEM OUTSIDE, THEY'D BECOME TOO VIOLENT TO HANDLE...
...SO ALL I COULD DO WITH THEM WAS LOCK THEM UP IN THE TREASURY.
BUT LOCKING THEM UP DOESN'T SOLVE ANYTHING!
IF MISTRESS VIOLA DOESN'T REALIZE SHE'S DOING IT, THEN TELL HER THE TRUTH!
IF I DID THAT, THIS TIME MISTRESS VIOLA'S MIND WOULD CRACK FOR SURE!

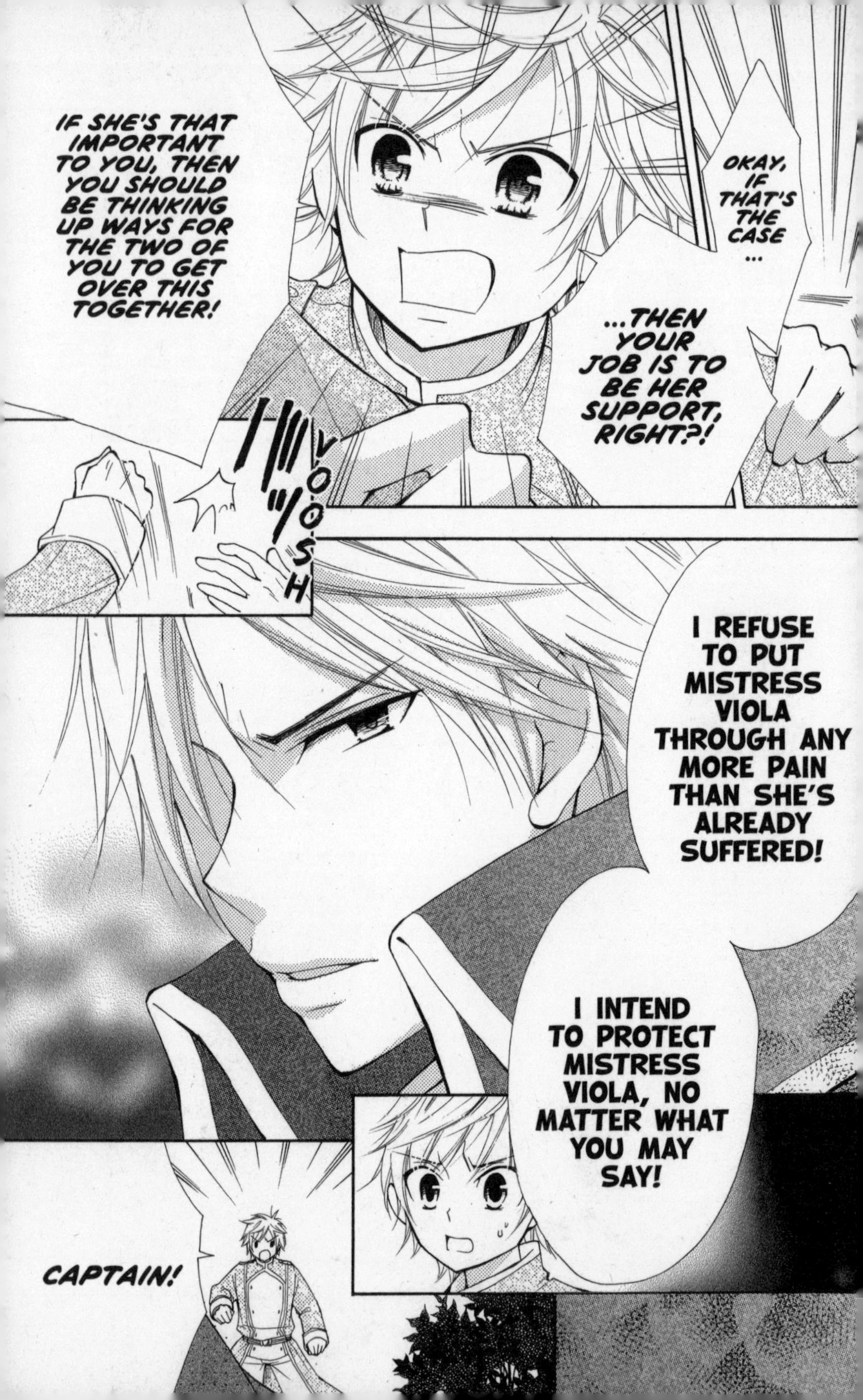
OKAY, IF THAT'S THE CASE...
...THEN YOUR JOB IS TO BE HER SUPPORT, RIGHT?!
IF SHE'S THAT IMPORTANT TO YOU, THEN YOU SHOULD BE THINKING UP WAYS FOR THE TWO OF YOU TO GET OVER THIS TOGETHER!
VOOOSH
I REFUSE TO PUT MISTRESS VIOLA THROUGH ANY MORE PAIN THAN SHE'S ALREADY SUFFERED!
I INTEND TO PROTECT MISTRESS VIOLA, NO MATTER WHAT YOU MAY SAY!
CAPTAIN!

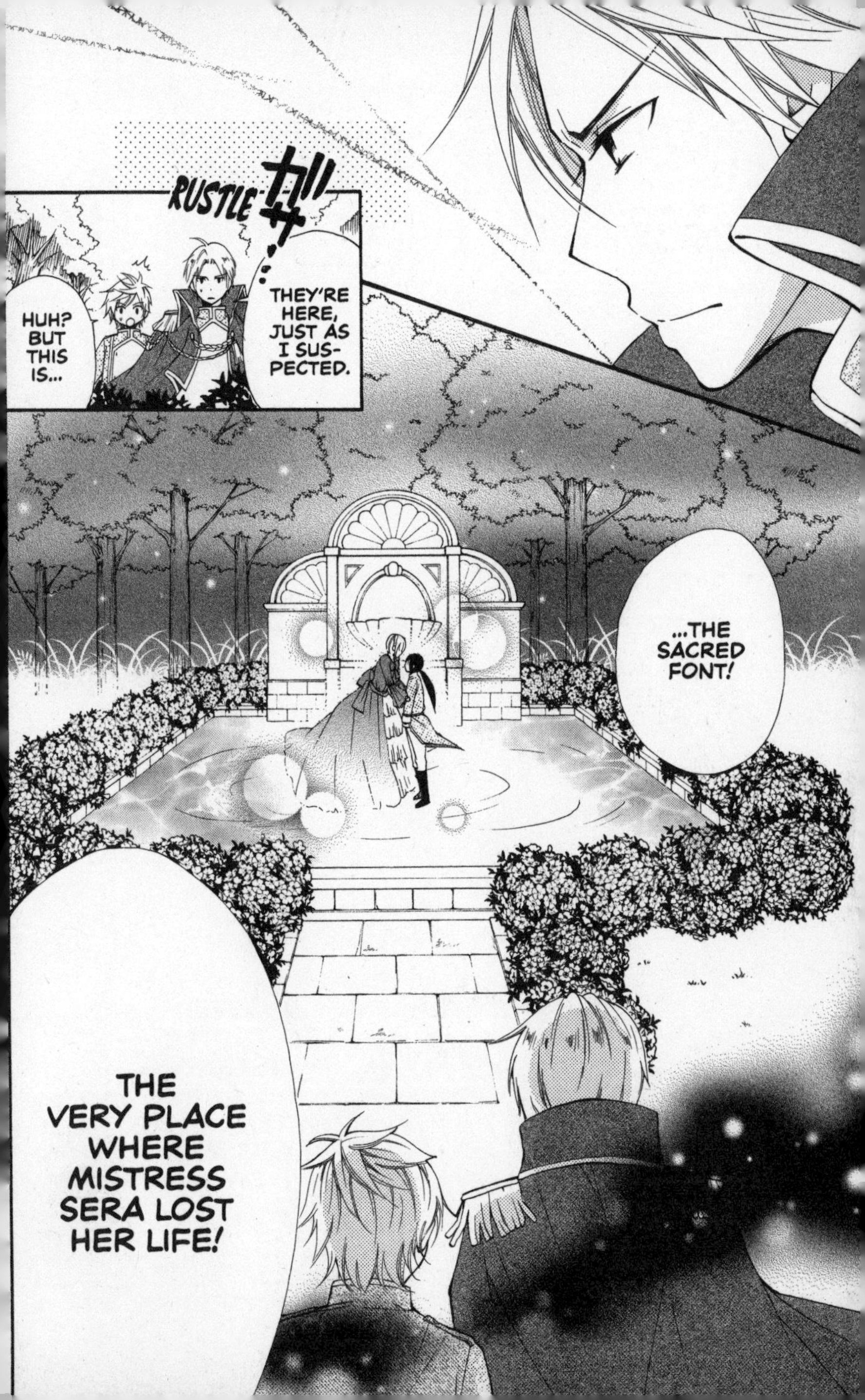
RUSTLE
THEY'RE HERE, JUST AS I SUSPECTED.
HUH? BUT THIS IS...
...THE SACRED FONT!
THE VERY PLACE WHERE MISTRESS SERA LOST HER LIFE!

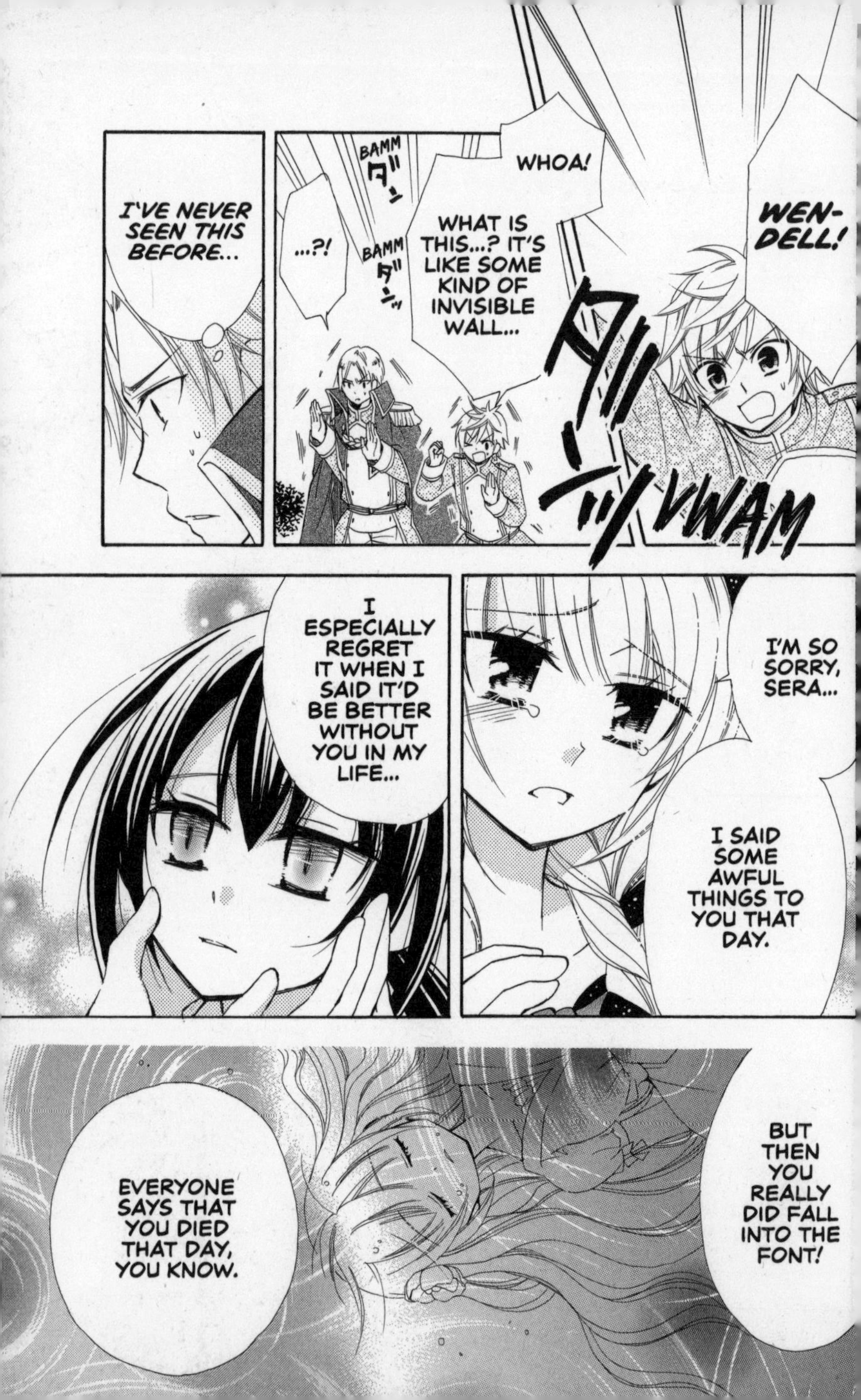
WEN-DELL!
VWAM
WHOA!
WHAT IS THIS...? IT'S LIKE SOME KIND OF INVISIBLE WALL...
BAMM
BAMM
...?!
I'VE NEVER SEEN THIS BEFORE...
I'M SO SORRY, SERA...
I SAID SOME AWFUL THINGS TO YOU THAT DAY.
I ESPECIALLY REGRET IT WHEN I SAID IT'D BE BETTER WITHOUT YOU IN MY LIFE...
BUT THEN YOU REALLY DID FALL INTO THE FONT!
EVERYONE SAYS THAT YOU DIED THAT DAY, YOU KNOW.

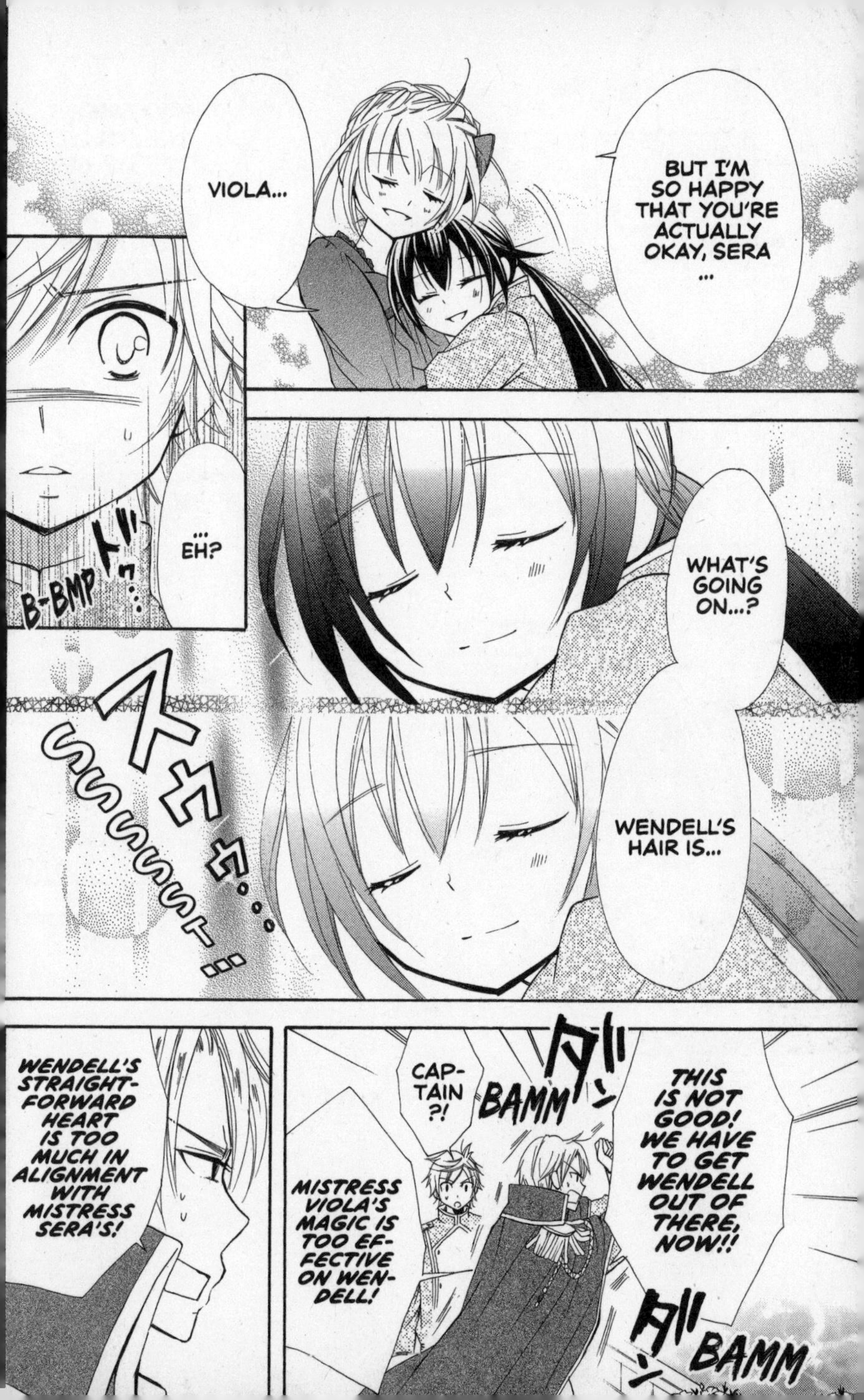
BUT I'M SO HAPPY THAT YOU'RE ACTUALLY OKAY, SERA ...
VIOLA...
WHAT'S GOING ON...?
... EH?
B-BMP
WENDELL'S HAIR IS...
SSSSSSST...!!
THIS IS NOT GOOD! WE HAVE TO GET WENDELL OUT OF THERE, NOW!!
BAMM
CAPTAIN?!
MISTRESS VIOLA'S MAGIC IS TOO EFFECTIVE ON WENDELL!
BAMM
WENDELL'S STRAIGHTFORWARD HEART IS TOO MUCH IN ALIGNMENT WITH MISTRESS SERA'S!

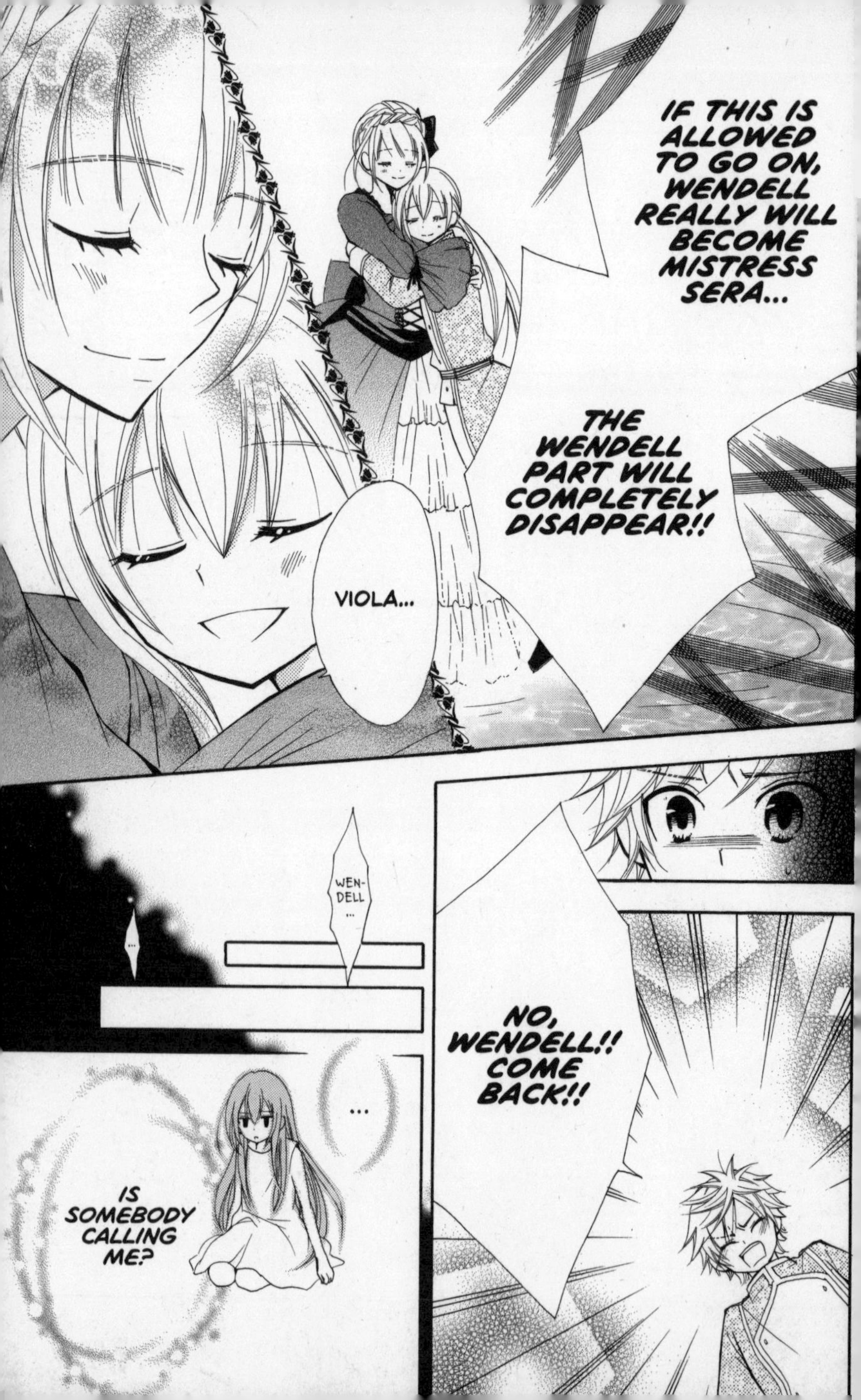
IF THIS IS ALLOWED TO GO ON, WENDELL REALLY WILL BECOME MISTRESS SERA...
THE WENDELL PART WILL COMPLETELY DISAPPEAR!!
VIOLA...
NO, WENDELL!! COME BACK!!
WEN-DELL ...
...
...
IS SOMEBODY CALLING ME?

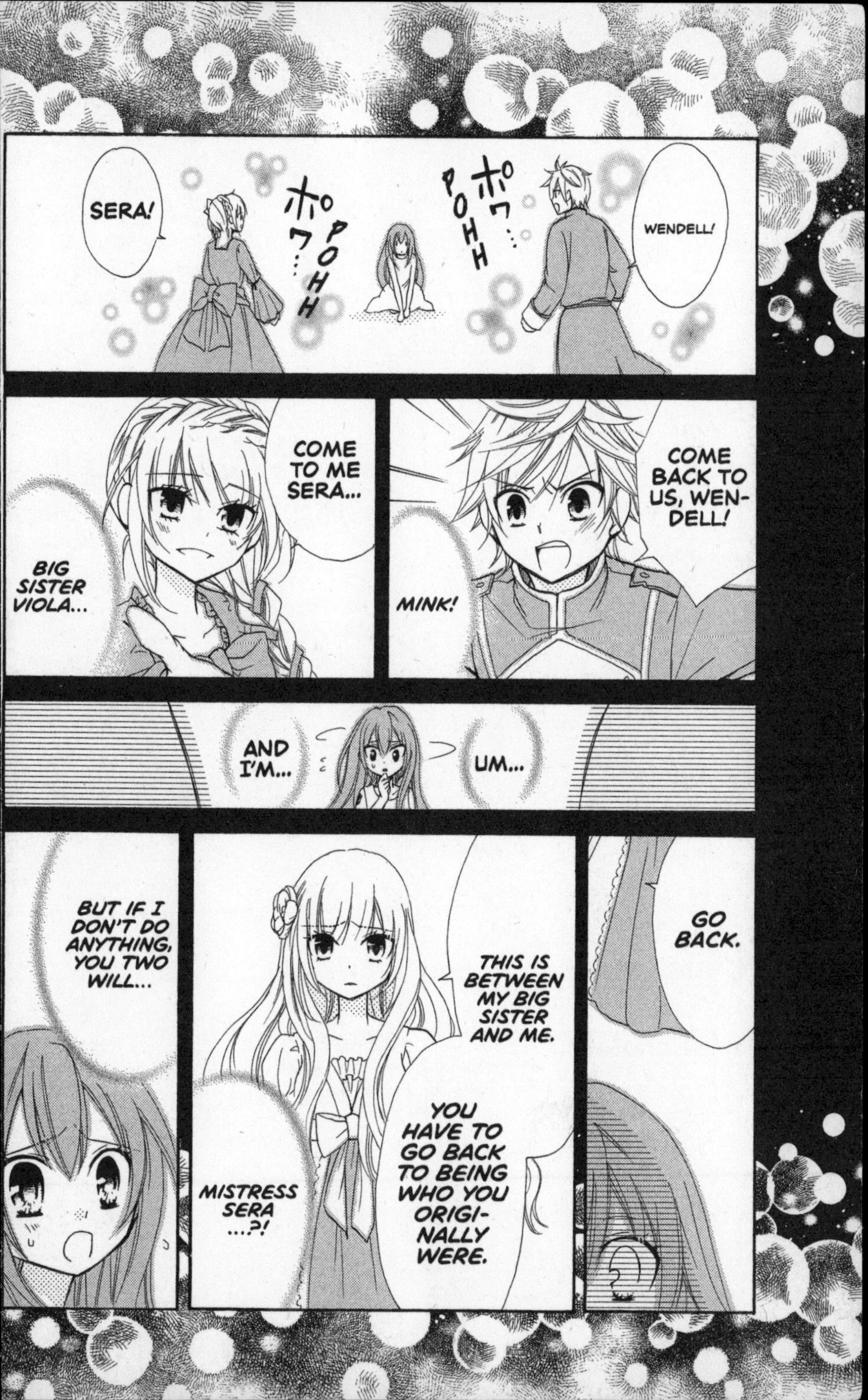
WENDELL!
ポワ… POHH
ポワ… POHH
SERA!
COME BACK TO US, WEN-DELL!
MINK!
COME TO ME SERA...
BIG SISTER VIOLA...
UM...
AND I'M...
GO BACK.
THIS IS BETWEEN MY BIG SISTER AND ME.
YOU HAVE TO GO BACK TO BEING WHO YOU ORIGI-NALLY WERE.
MISTRESS SERA ...?!
BUT IF I DON'T DO ANYTHING, YOU TWO WILL...

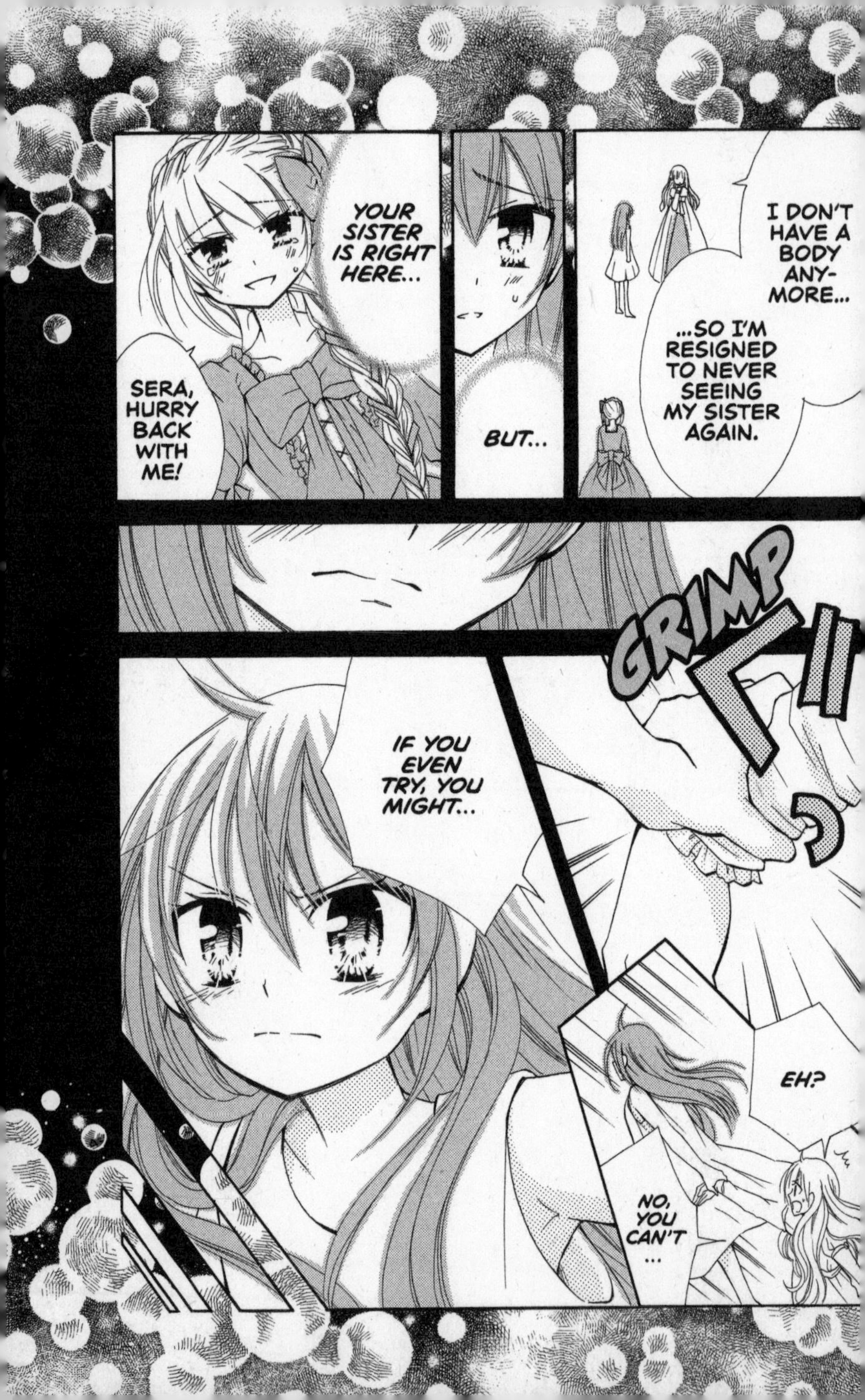
I DON'T HAVE A BODY ANYMORE...
...SO I'M RESIGNED TO NEVER SEEING MY SISTER AGAIN.
BUT...
YOUR SISTER IS RIGHT HERE...
SERA, HURRY BACK WITH ME!
GRIMP
EH?
NO, YOU CAN'T ...
IF YOU EVEN TRY, YOU MIGHT...

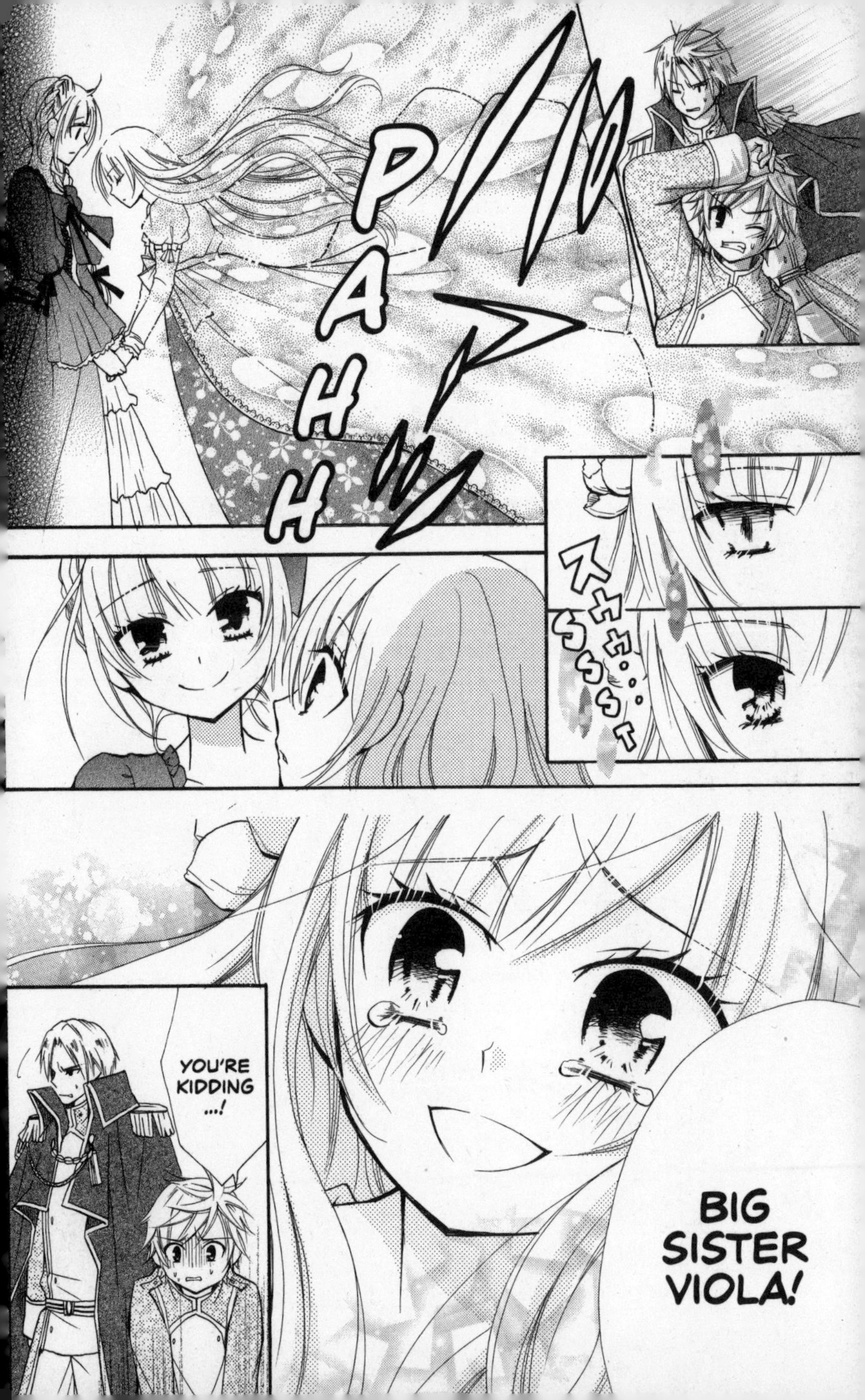
PAHHH
SSSST...
BIG SISTER VIOLA!
YOU'RE KIDDING ...!

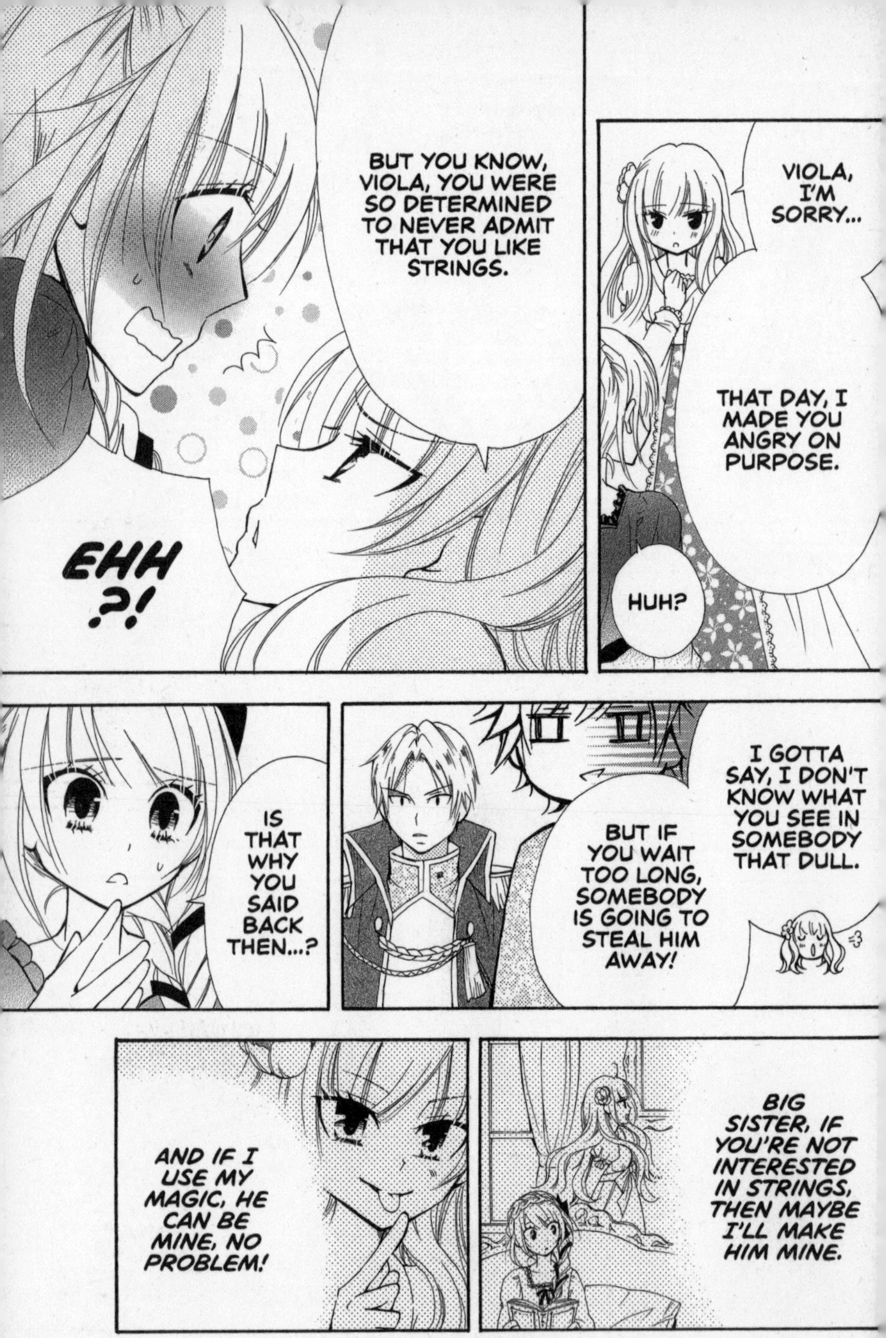
VIOLA, I'M SORRY...
THAT DAY, I MADE YOU ANGRY ON PURPOSE.
HUH?
BUT YOU KNOW, VIOLA, YOU WERE SO DETERMINED TO NEVER ADMIT THAT YOU LIKE STRINGS.
EHH ?!
I GOTTA SAY, I DON'T KNOW WHAT YOU SEE IN SOMEBODY THAT DULL.
BUT IF YOU WAIT TOO LONG, SOMEBODY IS GOING TO STEAL HIM AWAY!
IS THAT WHY YOU SAID BACK THEN...?
BIG SISTER, IF YOU'RE NOT INTERESTED IN STRINGS, THEN MAYBE I'LL MAKE HIM MINE.
AND IF I USE MY MAGIC, HE CAN BE MINE, NO PROBLEM!

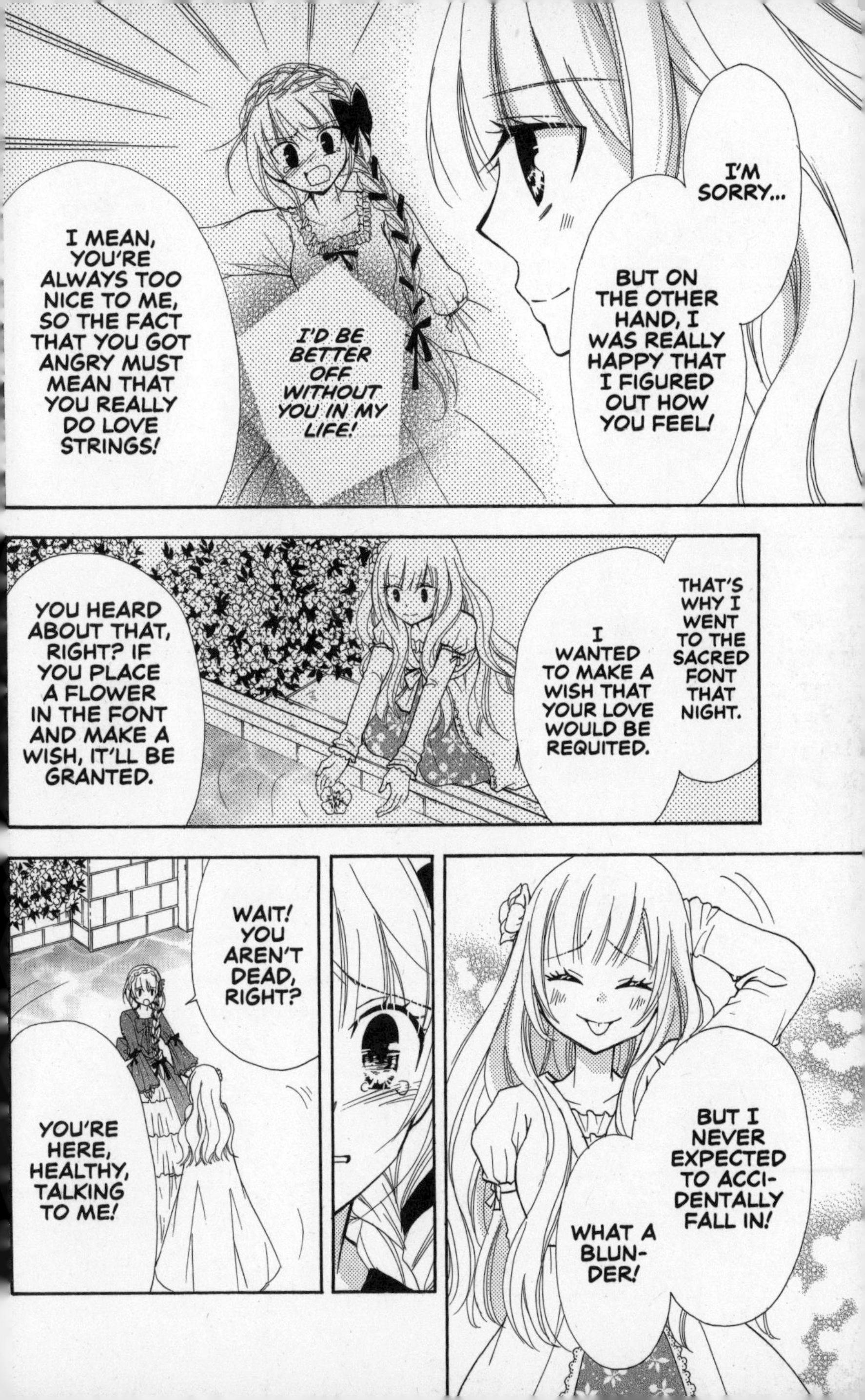
I'M SORRY...
BUT ON THE OTHER HAND, I WAS REALLY HAPPY THAT I FIGURED OUT HOW YOU FEEL!
I'D BE BETTER OFF WITHOUT YOU IN MY LIFE!
I MEAN, YOU'RE ALWAYS TOO NICE TO ME, SO THE FACT THAT YOU GOT ANGRY MUST MEAN THAT YOU REALLY DO LOVE STRINGS!
THAT'S WHY I WENT TO THE SACRED FONT THAT NIGHT.
I WANTED TO MAKE A WISH THAT YOUR LOVE WOULD BE REQUITED.
YOU HEARD ABOUT THAT, RIGHT? IF YOU PLACE A FLOWER IN THE FONT AND MAKE A WISH, IT'LL BE GRANTED.
BUT I NEVER EXPECTED TO ACCI-DENTALLY FALL IN!
WHAT A BLUN-DER!
WAIT! YOU AREN'T DEAD, RIGHT?
YOU'RE HERE, HEALTHY, TALKING TO ME!

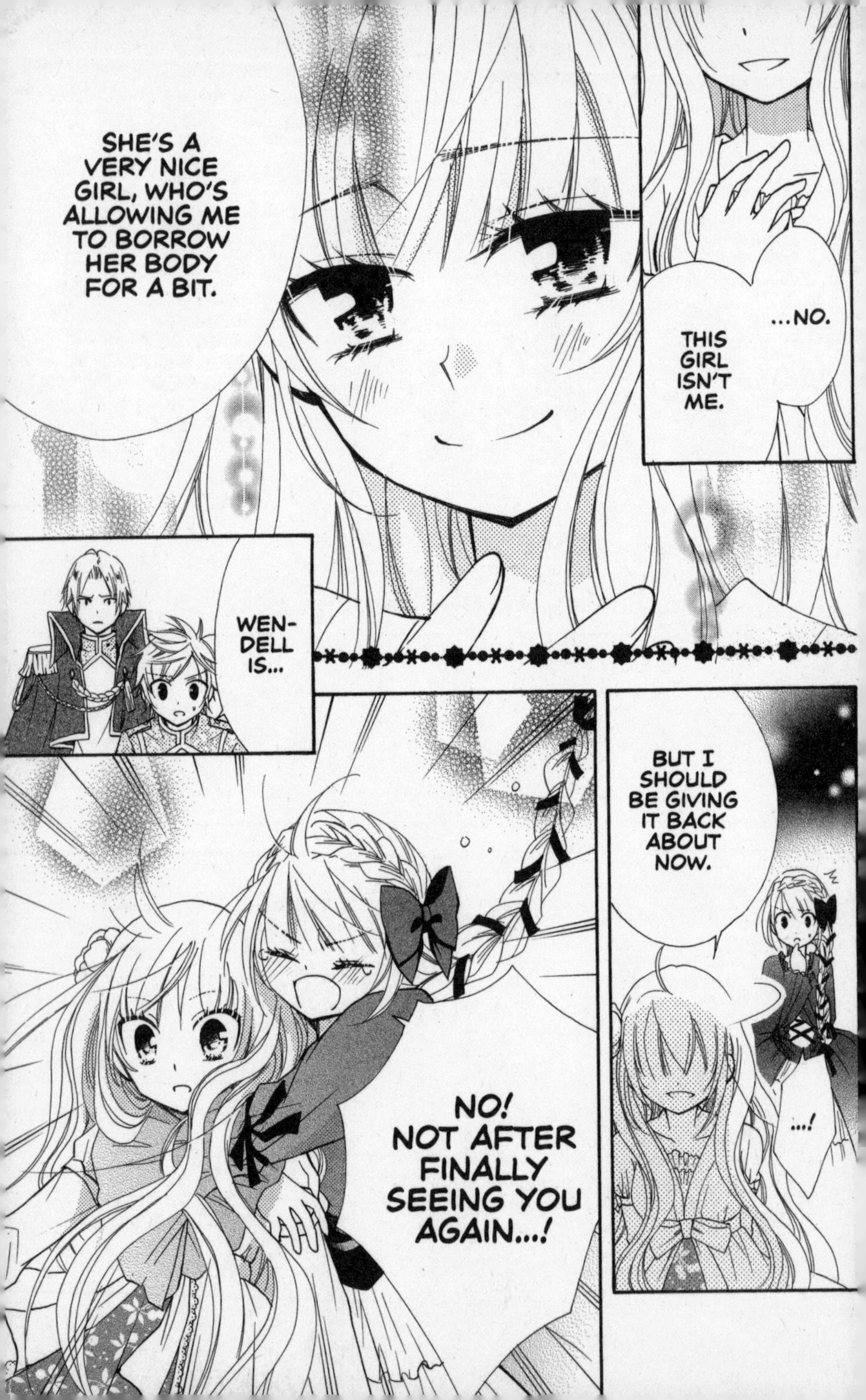
...NO.
THIS GIRL ISN'T ME.
SHE'S A VERY NICE GIRL, WHO'S ALLOWING ME TO BORROW HER BODY FOR A BIT.
WEN-DELL IS...
BUT I SHOULD BE GIVING IT BACK ABOUT NOW.
...!
NO! NOT AFTER FINALLY SEEING YOU AGAIN...!

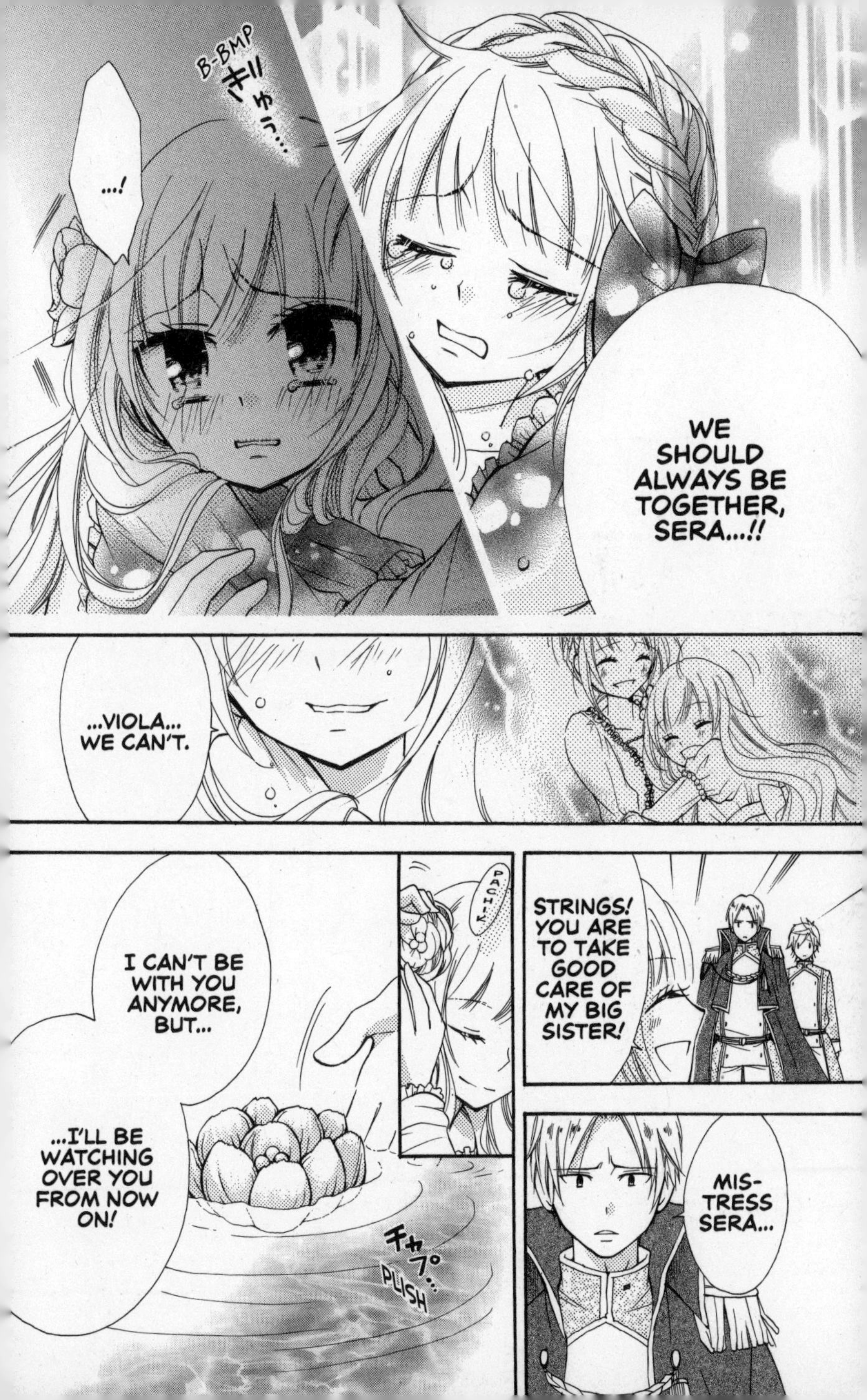
WE SHOULD ALWAYS BE TOGETHER, SERA...!!
B-BMP
...!
...VIOLA... WE CAN'T.
STRINGS! YOU ARE TO TAKE GOOD CARE OF MY BIG SISTER!
MIS-TRESS SERA...
PACHIK
I CAN'T BE WITH YOU ANYMORE, BUT...
...I'LL BE WATCHING OVER YOU FROM NOW ON!
チャプ…
PLISH

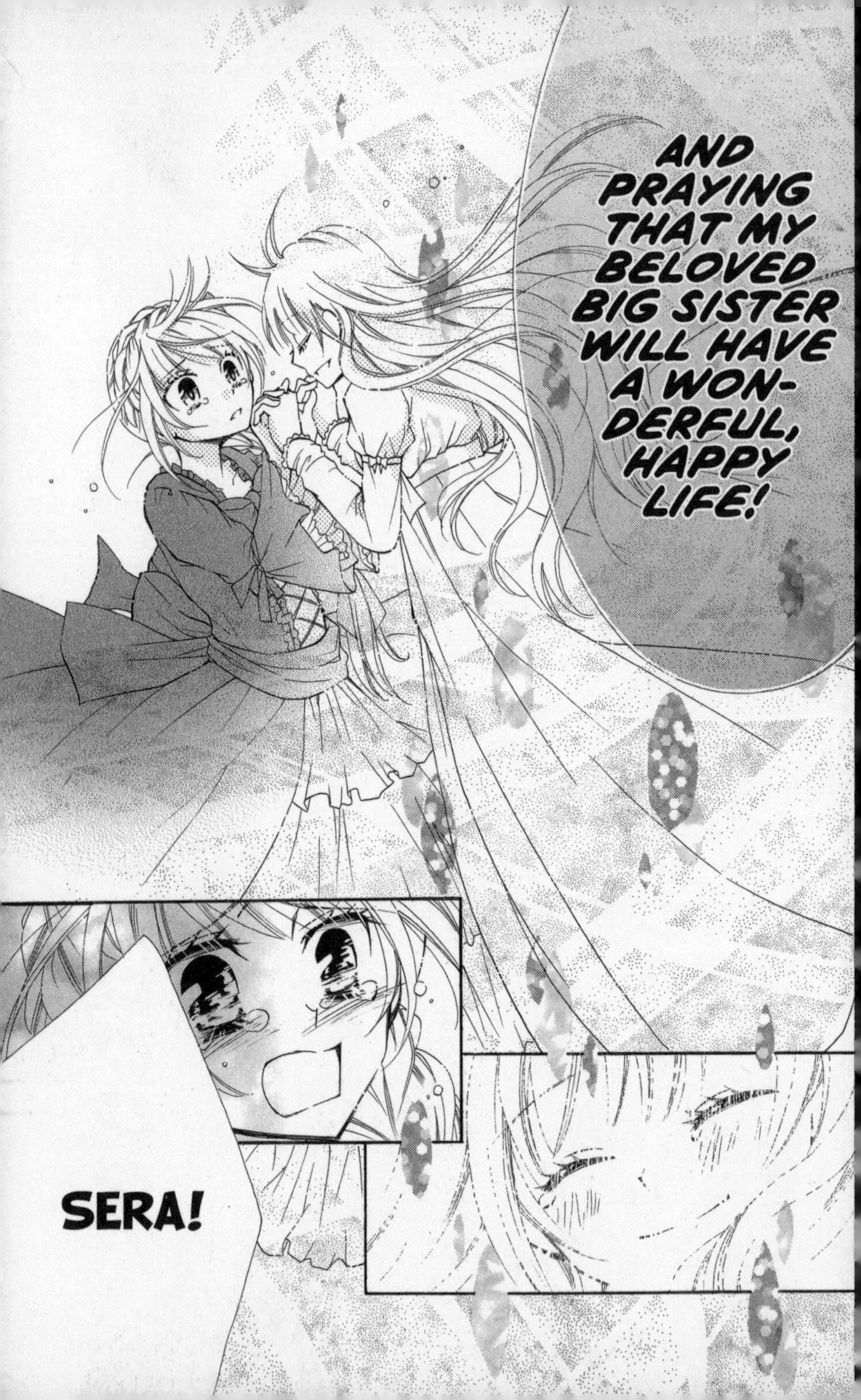
AND PRAYING THAT MY BELOVED BIG SISTER WILL HAVE A WON-DERFUL, HAPPY LIFE!
SERA!

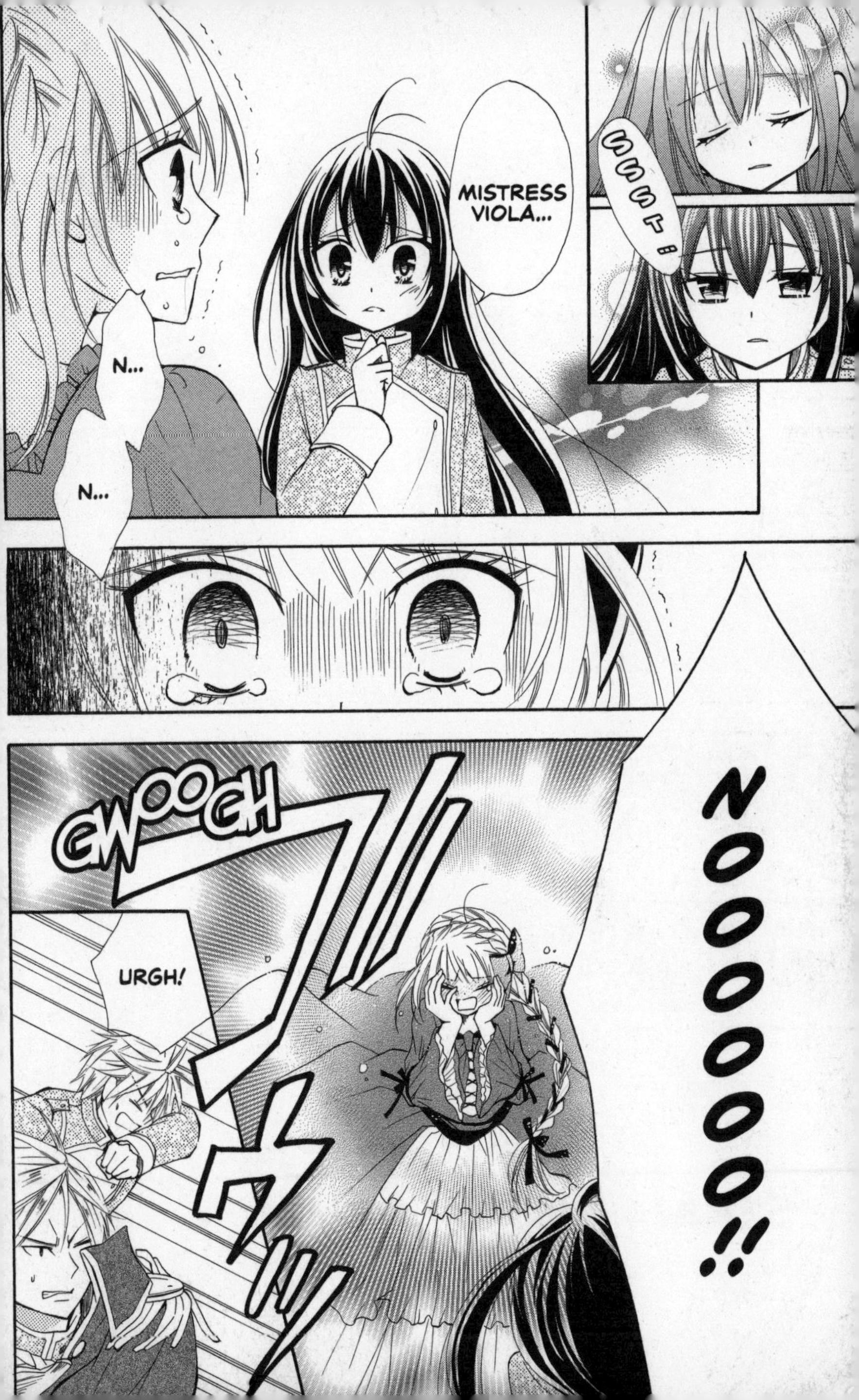
SSST!
MISTRESS VIOLA...
N...
N...
NOOOOOOO!!
GWOOGH
URGH!

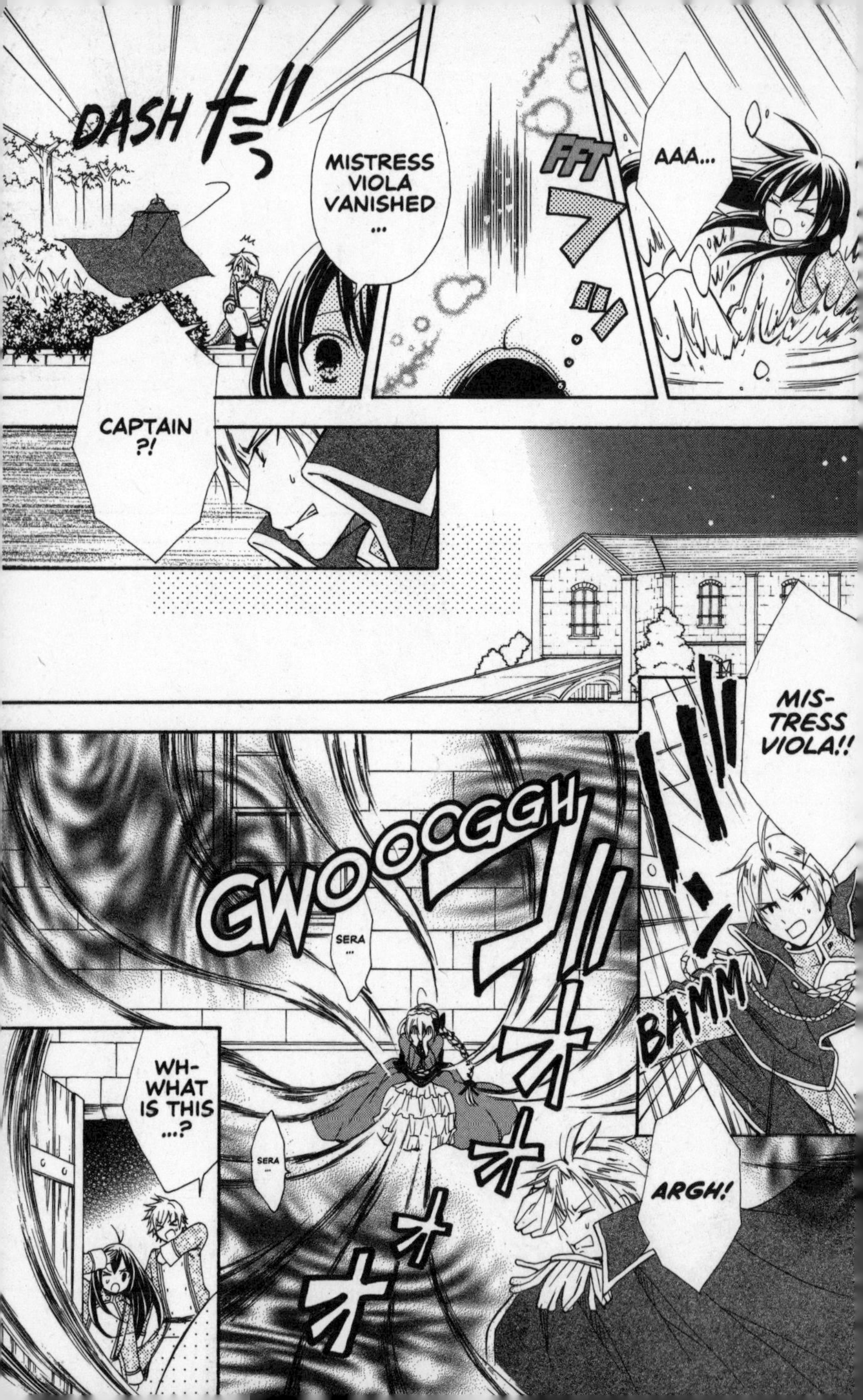

AAA...
FFT
MISTRESS VIOLA VANISHED ...
DASH
CAPTAIN ?!
MIS-TRESS VIOLA!!
BAMM
GWOOOGGGH
SERA ...
ARGH!
SERA ...
WH-WHAT IS THIS ...?

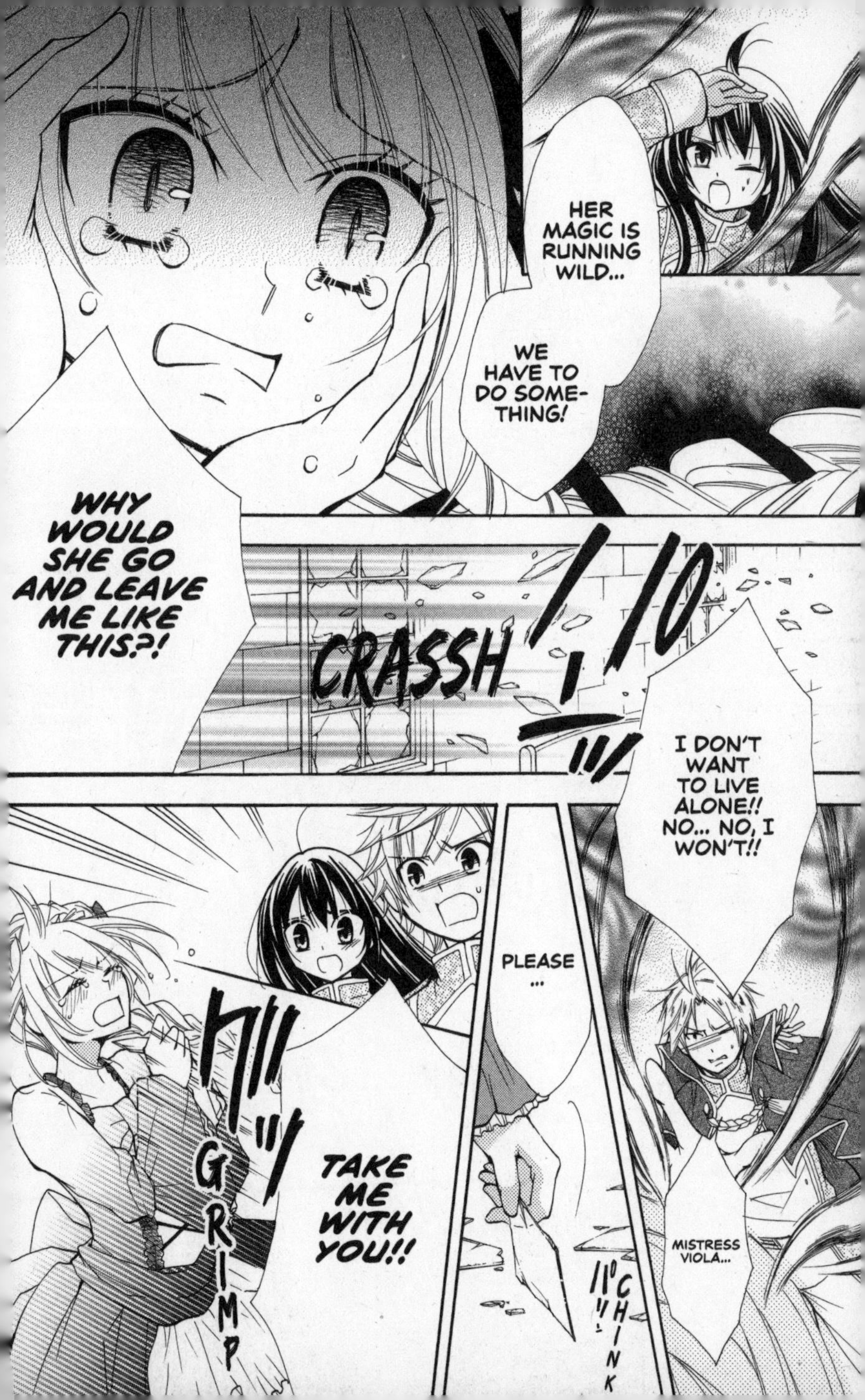
HER MAGIC IS RUNNING WILD...
WE HAVE TO DO SOME-THING!
WHY WOULD SHE GO AND LEAVE ME LIKE THIS?!
CRASSH
I DON'T WANT TO LIVE ALONE!! NO... NO, I WON'T!!
MISTRESS VIOLA...
PLEASE ...
CHINK
TAKE ME WITH YOU!!
GRIMP

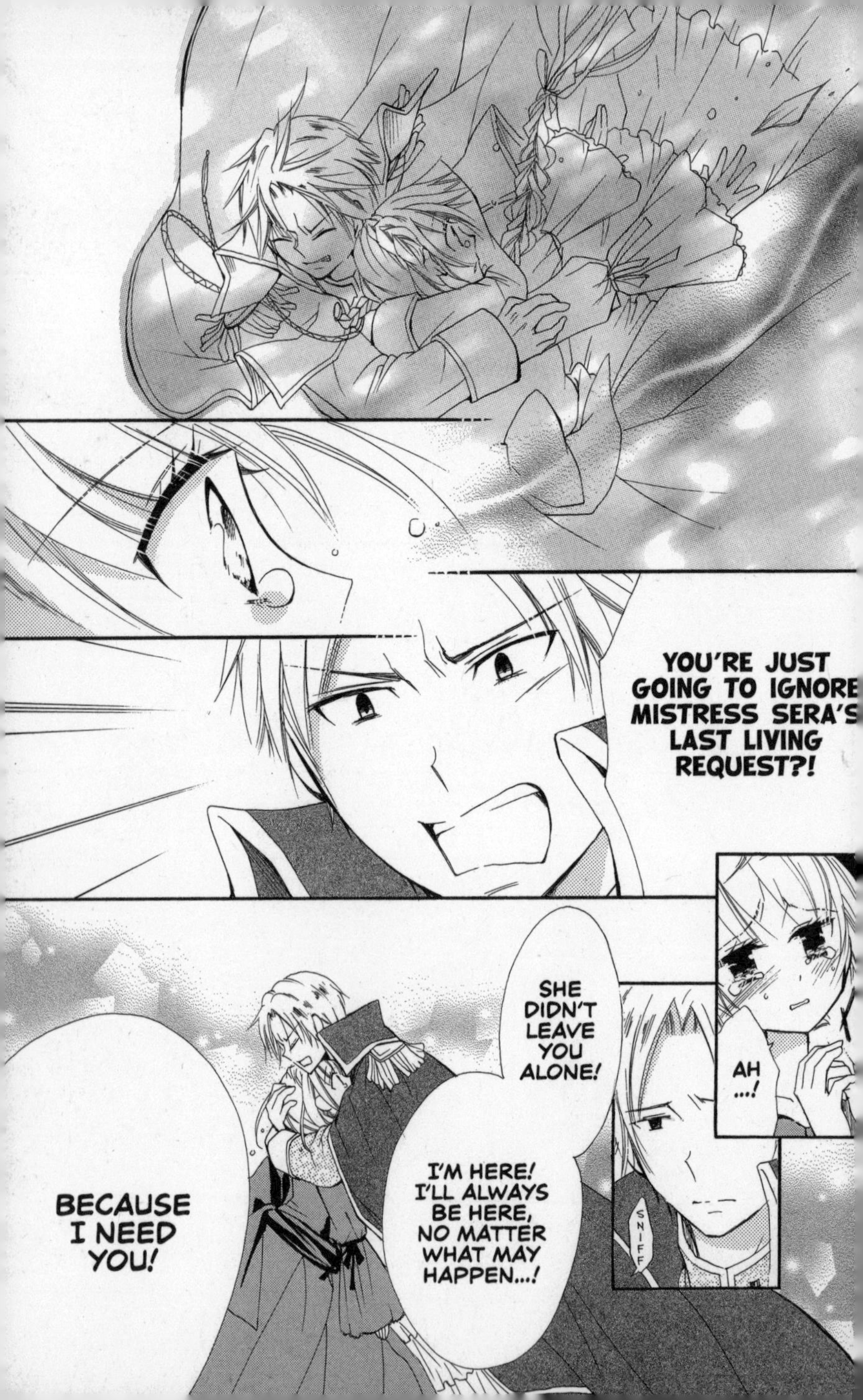
YOU'RE JUST GOING TO IGNORE MISTRESS SERA'S LAST LIVING REQUEST?!
AH ...!
SNIFF
SHE DIDN'T LEAVE YOU ALONE!
I'M HERE! I'LL ALWAYS BE HERE, NO MATTER WHAT MAY HAPPEN...!
BECAUSE I NEED YOU!

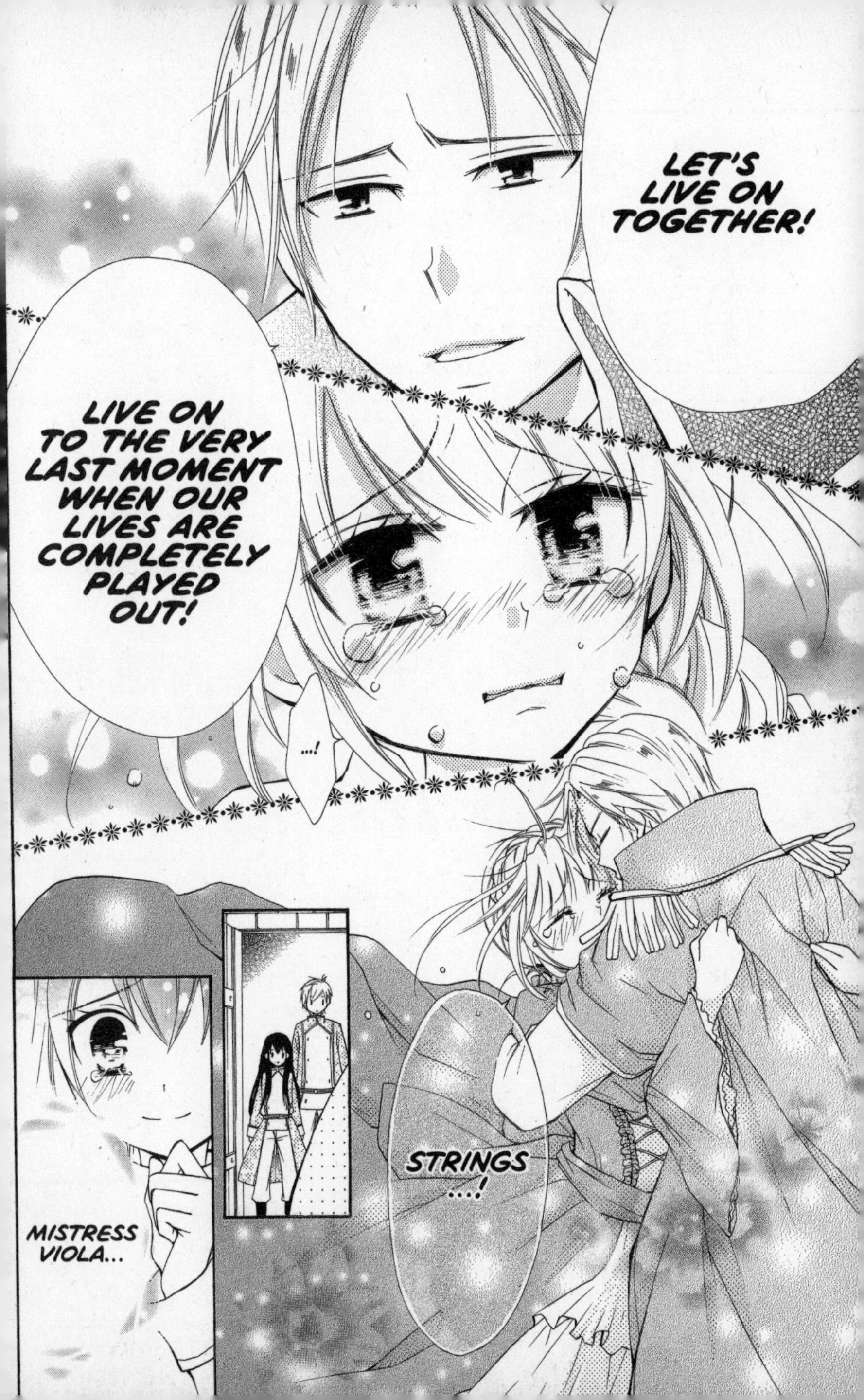
LET'S LIVE ON TOGETHER!
LIVE ON TO THE VERY LAST MOMENT WHEN OUR LIVES ARE COMPLETELY PLAYED OUT!
...!
STRINGS ...!
MISTRESS VIOLA...

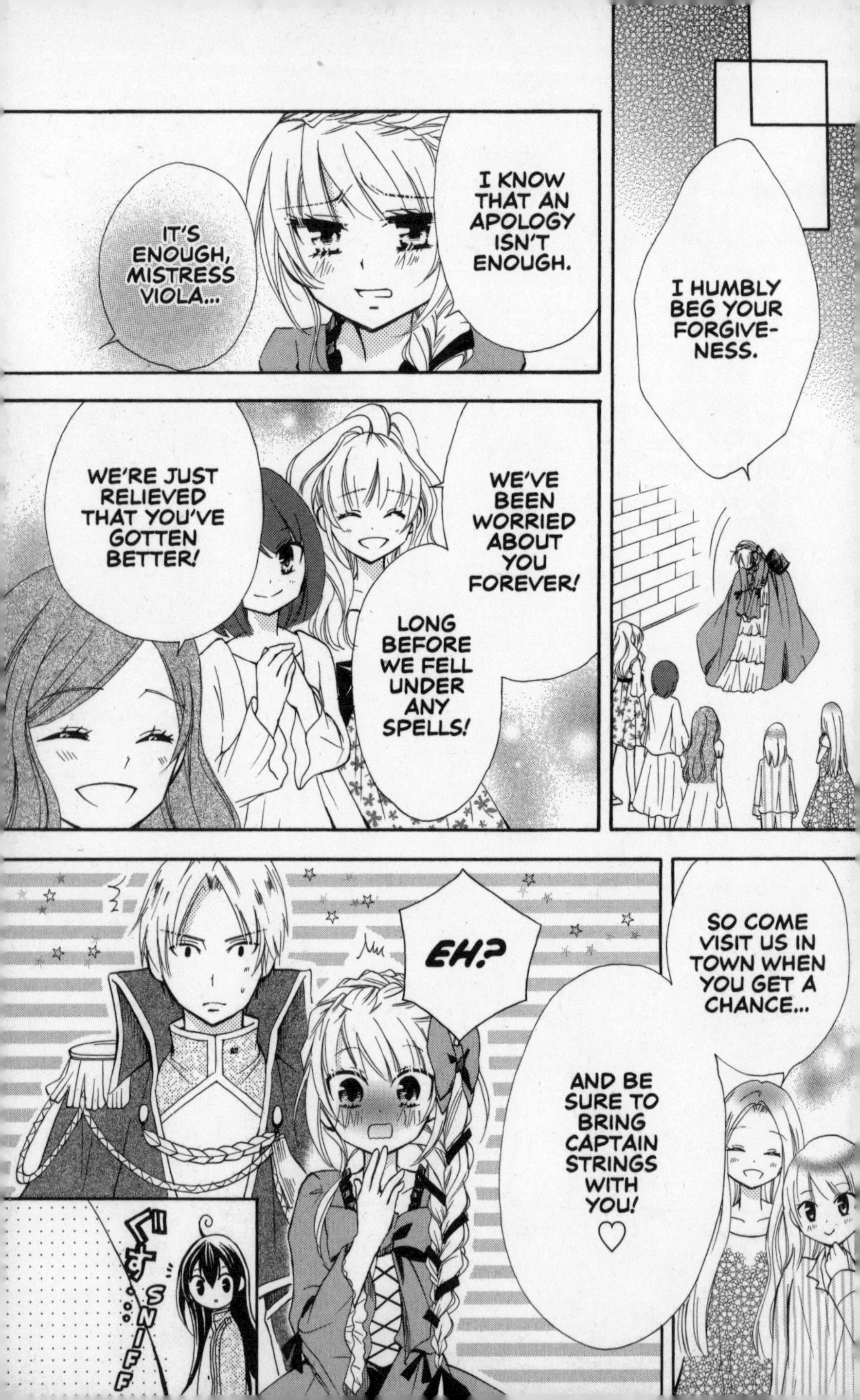
I HUMBLY BEG YOUR FORGIVE-NESS.
I KNOW THAT AN APOLOGY ISN'T ENOUGH.
IT'S ENOUGH, MISTRESS VIOLA...
WE'VE BEEN WORRIED ABOUT YOU FOREVER!
LONG BEFORE WE FELL UNDER ANY SPELLS!
WE'RE JUST RELIEVED THAT YOU'VE GOTTEN BETTER!
SO COME VISIT US IN TOWN WHEN YOU GET A CHANCE...
AND BE SURE TO BRING CAPTAIN STRINGS WITH YOU! ♡
EH?
SNIFF

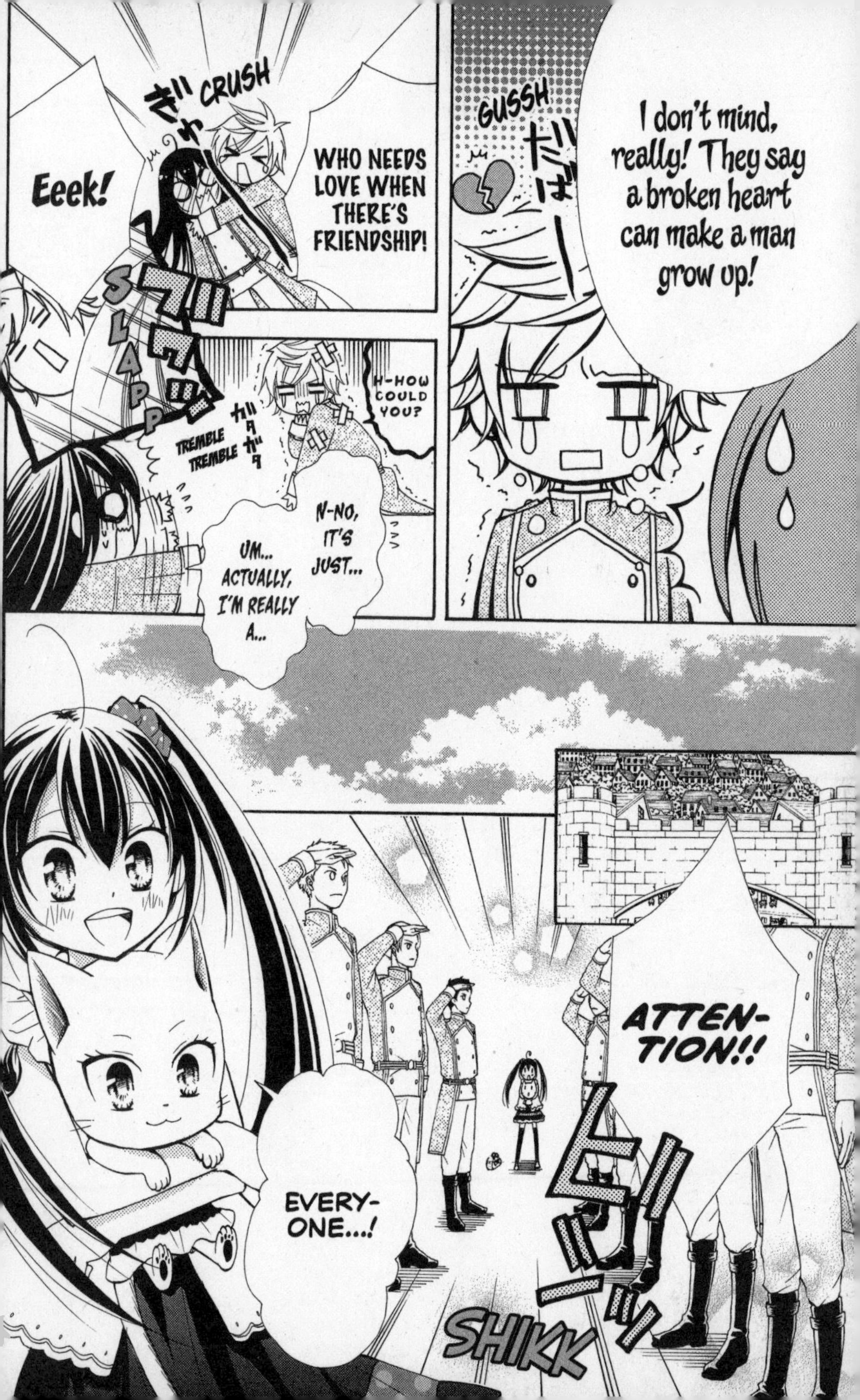
GUSSH
I don't mind, really! They say a broken heart can make a man grow up!
CRUSH
WHO NEEDS LOVE WHEN THERE'S FRIENDSHIP!
Eeek!
SLAPP
H-HOW COULD YOU?
TREMBLE TREMBLE
N-NO, IT'S JUST...
UM... ACTUALLY, I'M REALLY A...
ATTEN-TION!!
SHIKK
EVERY-ONE...!

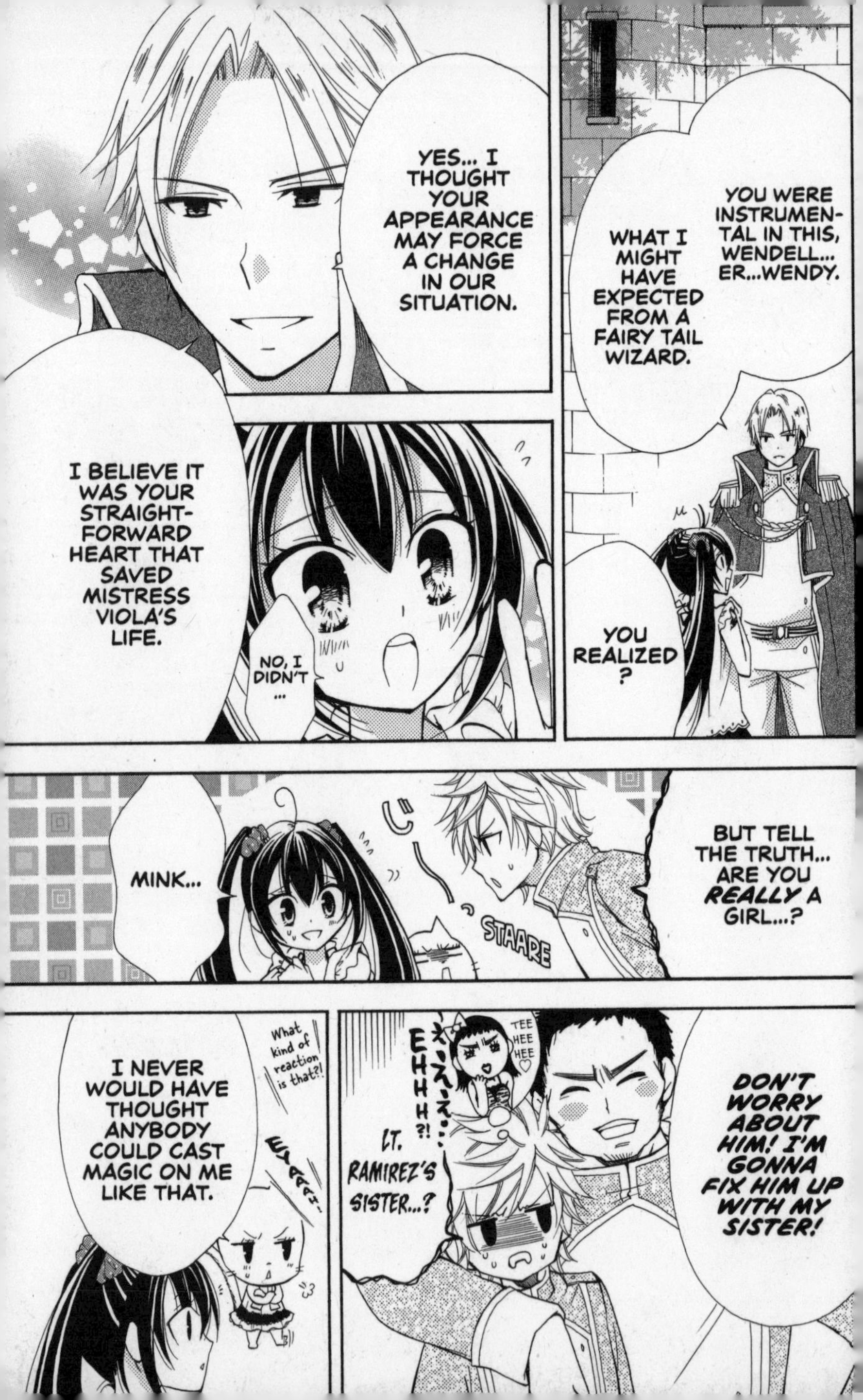

YOU WERE INSTRUMENTAL IN THIS, WENDELL... ER...WENDY.
WHAT I MIGHT HAVE EXPECTED FROM A FAIRY TAIL WIZARD.
YOU REALIZED?
YES... I THOUGHT YOUR APPEARANCE MAY FORCE A CHANGE IN OUR SITUATION.
I BELIEVE IT WAS YOUR STRAIGHTFORWARD HEART THAT SAVED MISTRESS VIOLA'S LIFE.
NO, I DIDN'T ...
BUT TELL THE TRUTH... ARE YOU *REALLY* A GIRL...?
STAARE
MINK...
DON'T WORRY ABOUT HIM! I'M GONNA FIX HIM UP WITH MY SISTER!
TEE HEE HEE ♡
EHHHH?!
LT. RAMIREZ'S SISTER...?
I NEVER WOULD HAVE THOUGHT ANYBODY COULD CAST MAGIC ON ME LIKE THAT.
EYAAAH!
What kind of reaction is that?!

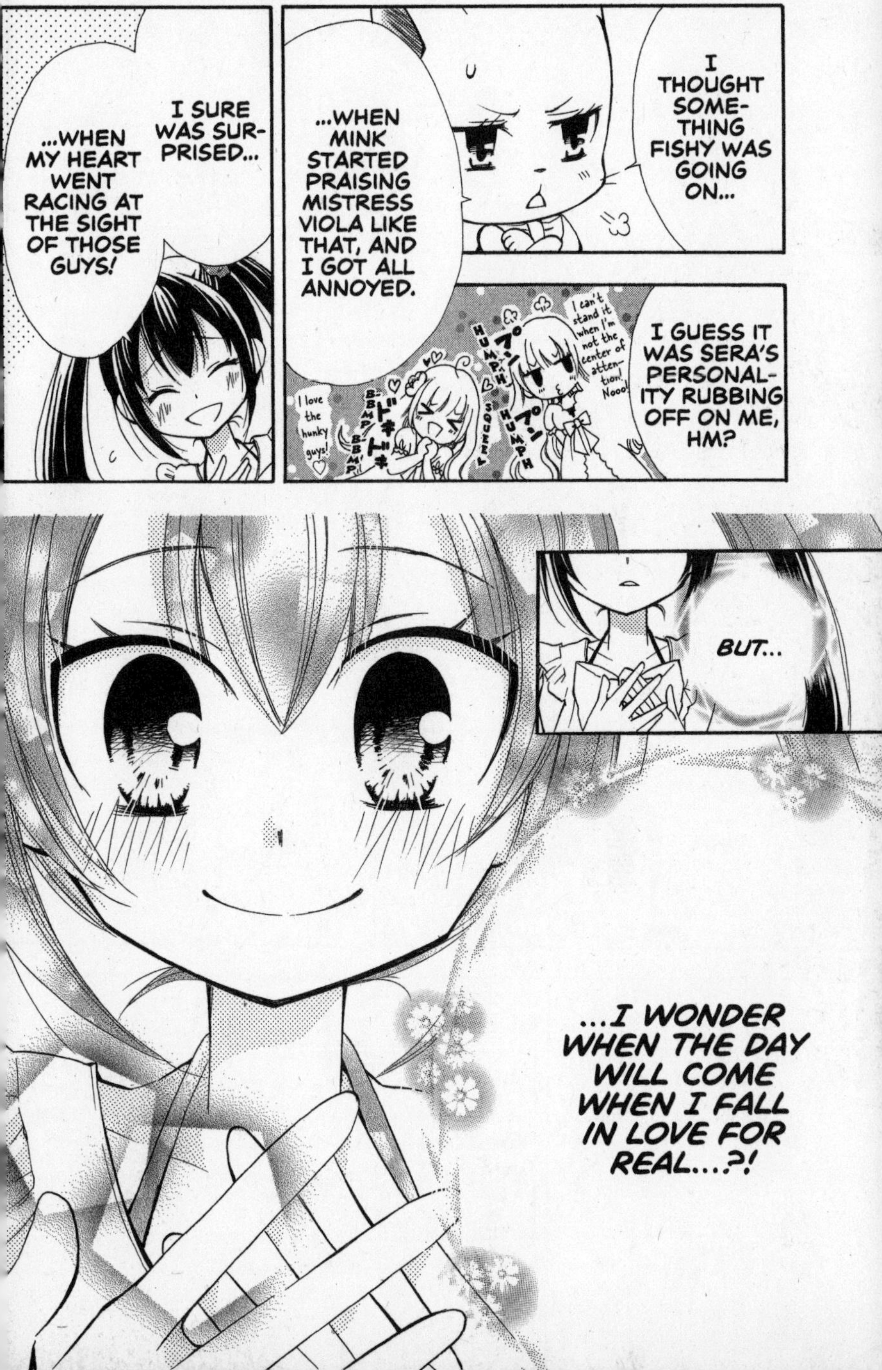
I THOUGHT SOMETHING FISHY WAS GOING ON...
...WHEN MINK STARTED PRAISING MISTRESS VIOLA LIKE THAT, AND I GOT ALL ANNOYED.
I GUESS IT WAS SERA'S PERSONALITY RUBBING OFF ON ME, HM?
I can't stand it when I'm not the center of attention! Nooo!
HUMPH HUMPH
SQUEEE
B-BMP B-BMP
I love the hunky guys!
I SURE WAS SURPRISED...
...WHEN MY HEART WENT RACING AT THE SIGHT OF THOSE GUYS!
BUT...
...I WONDER WHEN THE DAY WILL COME WHEN I FALL IN LOVE FOR REAL...?!

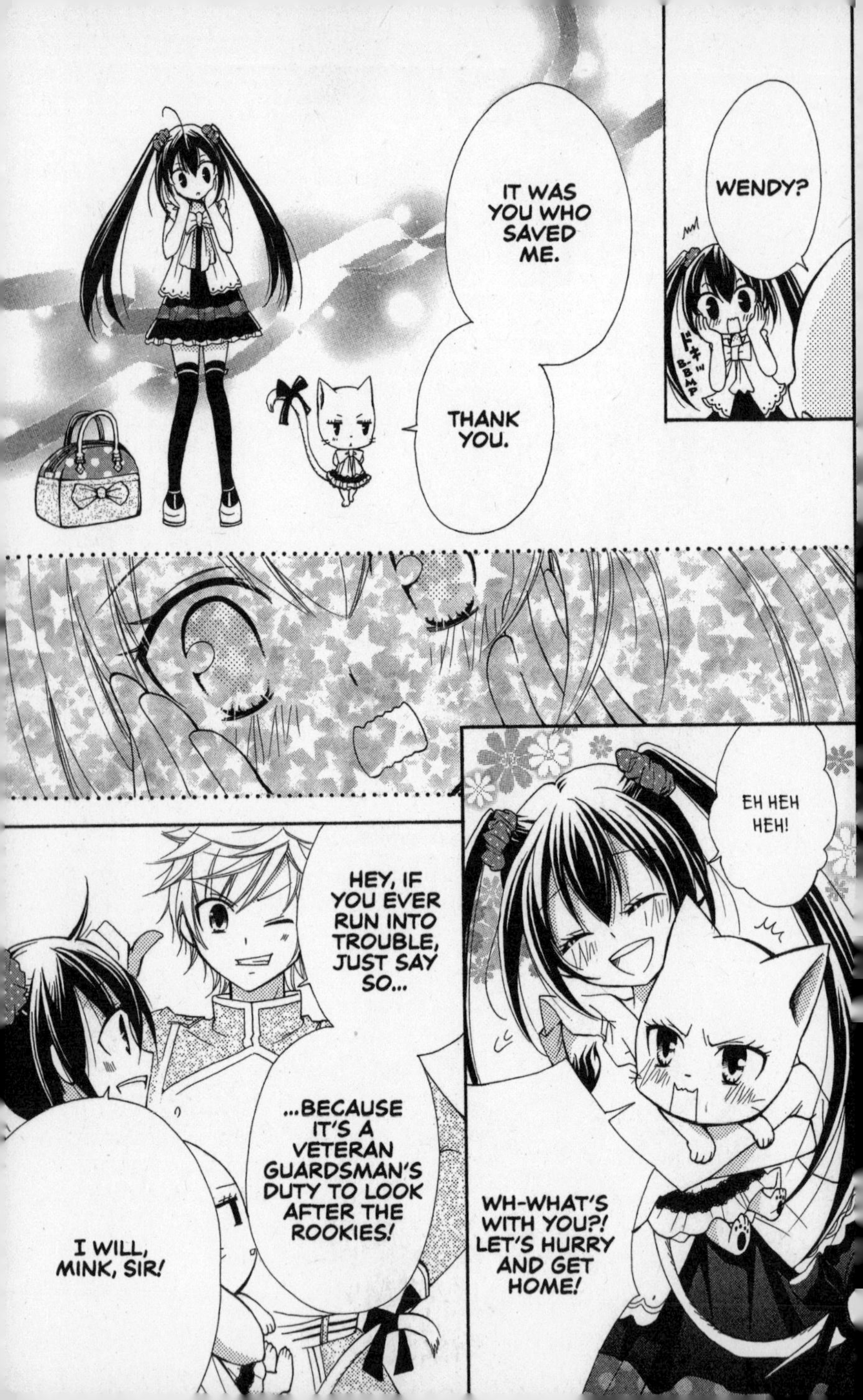
WENDY?
ドキ B-BUMP
IT WAS YOU WHO SAVED ME.
THANK YOU.
EH HEH HEH!
WH-WHAT'S WITH YOU?! LET'S HURRY AND GET HOME!
HEY, IF YOU EVER RUN INTO TROUBLE, JUST SAY SO...
...BECAUSE IT'S A VETERAN GUARDSMAN'S DUTY TO LOOK AFTER THE ROOKIES!
I WILL, MINK, SIR!

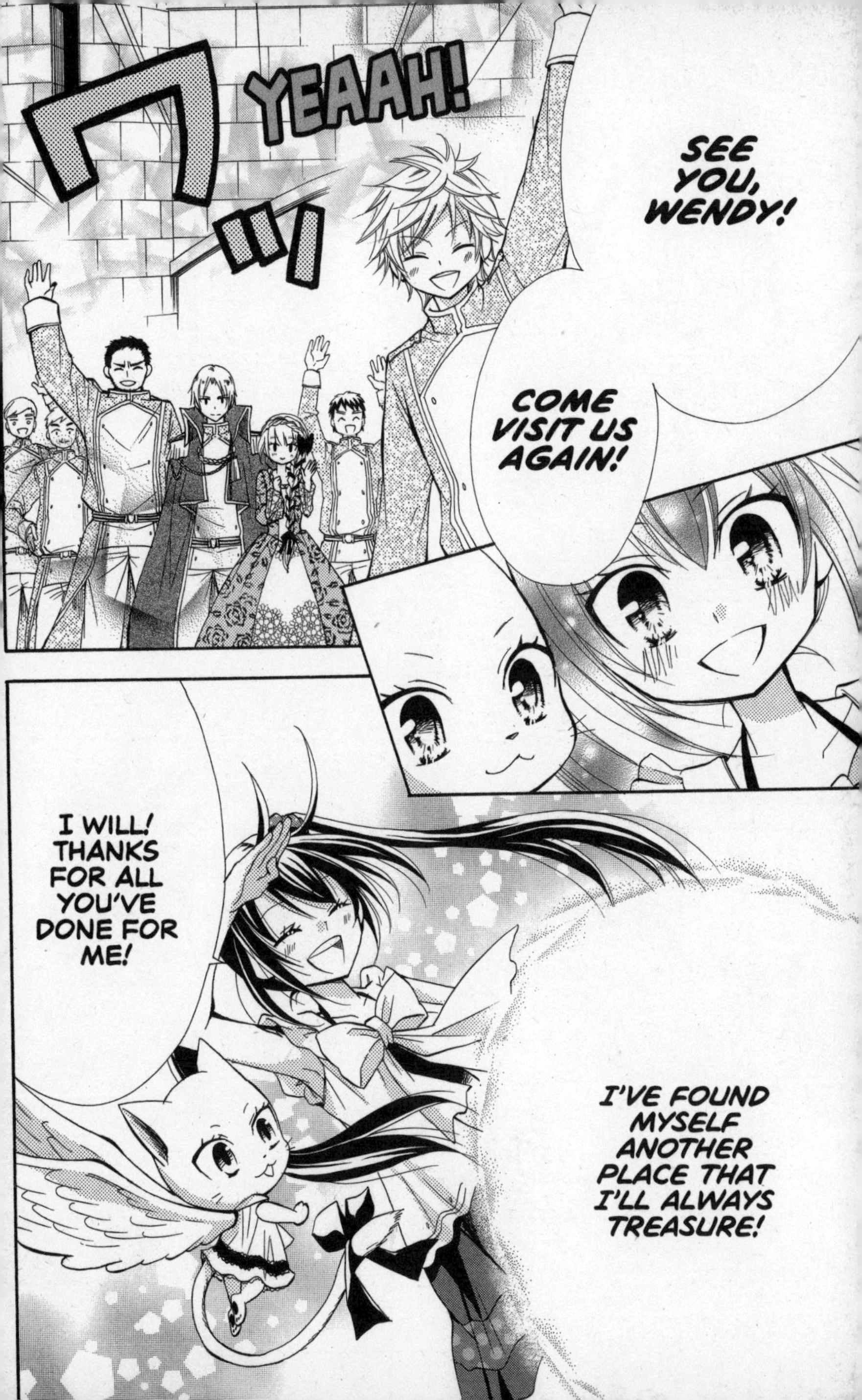
SEE YOU, WENDY!
YEAAH!
COME VISIT US AGAIN!
I WILL! THANKS FOR ALL YOU'VE DONE FOR ME!
I'VE FOUND MYSELF ANOTHER PLACE THAT I'LL ALWAYS TREASURE!

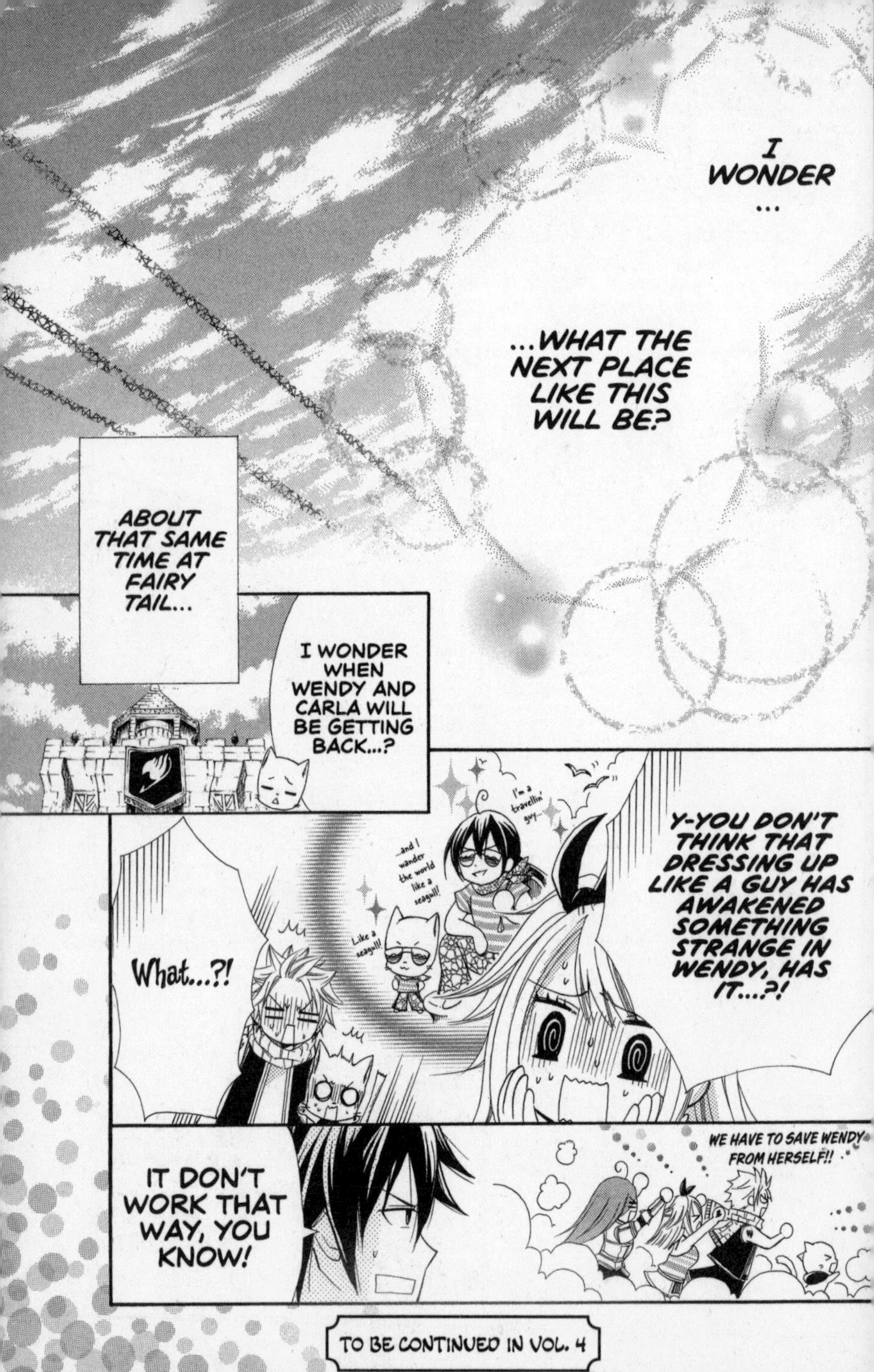
I WONDER ...
...WHAT THE NEXT PLACE LIKE THIS WILL BE?
ABOUT THAT SAME TIME AT FAIRY TAIL...
I WONDER WHEN WENDY AND CARLA WILL BE GETTING BACK...?
Y-YOU DON'T THINK THAT DRESSING UP LIKE A GUY HAS AWAKENED SOMETHING STRANGE IN WENDY, HAS IT...?!
I'm a travellin' guy...
...and I wander the world like a seagull!
Like a seagull!
What...?!
WE HAVE TO SAVE WENDY FROM HERSELF!!
IT DON'T WORK THAT WAY, YOU KNOW!

TO BE CONTINUED IN VOL. 4

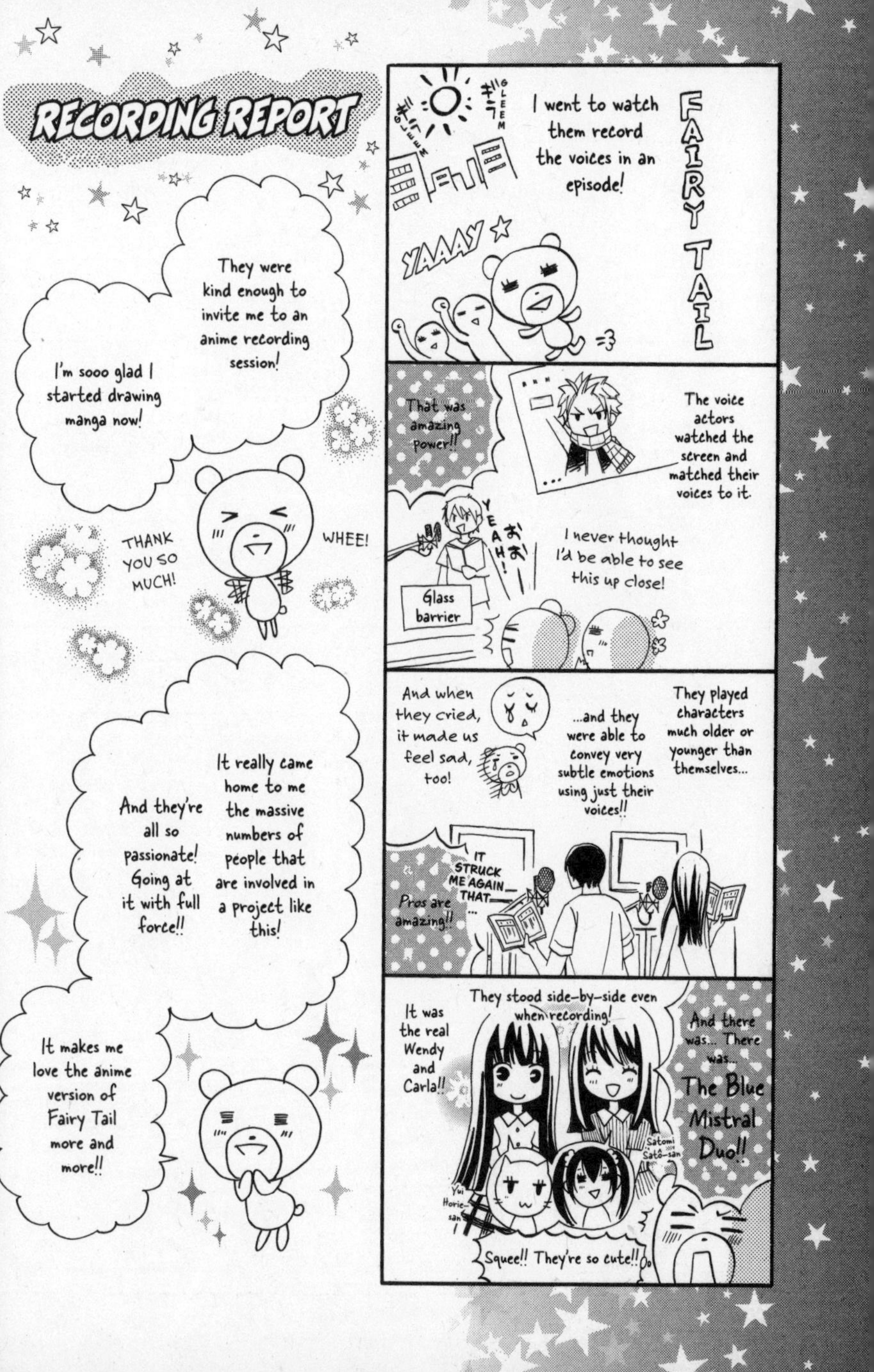
FAIRY TAIL
I went to watch them record the voices in an episode!
GLEEM
GLEEM
YAAAY
The voice actors watched the screen and matched their voices to it.
That was amazing power!!
I never thought I'd be able to see this up close!
YEAH!
おお
Glass barrier
They played characters much older or younger than themselves...
...and they were able to convey very subtle emotions using just their voices!!
And when they cried, it made us feel sad, too!
IT STRUCK ME AGAIN THAT...
Pros are amazing!!
And there was... There was... The Blue Mistral Duo!!
They stood side-by-side even when recording!
It was the real Wendy and Carla!!
Satomi Satō-san
Yui Horie-san
Squee!! They're so cute!!
RECORDING REPORT
They were kind enough to invite me to an anime recording session!
I'm sooo glad I started drawing manga now!
WHEE!
THANK YOU SO MUCH!
It really came home to me the massive numbers of people that are involved in a project like this!
And they're all so passionate! Going at it with full force!!
It makes me love the anime version of Fairy Tail more and more!!

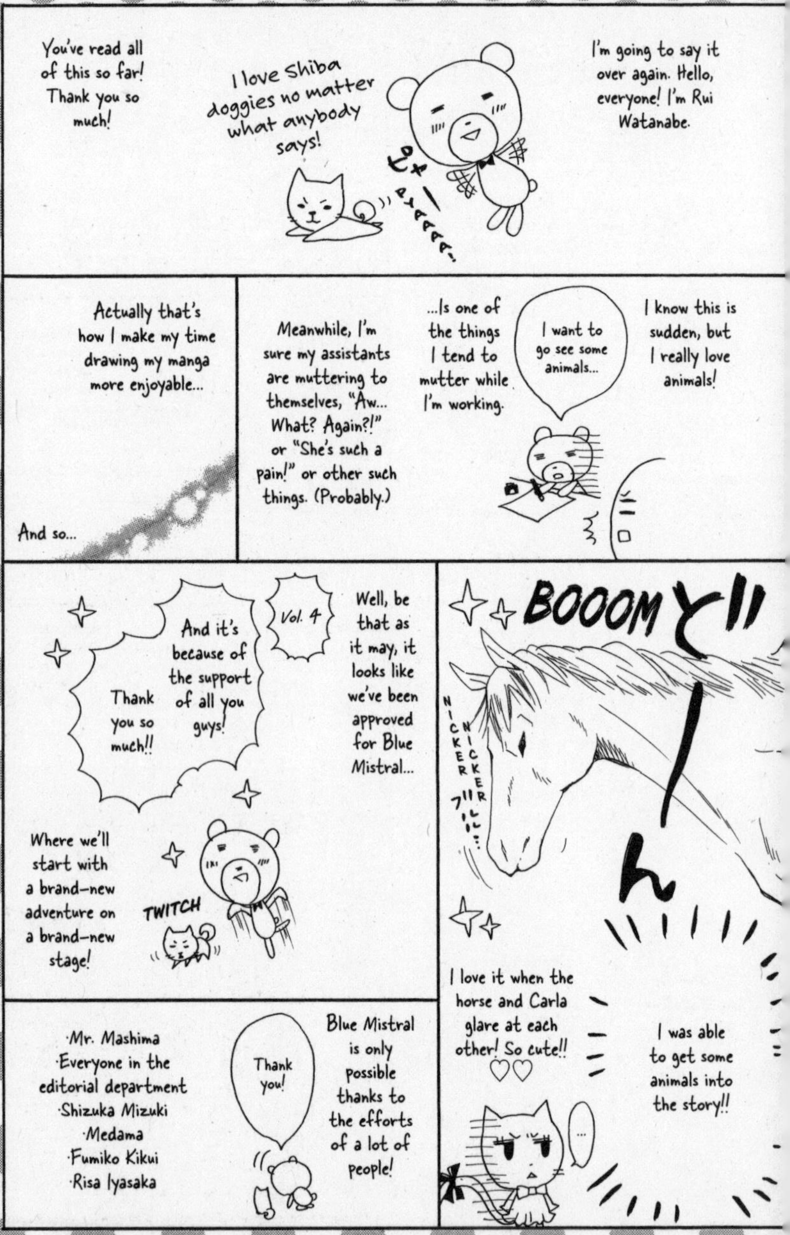
I'm going to say it over again. Hello, everyone! I'm Rui Watanabe.
I love Shiba doggies no matter what anybody says!
ピャー
PYAAAAA!
You've read all of this so far! Thank you so much!
I know this is sudden, but I really love animals!
I want to go see some animals...
...Is one of the things I tend to mutter while I'm working.
Meanwhile, I'm sure my assistants are muttering to themselves, "Aw... What? Again?!" or "She's such a pain!" or other such things. (Probably.)
Actually that's how I make my time drawing my manga more enjoyable...
And so...
BOOOM
NICKER NICKER
I was able to get some animals into the story!!
I love it when the horse and Carla glare at each other! So cute!! ♡♡
...
Well, be that as it may, it looks like we've been approved for Blue Mistral...
Vol. 4
And it's because of the support of all you guys!
Thank you so much!!
Where we'll start with a brand-new adventure on a brand-new stage!
TWITCH
Blue Mistral is only possible thanks to the efforts of a lot of people!
Thank you!
·Mr. Mashima
·Everyone in the editorial department
·Shizuka Mizuki
·Medama
·Fumiko Kikui
·Risa Iyasaka

HIRO MASHIMA

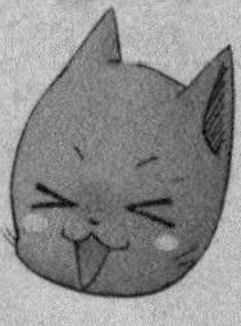

It's so cool to see brand-new charms added to Wendy's character! And in her adventure this time, the fun and her cuteness go on full display!! I hope you all have a blast with Blue Mistral Vol. 3!

RUI WATANABE

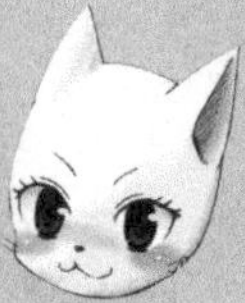

As I draw this manga, I actually can sense the love you all have for Wendy, Carla, and their friends... and my own affection for Wendy and Carla grows, too. It'd make me very happy if you can see the love that went into their adventures this volume!

Original Jacket Design: Hisao Ogawa

The cover art,
three seconds later...

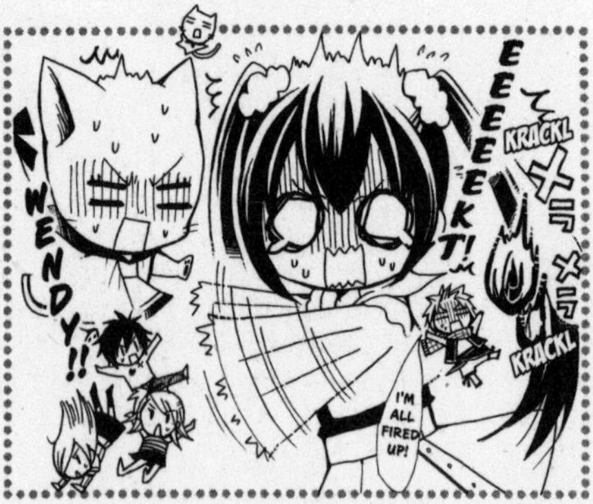
EEEEEEKT!
KRACKL
KRACKL
I'M ALL FIRED UP!
WENDY!!

Translation Notes:

Japanese is a tricky language for most Westerners, and translation is often more art than science. For your edification and reading pleasure, here are notes on some of the places where we could have gone in a different direction with our translation of the work, or where a Japanese cultural reference is used.

Page 3, Cakes

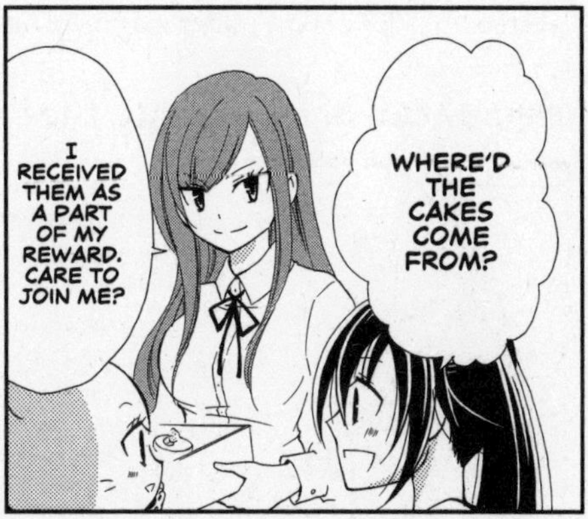
WHERE'D THE CAKES COME FROM?
I RECEIVED THEM AS A PART OF MY REWARD. CARE TO JOIN ME?

In the west, we usually think of cakes as big, round things meant to be cut and split up for a number of different servings. But while that version of cake is also available in Japan's bakeries, the more popular and fashionable type of cakes are those which are intricately decorated single-serving cakes, as seen in the beginning of this volume. They are especially popular with the ladies.

Page 20, Fie

In the Japanese original, Wendy used a version of, "that isn't true," that dates back to the Edo period of the Japanese feudal period…and the only place it is found today is in Samurai period dramas. But it is very rough and manly, so that's probably why Wendy used it. Similarly, "fie" is a word of rejection that dates back to the feudal period of the west, and you only hear it today in western period dramas.

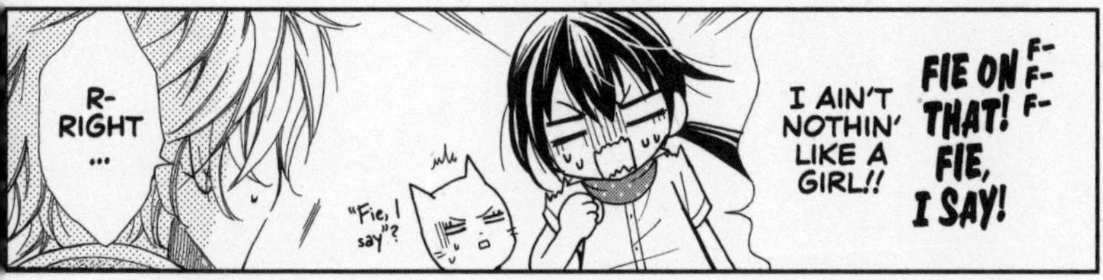
F- F- F-
FIE ON THAT! FIE, I SAY!
I AIN'T NOTHIN' LIKE A GIRL!!
"Fie, I say"?
R-RIGHT ...

Page 32, Lieutenant

The word, "lieutenant" here is not meant to represent the rank used in modern armies. In Japanese, Lt. Ramirez is called *fukutaichô*, where *fukutaichô* means "vice unit-leader." Since the world of Fairy Tail seems loosely based on Europe in the middle ages or renaissance, I am using ranks that were more common back then. A commander of

a unit of soldiers would be called its captain, and his sub-commanders were called his lieutenants.

Page 78, Captain

In much the same way as "lieutenant" above, I am using "Captain" in the sense of the archaic method of titling unit commanders, rather than "captain" as it is used in modern armies. In Japanese, the title is *taichô,* which means "group leader," and in the western middle ages, the leader of a unit of military men was called its captain.

Page 97, Out drinking with the captain

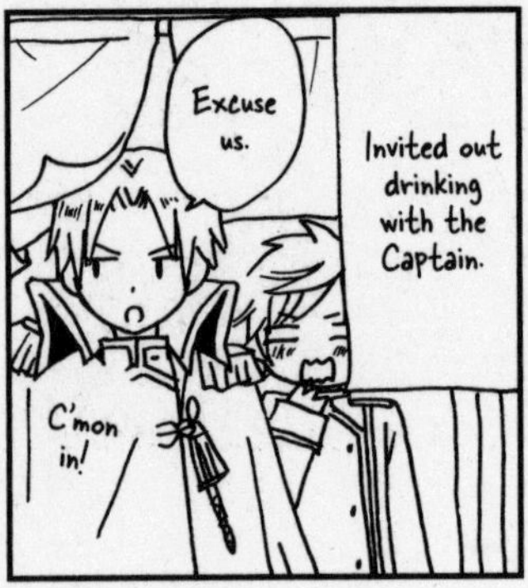
Invited out drinking with the Captain.
Excuse us.
C'mon in!

One of the Japanese customs that is fairly well known in the west is the custom of business-people going out drinking after work. This is supposed to build unity within the team, and the alcohol is also used as an excuse for some consequence-free complaining to the boss. But mostly when it is one-on-one, it is a chance for the boss to get to know his/her employees a little better. In this case, Mink is under aged, and so only drinks *mikan* (mandarin orange) juice.

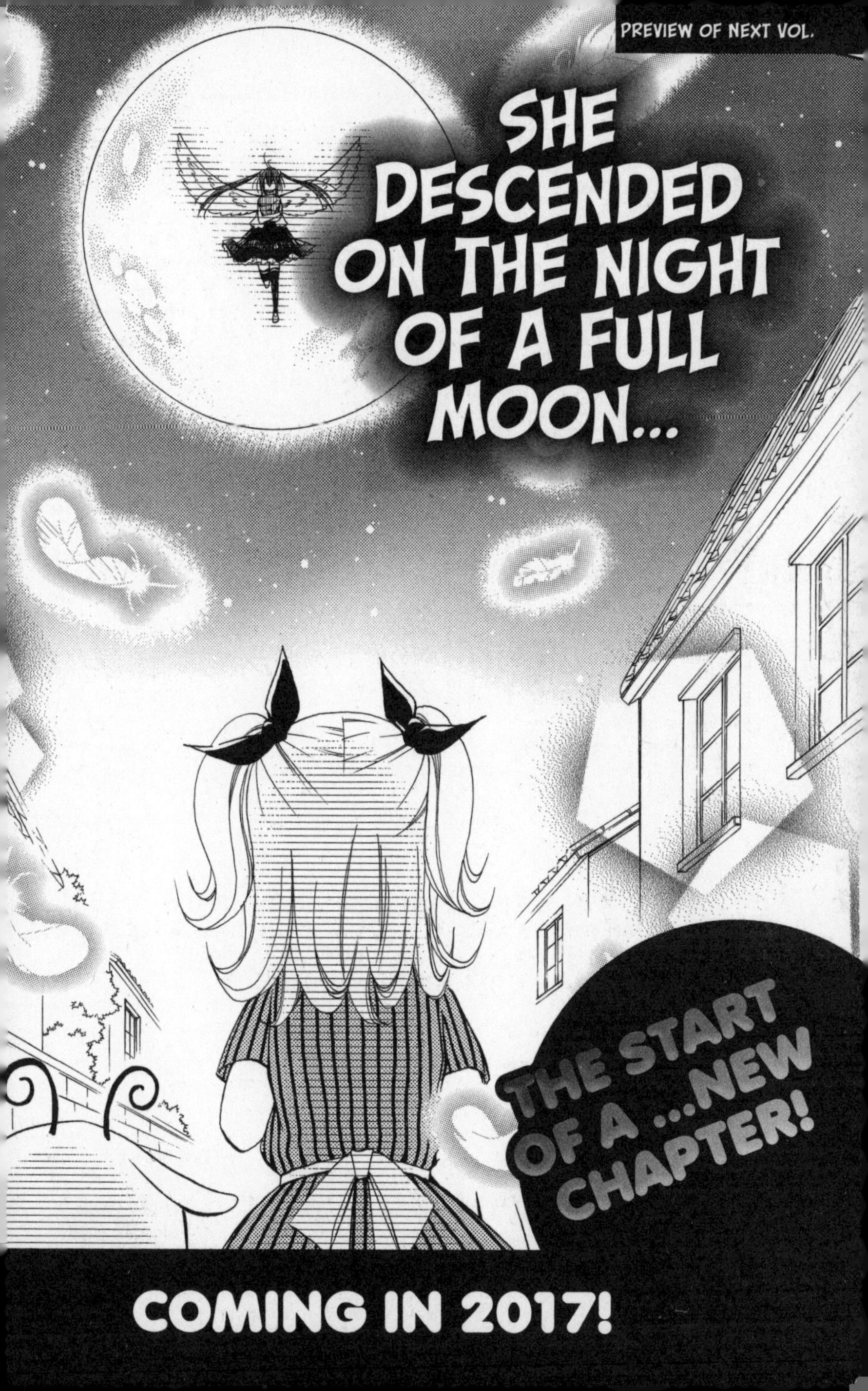
PREVIEW OF NEXT VOL.
SHE DESCENDED ON THE NIGHT OF A FULL MOON...
THE START OF A ...NEW CHAPTER!
COMING IN 2017!

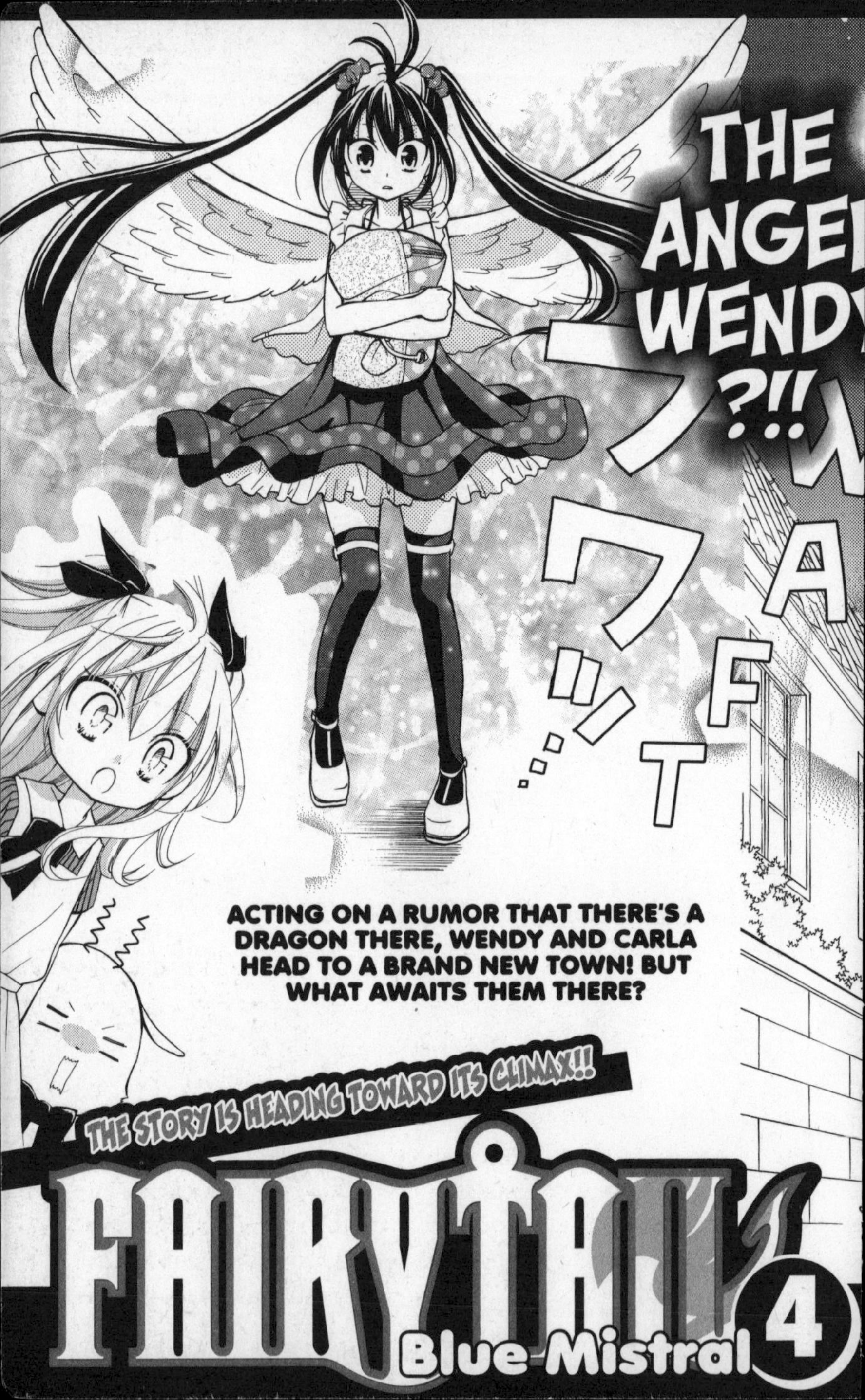
THE ANGEL WENDY ?!!
ワッ
WAFT
ACTING ON A RUMOR THAT THERE'S A DRAGON THERE, WENDY AND CARLA HEAD TO A BRAND NEW TOWN! BUT WHAT AWAITS THEM THERE?
THE STORY IS HEADING TOWARD ITS CLIMAX!!
FAIRY TAIL
Blue Mistral 4

a Silent Voice

KODANSHA
COMICS

"The word heartwarming was made for manga like this."
–Manga Bookshelf

"A harsh and biting social commentary... delivers in its depth of character and emotional strength." -Comics Bulletin

"A very powerful story about being different and the consequences of childhood bullying... Read it."
–Anime News Network

Shoya is a bully. When Shoko, a girl who can't hear, enters his elementary school class, she becomes their favorite target, and Shoya and his friends goad each other into devising new tortures for her. But the children's cruelty goes too far. Shoko is forced to leave the school, and Shoya ends up shouldering all the blame. Six years later, the two meet again. Can Shoya make up for his past mistakes, or is it too late?

Available now in print and digitally!

SHERLOCK BONES

DEDUCTIVE DOG DETECTIVE

When Takeru adopts a new pet, he's in for a surprise—the dog is none other than the reincarnation of Sherlock Holmes. With no one else able to communicate with Holmes, Takeru is roped into becoming Sherdog's assistant, John Watson. Using his sleuthing skills, Holmes uncovers clues to solve the trickiest crimes.

FINALLY, A LOWER-COST OMNIBUS EDITION OF FAIRY TAIL! CONTAINS VOLUMES 1-5. ONLY $39.99!

-NEARLY 1,000 PAGES!
-EXTRA LARGE 7"X10.5" TRIM SIZE!
-HIGH-QUALITY PAPER!

Fairy Tail takes place in a world filled with magic. 17-year-old Lucy is a wizard-in-training who wants to join a magic guild so that she can become a full-fledged wizard. She dreams of joining the most famous guild, known as Fairy Tail. One day she meets Natsu, a boy raised by a dragon which vanished when he was young. Natsu has devoted his life to finding his dragon father. When Natsu helps Lucy out of a tricky situation, she discovers that he is a member of Fairy Tail, and our heroes' adventure together begins.

FAIRY TAIL

MASTER'S EDITION

Fairy Tail Blue Mistral volume 3 is a work of fiction. Names, characters, places, and incidents are the products of the author's imagination or are used fictitiously. Any resemblance to actual events, locales, or persons, living or dead, is entirely coincidental.

A Kodansha Comics Trade Paperback Original.

Published in the United States by Kodansha Comics, an imprint of Kodansha USA Publishing, LLC, New York.

Publication rights for this English edition arranged through Kodansha Ltd., Tokyo.

First published in Japan in 2015 by Kodansha Ltd., Tokyo
ISBN 978-1-63236-318-3

Printed in the United States of America.

www.kodanshacomics.com

9 8 7 6 5 4 3 2 1

Translation: William Flanagan
Lettering: AndWorld Design
Editing: Lauren Scanlan
Kodansha Comics edition cover design by Phil Balsman

TOMARE!

止まれ
[STOP!]

You're going the wrong way!

Manga is a completely different type of reading experience.

To start at the *beginning,* go to the *end!*

hat's right! Authentic manga is read the traditional Japanese way—
om right to left, exactly the *opposite* of how American books are
ead. It's easy to follow: Just go to the other end of the book and read
ach page—and each panel—from right side to left side, starting at
e top right. Now you're experiencing manga as it was meant to be!